Frontier and Overseas Expeditions from India

Frontier and Overseas Expeditions from India

(in 7 Volumes)

Compiled in the
Intelligence Branch,
Army Headquarters, India

Vol. 5
Burma

Low Price Publications
Delhi-110052

Distributed by
D.K. Publishers Distributors (P) Ltd.
4834/24, Ansari Road, Darya Ganj,
New Delhi-110002
Phones: 23278584, 23278368, 23261465
e-mail: dkpd@del3.vsnl.net.in
url: www.dkpd.com

First Published 1907-11

Reprinted in **LPP** 2004

ISBN 81-7536-323-1 (Set)
ISBN 81-7536-328-2 (Vol.5)

Published by
Low Price Publications
A-6, Nimri Commercial Centre,
Near Ashok Vihar Phase-IV,
Delhi-110052
Phones: 27401672, 27452453
e-mail: lpp@nde.vsnl.net.in
url: www.lppindia.com

Printed at
D K Fine Art Press P Ltd.
Delhi-110052

PRINTED IN INDIA

CONTENTS.

PART I.

THE FIRST BURMESE WAR.

CHAPTER I.

THE COUNTRY AND ITS EARLY HISTORY.

CHAPTER II.

OUTBREAK OF HOSTILITIES: OPERATIONS ON THE N.-E. FRONTIER.

CHAPTER III.

THE EXPEDITION TO RANGOON.

CHAPTER IV.

FURTHER OPERATIONS ON THE NORTH-EAST FRONTIER.

CHAPTER V.

PAGE

BRITISH ADVANCE FROM RANGOON.

PART II.

THE SECOND BURMESE WAR.

CHAPTER VI.

CAUSES OF THE WAR.

CHAPTER VII.

THE MAIN OPERATIONS.

CHAPTER VIII.

PAGE

OPERATIONS AGAINST DACOITS.

PART III.

THE THIRD BURMESE WAR.

CHAPTER IX.

RELATIONS WITH BURMA FROM 1853 TO 1885.

CHAPTER X.

BRITISH PREPARATIONS FOR WAR.

CHAPTER XI.

DESCRIPTION OF THE SCENE OF OPERATIONS.

CHAPTER XII.

THE CAPTURE OF MANDALAY.

CHAPTER XIII.

PAGE

SUBSEQUENT OPERATIONS TO 31ST DECEMBER 1885.

CHAPTER XIV.

DACOITS.

CHAPTER XV.

OPERATIONS FROM 1ST JANUARY TO 31ST MARCH 1886.

CHAPTER XVI.

OPERATIONS FROM 1ST APRIL TO 31ST JULY 1886.

CHAPTER XVII.

GENERAL SITUATION IN JULY 1886.

CHAPTER XVIII.

PAGE

THE WINTER CAMPAIGN OF 1886–87, AND SUBSEQUENT OPERATIONS TO MIDSUMMER 1888.

CHAPTER XIX.

REVIEW OF THE SITUATION IN UPPER BURMA IN 1888.

CHAPTER XX.

THE WINTER CAMPAIGN OF 1888–89.

CHAPTER XXI.

OPERATIONS OF 1888-90-91.

PART IV.

THE CHINS, KACHINS, AND SHANS.

CHAPTER XXII.

THE CHINS.

CHAPTER XXIII.

THE KACHINS.

CHAPTER XXIV.

THE SHANS.

APPENDICES.

[redacted].

[redacted] [redacted]

CORRIGENDA.

Page 3, line 2, *for* Tolaing *read* Talaing.

" 20, bottom line, *for* 5 *read* 1.

" 55, line 18, *delete* brackets round word Sarawa.

" 63, marginal inset, *for* attacked *read* attack.

" 192, marginal inset, *for* 1906 *read* 1886.

" 276, line 12, *for* Migin *read* Mingin.

" 325, line 19, *for* 1889–90 *read* 1888–89.

Page 336, line 12, *for* Shwipi *read* Shwimpi.

" 351, line 25, *for* Botang *read* Botaung.

" 371, line 36, *for* Lepei *read* Lepai.

" 373, lines 6 and 29, *for* Lepei *read* Lepai.

" 426, line 25, *for* 1886 and 1887 *read* 1896 and 1897.

Throughout the book for *nullah* read *nala*.

PART I.

THE FIRST BURMESE WAR.

THE FIRST BURMESE WAR.

CHAPTER I.

THE COUNTRY, AND ITS EARLY HISTORY.

THE country now known as Burma is the most easterly of the provinces forming the British Empire in India, and, lying on the east coast of the Bay of Bengal, extends from Assam and Tibet in the north to the river Pak-Chan, on the frontier of Siam, in the south. It includes the once independent kingdoms of Burma proper (otherwise known as Ava), Pegu, Arakan, and Tenasserim. Of these the most important were Burma proper, or Ava, which comprised the middle reaches of the Irrawaddy; and Pegu which comprised the lower valley of that river. The two other kingdoms are both long, narrow strips of coast territory facing the Bay of Bengal, Arakan running northwards from the delta of the Irrawaddy to the river Naaf, and Tenasserim running south to the frontier of Siam on the river Pak-Chan.

Each of these four kingdoms has a history of its own; each grew out of the aggregation of petty states; and each, eventually coming into contact with the others, was deluged with blood in the attempts of the rulers to extend their dominions.

The people of Burma belong to the Indo-Chinese race, having Mongolian features, with tolerably fair complexions, varying from a dusky yellow to a clear whiteness, but always with non-transparent skin. In religion they are Buddhists. They are without caste, without hereditary rank except in the royal family, without an aristocracy, save what is official, and without any of the prejudices which prevail in India as regards early marriages and the seclusion of females. In comparison to the grave and self-contained Hindus they are a joyous race, taking pleasure in theatrical performances, singing, dancing, and merry-making in general. They are imbued with military sentiments akin to the Rajputs; and leave all menial appointments to slaves and captives.

Burma is a land of sun and rain. There is as a rule no cold weather as in the Punjab, and the south-west monsoon, which begins early in May and lasts till September, is far more severe than in India.

The villages are generally on the banks of rivers, and consist of wooden huts built on piles, so as to be above the floods during the rainy seasons.

Communications, at the beginning of British intercourse with Burma, were bad. The roads were mere tracks through swamp and jungle, and, in the rainy season, were impassable. The natives relied chiefly on water communications, and the whole prosperity of the country was due to the Irrawaddy, which was then, as it is in a minor degree still, the great national highway.

Early History.

The historians of the ancient kingdoms of Burma, in their efforts to attribute a miraculous origin to the founders of the reigning families, have so embellished their accounts with incredible myths and fictions that it is difficult to fix any period at which fable ends and history begins. For the purposes of this work, however, it will suffice to carry the reader back to the middle of the sixteenth century. At this time the whole country was being exposed to inter-tribal wars, chief amongst which was the constant rivalry between the Burmese people of Ava and the Talaings of Pegu. To this day the whole region of Pegu and Ava bears the marks of these desolating contests, and large tracts of culturable lands lie utterly waste from sheer want of population.

In the sixteenth century many Portuguese adventurers came to Burma from Goa and Malacca. One of them raised a fleet of pirate galleys which terrorised the coast of Arakan. Another obtained possession of a fort near Rangoon, and was the terror of the Burmese kings on the Irrawaddy. Others, again, entered the service of different kings of Burma and often turned the fortunes of war by their fire-arms and superior knowledge.

About 1540, Byin-noung, Governor of Toungoo, then an independent kingdom in the interior of Burma, came to the front. He made himself king of the country, and subsequently conquered the Tolaing kingdom of Pegu and slew the Talaing king. He next raised a large army and invaded Martaban, successfully capturing and laying waste the capital after a siege lasting six months. He then returned to Pegu, and, advancing up the Irrawaddy, captured Prome, and attempted the conquest of Ava. Two years later he invaded Siam, but was suddenly recalled by rebellion in Pegu. Hurrying back, he put down the revolt with his Burmese troops, but was assassinated in the hour of his triumph.

The story of this man is typical, and reveals the general conditions of life in Burma from remote ages down to our own times; it is consequently unnecessary to enter into detail about the reigns of his immediate successors.

During the early years of the eighteenth century the Talaing kings of Pegu conquered Ava. About 1755, however, a man of low origin, known as Alompra, the hunter, headed a popular insurrection, and sweeping down the Irrawaddy, threw off the Talaing yoke, subverted the Talaing dynasty, and founded a maritime capital at Rangoon. The English at that time had a factory at Negrais, off the coast, and the merchants were weak enough to court the friendship of Alompra, while selling ammunition to the Talaings. Alompra was informed of their misdeeds, and the result was that nearly every Englishman at Negrais was massacred by the Burmese.

At the end of 1759, Alompra invaded Siamese territories, and captured Mergui and Tenasserim. From here he advanced on the Siamese capital, but being seized with a mortal sickness he gave orders for a retreat, hoping to regain his own country and arrange about the succession, so that there should be no dispute after his death. He, however, died on the way, on 15th May 1760, before he had attained his fiftieth year. A petty farmer, he had raised himself to the throne of his country and established a dynasty which until lately reigned in Burma. He found his country conquered and oppressed by a foreigner; he left it extending from Mergui to Manipur.

The successors of Alompra followed in his steps. His second son, Sheng-hpyu-sheng, invading Siam, annihilated the Siamese army and captured the capital, the Siamese taking an oath of fidelity and agreeing to pay an annual tribute to the Burman rulers.

In 1767 he successfully defeated a Chinese army of 50,000 men who invaded Burma from the north. The Chinese made another invasion in 1769, and by the same route, but were again totally defeated by the Burmese. At this time, however, the Siamese rebelled and, successfully throwing off the Burman yoke, recaptured their lost dominions. Alompra's third son, Patodaw (Bhodaw) Paya, was the sixth sovereign of the dynasty. He reigned from about 1780 to 1819 and is regarded by the Burmans as only second in greatness to his father. He conquered Arakan as far as the frontier of Bengal, and Martaban and Tenasserim as far as the boundaries of Siam.

The successor of Patodaw (Bhodaw) Paya was Pagyi-daw, who invaded and conquered Assam and Manipur and brought on the Burmese war of 1824-25.

The kings of Burma, from Alompra downwards, were rude despots. They were utterly ignorant of foreign nations, regarding Burma as the centre of the universe, and all people outside the Burman pale as savages and barbarians.

Causes of friction with British Government.

The extensions of the Burmese frontiers to the north and west, beyond the mountain ranges forming the western watershed of the Irrawaddy valley, increased the national arrogance and proved a source of friction with British India. The situations which in this way arose from time to time were the preponderating causes of both the first and second Burmese wars. And, as neither of these very severe lessons could teach the Burmese court that the British Empire in India was of a more solid and resisting nature than any of the countries mentioned in their Royal Chronicles, similar causes in course of time led to the total extinction of the Burmese monarchy and of national independence.

CHAPTER II.

OUTBREAK OF HOSTILITIES: OPERATIONS ON THE N.-E. FRONTIER.

BRITISH and Burman interests first clashed at the end of the eighteenth century.

At this time the people of Ava, having successfully liberated themselves from the yoke of Pegu, were now masters of that kingdom, and having met with almost uninterrupted success in all their wars for the past fifty years, as has already been shown, they were arrogantly turning their attention to fresh conquests, including Arakan, Assam, and even Bengal itself.

In 1784, Bhodaw Paya, the king of Burma, invaded and annexed Arakan, but the Arakanese rebelling, some of them fled to Bengal to seek British protection. The Burmese governor of Arakan haughtily demanded their surrender, which Lord Wellesley refused on the grounds that having sought the protection of Great Britain, he was unable to give them up. Anxious, however, to avoid hostilities, a British mission was sent to Ava, under Lieutenant-Colonel Symes, to settle this dispute, and also "to procure for British traders immunity from the oppression and extortion to which they were continually subjected on their visits to Burman ports." Colonel Symes met with scant ceremony from the Burmese, but a treaty ensued, the beneficial results of which, however, only lasted a short time.

Other missions were sent to Ava, but they met with more indignity and less success than had Lieutenant-Colonel Symes, and in 1811, a serious rebellion having broken out in Arakan, the king of Ava believed it had been instigated by the English, and consequently laid an embargo on all British ships in Rangoon.

This was sufficient cause for hostilities, but owing to Lord Hastings' wars, which had secured the peace of India, having been so strenuously denounced in England, his successors were loth to enter on so expensive an alternative, and accordingly yet another mission was sent to Ava.

The natural consequence of this was that the Burmese, an ignorant, isolated people, mistaking clemency for fear, imagined the British to be powerless to resist them. Their arrogance increased accordingly, and after a period of apparent inaction, and while the East India Company was too much occupied over its troubles with Nepal and the Mahrattas to watch any powers in the south-east, the Burmese General Bandula invaded the countries between Burma and Bengal, conquered Assam and Manipur (then an independent State between Burma and Assam), threatened Cachar, and finally, invading British territory, captured a party of British sepoys.

At the same time the Burmese started levying taxes on British boats on the Naaf river (the boundary between Arakan and Chittagong), and landing an armed party on the British island of Shahpuri at its mouth, killed and wounded six of the garrison.

Thus Great Britain was at last forced into hostilities with this troublesome and turbulent neighbour, who was keeping the frontier provinces in constant dread and danger of invasion.

Declaration of War, 5th March, 1824.

At this juncture Lord Amherst arrived in India and immediately turned his attention to Burma; and a demand for an explanation of these continual offences against the British Government meeting with an aggressive reply, the Governor-General declared war on the 5th of March, 1824. The plan of campaign that had been decided on was as follows:—that three Brigades should be formed and placed at Chittagong, Jamalpur, and Goalpara for the defence of the Eastern Frontier, with a strong reserve at Dinajpur, and an efficient flotilla on the Brahmaputra, in the vicinity of Dacca. The course of operations on the frontier, owing to the lack of roads and consequent impossibility of moving troops by this route to Ava, was to be strictly defensive, or, at the utmost, limited to the re-establishment of the States subdued by the Burmese, while the offensive operations were to consist of an over-sea expedition against Rangoon and such portions of the enemy's coast as should offer the best prospects of success.

Cachar taken under British protection.

It should here be stated that a little previous to the outbreak of war, the Raja of Cachar had, owing to the threats of Burmese invasion, begged the British to take his country under their protection.

The Government, recognizing that the possession of this district would impede a Burmese advance into Sylhet and lessen the danger to British territories, had acceded to his request, and had advanced troops from Dacca for this purpose. This force, which consisted of part of the 1st Battalion, 10th Native Infantry, three companies of the 2nd Battalion, 23rd Native Infantry, four companies of the Rangpur Local Corps,[1] and a few guns, was posted in three detachments, under Major Newton and Captains Johnston and Bowen, at Badarpur, Jattrapur, and Tilain, in advance of the Sylhet frontier and covering that district against any threatened attack. Instructions were also sent to the Commissioner of the North-East Frontier to inform the Burman governor of Assam that Cachar had been placed under British protection and that any molestation of that country would be regarded as an act of hostility.

These arrangements had scarcely matured when events justified their policy. In the early part of January 1824, notwithstanding the representations of the Commissioner, a force of 4,000 Burmans advanced from Assam into Cachar to the foot of the Bhertika pass, and began to stockade themselves at Bikrampur. Another Burman force entered from Manipur, and a third crossed into Jaintia immediately to the north of the station of Sylhet. It consequently became necessary to resist their further progress before they occupied positions which would give them the command of the Sylhet Frontier, where their invasion of Cachar had already caused a general panic amongst the inhabitants. As it was evident that there was little hope of attention being paid to remonstrance, the British Officers were instructed by the Civil authorities to oppose the Burman advance by force, and hostilities shortly ensued.

Action at Bikrampur.

The first move was made by Major Newton, commanding the troops on the Sylhet Frontier. He decided to concentrate his forces at Jattrapur and advance against the Burmans from Assam before they had time to complete their dispositions for defence, and he accordingly advanced at 2 A.M. on the 17th of January and attacked the enemy at daybreak.

The main attack was made on the south face of the stockade and a secondary attack on the village adjoining. The Burmans

[1] Now the 6th Gurkhas.

in the village retired immediately, but those behind the stockade made a resolute resistance. The position, however, was successfully captured with a loss on the British side of only five sepoys killed and fourteen wounded, the enemies' casualties amounting to over a hundred. After this action Major Newton retired to Sylhet, withdrawing the whole of his troops from Cachar. The Burmans then advanced to Jattrapur, where their two divisions from Assam and Manipur effected a junction and erected stockades on both banks of the river Barak, connected by a bridge. Their united forces amounted to about 6,000 men, while a detachment of about 2,000 more was posted at Hailakandi in the southwest of Cachar.

Action at Badarpur.

The main body of the Burmese proceeded to push their stockades to about a thousand yards from Badarpur, garrisoned by a wing of the 10th Native Infantry, a company of the 23rd, and a small party of the Rangpur Local Corps, under the command of Captain Johnston. This officer determined to dislodge the enemy, and, with the consent of the Commissioner, moved against them on the 13th of February. The Burmese opened a heavy fire on him as he advanced, but the troops pressed on without hesitation and carried the position at the point of the bayonet with a loss of one killed and thirty-eight wounded. The Burman force from Assam fell back on the Jatinga river, while that from Manipur stockaded itself at Dudpatli.

Lieutenant-Colonel Bowen, who had joined and taken over command, now marched in pursuit of the first of these columns with a view to expelling it from Cachar. Finding it strongly entrenched at the foot of the Bhertika pass, he attacked and defeated it. Driving it into the hills, he freed Cachar from the enemy.

There now remained only the Manipur force to be dealt with, and Colonel Bowen next advanced against it at Dudpatli, which proved to be the strongest position yet assailed. The Burmese were stockaded on the north bank of a small river, their rear resting on steep hills. Each face of the stockade was defended by a deep ditch fourteen feet wide, a fence of bamboo spikes was constructed along the outer edge, and the approach on the land side was through dense jungle and high grass. After the post had been reconnoitred and an artillery preparation made, an assault was ordered on the western front. The Burmese remained passive until the troops reached the spikes, when they poured on the assailants a destructive and well-directed fire. After being exposed to this fire for some time in their efforts to break through the barrier, the British Commander, imagining that his troops had made no impression on the defence, unfortunately abandoned the attempt to carry the works and withdrew his force to Jattrapur. Lieutenant Armstrong and twenty men were killed, and Colonel Bowen, Captain Johnston, Ensigns Graves and Barberie and 131 men were wounded in this affair. On the 27th February, Colonel Innes joined the force at Jattrapur with four guns and the 2nd Battalion, 19th Bengal Native Infantry,[1] and assumed the command. In the meantime the Burmese, who had suffered far more severely at Dudpatli than the British had thought, abandoned their position and fell back to Manipur.

Action of Dudpatli.

Cachar being thus freed of the enemy, and the nature of the country rendering it difficult to procure supplies for the British troops, Colonel Innes left a small detachment there as a garrison, and moved his main body into cantonments in Sylhet. This was their position on the formal outbreak of war on 5th March, 1824.

The war being now formally declared by the British Government, measures were at once taken for its prosecution on the lines already mentioned. Of the plan of operations on the Eastern Frontier it appeared, in the first instance, only necessary to dislodge the Burmese from Assam, as Cachar was already cleared of them and the invasion of Arakan was not immediately proposed. In Sylhet and Chittagong therefore a strictly defensive line of conduct was pursued, Colonel Innes remaining in the former district and Colonel Shapland establishing himself in the latter with a force consisting of a wing of the 13th Native Infantry, five companies of the 2nd Battalion, 20th Native Infantry, and the 1st Battalion, 23rd Native Infantry, with the Provincial Battalion. A local corps was also raised, bringing up the total strength to about 3,000 men. Of these a detachment under Captain Noton, consisting of

[1] The late 39th Bengal Native Infantry.

five companies of the 23rd Native Infantry with two guns and some details, was left at Ramu to check any demonstration from Arakan. It was in Assam, however, that the first hostilities occurred after the war was proclaimed.

Operations in Assam.

The Assam force stationed at Goalpara under Brigadier M'Morine, consisted of the 2nd Battalion, 23rd Native Infantry, three local corps, three brigades of six-pounders, and a small body of mounted troops, besides a gunboat flotilla on the Brahmaputra. This force moved out on the 13th of March, their route lying along the bank of the Brahmaputra. Owing to thick jungle and long grass, and the number of rivers and ravines that had to be crossed, the advance was one of peculiar difficulty, but meeting with no opposition on the way Gauhati was reached on the 28th March. The Burmese had erected stockades here but evacuated them on the approach of the British. The Assamese, in answer to a proclamation assuring them of British protection, were most anxious to lend their aid against the common enemy, but their un-warlike character and smallness of numbers rendered their co-operation of no value, and Colonel M'Morine, owing to lack of information about the state of the roads and doubt of the capability of the country to maintain a large force, decided to halt at Gauhati, in spite of the fact that he seemed to have a great chance of expelling the Burmese entirely from Assam by only a partial advance of his force.

In the meantime Mr. Scott, the Political Agent, having crossed from Sylhet through Jaintia with a party of some strength, arrived at Nowgong, on the Brahmaputra, on the 15th April, and, leaving his escort there, proceeded to Gauhati to communicate with the head-quarters of the invading force. At his instigation a party, under Colonel Richards, was detached from Gauhati, and, joining the Commissioner's escort at Nowgong, succeeded in inflicting a series of small defeats on the Burmese, who retreated to Mara Mukh. The rains now setting in put a stop to the campaign in Assam, and as it was found impossible to transport supplies beyond Gauhati, the force consequently had to retire to that place. The result of the operations was decidedly successful, and the British authority established over a large tract of country between Goalpara and Gauhati, but it is probable that had an advance been made from the latter point earlier, the Burmese would have been expelled from a still greater portion of Assam; their force in that country never having been formidable either in numbers or equipment.

In prosecution of the offensive operations, a powerful force was being fitted out at this time in the Madras and Bengal Presidencies, but, to secure continuity, it will be as well, before beginning a history of these movements, to finish the account of the operations on the North-Eastern Frontier.

As has been already noticed, a large Burmese force of about 12,000 men had assembled in Arakan under the command of Bandula. Early in May about 8,000 of this force crossed the Naaf and advanced to Ratnapalung about fourteen miles south of Ramu. Directly intelligence was received at Ramu of the Burman approach, Captain Noton made a reconnaissance in force with the whole of his available troops to ascertain the enemy's numbers and object. In consequence, however, of the artillery elephants having thrown their loads and the ammunition coolies having deserted, the guns could not be brought into action, and as without them he could not make any impression on the Burmese, Captain Noton retired to Ramu, where he was joined by three companies of the 40th Native Infantry, making his whole force about 1,000 strong, of whom less than half were regulars. With these Captain Noton decided to hold on to Ramu until the arrival of reinforcements from Chittagong. On the 13th May the enemy advanced and occupied the hills east of Ramu, being separated from the British by the Ramu river. On the evening of the 14th they made a demonstration of crossing the river, but were driven back by the fire from the two British six-pounders. On the morning of the 15th, however, they effected their purpose, and crossing the river unobserved to the left of the British position, took possession of a tank, surrounded, like other tanks in this neighbourhood, by a high embankment which protected them from the fire of their opponents.

Action of Ramu.

Captain Noton drew up his force behind a bank about three feet high, which completely surrounded his camp. On his right flank, at about sixty paces distance, was a tank where a strong picquet was posted, and his right was further protected by the river. On his left and somewhat to the rear was another tank in which he stationed the Provincials and Mug Levy. The regulars, consisting of the 20th and 23rd Native Infantry with the two 6-pounders, occupied the front or eastern face of the embankment. From this face a sharp fire was brought to bear on the Burmese as they advanced from the river, but they made such good use of cover, and entrenched themselves so quickly that it was far less effective than might have been expected.

Having received information that reinforcements had already left Chittagong and would arrive the next day, Captain Noton was more than ever determined to hold on to his post, in spite of the superiority in numbers of the Burmese, and of the fact that they were evidently gaining ground.

On the morning of the 16th, it was found that the Burmese had considerably advanced their trenches during the night. Firing was kept up on both sides during the day, but neither combatant secured any important advantage. The officer in command of the British guns, however, was disabled, and it was with some difficulty that the Provincials were prevented from deserting their post.

On the morning of the 17th, the enemy's trenches were advanced to within twelve paces of the picquets and a heavy and destructive fire was kept on them. At about 9 A.M., the Provincials abandoned the tank entrusted to them, and it was immediately occupied by the enemy.

The position was now untenable: a retreat was ordered and effected with some discipline for a short distance. The increasing numbers and audacity of the pursuers, however, and the activity of a small body of mounted men attached to their force, soon filled the troops with an ungovernable panic which rendered the exertions of the officers to preserve order unavailing. Finally, on the arrival of the force, now little better than a mob, at a river which crossed their road, the sepoys threw away their arms and accoutrements and plunged headlong into the water.

In the retreat Captains Noton, Pringle, and Trueman, Lieutenant Grigg, Ensign Bennett, and Assistant Surgeon Maysmore were killed. The other officers engaged, Lieutenants Scott, Campbell, and Codrington, made good their escape, but the two former were wounded. The loss in men could not be ascertained, as many of them filtered back to Chittagong after some time. According to official reports between six and seven hundred reached Chittagong by the end of May, so that the whole loss in killed and captured did not probably exceed two hundred and fifty. Many of those taken prisoners were sent to Ava, where they served to confirm the belief of that Court in the irresistible prowess of the Burman troops, and anticipations of future victories.

The defeat of this detachment caused much alarm at Chittagong and Dacca and even in Calcutta itself, where, in consequence of the fear of invasion, the European inhabitants formed themselves into a militia, and a large portion of the crews of the East India Company's ships were landed to assist in the defence of the town.

This panic, however, was soon discovered to be groundless, for adequate preparations for the defence of the frontier had been made by ordering Colonel Innes' force from Sylhet to Chittagong. In addition to this, so lacking were the Burmese in enterprise that they never attempted to advance beyond Ramu. Bandula was shortly after recalled, with most of his troops, for the defence of Ava, and the enemy abandoned all their posts to the north of the Naaf, retiring into Arakan.

Meanwhile, however, the Burmese in Manipur profited by the temporary absence of British troops from the neighbourhood of Cachar by immediately invading that district once more; but the alarm consequent on the defeat at Ramu having subsided, Colonel Innes returned to Sylhet on the 12th of June with about 1,200 men. After having halted a few days there, to rest his troops from the fatigues to which the rainy season had exposed them, he again proceeded to Cachar to expel the invaders. On the 20th June he arrived at Badarpur from whence he proceeded by water along the Barak river to Jattrapur, where after much difficulty he arrived on the 27th.

Action at Tilain.

Having learnt while on the way to this place that the enemy was strongly stockaded on the hill at Tilain, a detachment of the force, with two howitzers and four 6-pounders, was dispatched to take this position. The guns having been brought on to rising ground about 600 yards south-west of the stockade, opened fire on the 6th July; the distance, however, was found to be too great for any impression to be made on the enemy's works, so the guns were removed on the 7th to a hill nearer the stockade, the occupation of which was unsuccessfully opposed by the enemy. On the 8th, the Burmese occupied the heights in rear of and commanding the battery, dislodging the troops who had been posted there for its protection, and frustrating an attempt made to turn their flank. The guns therefore had to be withdrawn, and the troops being exhausted by the fatigues they had undergone, and the rains making it every day more impossible to carry out military operations, Colonel Innes decided to fall back on Jattrapur. From here the increasing sickness of the men, constantly exposed to the rains, and surrounded as they were by swamp and jungle, compelled a withdrawal to a more healthy situation. The force consequently retired to Badarpur, where it was disposed along the river either in boats or in elevated places on the banks. The Burmese remained in their entrenchments, and no further movements took place on either side during the continuance of the rains. This terminated the first phase of the defensive operations, the results of which were on the whole satisfactory.

Observations.

In Assam a considerable advance had been made. In Cachar a forward position had been maintained, although the nature of the country, the state of the weather, and the smallness of the force had prevented the campaign from closing with the éclat with which it had opened.

The disaster at Ramu, though it might have been prevented by the more prompt dispatch of reinforcements, reflected no imputation on the courage of the regular troops, and except in the loss of lives, was devoid of important consequences.

In all the operations the Burmese had displayed neither personal bravery nor military skill. Their whole system of warfare resolved itself into a series of entrenchments, cleverly contrived no doubt, and behind which they at times certainly displayed considerable steadiness and courage, but as they studiously avoided individual exposure, they were but little formidable in the field as soldiers. Neither was much to be apprehended from the generalship that allowed the victory at Ramu to pass away without the least effort to take advantage of a crisis of such promise, and which restricted the fruits of that battle to the construction of a stockade.

CHAPTER III.

THE EXPEDITION TO RANGOON.

HAVING reached the end of the first period of defensive operations on the North-East Frontier, we will now turn to the more important enterprises of the war—the over-sea expedition to Rangoon—to which the former were entirely subsidiary.

Directly war was seen to be inevitable, preparations for this expedition were set on foot. The difficulty of collecting a sufficient force from Bengal—owing to the repugnance of the Native soldier to crossing the sea, where their prejudices exposed them to many real privations—led to a request for help from the Madras Presidency. Here there existed no local call for a large force, and the Native troops did not share the prejudices of the Pandies. This request was promptly acceded to, and a considerable force was speedily equipped. A similar activity pervaded the measures of the Bengal authorities, and by the beginning of April the expedition was ready to sail.

The time of the year at which this expedition was fitted out was recommended by various considerations of local and political weight. All available information pointed to the fact that a more favourable time for the voyage could not be selected, and from the accounts of those who had been to Ava, it appeared that if the expedition, on arrival at Rangoon, should be able to proceed into the interior without delay, the rising of the Irrawaddy and the prevalence of a north-east wind made June and July the best months for an enterprise which, it was asserted, could only be effected by water.

That no time should be lost in making the Burmese act on the defensive was also apparent, as by the extent of their preparations in Arakan, Assam, and Cachar, they were evidently about to invade the frontier with a force that would require the concentration of a large body of troops for the protection of British Provinces, in places where mountains, streams, and forests were certair to exercise a destructive influence on the physical energies of officers and men, and would prevent the full development of the military resources of the State. To have remained throughout the rains, therefore, entirely on the defensive, would probably have entailed a greater expense and a greater sacrifice of life than an aggressive movement, to say nothing of an inevitable loss of prestige.

These considerations were, to a great extent, justified by events; but it should be noted that so great was the ignorance at that time of the features and climate of Burma, that it was anticipated that access to the capital of the Empire from Rangoon would be a task of the easiest description. This hope, however, was doomed to speedy disappointment.

The following was the composition of the army :—

Brigadier-General Sir Archibald Campbell, K.C.B., 38th Foot, Commander of the Forces.

Lieutenant J. J. Snodgrass, 38th Foot, Military Secretary and Aide-de-Camp.

Ensign J. Campbell, 38th Foot, Aide-de-Camp.

GENERAL STAFF.

Bengal.

Lieutenant-Colonel F. S. H. Tidy, C.B., 14th Foot, Deputy Adjutant-General.

Major J. N. Jackson, 1-23rd Bengal Native Infantry, Deputy Quartermaster-General.

Lieutenant H. Havelock, 13th Foot, Deputy Assistant Adjutant-General.

Captain H. Waterman, 13th Foot, Deputy Assistant Quartermaster-General.

Madras.

Brigadier-General W. Macbean, C.B., 54th Foot, Commanding the Madras Division.

Captain B. R. Hitchins, 1-7th Madras Native Infantry, Military Secretary.

Captain J. Campbell, 49th Foot, Aide-de-Camp.

Lieutenant-Colonel E. W. Snow, 2-17th Madras Native Infantry, Deputy Adjutant-General.

Captain S. W. Steele, 2-12th Madras Native Infantry, Assistant Quartermaster-General.

Captain A. E. Spicer, 2–8th Madras Native Infantry, Deputy Assistant Quartermaster-General.

The troops were organised in brigades as follows :—

Bengal Artillery.

——————————Commanding.[1]
3rd Company, 5th Battalion, Bengal Artillery.[2]
4th " " " " "

Madras Artillery.

Major W. M. Burton, Madras Artillery, Commanding.
" B " Company, 2nd Battalion, Madras Artillery.[3]
One company of Golandaz.
Detachment of gun lascars.

Bengal Infantry Brigade.

Lieutenant-Colonel M'Creagh, C.B., 13th Foot, Brigadier Commanding.
His Majesty's 13th Foot, Light Infantry.
" " 38th Foot, " "
2nd Battalion, 20th Bengal Native Infantry.[4]

1st Madras Infantry Brigade.

Lieutenant-Colonel W. Smelt, 41st Foot, Brigadier Commanding.
His Majesty's 41st Foot.
2nd Battalion, 8th Madras Native Infantry.[5]
2nd " 10th " " " .[6]

2nd Madras Infantry Brigade.

Lieutenant-Colonel C. Hodgson, 1–9th Madras Native Infantry, Brigadier Commanding.
1st Madras European Regiment.[7]
1st Battalion, 9th Madras Native Infantry.[8]

[1] No commandant of the Bengal Artillery was nominated until towards the end of the year, when Lieutenant-Colonel G. Pollock was appointed.

[2] Late No. 3 Battery, 25th Brigade, Royal Artillery. Disbanded in 1871.

[3] Two companies of Madras Artillery formed part of the Expeditionary Force, but the identity of the second cannot be traced.

[4] The late 40th Bengal Native Infantry, which designation it obtained on the re-organization of the Indian Armies in May 1824.

[5] The present 72nd Punjabis.

[6] The late 18th Madras Native Infantry. Disbanded in 1864

[7] The present 1st Battalion, Royal Dublin Fusiliers.

[8] Now the 69th Punjabis.

3rd Madras Infantry Brigade.

Lieutenant-Colonel H. F. Smith, C.B., 2-10th Madras Native Infantry, Brigadier Commanding.

1st Battalion, Madras Native (Light) Infantry.[1]

2nd " 17th " " ".[2]

The 1st Battalion of Madras Pioneers[3] was also included in the force under the command of Sir Archibald Campbell.

These troops were followed shortly by the—

4th Madras Infantry Brigade.

Lieutenant-Colonel E. Miles, C.B., 89th Foot, Brigadier Commanding.

His Majesty's 89th Foot.

1st Battalion, 7th Madras Native Infantry.[4]

1st " 22nd " " ".[5]

The strength of these troops was:—

Artillery	916
Pioneers	552
European Infantry	3,969
Native	5,218
Total ..	10,655

The ordnance consisted of eight 18-pounders, six 12-pounders, ten 6-pounders, ten howitzers, and eight mortars.

It will be observed that this expedition was totally destitute of cavalry. Towards the end of the year, however, a portion of the Governor-General's Body-Guard (about 300 men), under the command of Captain R. H. Sneyd, was sent to join the forces under the command of Sir Archibald Campbell, and, rendered excellent service. Here it may also be noted that before the end of the war the following reinforcements had, from time to time, joined our forces in Ava:—

1st Troop, 1st Brigade, Bengal Horse Artillery.

2nd " 2nd " " " (the Rocket Troop).

Two companies of Madras Artillery.

1 Now the 63rd Palamcottah Light Infantry.

2 The late 34th Madras (Chicacole) Native Light Infantry. Disbanded in 1882.

3 The two battalions of Madras Pioneers are now represented by the 2nd Queen's Own Sappers and Miners.

4 The present 67th Punjabis.

5 The late 43rd Madras Native Infantry. Disbanded in 1864.

One company of Bombay Artillery.
The Governor-General's Body-Guard.
1st Madras Light Cavalry, two squadrons.[1]
2nd Battalion, 1st Foot (Royal Scots).
His Majesty's 45th, 47th, and 87th Foot.
1st Madras Native Infantry.
22nd " " "
26th " " "
28th " " "
30th " " "
32nd " " "
36th " " ".[2]
38th " " ".[2]

The naval part of the expedition was composed of the following vessels :—

H. M. S. *Liffey*	..	50 guns,	Commodore C. Grant, C.B.
" *Slaney*	..	20 "	Commander C. Mitchell.
" *Larne*	..	20 "	" F. Marryat.
" *Sophie*	..	18 "	" C. F. Ryves.
H. C. S. *Hastings*	..	32 "	Captain G. Barnes.
" *Teignmouth*	..	16 "	" H. Hardy.
" *Mercury*	..	14 "	" R. E. Goodridge.
" *Prince of Wales*	..	14 guns,	Lieutenant W. S. Collinson.
" *Thetis*	..	10 guns,	Commander G. Middleton.

Penang Government cruiser *Jessy*, Captain Poynton.

To these were added the *Diana*, the first steam vessel ever seen in the East, nineteen armed brigs and schooners of the Bombay Marine, and a flotilla of twenty row-boats, each armed with one 18-pounder.

The place of rendezvous was Port Cornwallis in the Andaman Islands, where the Bengal troops and the first division of the Madras force assembled by the 3rd May. From there, Sir Archibald Campbell sailed direct to Rangoon on 5th May, detaching one part of his force under Brigadier McReagh against the island of

[1] The present 26th (Prince of Wales' Own) Light Cavalry.
[2] Disbanded in 1882.

Cheduba (or Manaung), and another under Major Wahab against the island of Negrais.

On the 10th May the fleet anchored in the Rangoon river, and next day sailed up to the town in order of attack, meeting with little or no opposition on the way.

The town of Rangoon was at that time situated on the northern bank of a main branch of the Irrawaddy, about twenty-eight miles from the sea. It extended for about 900 yards along the river, and was about 600 or 700 yards wide in its broadest part. At either end extended unprotected suburbs, but the town itself was defended by an enclosure of palisades about twelve feet high. This palisade was in shape an irregular parallelogram, having one gate in each of three sides, and two gates in that of the north, from both of which were roads leading to the Shwé Dagôn Pagoda. At the river gate was a landing-place on which was situated the principal battery, and opposite to which the *Liffey* dropped anchor about 2 P.M. After a short pause a desultory fire was opened on the fleet, but was soon silenced by the guns of the frigate.

Capture of Rangoon.

In the meantime three detachments were landed from the transports, and attacked the town from three different sides. The Burmese, who were completely surprised by the arrival of the British, and quite unprepared for this sudden attack, fled on the advance of the troops; and in twenty minutes the town was in the undisputed possession of the British, without the loss of a single life.

A great quantity of ordnance, chiefly of an inferior kind, was captured,[1] but the amount of supplies that fell into the British hands was disappointing in the extreme. The town itself was found to be entirely deserted, the inhabitants having fled to the neighbouring jungles at the first news of the arrival of the British. This desertion was in a great measure due to panic, but it was promoted by the local authorities, in order to deprive their invaders of the resources of the population. It was a move that was attended by much success, for the absence of the inhabitants, and the impossibility of obtaining from them either aid or supplies, were productive of serious inconvenience to the expedi-

[1] See Appendix 5.

tion, and more than anything else disconcerted the expectations which had been formed of its immediate results.

The days immediately following the capture of Rangoon were appropriated to the landing and disposition of the troops, who were all accommodated in houses in the town, in huts along the roads leading to the Shwé Dagôn Pagoda, or in the pagoda itself. Parties of seamen from the men-of-war, with a detachment of the Madras European Regiment, were also employed in scouring the river in search of any armed boats or fire-rafts which it was thought likely the enemy would prepare. A stockade having been discovered by one of these parties at Kemmendine, it was stormed and captured, the enemy leaving sixty dead in the position. Detachments were also sent into the interior to try to find and bring back the population, but without success.

The prospects of the British force at Rangoon were not encouraging. So impossible was it to procure supplies of any sort, that the troops were entirely dependent on Bengal and Madras for every description of food; a state of things which had never been expected, and for which no preparation had been made. In addition to this, the rainy season, so peculiarly unhealthy to Europeans, was just beginning; and so far from the capture of Rangoon, and the two islands, already alluded to, having the expected effect of making the King of Ava sue for peace, it was ascertained that he was making active preparations to equip a force to recapture his lost possessions.

The Commander-in-Chief, therefore, finding that no practical benefits had as yet resulted from his success, and that, on the contrary, the jungles which surrounded Rangoon were rapidly filling with troops from all quarters, saw the necessity of having recourse at once to bold and vigorous measures. His first object was to obtain a large number of boats and pilots to take his force up the Irrawaddy. At that time this river was the principal artery of communication of the Burman Empire, and it was known that each village on its banks was obliged to keep up a certain number of war-boats. It had been hoped that some would have been procurable at Rangoon which was a city of Pegu, a conquered state of Burma; and as the most determined hostility had existed between these two countries for years, it had been anticipated, and not perhaps without reason, that the inhabitants of Pegu would do all in their power to assist the British against their old enemies. This hope, however, was entirely fallacious; at the appearance of a common foe all internal dissensions were forgotten, and not a single boatman acquainted with the navigation of the river was to be procured.

Meanwhile the rains had set in with great severity, making it impossible for the British troops to keep the field, and it soon became evident that no important operations could be attempted until the end of the year.

While thus situated, the force at Rangoon was joined by the detachments which had been despatched against Cheduba (or Manaung) and Negrais. The latter, a small island about six miles in circumference, was found to be uninhabited, but the enemy had erected a stockade on the opposite mainland, against which Major Wahab landed a small detachment. The stockade was captured without much trouble and the enemy put to flight. The British Commander, considering that no further advantage was to be gained by the occupation of Negrais, then set sail for Rangoon.

Capture of Negrais.

The capture of Cheduba was more vigourously contested. The transports reached the mouth of the river leading to the chief town on the 12th May. Early on the 14th, 200 of His Majesty's 13th Regiment, and 100 of the 20th Native Infantry proceeded up the river in small boats. They soon discovered the enemy in considerable force on the banks. The troops landed; whereupon the enemy, retiring before them, took up a position behind a strong stockade. The stockade having been breached by the British guns, the position was assaulted and the enemy defeated with heavy loss, the British casualties amounting to three men killed, and four officers and thirty-seven men wounded. The next day the Raja of Cheduba was captured by a reconnoitring patrol, and the remainder of the Burman force escaping to the mainland, the people of Cheduba readily submitted to British rule.

Capture of Cheduba.

Brigadier McReagh, therefore, leaving a small detachment of the 20th Native Infantry as a garrison, sailed for Rangoon, which he reached on 11th June.

Between this date and the arrival of the main body at Rangoon, several minor engagements had taken place with the Burmese, who, concealed in the dense jungles that grew close to the British posts, maintained a system of harassing attacks, cutting off stragglers, firing on the picquets, and creating constant alarms, both by day and night.

In order to put a stop to this mode of warfare, and to find out the numbers and position of the enemy, Sir Archibald marched out on the 28th of May with four companies of British troops, 250 sepoys, one gun and a howitzer, against the entrenchments in the neighbourhood of the camp, which were supported by a large body of troops under the command of the Governor of Shwédang. After proceeding some way, it was found impossible to take the guns any further; they were consequently sent back to camp, and the infantry continued the advance alone, their path lying along rice-fields some inches under water. After a most fatiguing march of about ten miles the enemy were discovered in great numbers at the village of Joazong, their front defended as usual by strong stockades. An attack was immediately ordered and the stockades carried at the point of the bayonet. The Burmans then retired into the jungle, where it being impossible to pursue them, the detachment returned to camp. The enemy are said to have left 300 dead in their defences.

Soon after this affair two deputies arrived from the Burmese camp under pretence of negotiating a peace, but in reality only with the view of gaining time for the main body to strengthen themselves. They were intended, perhaps, to act also as spies, but whatever was their object, nothing satisfactory was proposed by them in their interview with the British Commissioners, and they shortly after returned to their camp.

Several more minor successes were now scored against the Burmese, but the ease with which their stockades were captured and the heavy losses they were frequently suffering, did not cause them to change their plan of campaign against the British, namely to surround and destroy them. The next move on the part of the Burmans was to concentrate a large force at Kemmendine, at which place, about two miles above the stockade from which they had been expelled on the 10th May, they constructed an extensive system of fortifications of the same nature. From this place they became so generally troublesome that Sir Archibald Campbell found it necessary to advance against them without delay and a combined military and naval expedition accordingly proceeded up the river on the 2nd June.

Failure at Kemmendine.

The land force consisted of two independent columns under Lieutenant-Colonel H. F. Smith, C.B., and Lieutenant-Colonel Hodgson, respectively. The former was composed of detachments of the Madras European Regiment, 3rd and 12th Native Infantry, 15 Pioneers, two howitzers, and one mortar, while Colonel Hodgson's force included a detachment of the Madras European Regiment, and the 9th Regiment of Native Infantry. In addition to these troops the cruisers composing the naval part of the expedition were accompanied by three companies of His Majesty's 41st Regiment. The Commander-in-Chief also accompanied the fleet.

The two columns proceeded by separate roads, and after going five miles through thick jungle Colonel Smith arrived in front of a strong stockade about fourteen feet in height. His guns opened upon it, and the Grenadiers of the Madras European Regiment, led by Major Walker of the 3rd Light Infantry and Captain Kyd of their own Corps, supported by the 3rd Light Infantry, carried the place by mounting on each other's shoulders. Colonel Hodgson came up during the attack and moved round to the rear for the purpose of intercepting the fugitives but was too late. The march was now resumed; Kemmendine was reached shortly afterwards, and was found to be surrounded by a formidable stockade.

The howitzers and the mortar were brought into action but without result; the stockade was too high to be surmounted, and there being neither scaling ladders nor axes with the column all efforts to pull down the palisading were fruitless, and Colonel Smith after persevering for two hours was forced to retire. Colonel Hodgson's column co-operated in this attack. The British loss, some of which was caused by a heavy fire of grape from our own cruisers in the river, amounted to fifty-five Europeans and twenty-five natives killed and wounded.

The want of foresight in having neglected to supply the troops with either scaling ladders or axes and their loss from the fire of the cruisers was slurred over in the despatch in the following sentences :—" The two columns coming down from the Shwé Dagôn Pagoda met close to the stockade at Kemmendine and an effort was made to enter it which I have no doubt would have succeeded but for the occurrence of some mistakes."

Description of Burmese stockades.

It may be well to give here a general description of the stockades with which our troops had to contend. They were generally square or oblong enclosures, their strength varying according to the time allowed for their construction and the materials at hand; sometimes they consisted of solid beams of teak, previously prepared, sometimes of green bamboos and young trees cut from the surrounding jungle. The height varied from ten to twenty feet; the garrison firing from platforms or heaped up earth, on which *jingals*, or guns of small calibre, were also occasionally planted. In some cases an outer and an inner ditch were added to the defences; and outworks of small stockades, abattis, and bamboo spikes (*pangyis*) increased the difficulties of the attack. The nature of the materials, especially when consisting of green bamboo or other timber, enabled them to resist a cannonade better than more solid substances, and there was always some difficulty in breaching the palisades.

No time was lost in trying to repair the failure at Kemmedine and on the 10th June a force of about 3,000 men, with eight guns, proceeded to repeat the attack, two divisions of armed vessels being employed at the same time to attack the river face of the stockade.

The attacking force was formed into three columns organized as follows :—

No. 1 under Lieutenant-Colonel Mallet, 89th Foot.

41st Foot	.. ..	250 men.
89th "	.. ..	500 "
Madras European Regiment	..	250 "
1st Battalion, 7th Madras N. I.	..	450 "
2nd " 8th " "	..	350 "
" " 17th " "	..	200 "

No. 2 under Brigadier Hodgson.

13th Foot	.. ..	A detachment.
38th "	.. ..	"

Madras European Regiment	..	5 companies.
1st Battalion, 9th Madras N. I.	..	300 men.
1st ,, 22nd ,, ,,	..	500 ,,

No. 3 under Brigadier Smelt, 41st Foot.

21st Foot	..	4 companies.
1st Battalion, 3rd Madras N. I.	..	400 men.
2nd ,, 10th N. I.	..	200 ,,
2nd ,, Madras N. I.	..	250 ,,

On the march the land columns came across a strong stockade, about two miles from the town. Its front face consisted of a palisade about twelve feet high, strengthened by crossbars and railings of great solidity; the other sides were protected by the denseness of the surrounding jungle. It was speedily attacked, and a breach being made by the two 18-pounders, the assaulting troops made good their entrance, while at the same time another party clambered over the palisades on the left flank and co-operated in clearing the entrenchment. The enemy fled into the thicket, leaving 150 dead, including a chief of some rank, as indicated by his golden umbrella.

Capture of Kemmendine.

After carrying this work, the British moved forward to the river, where they came upon the chief stockade, which was immediately invested. By four o'clock the troops were in position in a thick jungle, and in spite of a heavy fall of rain, batteries were erected during the night, and opened fire at daylight on the 11th. After a cannonade of two hours, it was discovered that the enemy had evacuated the fort, the propinquity of the jungle having enabled them to carry out their retreat unobserved.

The stockade of Kemmendine, thus captured, being found convenient for the command of the river immediately above Rangoon, Sir Archibald Campbell determined to occupy it permanently, and a regiment of Madras Infantry and a small British detachment were accordingly posted in it. Subsequent events amply justified this step.

The enemy now withdrew from the vicinity of Rangoon, and concentrated their forces at Donubyu, about fifty miles up the river. For some time nothing of importance happened, and Sir A. Campbell had time to consider the position in which he was placed.

An advance up the river while both banks were held by the enemy in force was out of the question, as it was impossible to obtain supplies from the country, and equally impossible to maintain communication with Rangoon. It was clearly necessary, therefore, to begin by annihilating the force in the immediate neighbourhood, before any advance could be attempted. This, however, was no easy task. In the field the enemy were as little able as inclined to face the British force, but their dexterity in throwing up trenches rendered their expulsion from these an undertaking that involved great loss of time and sacrifice of life. The nature of the country and the time of year stood the enemy in the stead of discipline and courage. The vicinity of Rangoon was covered with swamp or jungle through which the men had to wade knee-deep in water, or force their way through harassing entanglements. The malignant influence of the climate, combined with the bad quality of food supplied to the troops was crowding the hospitals with sick, fever and dysentery being the principal maladies. So great indeed was the havoc played by these causes that by the end of the rains, the British Commander had scarcely 3,000 men fit to take the field.

General Campbell's difficulties.

Notwithstanding the number of the sick being a serious deduction from their available force, the British were, however, still able to undertake offensive operations and to successfully defend themselves against the Burmese, who had for some time been gaining strength in the vicinity; and during the month of June, they gained several minor successes. About the end of June the enemy began again to assemble in the neighbourhood of Rangoon. A new general had taken over command, and began his operations with an ineffectual attack on the British position on the 1st July, in which the Burman losses amounted to over a hundred.

This check, however, did not alter the Burmese plans, and they continued gaining strength in front of the lines, and giving constant annoyance. It, therefore, again became necessary to drive them back to a greater distance, and on the 8th a column about 1,200 strong, under Brigadier-General M'Bean, moved out to operate by land, whilst Sir Archibald Campbell, with another force of 800, proceeded by water. The boats found the enemy strongly posted at the junction of the Panhlaing and Hlaing rivers. The main entrenchment was on the tongue of land at their junction, while stockades on the opposite banks of both streams commanded the approach and afforded mutual support.

Notwithstanding these formidable preparations the position was captured without difficulty.

The land column was equally successful. Having advanced to Kamayut, about six miles from Rangoon, they stormed and captured seven stockades in rapid succession. The enemy, driven from their advanced positions, fell back on their main defence, consisting of three strong entrenchments, one within the other, in the innermost of which Thamba Wungyi, who commanded, had taken his stand. This position was also quickly assaulted and captured by the victorious column, the Burmese General being among the slain. The British casualties between the 16th June and 12th July amounted to ten killed and seventy-six wounded.

The capture of so many stockades by this force, without the aid of artillery, was an achievement unsurpassed during the war, and made a great impression on the enemy, who from this time began to think themselves insecure in the strongest positions.

The inundated state of the country now prevented the British undertaking any important movements, but the troops were not allowed to remain idle, and throughout July and August minor successes continued to be gained. Nevertheless, no thoughts of peace were entertained by the Burmese; and it was now evident that, whatever victories were gained, so long as our operations were confined to the neighbourhood of Rangoon no effect would be produced by them on the Court of Ava. Unprovided, therefore, as Sir Archibald was, with the means of advancing into the interior, he resolved to have recourse to the only other alternative open to him, which was to intimidate the Burmese still further by the capture of some of their southern maritime possessions.

Expedition against Tenasserim.

Accordingly, about the end of August, a force consisting of the 89th Foot, the 7th Madras Native Infantry, and a detachment of the Bombay Artillery, under the command of Lieutenant-Colonel Miles, C.B., 89th Foot, was despatched from Rangoon for the reduction of the

Tenasserim district, a narrow strip of land on the eastern shore of the Bay of Bengal, which the successor of Alompra had wrested from the Siamese some fifty years before the outbreak of our war with Ava.

Sailing from the Irrawaddy on the 26th August, the expedition arrived off the mouth of the Tavoy river on the 1st September, and on the 8th Tavoy fell into our hands without resistance. The expedition next proceeded to Mergui, which, after a sharp resistance, was captured on the 6th October. The capture of these two places involved the reduction of the whole province, which submitted without further opposition.

After leaving a small force to hold Tavoy and Mergui, Colonel Miles returned to Rangoon in November.

Martaban.

Similarly, in October, an expedition was detached against Martaban. The command was entrusted to Lieutenant-Colonel Godwin, 41st Foot, the force consisting of a part of that regiment, the 3rd Madras Native Light Infantry, and a detachment of the Madras Artillery, with H. M. S. *Arachne*, (lately arrived from England) and H. M. S. *Sophie*, as convoy.

Martaban was taken after some resistance on the 30th October, and the capture of that place was followed by the submission of the whole of the districts of Martaban and Ye.

Siamese incursions.

It should here be mentioned that the Siamese had never altogether given up hope of recovering Tenasserim from Ava, and for a long series of years had been making predatory incursions along the coast of that province. Early in 1825, a flotilla of Siamese boats arrived on the coast, and, as usual, began plundering and burning, and carrying off the inhabitants as slaves. Major Frith, commanding at Mergui, at once took measures to drive them off, and some skirmishes took place during February and March, in the last of which the enemy suffered so severely that they never again ventured to repeat these inroads.

To return to the operations around Rangoon: in September nothing of any importance took place, but the Burmese continued in force in the neighbourhood, and were evidently only waiting till the country should be more practicable for some important enterprise. In the meantime they harassed the British by perpetual night attacks on their picquets, whose muskets they frequently contrived to carry off.

British reverse at Kaiklu.

At the beginning of October, 1824, intelligence was received that a strong force of the enemy had stockaded themselves at Kaiklu, about fifteen miles from Rangoon. The light brigade, composed of the 3rd and 34th Madras Native Light Infantry, two howitzers, and a detachment of Madras Pioneers, under the command of Brigadier Smith, were immediately detached against this place, and marched from Rangoon on the 5th of the month. Contrary to the usual practice, no European troops formed part of the expedition. Sir Archibald Campbell, in order to gratify the sepoys, who "felt aggrieved that they had never as yet been allowed to lead the way to victory, but had always been employed in support of the Europeans,'' had resolved to entrust the enterprise to them alone. Towards evening a stockade was reached at Tadagyi. The enemy were shelled out of it, after an attempt to escalade the place had failed. Here Colonel Smith received information which induced him to ask for reinforcements, including a detachment of European troops. Three hundred more native infantry and two more guns were sent, but the Commander-in-Chief refused to allow any British troops to take part in the expedition. Thus reinforced, Colonel Smith pushed on, and on the 7th, about 2 P.M., came upon the enemy at Kaiklu.

Having successfully carried a series of breastworks, thrown across the road to impede their advance, the column reached the neighbourhood of the main position about 5 o'clock. On reconnaissance the position proved to be a strongly stockaded enclosure, its right resting on high ground, surmounted by a pagoda. A party, under Captain Williamson, was ordered to make a secondary attack through the jungle on the right flank, while the main attack was to be made by Major Wahab on the front of the position. The extreme silence that prevailed in the direction of the enemy now led the British Commander to believe that the position had been abandoned, but, owing to the lateness of the hour he would not wait for any further reconnaissance, and instead of postponing his attack till the next day, he unwisely decided to assault the position at once, and ordered the escalading party to advance.

As the British advanced into the open, a cannon was fired from the pagoda, but the troops in the stockades reserved their fire until the assailants had got to within fifty yards' range. They then poured down volleys of grape and musketry with an effect and regularity till then unequalled in the war. Major Wahab and the leading officers were shot down, and the men, panic-stricken, threw themselves on the ground and refused to advance. On fire being opened from the pagoda, which till then had been believed to be undefended, a detachment had been directed against it, but this party, too, was repulsed with great loss.

Owing to the lateness of the evening Colonel Smith, instead of bringing up his reserves, now sounded the retreat.

Complete loss of discipline was the result, and the whole of the troops broke and fled, in a confused mob, to a plain at the foot of the rising ground. Here, fortunately, the force under Captain Williamson which had been detached into the jungle, and which, on hearing the "retreat," had retired in good order, was formed up, and successfully covered the retreat of the fugitives. The column was, consequently able to re-assemble, and retired without molestation to Tadagyi, carrying their wounded with them. The British loss on this occasion was twenty-three killed, including Captain Allan and Lieutenant Bond, and eighty wounded, amongst whom were Major Wahab, Captain Moncrieff, and Lieutenants Sherman, Campbell, Chalon, and Lindesay.

No time was lost in endeavouring to remedy this mishap, and on the 9th a force under Brigadier McReagh, 700 strong, including 420 Europeans, was despatched from Rangoon to make another attempt on Kaiklu. The enemy appeared, however, to be satisfied with their success, for on arrival at Kaiklu the place was found to be evacuated. After destroying the stockades, the column returned to camp.

About the same time as the first expedition to Kaiklu, another started for Thantabin on the Hlaing river, and met with very different fortune. At this place, the commander of the Burmese forces had placed a detachment under the command of one of the principal

Expedition to Thantabin.

Ministers of State. The British force sent against this post consisted of detachments of the 38th Foot, the 18th Native Infantry and the Bengal Artillery, the whole under the command of Major Evans, 38th Foot, and accompanied by a naval force under Captain Chads. With the loss of three British wounded, the enemy were driven out of their stockades, and the detachment then returned to Rangoon.

During the rest of October and November, the troops enjoyed comparative rest, and this interval, together with the approach of a more healthy season, and improved supplies, contributed materially to improve the condition of the men, and diminish the number of the sick. The force therefore was gathering vigour for the renewal of operations.

On the 26th November, the Madras European Regiment with a detachment of 28th Native Infantry and some guns sailed from Rangoon for the purpose of taking possession of Pegu, which was effected without opposition on the 29th.

The Burmans meanwhile were not idle. The successful capture of the strongest stockades, and the prolonged occupation of Rangoon, had begun in the estimation of the Burmese themselves to alter the character of the war, and the King of Ava, at last realizing that the British could not be dislodged without a determined effort, had recalled his armies from Arakan and Assam, and, concentrating the whole of his power, gave the command to Bandula, whose reputation from his success at Ramu stood very high. This General's retreat from Ramu, and subsequent march through Arakan, which in the middle of the rains must have been a very arduous one, relieved the inhabitants of Calcutta, as has been already noticed, from considerable anxiety; and, shortly afterwards, enabled our troops in that quarter to advance into the very interior of Arakan, taking possession of the capital of that province.

Upon the arrival of Bandula at Ava, no expense was spared in equipping a large force for him, and by the end of October, it was estimated that 50,000 men were collected for the advance on Rangoon. After a short delay in the capital, this favourite General set out for Donubyu, accompanied by a large fleet of war-boats. His advance was hailed with delight by the British, and preparations were speedily made for his reception. At this time 500 artizans had arrived at Rangoon from Chittagong, to build boats for the British advance up the Irrawaddy. The arrival, likewise, of several battalions of British and Native Infantry, as well as some troops of cavalry, added considerably to our actual strength.

Discussion regarding the advance upon Ava.

It will be convenient to note here that the want of transport and deficiency of supplies at Rangoon had early suggested doubts to Sir Archibald Campbell of the possibility of penetrating into the interior of Ava by the line of the Irrawaddy. He had consequently suggested the adoption of one or other of two alternative plans—one to march upon the capital from Martaban, the other to embark for the coast of Arakan, after having left a strong garrison at Rangoon, and then to cross the Yomas into Ava. Neither of these plans met with the approval of the supreme Government, and both of them were strongly objected to by Sir Thomas Munro, Governor of Madras, who, in a letter to the Governor-General, dated August 1824, wrote as follows:—"I have already given my opinion on the main point, namely, that the plan of advancing by the Irrawaddy was preferable to that of marching south, or re-embarking and landing at Arakan. I can see no object in his going to Martaban, because it would not facilitate his advance to the capital, as, according to his own account, even if the Siamese and Peguers were to take part in the war, he would still require draught and carriage equipment from Bengal. With regard to the plan of re-embarking the Rangoon force, and landing at Arakan, nothing could justify such a measure but the certainty of being furnished there with an equipment of draught and carriage cattle. If they could not obtain it, they would be still more helpless than they are now, and we should have lost reputation, and given confidence to the enemy, by abandoning the original plan of operations."

Sir Thomas then went on to set forth the advantage of a simultaneous advance upon Prome by the river, and by land.

The result was that the supreme Government determined upon the line of the Irrawaddy, and preparations were eventually made for an advance in two divisions, one by water, the other by land.

The correspondence having been sent to the Duke of Wellington by the President of the India Board in March 1825, the

Duke, in returning it, observed :—" I return the box, having perused the papers last night. There is nothing in them except want of information of the nature of the country, climate, etc., of the proposed theatre of the war. The only paper which shows in the writer any knowledge of his subject, is Sir Thomas Munro's minute of the 24th August, and it is curious how all appear to have chimed in with his simple proposal, just as a pack of hounds do to the voice of the experienced dog."

Towards the end of November the Burmese army marched down from Donubyu, and made their appearance in the neighbourhood of Rangoon. The force was now estimated at 60,000 men, of whom more than half were armed with muskets, the rest with swords and spears.

A body of mounted men were attached to the force; which was provided with a considerable number of *jingals* throwing a ball of from six to twelve ounces in weight, whilst a large flotilla of fire-rafts accompanied the war-boats down the stream.

No opposition was made to the advance of the enemy to the vicinity of Rangoon, which took place on the 1st December. Encouraged by this seeming timidity, they formed a regular investment of the British lines, extending in a semi-circle from Dalla, opposite Rangoon, round by Kemmendine and the great pagoda, to the village of Pazundaung on the creek communicating with the Pegu branch of the river. Their extreme right was thus opposite to the town on one side, and their extreme left approached to within a few hundred yards of it on the other. In many places their front was covered by thick jungle, but where it was more assailable the Burmans entrenched themselves with their usual dexterity, throwing up these defences within a couple of hundred yards of the picquets.

The British force, reduced by sickness and casualties, was too small for the defence of the position it occupied, but their front was strengthened by the judicious disposition of the artillery in batteries and redoubts. The shipping protected Rangoon and the position on the river-side; while the extreme left was defended by the post at Kemmendine, supported on the river by H. M. S. *Sophie* and a strong division of gunboats.

The operations on the part of the enemy were commenced on the morning of the 1st of December, by a resolute attack on

Kemmendine, which was, however, successfully repulsed by the garrison under Major Yates and by the flotilla. Repeated attacks were made during the day, but with the same result, and a bold attempt after dark to float fire-rafts down the stream against the shipping at Rangoon was frustrated by the skill and bravery of the men-of-war's men. In the afternoon of the 1st, a reconnaissance of the enemy's left was made by a detachment of the 13th Foot and the 18th Native Infantry under Major Sale, which broke through their entrenchments, and, after killing a number of the enemy, destroyed their works. The same day was marked by two or three other successful skirmishes on the part of the British, but with these exceptions, and the reply to the enemy's fire by the artillery, nothing was attempted for a few days, Sir Archibald's policy being to encourage the Burmese to trust themselves completely within his reach. On the 3rd and 4th, therefore, the Burmese continued to push their position closer to the British lines unopposed. On the 5th they were so close that it was impossible for them to escape from a defeat, and Sir A. Campbell perceived that the right moment had come to strike a decisive blow.

With this view he ordered a division of the gunboats up the Pazundaung creek to attack the enemy in flank and keep their attention engaged in that quarter. At the same time he despatched two columns from the Rangoon side, one 800 strong, under Major Sale, and the other of 500, under Major Walker, against the enemy's left.

The columns advanced at 7 A.M. That under Major Walker was the first to come into action. The enemy began by offering some resistance, but the stockade being carried at the point of the bayonet, they quickly broke and fled: our casualties were few, but Major Walker was among the killed. The other column being equally successful completed the overthrow of the Burmese, the whole of whose left was driven in scattered parties from the field, leaving numbers of dead on the ground and all their guns and military stores in the hands of the British.

Bandula made no attempt to recover this position, but, collecting the fugitives on his right and centre, continued to sap up to the Shwé Dagôn Pagoda, until his trenches approached so close that his men's voices could be distinctly heard by the British. In order to end the contest, now that the chief part of the enemy's force was within his grasp, Sir Archibald, on the 7th, ordered an attack to be made by four columns,[1] whilst Major Sale, with his detachment operated against the enemy's left and rear.

The advance of the columns was proceeded by a heavy cannonade, during which they moved to their respective points of attack. Colonel Mallet's column moved against the right of the enemy, and Colonel Brodie against their left, while the other two under Captain Wilson and Lieutenant-Colonel Parlby advanced straight against the centre. No data is available concerning the individual strength and composition of these columns. After a moment's pause the enemy opened a heavy fire, but it was unable to stop the assailants, who rushed the entrenchments and put their defenders to rout.

During all this time Major Yates with his garrison of the 26th Native Infantry (now the 86th Carnatic Infantry) had successfully held the post of Kemmendine against repeated attacks of the enemy both by day and night. For the conspicuous gallantry displayed by the above regiment during this period, they were permitted, by a Resolution of the Governor-General in Council dated 21st January 1825, to bear the word "Kemmendine" inscribed on their colours.

Defence of Kemmendine.

The Burman army was now completely defeated. Their loss in the different actions is supposed to have exceeded 5,000 men, but they suffered most in their loss of arms and ammunition, which they could not easily replace: in all 240 pieces of ordnance were captured, in addition to a great number of muskets.

The loss of the British, throughout the seven days, was only about thirty killed and two hundred and sixty wounded. Amongst the former were Major Walker and Lieutenant O'Shea of the 13th Foot.

Notwithstanding the unexpected defeat which Bandula thus sustained, not many days passed before that indefatigable leader succeeded in rallying his scattered forces and, with a body of about 25,000 men, returned to Kokine, within three miles of the British

1 Her Majesty's 41st and 89th Foot; the Madras European Regiment; the 9th, 12th, 28th, 30th and 44th Native Infantry.

lines; here he, in the words of Sir Archibald Campbell's despatch, "commenced entrenching and stockading with a judgment in point of position such as would do credit to the best instructed engineers of the most civilized and warlike of nations.'' At the same time, he started harassing the British by floating fire-rafts down stream against the shipping at Rangoon, and employing incendiaries to set fire to Rangoon itself. So successful was he in this last project, that on the night of the 14th a great part of the town was in flames in different quarters. The garrison, after great exertions, succeeded in getting the fire under control, but not before half the town, including the quarters of the Madras Commissariat, had been destroyed.

It was thus necessary to advance against the new Burmese position, not only to confirm the impression made by the last victory, but also to open the country to the further advance of the army, and to secure the safety of Rangoon, with all the British stores.

Accordingly, on the 15th December, General Campbell moved out against the enemy in two columns. The right column consisted of 540 men under Brigadier-General Cotton, the left, 900 strong, was under the command of Sir Archibald Campbell himself. The former was directed to make a détour and take the work in rear, while the latter attacked in front. The position was found to be of great strength; it consisted of two large stockades on either flank, connected by a central entrenchment. Each wing was about 400 yards long by 200 broad, and the whole position was occupied by a force of 20,000 men.

The right column, having gained the rear, attacked the centre of the work, while the left, forming into two divisions, commanded by Brigadier Miles and Major Evans, stormed the flank stockades. In fifteen minutes, thanks to the admirable way the fire of the artillery was directed, the British were in possession not only of the enemy's work, but of his camp, which was left standing, the whole of his baggage, and a large proportion of his arms and ammunition. In this encounter the 13th Foot suffered severely, losing three officers and twelve men killed, and eight officers and fifty men wounded. The total British casualties amounted to eighteen killed and one hundred and fifty wounded.

It is worthy of notice that the number of the British force on this occasion did not exceed 1,440 men.

On the same day as this action was fought, an attack, under Captain Chads, R.N., was made on the enemy's fleet of war-boats. Of these, principally through the help of the *Diana* steam-boat, the sight of which filled the Burmese with the greatest consternation, thirty were captured, having been previously abandoned by their crews, who, upon the approach of the steam-boat, threw themselves into the river and swam ashore in an agony of terror.

In consequence of these continued disasters, Bandula led back his army, much shattered, to Donubyu, and the character of the war was changed. The Burmans no longer dared to undertake offensive operations, but restricted themselves to the defence of their positions along the river. The road was now open to the British force, which was prepared to advance, if necessary, to the walls of the capital, in harmony with the policy dictated by the course of events.

Before proceeding any further, however, with their future actions we must stop to notice the renewal of active hostilities on the north-eastern and eastern frontiers of the British Indian Dominions.

CHAPTER IV.

FURTHER OPERATIONS ON THE NORTH-EAST FRONTIER

CAMPAIGN IN ASSAM.

It has already been related that, on the commencement of the rainy season of 1824, Colonel Richards, with the force operating in Assam, fell back on Gauhati from the advanced positions he had taken up on first driving back the Burmese forces. Immediately on this retrograde movement, the enemy re-occupied Kaliabar and Nowgong, plundering the whole country, and even making incursions into Jaintia. It therefore became necessary to expel the Burmans once more from these districts.

Colonel Richards still commanded at Gauhati, and his force amounted to about 3,000 men, consisting of the 46th and 57th Native Infantry, the Rangpur and Dinajpur local Battalions, and the Champaran Light Infantry, with details of artillery and a detachment of Irregular Horse. The numbers of his force and the necessity of employing water transport prevented the advance of the whole body at one time, and it was consequently decided to start operations by detaching two parties to expel the enemy from the advanced positions they had taken up. Accordingly, at the end of October 1824, Major Waters, with a flotilla and part of the Dinajpur Battalion, was directed to proceed to Rahachauki and Nowgong; and the rest of the boats, with one wing of the Champaran Light Infantry and four guns, under Major Cooper, proceeded to Kaliabar. The latter arrived at his destination on the 29th October, surprising and defeating a small body of Burmese on his way. The former, after two or three minor successes, reached Rahachauki a few days later.

On the morning of the 3rd November Major Waters, hearing that the Burmese Governor of Assam was meditating retreat from Nowgong, made a forced march to that place in order to intercept him, but on arrival, he found that the enemy had retired the day before and had got too long a start to leave any chance of being overtaken. From information gained on the spot it appeared that the Burmese force amounted to about 3,000 men, and the hurried retreat of so large a body, upon the approach of a force not a third of their strength, clearly showed how little they were disposed to offer opposition to the British occupation of Assam.

The advanced posts being thus secured, Colonel Richards moved the remaining part of his forces up to Kaliabar, but his chief means of transport being by water, the advance of the army was necessarily slow. No difficulty, however, was experienced from any other cause, as the people were friendly and there were no enemy to be encountered. From Kaliabar, the force moved to Mara Mukh, where they arrived on the 6th January. At this place intelligence was received of the presence of various hostile bodies at Kaliana, Deogoru, Dhogaon, and on the Jorhat road, whereupon Colonel Richards at once despatched portions of his force against them. These operations having driven back the enemy at trifling loss to the British, a further advance on Jorhat was undertaken on the 17th January.

From here Colonel Richards marched to Gawrisagar, a few miles from Rangpur.[1] The boats had now to be left behind, the Dikhu river being too shallow for them to proceed any further. The guns and ordnance stores were consequently landed, and a party of the 46th Native Infantry being dropped to guard the boats, the rest of the troops advanced on Rangpur. On the morning of the 27th, the advanced guard was vigorously attacked by the Burmese who had taken up their position in thick jungle. Colonel Richards finding it impossible to get to close quarters, feinted a retirement, to tempt the enemy into leaving their position. The ruse was entirely successful; the Burmese rushed out into the open at this apparent exhibition of timidity, and the British, suddenly turning, charged the enemy and defeated them with heavy loss.

The British advance on Rangpur was then resumed. The approach to the capital had been strongly fortified. A stockade had been drawn across the road, the left of which was strengthened by an entrenched tank, and the right was within gun-shot of the

[1] Rangpur, the old capital, was situated about one mile south of Sibsagar. Only the ruins of the palace now remain.

fort; several guns were mounted in the position, which was defended by a strong garrison. On approaching the defences, the British were met with a heavy fire, which brought down half the leading troops and caused a momentary check: under cover of the artillery, however, the column again advanced and the stockade was carried at the point of the bayonet. The tank on the left was also occupied, and two temples, one on the left and another on the right, were seized, whereby the south side of the fort was entirely invested, and the enemy were driven in at all points. The loss on the side of the attackers was two men killed and fifty-one wounded.

The result of this action not only dispirited the Burmans, but gave renewed life to the internal dissensions that prevailed in their camp. The two chiefs and some of their troops were willing to sue for terms, but most of the garrison were bent on resistance and threatened the advocates of peace with extermination. The latter, however, so far prevailed as to despatch a priest to the British Commander to negotiate for the surrender of Rangpur, and the following terms were finally agreed upon through this man's mediation. Such of the garrison as continued hostile were allowed to retire into Burman territory, on their engaging to abstain from any act of aggression on their retreat, and those who were pacifically inclined were allowed to remain unmolested, with their families and property: their final destination was to await the decision of the Governor-General, but in the event of peace with Ava, they were not to be given up to that Government. Colonel Richards was induced to accede to these conditions by his conviction of the impossibility of preventing the escape of the garrison on the capture of the fort, or of pursuing them on their flight.

Occupation of Rangpur.

By the occupation of Rangpur on the terms granted much time was saved, much loss of life avoided, and the object of the campaign, *i.e.*, the expulsion of the Burmans from Assam, peacefully and promptly secured. Those who surrendered numbered 700; the rest about 9,000, of both sexes, and all ages, including 2,000 fighting men, withdrew to the frontiers.

By the fall of Rangpur the conquest of Assam was practically completed, for the enemy held no other posts within the province. It was some time, however, before the country was restored to law and order; numerous bodies of Burmans, joined by Singphos and other savage hill tribes, took advantage of the anarchy into which the country had sunk during the Burmese occupation, and began to plunder and murder on their own account. Detachments had frequently to be sent against these marauders, and several encounters took place. After two or three defeats, however, the enemy did not again assemble, and order was gradually introduced. .

OPERATIONS IN CACHAR, 1825.

At the beginning of 1825 the original plan of remaining on the defensive on the Sylhet frontier was abandoned and it was decided to march a large force into Ava through Cachar and Manipur. With this object a force of about 7,000 men was collected under Brigadier Shuldham, who was appointed to command the eastern frontier. The army consisted of six regiments of infantry (the 7th, 44th, and 45th Native Infantry forming the 3rd Brigade, and the 14th, 39th, and 52nd Native Infantry forming the 4th Brigade), two companies of artillery, four of Pioneers, the Sylhet Local Corps, a corps of Cavalry, Blair's Irregular Horse, and a body of Cacharis and Manipuris under Raja Gambhir Singh.

Directly after the rains had ceased, it was found that the Burmese had been compelled by sickness and want of supplies, to abandon their position at Tilain. There was, therefore, no likelihood of meeting with any opposition on the advance through Cachar, nor was it probable that the enemy would be met with in any strength in Manipur, the defence of Arakan and the Irrawaddy at that time employing all the available strength of Ava. Notwithstanding the fact that hostile opposition was not to be feared, the nature of the country to be traversed and its utter unproductiveness, afforded obstacles equally serious, and proved insurmountable to the numerous and heavily equipped British force.

The advance was begun in February 1825. A road from Badarpur to Banskandy was speedily made by the Pioneers, on which General Shuldham, with the artillery and the 3rd Brigade, advanced to the latter place, there to await the further work of the Pioneers and the arrival of transport and supplies.

Difficulties of the country.

The country from Banskandy towards Manipur was a continual series of ascents and descents, the route being intersected at right angles by ridges of mountains running nearly due north and south and by mountain streams swollen into deep and rapid rivers after every shower. For the first thirty miles the mountains were covered with dense jungle, and the soil was a soft alluvial mould, converted by the slightest rain into a quagmire; and to aggravate all these difficulties, frequent and heavy rains began early in February, and continued, almost without intermission, until the proximity of the real rainy season rendered the attempt to reach Manipur hopeless.

During February, the Pioneers contrived, with immense difficulty, to make a pathway through the forest to the banks of the Jiri *nullah*, about forty miles from Banskandy, but the nature of the soil, and the state of the weather, rendered their exertions of no avail, as the road continued impassable for guns and laden cattle. In the attempts to advance and to forward supplies to the Pioneers, several hundred bullocks, camels, and elephants were lost, partly from overwork, and partly from sinking so deeply into the mire that no efforts could extricate them.

Campaign abandoned.

After struggling in vain against these physical obstructions for two months, General Shuldham reported the impracticability of an advance to Manipur, in consequence of which the attempt was abandoned, and the force broken up. The head-quarters were removed to Dacca; a force under Colonel Donkin was posted at Sylhet; and two corps of native infantry, with the Sylhet Local Corps, and the Manipur Levy were left in Cachar.

That the difficulties, which had thus arrested the advance of the British, were not insurmountable to a small force, differently constituted, was speedily established; for later on in the year, Gambhir Singh was allowed to make an attempt to recover Manipur at the head of his own irregular troops. Accompanied by Lieutenant Pemberton of the Pioneers, he started on this expedition on the 17th May, and in less than a month he had succeeded in turning the enemy out of Manipur, and had driven him into the hills and jungles that lie between that country and Ava.

EXPEDITION TO ARAKAN.

It will be remembered that when the plan of operations against the Burmese was decided on in the early part of 1824, it was determined to maintain a strictly defensive attitude on the

Chittagong frontier. Later on, when the difficulties of the army at Rangoon made the success of the British force in that quarter a matter of some doubt, more enterprising counsels prevailed. Arrangements were made for the assembly, during the ensuing cold season, of a force at Chittagong to move forward from that place, clear Arakan of the enemy, and eventually cross into Ava, holding out a hand to Sir Archibald Campbell on his advancing up the line of the Irrawaddy, and aiding him in his movement on the enemy's capital. With this intention, orders were given in September 1824, for the assembly of about 11,000 men at Chittagong, the command of the expedition being entrusted to Brigadier-General Morrison.

Barrackpore mutiny.

It was in connection with the movements of these troops that the Barrackpore mutiny occurred—one of the most painful incidents in the annals of the Bengal army.

Amongst the regiments warned for service in Arakan were the 26th, 47th and 62nd Bengal Native Infantry, all at that time stationed at Barrackpore. These regiments took no pains to conceal their aversion to the service for which they had been detailed. Several causes were at work to make them discontented; the recent changes in the army had sent a number of officers to the regiments who were strangers to the men; the Ramu disaster had impressed them with an unreasonable and unreasoning dread of the Burmese, whom they had endowed with supernatural powers; despite assurances to the contrary, an impression prevailed that they would be forced, against their will, on board ship; and finally, there existed a real grievance in the difficulty of procuring the necessary amount of baggage animals, which, according to the custom then in vogue, the sepoy had to supply for himself out of an allowance given for that purpose. The nature of Arakan demanded bullock transport and at this time the drain on Bengal for the supply of the Rangoon expedition had made these animals almost unprocurable.

In the midst of this dissatisfaction, the 47th, the first regiment to march, was ordered to parade on the 1st November. On this they broke into open mutiny and refused to fall in. All attempts to soothe the excited feelings of the men proved fruitless, though it would appear that little consideration was paid to the peculiarities of the native temperament, for the first signs of discontent seem to have been met with harshness instead of reassurance. The men, however, having now become completely out of hand, there was no alternative left but to put down the mutiny by force. The next day, therefore, the Commander-in-Chief proceeded to the spot, and at daybreak the 1st and 47th (British) Foot, a troop of the Body-Guard, and a detachment of Bengal Horse Artillery were paraded opposite the sepoy lines.

The 47th Native Infantry formed up in front of their quarters, and were joined by about a 100 from the other two regiments under orders for Arakan. The mutineers were ordered to ground their arms, but refused to obey. On this, the artillery were ordered to open fire upon them. At the first discharge, the mutineers broke and fled, pursued by the Body-Guard. Many were killed on the spot, and most of the remainder were taken prisoners, of whom eleven were hanged, and the rest sentenced to hard labour in chains. The number of the regiment was effaced from the Army List[1] and the native officers dismissed the service, although none of these openly took part in the mutiny (G. G. O. No. 335 of 1824). It is evident that these sentences were considered more severe than the occasion warranted, for the mutineers who remained in custody were pardoned four months later (G. O. C. C., 22nd April 1825).

It should be noted that, though this mutiny was serious in that the sepoys openly refused to obey orders, no acts of violence were committed nor did the mutineers fire a single shot, although they were each in possession of forty rounds of ammunition. The mutiny was aptly described by the Court of Inquiry as "an ebullition of despair at being ordered to march without having the means of doing so."

The prompt and vigorous measures of suppression adopted took immediate effect. The chief difficulty, the provision of transport, having been overcome, the disinclination of the other two regiments to proceed on service was no longer openly expressed, and within a few days of the mutiny the 26th and 62nd marched

[1] It should be stated that to replace the 47th, a new regiment was raised and numbered the 69th. In 1829 this regiment was re-named the 47th, and under that title served in the Sutlej campaign, and in Burma, and remained faithful during the mutiny of 1857. The 69th regiment which mutinied in Multan in 1858 was raised in 1825 as the 1st Extra Regiment.

for Chittagong. At this place arrangements for the expedition had been proceeding actively, but it was the end of the year before all was in readiness for an advance to the southward.

When finally formed the expeditionary force was constituted as follows :—

Staff.

Brigadier-General J. W. Morrison, C.B., 44th Foot, Commanding.

Brigadier-General W. Macbean, C.B., 54th Foot, Second-in-Command.

Lieutenant W. B. Scott, 44th Foot, Deputy Assistant Adjutant-General.

Captain J. G. Drummond, 6th Bengal N. I., Deputy Assistant Quartermaster-General.

Artillery.

Lieutenant-Colonel A. Lindsay, Bengal Artillery, Commanding.

6th Company, 2nd Battalion, Bengal Artillery.

7th " " " " "

Pioneers.

"A" Company, 1st Battalion, Madras Artillery Pioneers.

Six companies of Bengal Pioneers.

Corps of Magh Pioneers.

Extra Pioneer and Pontoon Train.

Cavalry.

2nd Bengal Local Horse.

1st Bengal Infantry Brigade.

Lieutenant-Colonel W. Richards, 26th Bengal N. I., Commanding.

44th Foot.

28th Bengal Native Infantry.

49th " " ".

2nd Bengal Infantry Brigade.

Lieutenant-Colonel C. Grant, C.B., 54th Foot, Commanding.

54th Foot.

42nd Bengal Native Infantry.

62nd " " "

5th Madras Infantry Brigade.

Lieutenant-Colonel A. Fair, 10th Madras N. I., Commanding.

10th Madras Native Infantry.

16th " " "

Additional Corps.

1st Bengal Light Infantry Battalion.
2nd ,, ,, ,, ,,
1st Bengal Grenadier Battalion.
2nd ,, ,, ,,

The naval force assembled to co-operate with General Morrison, was commanded by Commodore Hayes, of the Bombay Marine, and consisted of the following vessels:-

Vestal	10-gun brig.
Research	Surveying vessel.
Investigator	,, ,,
Helen	6-gun brig.
Henry Meriton	,, ,,
Planet	,, ,,
Sophia	,, ,,
Asseerghur	,, ,,
Trusty	Ketch.
Pluto	Steam-gun vessel.

Ten pinnaces, each carrying two guns.

Eighty gun-boats, each armed with a 12-pounder carronade.

In addition, a number of other craft were got ready on the spot by the Political Agent, for the conveyance of the men and stores along the coast and across the many creeks and rivers by which the approach to Arakan was intersected.

Although no serious obstruction to the march was to be apprehended from the enemy, yet the advance to Arakan was impeded by the same difficulties which had been found the most formidable foes in every stage of the war. The country, thinly populated and overrun with jungle, afforded no resources, and all supplies and transport had to be brought from Bengal, at much trouble and expense. The rainy season of this particular year also, being protracted to the end of November, made it impossible to send supplies by land, and retarded the construction of a military road by which the artillery were to proceed. This road was completed as soon as the weather permitted, but a large part of the stores had not arrived as late as January 1825, in the beginning of which month General Morrison determined to move out,

The army, accordingly, began to advance on the 1st January, and in the course of the month, they were assembled in the vicinity of Cox's Bazar, to which place they were accompanied along the coast by the transports and other vessels.

Here it became necessary to decide whether to follow the road along the coast to the mouth of the Naaf, or, by taking a more easterly direction, to cross that river at a higher and more practicable part of its course. It should be noted that the rivers of Arakan rise in a range of mountains only a short distance from the sea coast, and are consequently neither of great volume nor depth. They are generally fordable, except after heavy rain; but as they approach the coast they suddenly change their character, and expand into vast estuaries, communicating with each other and the sea. The whole coast, indeed, may be considered to be indented by large inlets of the sea, receiving mountain torrents, rather than as broken by the mere passage of rivers. In spite, however, of the greater difficulties to be encountered in crossing these numerous estuaries, which would have been avoided if a route further inland had been selected, General Morrison determined to follow the direction of the coast. The existence of an inland road was doubtful, and there could be no question that it led through a wild and jungle covered country, which would be impassable for the artillery and baggage animals. Whilst proceeding along the coast, the fleet would ensure the receipt of supplies, and would, it was hoped, be able to take the army across the mouths of the different rivers without delay.

The army reached Tek Naf on the 1st February. A detachment was immediately sent across the river and occupied Maungdaw. No enemy appeared, and the population was decidedly friendly.

The rest of the troops were gradually taken across the river, but the difficulties of this operation greatly exceeded anticipation, and it was the 12th of the month before a further advance could be made. Even then a great part of the baggage was still on the western bank, and a lot of the transport had not even reached the Naaf. From Maungdaw an inland road led *viâ* Lawadong (Rathedaung ?) to Arakan, which was a better route than that from Ramu; but acting on the plan first adopted, General Morrison continued his march along the coast to the mouth of another large river, the Mayu, about fifty miles south of the Naaf. To this place the 54th Foot, the 10th Madras Native Infantry, and the left wing of the 16th Madras Native Infantry proceeded by sea, the rest of the force, with the exception of a detachment under Colonel Richards, moved by land. Colonel Richards was left at Maungdaw, with directions to follow as soon as enough transport to carry three weeks' supplies had crossed the Naaf. The land column reached the Mayu river on the 22nd February, but owing to the delay caused by a squall, the transports did not arrive till five days later. The Mayu was about five miles broad at its mouth, and was only twelve miles from the Arakan (Kaladan) river, from which it was separated by the island of Akyab. A series of creeks to the north of this island offered water communication between the two rivers. General Morrison now began to throw his force across the Mayu, whence he directed them through these canals or creeks to a small island on the eastern side of the Arakan river where he placed his camp. The difficulties of this movement, however, were so great that it was the 20th March—nearly a month afterwards—before the whole force was across and a further advance could be undertaken. Meanwhile Commodore Hayes, with the greater part of the fleet, had sailed direct for the Arakan river. Arriving at its mouth on the 22nd February, he sailed up in the direction of Arakan,[1] but was stopped by the enemy's works at Kangyaung-bya (Hkyoung Pala), and after a sharp engagement, was obliged to drop down the river.

General Morrison, after four days spent in improving the road across some *nullahs* on the left bank of the river Arakan, ordered an advance on the 24th February. The route lay along the east bank of the main branch of the Arakan river (the Kelabôn river), and the march was made under auspicious conditions, the weather being favourable, the country productive, and the people warm in the cause of those who were likely to liberate them from Burman oppression.

On the 24th March, the army encamped on the southern bank of the Chabatti *nullah*. The 25th was occupied in preparing to cross this and another *nullah* about a mile in advance, beyond

[1] The ancient capital of Arakan, now called, and shown on most maps as, Mrohaung or Myahaung.

which the enemy were said to be posted on the Pade (Padha) hills. The *nullahs* being crossed on the morning of the 26th, the force was formed into four columns, the right commanded by Brigadier Grant, the centre by Brigadier Richards, the left by Captain Leslie and the reserve by Lieutenant-Colonel Walker. The left column proceeded up the main branch of the river, but the boats soon grounding, the men were landed, and were ordered to turn the hills on the enemy's right. The right and centre columns moved towards the passes which had been found to lead through the range.

The enemy were completely concealed by the forests which crowned the hilltops. The light companies were directed to turn them out, and climbing the slopes in the most gallant manner, they carried several intrenched posts with a loss of only sixteen wounded. Meanwhile the columns below had captured the passes, and the army crossing to the northern side of the range, bivouacked within a mile and a half of the enemy's main position at Mahati.

The advance was resumed on the 27th. The enemy held a strong position, heavily fortified, and protected on two sides by broad rivers, but on the approach of the British they retired without firing a shot and fled towards Arakan.

On the 28th, the whole of the troops in rear, and the flotilla, with Commodore Hayes, having joined head-quarters, the British advanced on Arakan. After a careful reconnaissance, an attack was ordered on the eastern side of the town. The defences here consisted of a series of stockades, carried along the crest of some hills about 400 feet high, which, running parallel with the town, had been strengthened by escarpments, abattis, and masonry. Only one pass led through these hills to the capital, and this was defended by about 3,000 men and several guns. The total strength of the enemy was estimated at 9,000 men. The ground in front of the hills was a long narrow valley, devoid of cover, and commanded by the enemy's artillery. A narrow belt of jungle skirted the foot of the hills, but above this the ground was again bare and open.

With incredible folly the British Commander decided to try and carry this strong position by a frontal attack on the pass. This well-nigh impossible task was entrusted to Brigadier Macbean.

The assault was led by the Light Infantry company of the 54th Foot, four companies of the 2nd Light Infantry Battalion, and the Light Infantry companies of the 10th and 16th Native Infantry, but notwithstanding the utmost gallantry of the troops, the attempt failed, and after a fruitless struggle, in which every officer was wounded, a retirement was ordered, and the force took up a defensive position for the rest of the day.

After this failure, another reconnaissance was made, as the result of which it was decided, while holding the enemy in front, to direct the main attack on the hill on their right flank, which was now discovered to be the key of the position. The next day was spent in the construction of a battery to play on the defences of the pass, and on the 31st, at daylight, the guns opened and maintained a heavy cannonade throughout the day, which effectually checked the enemy's fire. At eight in the evening Brigadier Richards moved off with the column for the attack of the right flank, his force consisting of six companies of the 44th Foot, three of the 26th, and three of the 49th Native Infantry, thirty seamen, and thirty dismounted men of Gardener's Horse. Though there was moonlight it was evident from the silence of the Burmese that this movement had not been detected from the heights. The hill was about 500 feet high, and the road by which the party advanced was winding and precipitous. The results of this movement were anxiously awaited by the remainder of the force in camp. Suddenly, about 11 o'clock, a shot from the hilltop proclaimed that the enemy had discovered the advance of the assailants. A yell or two from the Burmese was followed by a short, sharp rattle of musketry, and then the drums and fifes of the 44th announced that the position was won.

The next morning, as soon as a 6-pounder, dragged up the hill with much difficulty, had opened fire on the enemy, Brigadier Richards assaulted the trenches on the adjacent height, whilst a simultaneous movement was again made against the pass by Macbean. The enemy now abandoned the hills after a feeble resistance, and the capital of Arakan fell into the hands of the British. The loss in General Morrison's column during the ten days' fighting amounted to twenty-nine killed and one hundred and thity-seven wounded.

Capture of Arakan.

On taking possession of the city, it was found that most of the inhabitants had abandoned the place on its occupation by the Burmese, but they now speedily returned to their homes, and showed themselves well pleased with the change of government.

The next few days were occupied in preparing for further operations, the nature of the unmolested country having assisted the enemy to effect their escape across the mountains through the passes of Dalet (Talak) and Aeng. Two of the four provinces of Arakan were therefore now clear of the Burmese, and it only remained to dislodge them from Sandoway and Ramree, for which purpose a force under Macbean was despatched on the 8th April.

The detachment arrived in the Cheduba roads on the 18th April, and found Ramree undefended; and on proceeding to Sandoway, where they arrived on the 30th April, they found that the river had been staked and stockades erected, but the enemy had withdrawn all their troops on hearing of the fall of the capital.

In just three months, therefore, one object of the expedition, the entire occupation of the province of Arakan, had been fulfilled. It was found impossible, however, to carry out the main object, a junction across the mountains with Sir Archibald Campbell.

Little was to be feared from the enemy on this side of the Burman boundary, for they had retreated over the mountains with great haste, losing hundreds on the way, from want, fatigue, and the onslaughts of local tribes. They had halted at Chalain, in the Ava country, and had been strongly reinforced at this place; but it was the nature of the country and the time of the year, rather than the presence of this force, which impeded the further advance of the British. More than eighty miles of jungle, cut up by numerous rivers, intervened between the capital and Dalet (Talak); thence the road passed over ninety miles of lofty and rugged precipices, where no supplies could be procured, and even water was scarce. A force, under Major Bucke, was sent to explore this route, and proceeding to Talak by water, they made four marches over the mountains, in which the men and cattle underwent extreme fatigue. When arrived at Akowyn, within one march of the Burman frontier, they heard of the proximity of the Burmese in strength, and the exhausted state of his detachment, and the impracticable nature of the road, then induced Major Bucke to retire to Talak. At a more favourable time of year the army might have been able to negotiate this country, but it was now too late, as the rains had set in, making military operations impossible.

The season now brought with it its pestilential influence, and although the precaution had been taken to put the troops into cantonments at Arakan, fever and dysentery broke out amongst them to an alarming extent, and with most disastrous results. Sickness was so universal and the chance of subduing it so hopeless that the Government was at last compelled to abandon the expedition and recall the troops altogether, leaving detachments only at the more healthy stations of Ramree, Sandoway, and Cheduba.

General Morrison himself fell a victim to the climate, dying of fever on his way to Europe.

From these expeditions we will now return to the operations of the army at Rangoon.

CHAPTER V.

BRITISH ADVANCE FROM RANGOON.

We have already seen how, after the capture of the stockades at Kokine on the 15th December, which was followed by the complete dispersion of the Burman army, Bandula retreated to Donubyu, where he succeeded in collecting a considerable force. Despite the severe defeat which he had suffered, this General seems to have carried out his retreat in a masterly manner, leaving detachments on the Lain and Panlang rivers to detain the British advance.

Active preparations were now made for the advance of the British force into the interior. Besides the continual arrival of transports from India, these preparations were assisted by the return of many of the inhabitants to Rangoon, and their consent to bring in food, and also by the fact that many watermen had now entered the service of the British, thus obviating the difficulties which they would otherwise have had in the navigation of the Irrawaddy.

Despite these favourable changes in the prospects of the British force, the advance into the heart of the country was not, however, without its unpropitious accompaniments. There was no doubt that all the local resources would be removed from the reach of the invaders, and it would therefore be necessary to keep up uninterrupted communication with Rangoon. For this purpose a large force would have to be left there, and at different points on the line of march; and above all, the line of the Irrawaddy would have to be defended by a large and well equipped flotilla. Another difficulty was that all transport for the force had to be brought by sea from Bengal and Madras, from whence few coolies would consent to embark, and the shipment of cattle was attended by much delay and loss.

The Bengal cattle, too, were found to be too small and feeble for field service, and the army was chiefly dependent on those sent from Madras; and although the Madras Government did their utmost to supply a sufficient number, the amount of available transport was quite inadequate for the requirements of the expedition. For this reason, Sir Archibald Campbell was obliged to reduce his striking force materially, leaving a far larger number at Rangoon than he had contemplated, with orders to join him as opportunity offered.

His determination to advance, however, was unaffected by these embarrassments, and by the first week in February, he had completed his arrangements for a forward movement on Prome.

Detailing for Rangoon a garrison of native infantry, and such of the Europeans as were unfit for immediate service, he had formed as many troops as he possessed transport for into two columns. With one, about 2,400 strong, he decided to move by land, while the other, about 1,170 strong, was to proceed by water, and, capturing Panhlaing and Donubyu *en route*, was to meet the land force at (Sarawa) some distance further up the Irrawaddy.

Of these two columns, the first, under the command of the Chief himself, consisted of two troops of Bengal Horse Artillery, the Madras Pioneers, the Governor-General's Body-Guard, the 38th, 41st, and 47th Foot, and the 26th and 43rd Madras Native Infantry. The second column was commanded by Brigadier-General Cotton and was composed of the Rocket Troop, a detachment of Madras Artillery, the 89th Foot, the 1st Madras European Regiment, and a few of the 18th Madras Native Infantry, together with a flotilla of about seventy boats under Captain Alexander, R.N.

A third column, of about 800 men, under Major Sale, was formed at the same time, with orders to move against Bassein, clear that country of the enemy, and then join head-quarters at Henzada. The rest of the army, nearly 4,000 effective men, was left in Rangoon, under Brigadier M'Creagh, who was to follow up the Commander-in-Chief as soon as sufficient transport could be obtained.

Before the British force left Rangoon, Colonel Elrington was sent to drive out the Burmese who had re-occupied Syriam; and thus, with no enemy in his rear, the Commander-in-Chief felt himself in a position to advance. The land column, therefore, left Rangoon on the 13th February, the water column followed on the 16th, and Major Sale started for Bassein one day later. The movements of this last force will be first narrated.

Having arrived off the mouth of the Bassein river, they proceeded up stream on the 26th February. Bassein itself was reached on the 3rd March and occupied without resistance, the enemy having fired the place and fled to Lemyethna (Lamina,) a town about 150 miles higher up the river. Thither Major Sale followed, but only to find the place deserted. He then returned to Bassein and was soon after recalled to Rangoon, the movement to Henzada, having in the meantime become unnecessary. From Rangoon the detachment afterwards proceeded to join the main body under the Commander-in-Chief.

The land column, under Sir Archibald Campbell, leaving Rangoon on the 13th February, marched through Hmawbi and Hlaing without incident, and reached Sarawa on the 2nd March.

General Cotton's advance.

The river column, proceeding up the Rangoon river, arrived on the 19th February at Panhlaing. Here the enemy had constructed some strong stockades, but abandoned them on the approach of the British. Leaving the detachment of the 18th Native Infantry to hold this place, and keep open the communication with Rangoon, General Cotton continued his advance up the river, entered the main stream on the 27th, and next day came in sight of Donubyu. Here Bandula was strongly entrenched, with all the troops he could muster, amounting to about 15,000 men. The position consisted of a series of formidable stockades extending for a mile along the bank, beginning at the Pagoda of Donubyu, and increasing in strength until completed by the main work, situated on a commanding height, and surrounded by abattis and the usual defences.

Some delay having occurred in getting the whole of the artillery up the river, the British force was not in position till the 5th March. On the 6th General Cotton advanced to within two miles of the Burmese, and sent a summons to surrender, to which a refusal was returned. On the receipt of the reply, a party of the 89th was landed opposite the main stockade to reconnoitre. On the 7th, 500 men were disembarked a mile below the pagoda, and formed into two columns, under Colonel Donoghue and Major Basden, with two 6-pounders and a detachment of Rocket Artillery; the first stockade was captured with a loss of about twenty killed and wounded, and the enemy fled to their second line, leaving 280 prisoners in the hands of the British.

The second line of defence was about 500 yards in rear of the first, and about the same distance from the main position, by which it was commanded. Two more 6-pounders and four mortars were now brought into action; and when it was thought that a sufficient impression had been made, the storming party of 200 men was ordered to advance.

Cotton's reverse at Donubyu.

The enemy held their fire until this party had got within close range, when they opened such a destructive fusillade, and inflicted so severe a loss upon them that Captain Rose, who was commanding, had to order a retreat. Captains Rose and Cannon were killed, and nearly the whole of the party killed or wounded. In consequence of this reverse, in which his total casualties amounted to 139, General Cotton decided to make no further attack until reinforced by General Campbell, and he therefore re-embarked the men and guns, and dropped down stream to Yandoon, to await orders from the Commander-in-Chief.

Meanwhile, taking it for granted that the river force had captured Donubyu, but without making any effort to communicate with that column, General Campbell had unwisely advanced twenty-six miles beyond the rendezvous,[1] to Yuadit, near Monyo. On hearing on 11th March of General Cotton's reverse, he decided to retrace his steps and attack Donubyu with the whole of his force. He accordingly returned to Sarawa, at which place he had to cross over the Irrawaddy. Owing to lack of boats this proved a task of great difficulty, and it was five days later before he was able to continue his advance, and the 25th of March before he arrived in front of Donubyu. He then opened communication with General Cotton, and started vigorous measures for the reduction of the Burmese stronghold, his plans including the

[1] This appears to be an excellent instance of the necessity of columns operating on parallel lines keeping up communication with each other. Had the Burmese shown any initiative they could now have defeated the British force in detail: first crushing General Cotton's weak column, and then advancing against General Campbell, who would have been entirely cut off from his base and food supplies.

construction of several batteries, armed with heavy artillery. The Burmese made frequent sorties from the fort, to try and interrupt this work, and on one occasion the working-parties were charged by seventeen elephants, ridden by sharp-shooters, and supported by a body of infantry. They were, however, driven back by the Horse Artillery and Rocket Troop, and, the elephant-drivers being killed, the animals made off into the jungle, while the luckless sharp-shooters, throwing themselves to the ground, retreated precipitately behind their defences.

Capture of Donubyu. Death of Bandula.

The mortar and enfilading batteries opened fire on the 1st April, and the breaching batteries at daybreak on the 2nd, shortly after which the enemy were seen in full retreat. The position was immediately seized, and a large amount of grain, ammunition, and guns fell into the British hands. It was ascertained that the sudden retreat of the enemy was due to the death of Bandula, who had been killed by a shell on the preceding day. With him fell the courage of the garrison, and the surviving chiefs had found it impossible to animate the men to further resistance.

The death of Bandula was a severe blow to the Burman cause. He was the chief instigator of the war, and its strenuous advocate, and in courage and readiness of resource he had displayed great abilities. The management of a Burmese army for so long a period, evinced no small degree of talent, while the position and defences of Donubyu, as a field work, would have done credit to the most scientific engineer. He was an illiterate man, who had risen to power by his bravery and audacity. When the war broke out he professed, and doubtless believed himself, able to lead his army to the capital of British India, and actually took with him a pair of golden fetters "to bind the Governor-General." Although not actually present at Ramu, he commanded in Arakan, and derived additional reputation from the result of that campaign. When called to the defence of Burma, he anticipated fresh triumphs, but the operations round Rangoon taught him a different lesson, and although they seem not to have shaken his pertinacity, they inspired him with a new spirit, and added courtesy to his other merits. Of this the reply he sent to General Cotton's summons, is a remarkable instance. He is said to have answered, "each of us is fighting for his own country, and you will find me as steady in defending mine as you are in maintaining the honour of yours. If you wish to see Donubyu, come as friends and I will show it to you."

Immediately after the fall of Donubyu, Sir Archibald Campbell resumed his advance on the capital, and was again at Sarawa on the 10th April. Here he was joined by General M'Creagh, with the reserve column from Rangoon, and a number of elephants and bullock transport. On arrival at Tarok-maw, envoys appeared who professed to desire peace. General Campbell, in reply, said he was ready to enter into negotiations, but asserted his intentions of continuing his advance on Prome. When within eight miles of the town, he received an answer proposing that he should halt, but he continued his march, and found the place abandoned. Half finished defences on all sides clearly showed that the Burmans had only wanted to try and gain time, and that, but for General Campbell's hurried advance, they would have made a stubborn defence. The rains now commenced and the Commander-in-Chief, therefore, seeing that further operations were impossible, placed his army in cantonments in Prome.

British advance on Prome.

Colonel Godwin was sent with a force of about 1,000 men to cross the Yomas to Toungoo, but finding the hills impassable he turned northwards and returned to Prome *viâ* Mya-wa-di, without coming across a trace of the enemy.

During the stay of the army at Prome, law and order were re-established in the town, and the people flocked back and lived in peace,—entirely satisfied with British rule; in fact the whole of Pegu, as well as a considerable part of Ava proper, may be considered as having, at this time, been under British jurisdiction. The months of June, July, and August, were necessarily spent in inactivity, owing to the inundated state of the country; the monsoon, however, was by no means so severe as that of the previous year at Rangoon, and thanks to the troops being comfortably hutted, and to supplies being plentiful, the numbers of deaths from sickness were few.

Operations delayed by the monsoon.

The death of Bandula, and the defeat at Donubyu, followed by the British advance to Prome, had caused the utmost consternation at the Burman court, but the necessity of our army remaining in cantonments during the rains had given the war party time to regain the ascendancy, and all ideas of peace vanished. The impression made upon the people, on the other hand, was more permanent, and large bounties had to be given to the men to induce them to enlist in the army. The necessary money was, however, forthcoming, and at the beginning of August it was estimated that about 20,000 of the enemy were in the vicinity of Prome.

Peace overtures.

Although prepared for the renewal of hostilities,[1] General Campbell at this time, by order of the Bengal Government, sent a letter to the Burman court, informing them that the British were ready to listen to overtures for peace. This letter promised to produce the happiest results, for in answer to it, on the 6th September, Burmese deputies arrived at Prome with a flag of truce. After some discussion, an armistice till the 18th October was agreed upon, and a meeting was arranged to take place between General Campbell and the Burman authorities on the 23rd September at a village half-way between the two camps. The meeting duly took place, and the terms proposed by the British were as follows :—"The non-interference of the Burmese in the affairs of Assam, Manipur and Cachar; the cession of Arakán; the payment of two crores as an indemnity, (one-half to be paid at once, and the Tenasserim provinces of Moulmein, Tavoy, and Mergui to be retained till the second half was delivered); permission for a British Resident to reside at Ava; and the signature of a liberal commercial treaty." To these terms the Burman Commissioners at first demurred, but finally asked for a prolongation of the armistice till the 2nd November, to give them time to submit them to their sovereign; this was readily agreed to, and matters thus remained till the end of October, when the British were informed that the demand for money and territory precluded all possibility of a friendly arrangement. Sir Archibald, therefore, at once prepared to resume active operations. The information of the last few weeks had given notice of the assemblage of a large force along

1 See Appendix 2 for "present state" of the army at this time.

the line of the river, which was gradually concentrating on Prome. From a direct attack there was nothing to fear, but any large movement on either flank might be attended by great inconvenience. In order to oppose an advance on the right, Colonel Pepper was stationed at Old Pegu, while it was thought that the presence of the detachment at Bassein would be a sufficient protection to the left. The chief point was to hold the enemy to his immediate front, and draw his attention as much as possible to Prome.

Upon the close of the armistice, the state of the country, and the yet incomplete concentration of the army, rendered a forward movement of the whole force impracticable, but General Campbell lost no time in detaching a column to drive back the enemy from an advanced position they had occupied at Wet-ti-gan, about twenty miles from Prome. With this view, Colonel Macdowall marched with two brigades of native infantry to attack the post from the left, and Major Evans, with the 22nd Native Infantry, was ordered to move on the front of the position, while the 18th Native Infantry were to support the 22nd if required. The 38th Native Infantry was also sent round by Sangwè to make a diversion in that quarter. The state of the roads prevented artillery forming a part of any of these columns.

The result of this attack was a repetition of the reverse at Kaiklu. The main body under Colonel Macdowall marched on the evening of the 15th November. On the morning of the 16th, they encountered the Burmese in great force, who, although driven back, kept up a heavy fire as they retreated to their position in the rear. This position proved to be too strong for the attacking force to storm, and their want of artillery prevented them from breaching it. In the abortive attack, Colonel Macdowall was killed and four officers severely wounded. Lieutenant-Colonel Brooke, who succeeded to the command, finding it impossible to make any impression on the enemy, then ordered a retreat. This was effected with as much regularity as circumstances would permit, the country being a thick jungle in which the enemy lurked in great numbers and kept up a galling fire. After a severe march, in which a number of the wounded were unavoidably left behind, the detachment came to a *nullah* about nine miles

British reverse at Wet-ti-gan.

from Prome, where the enemy stopped their pursuit, their attention having been diverted by the movements of the other detachments.

Major Evans, having moved out on the night of the 15th, fell in with the enemy's picquets at daybreak on the following morning. After driving them back, he advanced to an opening in the jungle, when he was checked by a very heavy fire from a strong stockade, by which his leading company was almost annihilated, and severe casualties sustained by the other companies. Firing in the direction of Colonel Macdowall's column had been heard early in the morning, but as there was no sign of their co-operation, and as the enemy were too strong for one battalion to attack, Major Evans also retreated. The enemy pursued for about three miles and harassed the rear, but the regiment successfully effected its retreat in good order. In this column, as in Colonel Macdowall's, many of the wounded had to be left behind, the dooly-bearers having, at the beginning of the retreat, thrown down their loads and bolted into the jungle.

The 38th Regiment under Colonel Smith reached Wet-ti-gan about 12 o'clock on the 16th, and then fell in with what appeared to be the rear of the enemy, at this time in pursuit of the main body of the British. The Burmese fled on the appearance of this corps, but the firing having ceased and no traces of the other two columns being visible, Colonel Smith also retired on Prome.

Our total loss in this affair was Colonel Macdowall and fifty-three rank and file killed, thirteen officers wounded, of whom one, Lieutenant Ranken, subsequently died, and 150 rank and file wounded or missing. Our defeat was, at the time, attributed to ignorance of the enemy's strength, as, instead of 2,000 or 3,000 men, as expected, Major Evans estimated those opposed to him to be not less than 5,000, while those engaged by the main division, under Colonel Brook, were reckoned at between 10,000 and 12,000. It would appear, however, that had some method of communication between the columns been arranged, the expedition would, despite the number of Burmese, have had a very different result. The ultimate consequences of this disaster were not unfavourable, as it encouraged the Burman Generals in the high opinion of their own power, and induced them to adopt a system of confident warfare, which brought them within the reach of the British Commander.

Relying on the manifestation of their purpose to attack him in his position, General Campbell determined to await their advance, and the enemy soon made their appearance round Prome to the extent of between 50,000 and 60,000 men. As their numbers enabled them to extend over a considerable tract of country, they were able to detach parties to both flanks of the British position, by which the communications with Rangoon were threatened, and the districts below Prome exposed to the depredations of irregular and marauding bands. The command of the river was, however, an important advantage to the British, and some successes gained by the flotilla, and by a detachment at Padaung on the right bank, soon dispelled all fear with regard to the communications with Rangoon being cut.

After awaiting for some days the expected approach of the Burman force, General Campbell finding that they were reluctant to leave the cover of the jungle, and that they merely continued to harass his flanks, determined to make a general attack on the enemy's position, which extended from the Napadi hills, a commanding ridge on the bank of the river, to the villages of Sinbaik and Sangwè inland, about eleven miles north-east of Prome.

General attacked on Burmese position.

The Burman army was divided into three bodies; the right was formed on the western bank of the Irrawaddy; the centre was on the Napadi hills, and communicated through a thick forest, by a line of detached posts, with the left, which was drawn up at Sinbaik on the Nawin river. Each body was strongly stockaded and occupied a position difficult of approach.

Leaving four regiments of native infantry for the defence of Prome, General Campbell marched early on the 1st December against the enemy's left, while the flotilla, under Sir James Brisbane, by a cannonade of the works on the river, diverted the attention of the centre from the real point of attack.

Upon reaching the Nawin river, the force was divided into two columns. The right, under General Cotton consisting of the 1st, 41st, and 89th Foot, the 18th and 28th Native Infantry, and some artillery, proceeding along the left bank, found the enemy occupying a strong position with about 10,000 men. The post was immediately stormed and carried at the point of the bayonet, the Burmese leaving 300 dead in their trenches. The left column which included the 13th, 38th, 47th, and 87th Foot, and the 38th Native Infantry came up as the enemy were retreating and completed their rout.

Following up the advantage thus gained, Sir Archibald Campbell determined to attack the position on the Napadi hills without delay. The army accordingly resumed their march on the following morning.

The nature of the country admitted of no approach to the enemy's defences on the hills, except in front, and that only by a narrow path. Their posts at the foot of the hills were more accessible, and from these they were speedily driven, but the attack of the heights was a more formidable task, as the narrow path was commanded by the Burman artillery and by numerous breastworks. After the position had been bombarded by our guns, the 1st Bengal Brigade were ordered to storm the heights, and rushing up the steep slopes in the teeth of a heavy fire, they drove the enemy from hill to hill until they had cleared the whole of the formidable entrenchments.

Total defeat of Burmese. 1st to 4th December 1825.

On the 4th December, a detachment under General Cotton, proceeded across the river and drove the left wing of the enemy from their position with heavy loss, thus completing the entire dispersal of the Burman army.

On the 6th December commenced the advance on Ava, one division, under General Cotton, moving along the bank of the river, and keeping touch with the flotilla, the other, under General Campbell, advancing in a circuitous direction so as to turn the entrenchments which the Burmese had erected at Mya-wa-di, and for some miles beyond.

Mya-wa-di was found to be deserted. General Campbell fixed his head-quarters there on the 19th December, and was soon afterwards joined by the flotilla and General Cotton's column.

Continuing his advance towards Malun, whither the Burmese had now fled, the Commander-in-Chief, on the 26th December, received a letter expressing the wish of the Burman Commander to conclude peace.

More peace proposals.

Lieutenant-Colonel Tidy and Lieutenant Smith, R.N., were deputed to ascertain the terms proposed by the Burmese, and in the meanwhile the column continued its march, and arrived at Patanaga, opposite the Burmese post of Malun on the 28th, while the flotilla, unmolested, anchored above the Burman position.

There is no doubt that the prevailing feeling amongst all ranks of Burmans was now a desire for peace. The war had long been most unpopular; the best troops of the State had been destroyed; the new levies raised to take their place were of the worst description, procured at great expense, and decimated by desertion directly they took the field. Most of the members of the King's council and his own relations warmly advocated peace, and he was well inclined to listen to their advice. The Queen and her kindred, on the other hand, still counselled opposition, and the pride of a barbaric sovereign could ill stoop to make the sacrifices by which alone tranquillity could be restored. The advance of the British army from Napadi seems, however, to have turned the scale in favour of pacific councils, and Kolein *Wungyi* was in consequence sent from Ava to Malun to negotiate.

After some unimportant preliminary discussions, it was arranged that General Campbell, Mr. Robertson, lately appointed Civil Commissioner, and Sir J. Brisbane, should hold a conference with the Burman envoys in a boat moored in the centre of the river between Malun and Patanaga.

The Burmese Commissioners, true to their national character, could not conduct the negotiations without fraud, and solemnly declared that they had full powers to agree to terms. The proposals made by the British Commissioners were the same as those made by General Campbell in the previous September, except that the permanent cession of the Tenasserim Provinces, with the Salween as a boundary, was insisted on, and the amount of the indemnity was reduced by one-half. After much discussion these terms were accepted and the English copy of the treaty was signed on the 2nd, and the Burmese copy on the 3rd January 1826. An armistice was agreed upon until the 18th to enable the envoys to obtain the necessary ratification.

British terms.

During all the conferences the Burmans had repeatedly declared that the King would ratify whatever they agreed to, and had expressed their entire satisfaction with the spirit in which the negotiations had been conducted, and their gratification at the prospect of a speedy renewal of friendly relations. They had frankly confessed that the King had been ruined by the war, that the resources of the country were exhausted, and that the road to Ava was open to the British army. There appeared every reason to credit their assertions, and all who had seen them, believed that peace was now assured.

Operations in Pegu.

While these transactions were taking place the province of Pegu had been the scene of some military operations, which we must here pause to notice. Colonel Pepper's force at Pegu was mainly intended for defensive purposes, and to prevent the enemy interfering with the British communications; but finding the Burmese becoming troublesome, this officer now decided to take the offensive. Accordingly, on the 23rd December, he marched on Shwégyin, on the left bank of the Sittang river, which was occupied without resistance. Thence a force under Colonel Conry was detached to capture the fortified post of Sittang, also on the left bank. This attack failed and Colonel Conry and Lieutenant Adams, one native officer, and nine men were killed, and Lieutenants Harvey and Power, and eighteen men were wounded. Colonel Pepper then advanced with reinforcements and captured the position on the 11th January, but not without severe loss. Captains Cursham and Stedman and fourteen rank and file being killed, and Major Home, Lieutenants Fullerton and Gower, and fifty-three men wounded. Colonel Pepper was quickly reinforced by about 800 men from Rangoon, and all fears for the security of that part of the country were set at rest; and the establishment of peace shortly after suspended further operations.

During the armistice at Malun a friendly intercourse was carried on between the two camps, only at times interrupted by the enemy working at and strengthening his defences, as if aware that nothing conclusive would result from the negotiations. Strong remonstrances were made to the Burmese on this subject, but they with their usual dexterity parried the accusations of double-dealing, attributing to every cause, except the right one, the proceedings complained of. Scarcely a day passed without a visit from some chief of rank, to expatiate upon the blessings which would result from the ensuing peace, and to repeat their conviction that the ratified treaty would arrive long before the period specified. At length, however, on the 17th, the day before the armistice was to expire, three Burmese officers arrived in the British camp, and, while offering to pay the first instalment of the indemnity, stated with much circumlocution that they had as yet received no answer from the capital, and begged for an extension of the armistice for seven or eight days.

This statement was obviously untrue, as the chiefs were known to be in daily communication with Ava, boats from whence frequently passed the British picquets on the river. Sir Archibald, therefore, refused their request, but told them that if they would evacuate Malun, and continued retiring before the British army to Ava, hostilities would not be recommenced, and the march would be suspended as soon as the ratified treaty should be received.

This proposition was peremptorily rejected, and the armistice having expired, three officers were next day sent over to Malun, who formally told the *Wungyi* that, having again deceived us, no more forbearance would be shown by the British, and that after 12 o'clock that night hostilities would be once more resorted to.

At the specified hour of midnight the British began to erect batteries opposite the selected points of attack, and by 10 o'clock next morning twenty-eight pieces of artillery were ready to open on the enemy's defences. Shortly after 11 A.M., the guns began the bombardment, and, two hours later, the troops intended for the assault were embarked in boats at some distance above the place, to ensure their not being carried past it by the force of the stream.

The 1st Bengal Brigade, consisting of the 13th and 38th Foot, under Lieutenant-Colonel Sale, was directed to land below the stockade, while three brigades were to land above the place, and, after carrying some outworks, to attack it by the northern face. Despite all precautions, however, the force of the current, aided by a strong north wind, carried the 1st Brigade, under all the enemy's fire, to its destined point of attack before the other brigades had reached their position. Landing under cover of a shelving bank, this brigade at once pushed forward without waiting for the co-operation of the other troops, and, assaulting the works with great gallantry, drove the enemy from their position

Capture of Malun.

The other brigades cutting in upon the Burmans' retreat completed their discomfiture, and they were driven with much loss from the whole of their stockades, leaving all their artillery and military stores in the hands of the British, whose losses amounted to nine killed, and three officers and thirty-one wounded. In the house of Prince Memiabu, a half-brother of the King, who had taken the command, was found money to the amount of from Rs. 30,000 to Rs. 40,000, and, what was still more surprising, though perhaps not so agreeable, both the English and Burmese copies of the treaty lately made, signed and sealed as they had been at the meeting, and bearing unmistakable evidence of their never having been seen by the King.

It is difficult to divine what object the Burmese Court could have had in opening negotiations they had no intention of abiding by, or what possible result they could have anticipated from a short and profitless delay, which to us was in every way desirable, as much to rest the men from their late fatigues as to afford time for collecting sufficient supplies to prosecute our advance on the capital. It is, however, more than probable that the envoys had exceeded their power, and that, on the terms of the treaty being made known to the King, the war party again prevailed.

The Burmese army now retired with all possible haste, and the British prepared to follow them up without delay.

Before, however, commencing his march, General Campbell sent a messenger with the unratified treaty to the *Wungyi*, both to show the Burmese that their perfidy was discovered, and to give them the means of still performing their engagements. In his letter to the *Wungyi* he merely told him that in the hurry of his departure from Malun he had forgotten the enclosed document, which he might now find more acceptable to his Government than they had a few days previously considered it. The *Wungyi* politely returned his best thanks for the paper, but added that the same hurry which had caused the loss of the treaty had compelled him to leave behind a large sum of money, which he also much regretted, and which he was sure the British General only waited an opportunity of returning.

The British force now resumed its march upon Ava. On the 31st of January it was met by a Doctor Price, an American

Missionary, and an Englishman of the name of Sandford, both of whom had been taken prisoners some months before, and who were now sent on parole to communicate the sincere desire which the Burman King at last entertained for peace, and to ascertain the lowest terms upon which it would be granted. The terms offered at Malun were renewed, and the British General having promised not to advance beyond Pagan-Myo for twelve days, the delegates returned to Ava.

There can be little doubt that the Burman monarch now saw the necessity of peace, and was therefore anxious to secure it; but the terms proposed, lenient though they were, were so galling to his pride that he resolved upon one more effort. If that failed, peace was to be immediately concluded. He, therefore, by means of large bounties, collected a new force, to whom he gave the honourable appellation of "Retrievers of the King's Glory," and entrusted the command of this army to a warrior bearing the formidable titles of "Prince of Darkness," "King of Hell," and "Prince of the Setting Sun."

Final defeat of the Burmese. 9th February 1826.

The Burmese took up their position at Pagan Myo, where they were attacked by the British on the 9th February. The enemy were routed with great slaughter, and the "Retrievers of the King's Glory" fled in detached parties over the country. The unfortunate "Prince of the Setting Sun" ventured to return to Ava after his defeat, where he was immediately put to death by order of the King. Peace was now inevitable.

The British army continued its advance, and was met at Yandabo, only four marches from the capital, by Doctor Price and Mr. Sandford, accompanied by two Ministers of State and all the British prisoners who had been taken during the war. The delegates brought the first instalment of the indemnity (twenty-five lakhs of rupees), as well as powers to accept whatever terms the British might propose.

The terms offered at Malun (with an additional article sanctioning the payment of the indemnity in four instalments) were agreed upon and peace was signed on 24th February, 1826.[1]

Treaty of Yandabo—24th February 1826.

[1] *See* Appendix III.

On the 7th March the Commander-in-Chief and the 1st Brigade embarked in boats for Rangoon, where they arrived on the 24th. By the end of April, the whole force, with the exception of the detachment left in Rangoon until the payment of the second quarter of the indemnity, was on its way to Bengal and Madras.

Thus closed the first Burmese war, engaged in by the British Government much against its inclinations, and resulting in the loss to the Burman monarch of all the territories which his ancestors had taken from the Siamese, and of Arakan, which had been conquered by his father; in his exclusion from all interest in Assam, Cachar, and Manipur, where his predecessors had been paramount; and in the loss of the sum of ten million rupees.

There are, however, always two sides to a story, as is clearly shown by a perusal of the Royal Chronicles of the Burmese, in which work the following remarkable account of the war and subsequent peace is to be found:—"In the years of 1186 and 1187 (of the Burman era) the white strangers of the west fastened a quarrel upon the Lord of the Golden Palace. They landed at Rangoon, took that place and Prome, and were permitted to advance as far as Yandabo; for the King, from motives of piety and regard of life, made no preparation whatever to oppose them. The strangers had spent vast sums of money in their enterprise, so that by the time they reached Yandabo their resources were exhausted, and they were in great distress. They then petitioned the King, who, in his clemency and generosity, sent them large sums of money to pay their expenses back, and ordered them out of the country."

The loss to the British in men and in money in this campaign was enormous. The total expenditure was about five millions sterling, of which one was recovered from the Burmese. The number of lives lost was considering the few who were killed in action, almost incredible. The whole number of British troops who landed in Rangoon in the first instance, comprising the 13th, 34th, 41st, 45th, 49th, and 89th Foot, was, exclusive of officers, 3,586; the number of reinforcements does not appear, but that of the deaths was 3,115, of which not more than 150 occurred in action or from wounds. Of about 150 officers sixteen were killed in action or died from wounds, and forty-five died from disease. In

Arakan the loss in action was none, but of the two British regiments quartered there, whose total average strength was 1,004 men, 595 died in the country in the course of eight months, and of those who quitted it, not more than half were alive at the end of the year. Had there been no reinforcements the British portion of the force would have been entirely annihilated by disease.

In recognition of their services during the war, permission was given for the words "Ava," "Arakan" and "Assam" to be borne on the colours of corps engaged, a medal and six months' *batta* were granted to the troops, and a further donation of an equal amount was paid to them the following year by order of the Court of Directors.

BIBLIOGRAPHY.

Documents illustrative of the Burmese War—H. H. Wilson, 1827.

Our Burmese Wars—Colonel W. F. D. Lawrie, 1880.

Narrative of the Burmese War—Major Snodgrass, 1827.

History of the Madras Army—Colonel W. J. Wilson, 1888.

Services of the Bengal Native Army—Lieutenant F. G. Cardew, 1903.

British Burma Gazetteer, 1880.

PART II.

THE SECOND BURMESE WAR.

THE SECOND BURMESE WAR.

CHAPTER VI.

CAUSES OF THE WAR.

THE Treaty of Yandabo guaranteed the security of our merchants and of our commerce, and seemed to hold out promise of a lasting friendship between British and Burmese. So quickly, however, did the latter nation forget the losses they had incurred in the first war, and so quickly did all their former arrogance return to them, that in a very few years it became evident that the British Indian Government would, sooner or later, be once again compelled to assert its rights by force of arms.

Phagyi-daw, the King who had brought on the first war, developed insanity shortly after the conclusion of peace, and was deposed by his brother, who adopted the title of King Tharrawaddy. This monarch absolutely refused to be in any way bound by his brother's treaty. Resident after Resident was treated with such indignity by the King and his ministers that it was at last found necessary to remove the Residency to Rangoon, and, shortly after, to withdraw it from the country altogether.

Removing his capital to Amarapura King Tharrawaddy reigned for nine years. But soon after his usurpation of the throne, he too developed symptoms of madness, and, eventually put under restraint by his sons, died in confinement in 1846.

The throne was seized by his eldest son, Pagan Min, who followed his father's footsteps in ignoring the provisions of the treaty of 1826. At the same time, the various Governors and Viceroys of provinces, feeling confident of the support of their own Government, recommenced those exactions from British traders which had so often provoked remonstrance from the Indian Government, and which had helped to bring on the first war.

These indignities offered to our representatives and merchants might, at any time, have served as a valid excuse for the renewal of hostilities, but the truth seems to be that our hands were too

L 2

full just then to pay any attention to Burma. The disastrous Kabul campaign of 1842, followed by the Sikh War, which, although successful, shook our Eastern Empire to its very foundations, demanded all the troops we could muster.

At last, however, in 1851, Lord Dalhousie, the then Governor-General, found himself able to turn his attention to the Eastern Frontier, and the report, at this time, of two more than usually outrageous cases of extortion, together with a memorial from the British residents at Rangoon, brought matters to a head.

Rangoon Residents' Memorial.

The memorial set forth that two British subjects, Messrs. Sheppard and Lewis, masters of British ships, had been arrested by the Governor of Rangoon on several successive false charges; that they had been ill-treated and imprisoned; that Captain Lewis had been threatened with the stocks; and that large sums of money had been extorted from them before they could get their port clearance. It further set forth that all "all your memorialists have for a long time suffered from the tyranny and gross injustice of the Burmese authorities; that trade is seriously obstructed and almost suppressed in consequence; that neither life nor property is safe, as the Governor has publicly stated to his dependents that he has no money to pay them for their services and has granted them his permission to rob the inhabitants, and 'to get money as they best can'; that, in consequence, robberies and false charges are of almost daily occurrence; that the Governor has frequently demanded money without pretext, and has tortured the parties till his demands were complied with; that now affairs have arrived at such a crisis that, unless protected, your memorialists will be obliged to leave the country, and, in doing so, must sacrifice their property; that they are here under the provisions of the Treaty of Yandabo, and beg to state, with all due deference and respect, that they claim the right to seek your protection."

Directly Lord Dalhousie received this memorial he gave the matter his most urgent attention and at once despatched Commodore Lambert with his squadron to Rangoon, with instructions to address a note to the Governor of Rangoon, setting forth the details of each case, pointing out that they constituted a very grave infraction of the existing treaty, informing him that the

British would not allow the liberty of its subjects to be violated, and finally demanding the payment of £900 sterling as compensation for the losses sustained by Messrs. Lewis and Sheppard.

Should the Governor refuse to comply with the demand, the Commodore was to forward to the King of Burma a letter from the President in Council, and await a reply. He was, however, specially instructed not to commit any act of hostility until definite instructions were issued by the Government of India.

The above-mentioned letter from the President in Council was dated 17th November 1851. It alluded to the fact of numerous complaints having been received regarding the conduct of the Governor of Rangoon, demanded compensation for the various outrages complained of, and further required that that officer should be removed. The letter concluded by stating that if these demands were not immediately met, the British Government would take measures to enforce the rights it possessed in virtue of existing treaties.

On the squadron arriving in the Rangoon river it was met by a Mr. Crisp, an English resident in Rangoon, who had been sent down by Maung Oot, the Governor, to ask the reason of an armed force arriving in Burman waters. In reply, the Commodore said that he brought a communication for the Governor from the Governor-General of India. On Mr. Crisp's return, Maung Oot issued orders that no European was to communicate with the squadron, on pain of death; a threat which his previous cruelties led them to think he would certainly carry out. Maung Oot fixed a day for the reception of the Commodore's letter, but, before the day arrived, it was rumoured that he was contemplating the seizure, as hostages, of the officers who might land, and threatening to put them to death if the squadron did not at once leave Rangoon. At the same time, Maung Oot treated the British squadron with many petty annoyances, and another long list of his extortions was handed to the Commodore by the British residents. The Commodore, therefore, thinking that the payment of compensation for the cases of Lewis and Sheppard would not now be considered sufficient by the Supreme Government, and feeling that no good object would be served by having any dealings with the Governor, decided to withold his demand on that man, and to at once forward the President in Council's letter to the King calling for a reply in thirty-five days. This he reported to the Government of India.

Within the time fixed, a satisfactory reply was received from the Burman King, announcing the removal of Maung Oot from Rangoon, and the appointment of a successor, and promising an enquiry into the cases of Messrs. Sheppard and Lewis.

Both Commodore Lambert and the Governor-General now hoped that all differences would be amicably arranged, but this was by no means the intention of the Burmese Government. The arrogance of the court had again reached all its former height, and the King determined on measuring his strength once more with that of the British power in India. The new Governor was one Maung Hmoon, who brought with him 3,000 men, whilst at the same time 10,000 men under Maung Gnyo, and a large force under Maung Bwa were sent to the Bassein and Martaban districts respectively.

In the meantime the Government of India had received the Commodore's despatch informing them of his having sent on the letter to the King of Burma, and, approving of the course he had taken, had authorized him to blockade the Burmese rivers if the King's reply was unfavourable. Lord Dalhousie was not to be played with. On the 4th January 1852 the new Governor arrived at Rangoon, and it was at first expected that the late one would be subjected to a trial. But on the 5th it was learnt that he was in high favour with his successor, and on the 6th he departed for Ava with every mark of honour. No intimation of the new man's arrival was officially made to the Commodore, but it was soon found that he intended to follow his predecessor's example, for his first official act was to send a written notice to all British residents, threatening them with death in the event of their holding any intercourse with the squadron.

On the 6th January Commodore Lambert, by appointment, sent Commander Fishbourne and Captain Latter on shore with a letter to the Governor, containing the demands which he had been directed to make, which had now, by order of the Government, been increased by one made, under Article VII of the Treaty of Yandabo, for the honourable reception of a British Resident at Rangoon with a guard of fifty men. This deputation was treated with the utmost insolence, and was denied admittance to the Governor on the plea that he was asleep; and finally the officers had to return to their ship without delivering the letter. No apology was ever offered for this treatment, but the Governor sent on board a letter to the Secretary of the Government of India, accusing the officers of the deputation of having been drunk and of using violent and abusive language. Commodore Lambert at once declared the blockade of the rivers, and, in retaliation for the insults offered to the British Government through the officers of the deputation, seized a royal ship which happened to be lying off Rangoon.

British deputation insulted.

The same afternoon he sent a message ashore, telling all British merchants and residents to come on board the frigate immediately as the town was to be placed under blockade. By eight o'clock all the British subjects had embarked, and the next day, 7th February, all merchant ships were ordered to prepare to leave Rangoon. The same day a letter arrived from the Governor stating that "if the Commodore attempted to take the King's ship past the two stockades which had been erected down the river, he would be fired on." The Commodore replied that if even a pistol were fired he would level the stockades to the ground; and with this mutual determination may be said to have commenced the Second Burmese War.

On the 8th January the *Proserpine* left Rangoon with about 200 refugees and the next day the fleet proceeded down the river, accompanied by the merchantmen and with the Burman Royal ship in tow. Directly the stockades were reached a heavy fire was opened by the Burmese. This was quickly silenced by the guns of the men-of-war, and the enemy were driven from their entrenchments with a loss of over 300 killed and wounded. It was afterwards remarked by some that if the British had not carried away the Royal ship, the Burmese would probably not have offered any resistance, and that they only opened fire on seeing the King's property being taken away. Another authority, however, holds that the Governor stated he would fire on the Commodore if he attempted to remove "any British property," so there is reason to believe that the stockades would have offered resistance even if the King's ship had not been touched.

British squadron fired on by the Burmese.

After this engagement, the *Serpent*, Commander Luard, was sent to carry out the blockade of the Bassein river, and Commodore Lambert himself proceeded to Calcutta to confer with the Government.

The unsatisfactory aspect which affairs had now assumed rendered it advisable to at once reinforce the garrisons of Tenasserim and Arakan. A wing of the 18th Royal Irish and a company of European artillery were consequently sent to Moulmein, and a regiment of Bengal Native Infantry and some artillery were conveyed to Kyaukpyu, so as to be available for any duty on which it might be necessary to employ them.

Lord Dalhousie was at Benares when Commodore Lambert returned to Calcutta, but on receipt of his despatches, he made another attempt to avert war, and in a letter to the Secret Committee of the Court of Directors he expressed his belief that a peaceable adjustment was still possible. The President in Council, accordingly, again addressed the Governor of Rangoon, briefly recapitulating the occurrences in Rangoon since his arrival, and demanding that he should at once apologize to the Government of India, should pay the compensation claimed, and should consent to receive with due honour a British Agent at Rangoon. The despatch ended with the statement that if these demands were not complied with, the British Government would exact for itself the reparation due to it.

This communication was conveyed to Rangoon by the Commodore, but was not delivered without bloodshed, for as the British frigate was proceeding up the Rangoon river under a flag of truce, she was fired on by the Burmese batteries in the lower stockade. The enemy's fire was quickly silenced by the guns of the *Fox*, but not before a British seaman had been killed. The reply to this letter was sent to Commodore Lambert on 2nd February. Not only was every demand evasively refused, but the British officers were accused of falsehood in their assertions regarding their treatment at the Governor's house.

Final letter to the King.

On the receipt of this reply Lord Dalhousie determined to despatch a force to Rangoon, but at the same time decided to give the King one more opportunity of avoiding war. On the 18th February, therefore, he addressed his last communication to the Burman Court. The whole of the occurrences at Rangoon were recapitulated, and it was stated that active preparations were now being made by the Indian Government to enforce its rights. The King was, however, told that he could still avert war by complying with the following demands :—

1. An apology for the insults offered to the British deputation on 6th January.
2. The payment of a fine of one million (ten lakhs) of rupees, in compensation for the losses incurred by British merchants, and in part payment of the expense of preparation for war.
3. Permission for a British Resident to reside at Rangoon.
4. The removal of the present Governor of Rangoon.

If these conditions were not complied with before 1st April the King was informed that the British would at once commence hostilities. Up to the time of receiving this despatch the Burmese Government had not believed that the British would really go to war with them, and had consequently made no preparations beyond the erection of the stockades already mentioned, in the neighbourhood of Rangoon. They now, however, flatly refused to accede to the British terms, and, in light-hearted forgetfulness of the power of their western neighbour, and in ignorance of the feelings of their subjects, they at once began to make their arrangements for the coming campaign.

Meanwhile Lord Dalhousie's preparations were almost completed before the Court of Burma had received his letter. On the 5th April the first blow was struck, and was followed up by attack after attack, without allowing the enemy time to collect an army.

At the same time the Shans in the north-east positively refused to join the King of Burma's standard, while his Talaing and Southern Burmese subjects everywhere sided with the invading force.

CHAPTER VII.

THE MAIN OPERATIONS

WARNED by the first war, the Governor-General was determined not to wait for the King's answer to his letter. No sooner had it been despatched than, with his usual energy, he took immediate steps to ensure that the expeditionary force should be at Rangoon by the 1st April, ready to take action on that date if the Burman King should refuse to accede to the British demands. By the 23rd March, therefore, some of the troops had already sailed, and the rest were ready to embark.

Composition of expedition.

The force detailed for the expedition was taken partly from Bengal and partly from Madras. The former presidency contributed one company of artillery and a brigade of infantry, consisting of the 18th (Royal Irish) and 80th Foot, and 40th Native Infantry, under the command of Brigadier-General Warren, while the Madras force was composed of three companies of artillery, two companies of Sappers, and a brigade of infantry, consisting of the 51st Foot and three regiments of native infantry. The 38th Native Infantry was also detailed for this service, as, wearing the designation " Volunteers " on their appointments, it was thought at the time that they were General Service Troops. They, however, when warned for the service, refused to go on board ship, though they expressed their willingness to march wherever they were ordered. It was then discovered that, by the terms of their enlistment, they were not liable to service over seas, and the orders for them to proceed were consequently at once cancelled.

In connection with this subject it is interesting to note that, very shortly afterwards, the following regiments, of their own accord, came forward and informed their officers of their willingness to proceed by sea to Burma should reinforcements be required :—the 3rd and 4th Sikh Local Infantry (now the 53rd and 54th Sikhs), the regiments of Ferozepur and Ludhiana (now the 14th and 15th Sikhs), the Ramghur Local Force, the 1st Light Cavalry, the 10th, 33rd, and 37th Native Infantry and the Hariana Light Infantry. On the 21st May 1852 a General Order was published expressing the satisfaction of the Governor-General in Council at this exemplary conduct, and later on, when reinforcements were required, several of these regiments were employed in Burma.

The command of the expedition was given to Major-General H. Godwin, C.B., who had served with the 41st Foot in the former war. The total number of troops amounted to 5,800, and they were escorted by a fleet of nineteen steamships, carrying 159 guns.

General Godwin was instructed to ascertain by a flag of truce, on arrival at Rangoon, whether any reply had been received to Lord Dalhousie's last letter, and if a reply acceding to the demands had arrived he was to refrain from hostilities. In any other case he was to take immediate action, and if the Burmese should then sue for peace, he was authorized to accept as terms the payment of Rs. 15,00,000, with an addition of Rs. 3,00,000 for every month's delay in the payment, and the cession to the British of every place captured by them, until the whole amount had been paid.

Hostilities commence: 2nd April 1852.

The Bengal Brigade, with General Godwin, arrived off the mouth of the Rangoon river on the 2nd April. The same day the *Proserpine* was sent up the river with a flag of truce, but she was fired on and obliged to return. Thus the last hopes of a peaceful settlement vanished, and hostilities now began.

Capture of Martaban.

The Madras force not having arrived at the place of rendezvous,[1] the General proceeded to Moulmein in order to make arrangements for the reduction of Martaban, where the Burmese were said to be in considerable force. He arrived at Moulmein on the 4th, and on the

[1] Great dissatisfaction was expressed by Lord Dalhousie at the delay of this Brigade. He had given detailed instructions that all was to be in readiness for the Brigade to sail as soon as orders were received, and had sent transports for Bombay to take a portion of the troops, requiring the Madras authorities to make arrangements for the balance required. The Governor of Madras, however, apparently with intention, misread his instructions, and the extra ships required had not been chartered by the day sailing orders were received, with the result that instead of leaving for Rangoon on the 24th March, as was intended, no movement was possible till the 31st.

5th, the naval squadron bombarded the works of Martaban. The troops, consisting of a wing each of the 18th and 80th Foot and the 26th Native Infantry, were then landed, and after a sharp but ineffectual resistance on the part of the Burmese, carried the place by storm, with the trifling loss of eight men wounded. Leaving the 26th Madras Native Infantry to hold Martaban, General Godwin with the rest of the troops returned to the mouth of the Irrawaddy on the 8th April. The Madras troops having now arrived, the expedition proceeded up the river on the 10th.

On the 11th the squadron arrived off Rangoon, and being fired on by the Burmese, replied with broadsides, completely silencing the enemy's batteries on the river, and blowing up and destroying most of his stockades. At the same time, under cover of the guns of the fleet, a detachment of the Royal Irish and some marines was landed at Dalla, opposite Rangoon, and captured and destroyed the stockades on that side.

Everything was now ready for the landing of the troops and this began at 4 A.M. on the 12th April. By 7 A.M. the 51st King's Own Light Infantry, the Royal Irish, the 40th Bengal Native Infantry, and some of the artillery were disembarked and marched at once against the enemy's position at the Shwé Dagôn Pagoda. They had not proceeded far when, on reaching some rising ground, heavy guns opened on them, and to the surprise of all who had taken part in the first war, strong parties of skirmishers attacked the flanks of the column. This was the first occasion that the Burmese had been known to leave their stockades and take the offensive, and it was evident that they had made a considerable advance in the art of war since their first campaign against the British. The skirmishers were driven off, and the advance being resumed, the enemy were found strongly posted in a work known as the White House stockade, which it was found necessary to capture before a further progress could be made. A battery of four guns was at once opened on the position, under cover of which the place was carried by storm by four companies of the 51st and a detachment of the Madras Sappers, though not without considerable loss. It was now 11 o'clock, the heat of the sun was terrific and the troops, who had been under arms since 4 A.M., were so exhausted that

Action at White House stockade.

it was determined to halt, and to defer the advance till the next day. Of those struck down by the sun, Major Oakes and Major Griffith died the same evening, and Brigadier Warren,[1] Lieutenant-Colonel Foord, and Lieutenant-Colonel St. Maur suffered severely. The following morning it was deemed inadvisable to continue the advance, as the Commissariat were unable to get the troops rationed in time for them to march before the heat of the day began. The day was therefore occupied in bringing up the heavy guns and in further reconnoitring the enemy's position, while the ships kept up an occasional fire on various stockades. On the 14th April the troops were under arms at 5 A.M. and advanced in a north-westerly direction to attack the Burmese in their position at the pagoda. The enemy had assumed that our advance would be by a road leading from the town to the southern face of the pagoda, and here every preparation had been made to receive us, the defences being armed with nearly 100 guns, and held by a garrison of at least 10,000 men. General Godwin, therefore, decided to turn the position, and taking a circuitous route brought his troops opposite the eastern face of the pagoda. After some delay, occasioned by the difficulty of bringing the heavy guns through the jungle and of finding a suitable position for them, the artillery opened fire and made very good practice on the pagoda and town. Meanwhile a galling fire was kept up by the Burmese, which occasioned many casualties, especially among the Staffordshires and Royal Irish, who, owing to the nature of the ground, were in close order.

At 11 o'clock, a favourable opportunity presenting itself, General Godwin determined on an immediate assault. The storming party was composed of a wing of the 80th Foot, two companies of the Royal Irish, and two of the 40th Bengal Native Infantry, the whole under Lieutenant-Colonel Coote of the Royal Irish. The advance to the pagoda was over an open space of about 800 yards, which the troops crossed in splendid order, notwithstanding a deadly fire under which many officers and men went down. When the steps of the pagoda were reached, the storming party, making a gallant and determined rush, carried the upper terraces, when the enemy gave

Capture of Shwé Dagôn Pagoda.

[1] Brigadier Warren was shortly afterwards invalided on account of this sunstroke, his place being taken by Brigadier Reignolds.

way and fled in wild confusion through the southern and western gates, leaving the British in possession of the Shwé Dagôn Pagoda for the second time in history.

The British casualties during the operations, from the 11th to the 14th April, amounted in all to 17 killed and 132 wounded as is shown by the following returns :—

Return of killed, wounded, and missing, at the attack and storming of Rangoon on the 11th, 12th, and 14th April 1852.

Corps or Department.	Killed.	Wounded.
Personal Staff ..	....	One officer.
General Staff ..	....	One officer.
Madras Engineers ..	....	Three officers, 1 non-commissioned officer.
Madras Sappers ..	Three men ..	Two officers, 1 sergeant, 8 men.
Artillery.		
Bengal contingent ..	One non-commissioned officer.	Six non-commissioned officers.
Madras contingent ..	One non-commissioned officer.	One non-commissioned officer, 1 lascar, 3 syces.
Infantry.		
The Royal Irish ..	One officer, 1 sergeant, 2 men.	Three officers, 1 non-commissioned officer, 1 trumpeter, 37 men.
80th Foot	One non-commissioned officer.	One officer, 3 non-commissioned officers, 1 trumpeter, 21 men.
40th Native Infantry	One trumpeter, 3 men ..	Eleven men.
51st Foot	One officer, 1 man	One officer, 3 non-commissioned officers, 13 men.
9th Madras Native Infantry.	One man	One officer.
35th Madras Native Infantry.	....	One officer, 1 non-commissioned officer, 5 men.

Officers killed and wounded.

Corps or Department.	Killed.	Wounded.
18th Royal Irish ..	Lieutenant R. Doran, 14th April.	Lieutenant-Colonel C. J. Coote, (severely). Captain W. T. Bruce (slightly). Lieutenant G. H. Elliott (slightly).
51st Foot	Ensign A. N. Armstrong, 11th April.	Captain W. Blundell (dangerously).
Personal Staff ..	....	Lieutenant Chads, W. J. (slightly).
General Staff ..	....	Captain G. Allen (severely).
Engineers	....	Lieutenant E. C. S. Williams (slightly).
"	....	Lieutenant L. Donaldson (mortally), 12th April.
"	....	Lieutenant W. S. Trevor (severely).
Madras Sappers ..	....	Captain J. W. Rundall (slightly).
" " ..	....	Lieutenant B. Ford (slightly).
His Majesty's 80th Foot	....	Lieutenant J. L. W. Nunn (slightly).
9th Madras N. I. ..	....	Ensign G. F. C. B. Hawkes (slightly).
35th " " ..	....	Lieutenant W. C. P. Haines (dangerously).
Commissioner of Tenasserim Provinces.	....	Lieutenant-Colonel A. Bogle (severely).

After the capture of the pagoda the Burmese army retired northwards, and the people of Rangoon, relieved from oppression, readily returned to their homes, while the inhabitants of the neighbouring villages brought in supplies and offered themselves as coolies to the British. Forewarned by the first war, Lord Dalhousie had taken every precaution against any outbreak of disease at

Rangoon. A large stock of cattle had been procured by the civil officers before the arrival of the troops, so that there was no scarcity of animal food, and large wooden barracks, built in Moulmein, were sent across in sections to Rangoon, by means of which plenty of shelter was available for the whole army. At the same time several hospitals were established at Amherst, to which the sick and wounded were sent as soon as convalescent. The result of these precautions, which would have saved thousands of lives in 1824, was that the health of the troops remained good throughout the stay of the army in that part of the country.

Medical precautions.

The absorbing interest which Lord Dalhousie took in the welfare of the troops, and in all matters connected with this war, was indeed its most noticeable feature. It was a war which he had done all in his power to avoid, but when once it became unavoidable, he, with vigilant forethought, exerted himself to the utmost to bring it to a rapid and successful conclusion. Reading his original minutes on the subject one cannot fail to be struck by the masterly way in which he foresaw and arranged for all contingencies. From first to last he personally arranged for everything—no item was too small or too large for his attention; now we see him dictating, in short, crisp sentences, the number of reinforcements to be despatched—now hurrying off to Rangoon to decide matters on the spot—now, again, deciding whether *dâk* expenses should be allowed a 2nd-Lieutenant travelling to Calcutta *en route* to the front. True, there was little decentralization of command, but with such a man as this great Pro-Consul, one is prone to think how unnecessary this may sometimes be.

Lord Dalhousie.

The Burmese troops from Martaban did not retire to any great distance after the capture of that place, and on the 11th and 14th April they returned and attacked the British picquets. They were, however, driven off with slight loss, and on hearing of the fall of Rangoon, they fell back northward, leaving the British garrison unmolested.

With Martaban and Rangoon thus in our hands, General Godwin, partly with a view to seize the whole coast-line, partly to prevent any attack on the south of Arakan, next turned his attention to the capture of Bassein. He consequently sailed from

Rangoon on the 17th May with a force consisting of 400 of the 51st Foot, 300 of the 9th Madras Native Infantry, and some details of sappers and artillery. On the 18th, the flotilla arrived off the Burmese position, which consisted of a well-built mud fort, mounting several guns. Not a shot was fired by the enemy, who appeared completely surprised by the arrival of the British. The troops were at once disembarked, a company of the 51st proceeding to the right of the position, and the remainder of the regiments being directed against the centre. The Burmese now opened fire on the attacking columns, but the troops, breaking into a double, stormed the position with great gallantry, and in forty minutes the whole place was in the hands of the British. The loss on the part of our troops was two men killed, and five officers and eighteen men wounded. Leaving a garrison of two companies of the 51st, 300 of the 9th Native Infantry, and two howitzers, under the command of Major Roberts, at Bassein, General Godwin returned to Rangoon.

Capture of Bassein.

During the first fortnight of May the Talaings of Pegu rose against the Burmese and captured the town of Pegu. By the end of the month, however, the Burmans had recaptured the place. General Godwin, regarding the former as allies, now determined to send a force to once more expel the common foe. Major Cotton was placed in command of this expedition, and left Rangoon on the 2nd June with a force consisting of 100 men of the 80th Foot, 100 of the 67th Native Infantry, and thirty Madras Sappers, accompanied by the boats of the *Fox* under Commander Tarleton. After some sharp fighting on the right bank of the river, the enemy was driven across it, and the next day the town of Pegu was captured without loss, the enemy having fled at the approach of the British without offering any resistance. The town was, however, owing to paucity of troops at head-quarters, not held by the British, but was handed over to the Talaings, and Major Cotton, having destroyed the fortifications, returned to Rangoon.

First capture of Pegu.

In the early part of July, a small naval expedition, consisting of four ships, was sent up the Irrawaddy under the command of Commander Tarleton. At Kanoung, forty miles above Henzada, they found a force of 1,500 of the enemy who opened fire on them, but the small

Naval reconnaissance to Prome, July 1852.

squadron, after shelling the Burmese for an hour, continued its course and, next morning, came across the main Burman army, under the command of the son of the Burman General Bandula, who had been killed at Donubyu in the first war. So rapid had been the approach of the British from Bengal and Madras, and so little preparation had the Burmese made for war, that this army, which was to bar General Godwin's further progress, only consisted of 7,000 men.

Commander Tarleton at once pushed on, so as to get above this force, and at midnight on the 9th July he reached Prome, which he found undefended, the garrison having fled at his approach. It was impossible to hold the town, however, with so small a force, so the following day, having captured nineteen guns in the town, Captain Tarleton started on his return journey to Rangoon.

At Akouktoung (Kyauktan) he found the enemy crossing the river, and succeeded in capturing thirty-three more guns, and in destroying a great number of war-boats containing arms and ammunition. He then returned to Prome, where he found that Bandula (the son had taken his father's title) was encamped six miles inland with only 2,000 men, the remainder of his force having deserted.

The total result of this very successful little expedition was that fifty-six guns were captured; and the whole delta of the Irrawaddy was cleared of the enemy, whose force, reduced from 7,000 to 2,000, was assembled near Prome without defences or guns of any kind.

Lord Dalhousie, at this time, wrote to the Court of Directors of the East India Company, setting forth his views with regard to the continuance of the war. He pointed out that the Court of Burma had as yet made no sign of submission, and that it was absolutely necessary that the war should be continued until the British Government had obtained effectual pledges against a repetition of the outrages which had led to the despatch of troops. He reviewed the whole of our intercourse with the Burmese, and declared as his opinion that the only course for the British to adopt was to retain and permanently occupy as British territory the whole province of Pegu as far north as Prome. The Court of Directors, in reply to this letter, stated that both they and Her Majesty's Government fully approved of all Lord Dalhousie's measures and suggestions,

Lord Dalhousie's policy.

and were of opinion that the province of Pegu should certainly be annexed. Later on in the year, the Court of Directors further stated it as their opinion that, if, after the annexation of Pegu, the King should refuse to sign a treaty of peace, an advance on Ava should be made. The Governor-General, however, dissuaded them from this course. He pointed out that the extra expense would be stupendous, and that if it was contemplated to hold the whole country we should have to provide a large military force which we could ill spare. He urged that the occupation of Pegu would effect reparation for the past and security for the future, that we should "hold the kernel of the Burmese Empire without encumbering ourselves with an armful of worthless rind," and that if, in years to come (as Lord Dalhousie himself foresaw), the course of events should compel us to advance, we could do so without having lost anything by delay.

Nothing, therefore, remained but to occupy the deltas of the Irrawaddy and the Sittang as far north as Prome, and the Governor-General himself now visited Rangoon to confer with the civil, naval, and military authorities about the future plan of campaign.

General situation in August 1852.

Lord Dalhousie reached Rangoon shortly after the return of the naval expedition from Prome, and the state of affairs in Burma at this time, five months after the beginning of the war, could not be more clearly described than in the following minute which he wrote on the 10th August 1852, after his return to Calcutta:—

We are masters of the sea coast from east to west. We control by our steamers the whole of the streams of the Irrawaddy from Prome to the sea. With the exception of a few thousand men near Prome, and a still smaller body towards Martaban, no Burmese troops can be heard of in the Lower Province. In the Upper Province no army has been collected. No defences have been constructed at Prome, and no force remains there.

The Burmese have betrayed a total want of enterprise, courage, power, and resource. Large bodies of men retire at the sight of a steamer or a few Europeans. At the same time no sign has been shown of any intention to submit, or to treat, nor is there the slightest ground for believing that any such overtures will be made.

The Talaings of Pegu, while they evidently cannot be depended on to fight either for us or themselves, have everywhere shewn the strongest desire to aid our operations, to furnish us with supplies, and to obtain our protection.

The result of the Governor-General's visit, and of the consultations with the Home Government, was that on the 13th August, General Godwin was directed to advance on Prome in September, and to confine his operations to Pegu. Arrangements were at the same time made to reinforce him with a brigade from Bengal and one from Madras.

A strong flotilla of Burmese boats was now got ready to convey the troops up the Irrawaddy, and as soon as the reinforcements arrived, the army was reorganised in two divisions as follows [1]:—

Bengal Division.

In Command—Brigadier-General Sir John Cheape, K.C.B.

1st Brigade—under Brigadier Reignolds, The Royal Irish.

The 18th (Royal Irish).
40th Native Infantry.
67th ,, ,,

2nd Brigade—under Brigadier Dickenson, 10th Native Infantry.

The 80th Foot.
10th Native Infantry.
4th Sikh Local Infantry.

3rd Brigade—under Brigadier Huish, 37th Native Infantry.

The 1st European Bengal Fusiliers (now the 1st Royal Munster Fusiliers).
37th Native Infantry.
The Regiment of Ludhiana.

Madras Division.

In Command—Brigadier-General S. W. Steel, C.B.

1st Brigade—under Brigadier W. H. Elliott, 51st Foot.

51st King's Own Light Infantry.
9th Native Infantry.
35th ,, ,,

2nd Brigade—under Brigadier McNeill.

1st Madras Fusiliers (now the 1st Royal Dublin Fusiliers).
5th Native Infantry.
79th ,, ,,

[1] No Bombay troops were employed, partly on account of the greater distance they were from the scene of operations, and partly because, to quote the Governor General's minute, "they have had the privilege of contributing to the successes of the Indian Army in the Afghan wars, in the conquest of Scinde, and in the late war in the Punjab, whereas the Madras troops have enjoyed far fewer opportunities of distinction."—(*Governor-General's Minute dated* 23rd *June* 1852.)

3rd Brigade—
The 84th Foot.
30th Native Infantry.
46th „ „

All his arrangements for the advance being satisfactorily completed General Godwin embarked at Rangoon on the 27th September with the following troops:—one company of Madras Artillery with two howitzers and four 9-pounders, the Royal Irish, the 80th Foot, the 35th Madras Native Infantry, and 119 sappers. After an uneventful journey up stream, the flotilla arrived off Prome on the 9th October and were immediately fired on by the Burmese. At 4 P.M. the troops were landed, and after some very slight resistance on the part of the enemy, who were estimated to be about 4,000 strong, captured the town with the loss of only one man killed and eight wounded. Next morning the British advanced to storm the great pagoda, and the heights to the eastward, but found that the enemy had abandoned all their positions during the night.

General advance on Prome.

Meanwhile Bandula had been reinforced, and was now entrenched at Rathai-myo with about 18,000 men. General Godwin decided to leave him unmolested till the rest of the British force arrived from Rangoon, but on the 15th October, three days after the capture of Prome, Bandula surrendered and his troops dispersed.

After the first capture of Pegu in June, it was handed over to the Talaings, who undertook to hold it against the Burmese. They kept this promise for just one week, after which the town was recaptured by the enemy and the defences strengthened.

General Godwin, therefore, after the capture of Prome, and before the main body of the army was moved forward from Rangoon, despatched a column to retake the town. The column consisted of 300 of the 1st Bengal Fusiliers under Lieutenant-Colonel Tudor, 300 of the Madras Fusiliers, 400 of the 5th Madras Native Infantry, seventy sappers, and two 24-pounder howitzers, and it embarked on the evening of the 18th in four Bengal Marine steamers. The expedition was nominally under the command of Brigadier McNeill, but was accompanied by General Godwin. Sailing on the morning of the 19th, the fleet anchored two miles below Pegu the next day, when a reconnaissance proved that the Burmese position was strongly fortified.

On the 21st the troops were disembarked and advanced against an advanced post on the left of the enemy's position. This was stormed and carried by the 1st Bengal Fusiliers under Colonel Tudor. The party then changed direction, and cutting their way through thick jungle, in company with the Madras Fusiliers and the 5th Madras Native Infantry, they arrived, after a fatiguing march of two miles, in front of the main gate. Here the Burmese were in great strength, and opened a heavy fire, but the troops pressed on with vigour, and charging the gate with fixed bayonets, drove the enemy headlong from their defences. An advance was now made on the pagoda from which the Burmese speedily retired, and Pegu was once more in the hands of the British.

Second capture of Pegu.

A garrison of 200 Madras Fusiliers, and 200 5th Madras Native Infantry, with two howitzers, the whole under Major Hill, Madras Fusiliers, was left in the pagoda, and General Godwin returned with the rest of the troops to Rangoon. In leaving such a small garrison, General Godwin appears to have made the mistake of underestimating his enemy. He could easily have spared a larger force from Rangoon, and the speedy investment of Pegu by the Burmese shows that he should certainly have done so.

The Burmese, under more energetic leadership than those near Prome, had no intention of leaving this small British garrison unmolested, and, on the 27th, a strong force advanced to attack it, but were successfully driven off. As soon as General Godwin heard of this attack he despatched a small reinforcement to Pegu, but even with this addition the garrison there was still too small, and on the 9th December information was received that Major Hill was again beleaguered by a large force, was in want of ammunition, and was cut off from the river. More ammunition and 240 Madras Fusiliers were now sent to his relief, but on arriving at Pegu they found the enemy in such strength that they were obliged to retire without communicating with the garrison. General Godwin was now fully alive to the gravity of the situation, and immediately started up the river for Pegu, at the head of 1,300 men. At the same time he despatched a land column under the command of Colonel Sturt, to clear the line between Rangoon and Pegu, where parties of Burmese were harassing the villages.

Pegu besieged.

General Godwin's force consisted of—600 of the 1st Bengal Fusiliers, 300 of the 4th Sikh Infantry, 200 of the 10th Bengal Native Infantry, and 250 Madras Fusiliers, while the land column included some artillery and sappers, half a troop of the Ramghur Irregular Cavalry, and a wing of the 67th Bengal Native Infantry. General Godwin arrived at Pegu on the 14th, and disembarking six miles below the pagoda, advanced next morning to attack the enemy on the eastern face. The Burmese, finding themselves between two fires, retired before they were attacked, leaving only a party of skirmishers to oppose the advance, who were put to flight with trifling loss. The garrison of Pegu was thus successfully relieved after having been hard pressed from the 5th December. The Burmese force that had invested the pagoda was estimated at between 6,000 and 8,000 men, and they had kept up an incessant fire on the British, day and night. Major Hill's task had also been made the heavier by the fact that about 2,000 Talaings (men, women and children) had sought refuge from the Burmese under the walls of the pagoda, and had to be rationed and guarded by the British troops. The total loss of the British garrison during the investment was forty-five killed and wounded.

Composition of relief columns.

The following description of the pagoda will further show the difficulties with which the small British garrison had had to contend. It is raised on three terraces, each face of the lowest terrace being about 450 yards long. Outside the stockade high grass and jungle impeded the view of the sentries, and numerous small pagodas to the east and west gave shelter to the enemy; while on the north and east sides the interior of the stockade was commanded by ground higher than the platforms.

It was generally expected that no further movement would be made by General Godwin until the arrival of the land column from Rangoon, as the surrounding country was admirably adapted to cavalry, of which arm there were at present none at Pegu. The General, however, decided otherwise, and started in pursuit of the enemy, without waiting for Colonel Sturt, on the 17th December. The same day he came upon the Burmese position, which proved to be three lines of strong entrenchments, their right resting on the river, and their centre protected by a jungly *nullah*. The General determined to attack the left of the line, and made his dispositions accordingly. He, however, seems to have waited too long before pressing home his attack, for, after carrying the first line of trenches with a detachment of Bengal Fusiliers, a considerable time was spent in forming up his troops in two columns to storm the second line, with the result that when he was at last ready to advance, it was found that the enemy had entirely disappeared, nor, owing to his lack of cavalry, was he able to pursue them.

This delay was very keenly felt by the right of the British line, under General Steel, who asserted that if only he had been allowed to advance as soon as he was ready, he would have been able to cut off the whole Burman army. General Godwin pressed the pursuit with vigour, but on the 20th his supplies failed and he was obliged to return to Pegu. Here he left a new garrison of 750 men, and embarked the next day for Rangoon, *en route* for Prome.

While these events were taking place in Pegu, the dispersed troops of the Bandula were giving some trouble at Prome, and bodies of the enemy had appeared as low down as Akouktoung (Kyauktan) and Myanaung. On the 11th November two Burmese stockades opposite Prome were attacked and taken, and several detachments were sent out, which succeeded in destroying the enemy's numerous works in the neighbourhood. In one of these affairs, on the 18th November, Captain Gardner of the 40th Native Infantry, was unfortunately killed, being shot down while advancing with his men in single file through the jungle.

Lord Dalhousie decides to proclaim annexation of Pegu.

On receiving the despatches informing him of the occupation of Prome and Pegu, the Governor-General in Council felt that as it had been determined not to advance far beyond the former place, the time had come to declare the annexation of Pegu. On the 3rd December he wrote to Captain (afterwards General Sir Arthur) Phayre, appointing him Commissioner of Pegu. At the same time he forwarded him a letter for the King of Burma, and a proclamation to be issued whenever he considered best.

The proclamation was short; after very briefly recapitulating what had occurred, it declared the province of Pegu to be a portion of the British territories, and added that such Burmese troops as still remained in the province would be driven out.

The proposed treaty was still shorter, and consisted of only four articles. The first declared that there should be perpetual peace between the two States; the second that Pegu was ceded to the British; the third that trade should be perfectly free and unrestricted; and the fourth fixed the period within which the treaty was to be ratified.

The letter to the King, after declaring the annexation of Pegu, warned him that if he attempted to interfere with the British occupation of that province, the British Government would continue hostilities until the entire kingdom of Burma was subjugated.

The proclamation was issued on the 20th December 1852, eleven months after the first shot was fired at Rangoon, and as soon as possible afterwards the letter was forwarded to the King of Ava.

Meanwhile desultory fighting continued, and on the 8th December the Burmese made a daring night attack on Prome, which was, however, successfully repelled by the garrison under Sir John Cheape, who succeeded in inflicting a severe loss on the enemy.

Revolution at Ava.

Shortly after this all the Burmese troops suddenly disappeared from the vicinity of Prome, and bands of marauders alone were left to be put down by the British. The cause of this sudden cessation of hostilities was the outbreak of a rebellion at the capital. The reigning sovereign, Pagan Min, had two half-brothers, one of whom, the Mindun Min, he began to regard with disfavour. On the 17th December, that prince, feeling that his life was no longer secure, and knowing the hatred with which the people in general regarded the present King, followed the time-honoured custom of the country and fled with his brother to Mootsho-bho (Shwebo). This step, a sign of rebellion, was not taken hurriedly, but after much preparation; and on reaching the right bank of the Irrawaddy the brothers found themselves at the head of an army of sufficient size to warrant their resisting the force sent against them. This force they completely defeated and then continued their move on Moot-sho-bho. Here they quickly collected a large enough army to advance on the capital, and on the 1st January 1853 their troops were in possession of the suburbs of Amarapura, the Mindun Min himself remaining for the present at Moot-sho-bho. At first the court was paralysed, but after three days of inaction the gates of the capital were shut and the King prepared for defence. The fighting on both sides, however, was so miserable that neither combatant had gained any advantage up to the 18th February. On that day the *Mingyi* seized the King's chief ministers, and in the resulting confusion the rebel troops got over the walls and made themselves masters of the city and palace.

The Mindun Min was a strict Bhuddist, and kept out of the way until all the innumerable executions which invariably follow a Burmese insurrection had taken place, in order to persuade his future people that he was not responsible for any of the bloodshed. When all was over, and when blood had been shed like water, this highly religious prince entered the capital and was duly proclaimed King.

Mindun Min's policy.

Mindun Min had been averse to the war from its commencement, and was anxious for peace, but he declined most positively to sign away any of his territory, and would agree to no treaty. Taking warning, however, from Lord Dalhousie's threat, he never ventured to attempt to disturb us in our possession of Pegu. He felt strongly, and more than once expressed his feelings, that he, who was most anxious to stop the war, and after his accession forbade any open attack on us, should have been threatened with the extinction of his kingdom. But Lord Dalhousie's letter was intended for Pagan Min, and it was only owing to Mindun Min's successful rebellion that it was delivered to him.

From this digression we must now return to the doings of a column under General Steel, who during the rebellion had been busy carrying out the most important part of the proclamation, namely, "driving out from the province of Pegu such Burmese troops as were still remaining there."

Expedition to Toungoo.

On the 29th December General Steel, commanding at Rangoon, issued orders for the embarkation of a field force to start immediately for Martaban, to expel the Burmese from the valley of the Sittang and to give confidence to peaceful subjects as far as Toungoo.

The column was to be under the command of the General himself, and the following details were ordered to be furnished from Rangoon:—One European company of Madras Artillery, one company of Sappers and Miners, 450 of the 1st Bengal Fusiliers under Major Gerrard, 150 Madras Fusiliers under Major Geiles, a wing of the 10th Bengal Native Infantry, a wing of the 5th Madras Native Infantry, and a detachment of Ramghur Irregular Cavalry.

This force sailed from Rangoon on the 4th January and arrived off Martaban on the next day, but owing to lack of transport, it was the 14th of the month before an advance could be made into the interior. At 6 o'clock on the morning of that day the column moved out of Martaban, the total strength of the force, including some reinforcements from Moulmein, now numbering 2,100 men.

On the 18th a skirmish took place at Gangaw (Gongoh), in which the British lost one man killed and seven wounded. No further opposition was experienced, the Burmese everywhere abandoning their positions on the approach of the British, and on the 22nd February the column reached Toungoo, having driven the enemy out of the whole country between that place and Martaban. This march may be considered a very fine performance, as the column, accompanied by a long and heavy train of artillery, forced its way through 240 miles of unknown forest in thirty-four days.

Mention should here be made of a very creditable affair which occurred on the 6th January. On this day, at Naraghain, on the Burma–Arakan frontier, Captain Nuthall with a force of 150 of the Arakan Local Battalion, succeeded in surprising and capturing a large Burmese stockade which guarded the Aeng pass. It should also be stated that in the summer of the previous year, instructions had been given by Government for the improvement of the Aeng pass, and for the construction of tanks along the road where water was scarce, in order to improve the communication between Burma and Arakan.

CHAPTER VIII.

OPERATIONS AGAINST DACOITS.

It is now necessary to turn to the operations against the bands of marauders which were the only enemy left in the neighbourhood of Prome after the Burmese army disappeared at the beginning of the revolution.

Parties of these lawless freebooters sprung up in all directions, and were in some cases, owing to their numbers and resolution, dangerous opponents. The Bassein district, which was overrun by dacoits, was successfully cleared by the Commissioner, Captain Fytche, with the help of a small local force which he raised for this purpose, but a dacoit named Myat Tun, who commanded a large following, gave us a considerable amount of trouble before he was finally subdued.

This man had won for himself an all-powerful name in Donubyu (the scene of Bandula's death in the first war) and its vicinity. He had captured our boats in their progress up and down stream, and had proved himself so dangerous to our tranports that it was deemed necessary to send a considerable force against him. The expedition for this purpose consisted of 185 seamen, 62 marines, and 300 of the 67th Bengal Native Infantry, the whole under the command of Captain Loch, C.B., R.N. Leaving Rangoon at the beginning of February, Captain Loch found on arrival at Donubyu that all the creeks had been staked and rendered unnavigable by the enemy. He consequently decided to abandon his boats and make an inland march.

Captain Loch's expedition against Myat Tun.

After proceeding twenty-five miles through thick jungle without coming across any trace of the enemy, the column arrived at a *nullah,* partly filled with water, and with precipitous sides about thirty feet high. The road along which they had advanced through the jungle was at this point only broad enough for two men to walk abreast, and owing to the thickness of the bush it was impossible to have scouts on either flank.

As soon as the leading files arrived at this *nullah* they were met by a very heavy fire from a masked stockade on the opposite bank, from marksmen concealed in the trees, and from the jungle on each side of the path. All those in front, including Captain Loch, were immediately hit, and Captain Price and Lieutenant Kennedy were among the killed. The men continuing to drop on all sides, a retreat was now ordered, and thanks to the gallantry of the rear-guard of the 67th Native Infantry, who succeeded in repelling the repeated attacks of the pursuing enemy, the column arrived safely at Donubyu, though it was found necessary to abandon the guns on the way.

British reverse near Donubyu.

Out of the 225 Europeans who advanced to the attack, six were killed and fifty-three wounded, of whom Captain Loch died of his wounds a few days later. It is impossible to read the account of this reverse without noticing how little care seems to have been exercised by the British Commander. Though it was not feasible to have scouts out on the flanks, there seems to be no reason why the road should not have been previously reconnoitred or why a few scouts should not have marched in advance of the column; and it is plain that but for the lack of this obvious precaution, the troops would not have blundered into the enemy's trap and the consequent disaster would most certainly have been avoided. One cannot but think it an error that after the boats were abandoned the command should still have been in the hands of a sailor with probably no experience of land operations; and that General Godwin shared this view is shown by an order which he issued shortly after this reverse, to the effect that in all future combined naval and military operations on shore, the senior military officer should have the chief command, no matter what his rank might be relatively to that of the senior naval officer present.

After this reverse, immediate steps were taken to send a considerably larger force against Myat Tun, and on the 18th February Brigadier-General Sir John Cheape left Prome for this purpose at the head of a column composed of 200 of Her Majesty's 18th Royal Irish, under Major Wigston, 200 of Her Majesty's 51st Regiment under

Sir John Cheape's operations against Myat Tun.

Captain Irby, the Rifle Company of the 67th Bengal Native Infantry under Captain Hicks, 200 of the 4th Sikh Locals under Major Armstrong, seventy Sappers and Miners under Lieutenants Mullins and Trevor, and two guns.

Sir John landed at Henzada on the Irrawaddy, about thirty-five miles north of Donubyu, determining to start against Myat Tun's stronghold from this quarter. Henzada was a large and prosperous place, and here all the transport required for the expedition was available.

From information received from the Commissioner, Sir John was led to expect that he could reach Myat Tun's position in three or four days, then march into Donubyu and embark again in the steamers. The column consequently advanced from Henzada on the 22nd February, taking seven or eight days' rations with them. On the 26th the General found himself, as he believed, still at a considerable distance from the Chief's stronghold, and as provisions were running short, and he had no knowledge of the intervening country, he determined to regain the river. He accordingly made a flank march to Zalun, where the force arrived on the afternoon of the 28th. The steamers, having been warned, were waiting for the troops at Zalun, and the following day the force proceeded down stream towards Donubyu. The empty carts and the horses of the battery were escorted thither by 100 of the Royal Irish, 100 Sikhs, and a detachment of irregular cavalry who had now joined the column from Prome.

Arriving at Donubyu on the 3rd March it was found that the whole town had been burnt by Myat Tun, and that not a house nor an inhabitant remained. Owing to the reported strength of the enemy's position General Cheape decided to defer his advance until the arrival of reinforcements which were expected from Rangoon. These reinforcements, consisting of 130 of Her Majesty's 80th Foot, 300 of the 67th Native Infantry, two mortars, and a large supply of commissariat stores duly arrived on the 6th, and the next day the general advance began. A small body of troops were left at the base, and the column now consisted of about 500 Europeans, 500 natives, two guns, three rocket tubes, and two mortars, with the detachment of irregular cavalry and seventy sappers.

It was considered that three days' march would bring the column to the enemy's stronghold, so only seven days' provisions were taken, General Cheape wishing to have as small a transport train to guard as possible. About seven miles out from Donubyu a broad *nullah* was reached, from the opposite side of which the enemy opened a heavy fire which was however quickly silenced by the British guns. The troops passed the night behind a belt of jungle parallel to the *nullah*, and although the enemy sniped them all night only two men were wounded. On the 8th, rafts having been constructed by the sappers, the column was ferried across the *nullah*, an operation which was not finished till late at night.

It should be noted that the morning fogs were particularly heavy in this neighbourhood and never cleared away till about 9 A.M. It was consequently the usual practice to let the force breakfast before starting the day's march. The following day a start was made about 9 A.M., but about midday it was thought that the guide was taking the wrong road. He was consequently sent to the rear and another one called up to take his place. The new guide turned to the left, and after a most tedious march under a glaring sun, brought the wearied troops back to the identical place from which they had started. Such were the difficulties with which the unfortunate General, without maps, and compelled to trust himself to guides, had to contend. The right road was now found, and the column setting out once more arrived by nightfall at Kyon-tani, where it was decided to halt.

The whole of the 10th was occupied in crossing another *nullah*. On the morning of the 11th the enemy, taking advantage of the usual fog, sniped the camp at close quarters, but were soon driven off. The column advanced at the usual hour, and it was expected that the enemy's position would be reached that day. The difficulties of the march, however, were so great and the Burmans had made so many obstacles by felling trees across the road, that by 4 P.M. the troops were too fatigued to proceed any further, and it was decided to bivouac for the night where they were. Myat Tun's stronghold was said to be only two miles to the left, but there was no road to it through the bush. The guide, who had committed himself on the 9th, and who was now with the rear-guard, had pointed out a spot some way back where he asserted the road to the enemy's position branched off, but no one would believe him, which was unfortunate, as in this case he turned out to be speaking the truth.

The next day the column retraced its steps, and on passing the place where the road branched to the left, it was at first decided to advance straight on Myat Tun's position. Owing, however, to provisions running short it was thought prudent to return to Kyon-tani, and wait for a further supply. This was accordingly done, and the next day Colonel Sturt, with all the carts and 300 men, went into Donubyu for provisions, taking the sick and wounded with him. Meanwhile the troops were placed on half-rations and, to add to the General's difficulties, cholera now broke out in the camp, thirteen deaths occurring on the 13th.

The British force remained at Kyon-tani until the 16th when Colonel Sturt arrived with about twelve days' provisions. The Burmese had fired a few shots into camp every night, but fortunately without hitting any one.

The General now decided to advance as quickly as possible so as to give the enemy no more time for preparation. Accordingly on the afternoon of the 17th he sent a force consisting of the Royal Irish, the 80th Foot, and the 4th Sikh Local Regiment, the whole under the command of Major Wigston, Royal Irish, to take up a position at a stockade about three miles up the road, so that the rest of the force could move out of camp early on the 18th without waiting for the fog to lift.

Major Wigston found the stockade occupied by the enemy, but it was gallantly stormed by the Royal Irish, and the force bivouacked there for the night undisturbed. The following day the rest of the column came up and a general advance was begun, the road taken being the one previously pointed out by the guide as leading to Myat Tun's position. Owing to the number of obstacles constructed by the enemy, the march was one of peculiar difficulty, the rate of advance being only about one mile in two hours. In the afternoon the enemy were found holding a stockade on the left flank, concealed in the dense bush. This position was stormed and captured by the 51st Foot, with a loss of one officer killed and six men wounded. The advance was now continued to a *nullah* about a mile further on, where, as it was then 5 o'clock, a halt was made for the night. In the evening three signal rockets were fired for the information of Captain Fytche, who had promised to co-operate to the westward of the position, and these signals were replied to by guns. Next morning, after advancing about a mile, the enemy were found in position on the opposite side of the *nullah*, along the edge of which the road, having branched off to the left, lay.

The General determined to attack the right of the position at the head of the *nullah*, and immediately formed up his troop accordingly; the 80th Foot in advance, supported by the Sikhs, with the Royal Irish in reserve.

On arrival opposite the proposed point of attack, it was found that the only access to the stockade was along a narrow path with thick jungle on either side, and down this path the enemy were sending a heavy and well directed fire. Major Wigston, Captain Armstrong, and all the officers of the Sikhs but one, were quickly shot down, and the troops could make no headway. Several attempts were made to turn the position, but owing to the density of the bush this was found impossible. A 24-pounder howitzer was now dragged up to the front and began shelling the breastwork at twenty-five yards' range. Meanwhile reinforcements were hurried forward, and the enemy being shaken by the fire of the howitzer, volunteers were called for, and a desperate charge was at last made down the path, headed by Lieutenant Taylor and Ensign Garnet Wolseley.[1] This time the men were not to be denied, and, pressing on, they rushed the stockade at the point of the bayonet, and the position was won. Lieutenant Taylor was mortally, and Wolseley severely, wounded in the charge, and our total losses in the action amounted to eleven killed, and nine officers and seventy-five men wounded. Quantities of arms and ammunition were captured, including the two guns lost by Captain Loch at Donubyu, but Myat Tun himself succeeded in effecting his escape. The strength of the enemy on this occasion was estimated at 4,000.

Capture of Myat Tun's stronghold.

After the action a party was sent on to Kyaukazin, Myat Tun's own village, but neither there nor in another village passed on the road was a soul to be seen. Captain Fytche joined the main body about midday, at the latter village. On the 21st all the sick and wounded were sent down the river in boats which Commander

[1] Now Viscount Wolseley.

Tarleton had now managed to get up the creek, and on the 2nd the army started their return march to Donubyu, which they reached without incident on the 24th. The troops then embarked and returned to Prome.

In these operations against Myat Tun the British loss amounted to 140 killed and wounded, and upwards of 100 died of cholera, making the total casualties nearly 250.

This may be said to be the last episode of any importance in the war. The Burman King, though he refused to sign any treaty, kept his promise to make no efforts to resist the British occupation of Pegu, and sent a messenger to Prome to say that he wished the blockade on the Irrawaddy withdrawn, and free trade to be established between the two nations. Lord Dalhousie, therefore, decided to refrain from pressing for a treaty which he felt, from such a King, would not be worth the paper it was written on, and on the 30th June 1853 he issued his own Proclamation of Peace, and fixed, on his own authority, a parallel of latitude to be the frontier line between British and Burmese territory. The frontier pillars were duly erected and the King of Burma abided by Lord Dalhousie's proclamation.

Notwithstanding the conclusion of peace it was, however, several months before the various bands of marauders were finally driven out of Pegu, many small skirmishes taking place before real pacification was effected.

The corps engaged in the campaign were subsequently (in 1855) authorized to inscribe the word "Pegu" on their colours, and, by G. O. No. 88 of 23rd January 1854, a medal (afterwards known as the "India Medal of 1854"), and six months' *batta*, were granted to all ranks.

BIBLIOGRAPHY.

Our Burmese Wars—Colonel W. F. Lawrie, 1880.

British Burma Gazetteer—1880.

PART III.

THE THIRD BURMESE WAR.

THE THIRD BURMESE WAR.

CHAPTER IX.

RELATIONS WITH BURMA FROM 1853 *TO* 1885.

IN order to fully explain the causes which led up to the third Burmese war, it is necessary to touch on the political and commercial relations between British India and Upper Burma from 1853 to 1880.

After the second war of 1852, when the kingdom of Ava was shorn of all its coast-line and became a purely inland territory, a special mission was sent to Amarapura, where it was suitably received, but no real diplomatic representation of the Government of India was resumed till many years afterwards.

In 1862 Sir Arthur Phayre, the first Chief Commissioner of British Burma, negotiated a new commercial treaty with King Mindon at Mandalay, by which mutual concessions were agreed upon. To promote trade the British abolished certain customs duties levied on the southern side of the frontier, but the Burmese, true to their national characteristics, indefinitely delayed performance of their part of the agreement. Matters soon relapsed into such an unsatisfactory state that the Government of India intimated to the Court of Ava that they would restore the frontier duties unless negotiations were entered into for a new treaty. A new commercial treaty was accordingly concluded by Colonel Fytche in 1867. Notwithstanding certain defects this new convention secured several valuable commercial arrangements, and conferred on the British Resident recognized powers to watch over British interests, by securing for him certain civil jurisdiction over cases concerning British subjects in Avan territory; it also provided for a political agent, subordinate to the Resident at Mandalay, being stationed at Bhamo, the town in the north through which the bulk of the trade with Yunnan was carried out.

From 1867 to 1879 the Government of India was continuously represented by a Resident at Mandalay, but owing to the Burmese custom of neglecting obligations whenever possible, and of evading in practice the agreements which they accepted in theory, neither the political nor commercial relations can be said to have been satisfactory during any part of this time.

Apart from the question of concessions to British traders, other great causes of friction existed in the "Shoe Question," which will be dealt with later; in the improper treatment of British subjects in Upper Burma; and in certain territorial discussions. These four questions varied in urgency, but towards the close of King Mindon's reign they had all assumed the status of pending cases which it was necessary to bring to some practical issue. The hope of solving them by friendly negotiation was futile. The attitude of the Government of India, reluctant to proceed to force, merely encouraged the Burmese to maintain an attitude of indifference with regard to all proposals and remonstrances, and it became perfectly clear that unless they were urged in peremptory terms, and if necessary, enforced, the mere arrangement of a new commercial agreement would of itself be of no avail.

Causes of friction.

The "Shoe Question" above referred to was an indignity of long standing. The British Minister at Mandalay had always submitted, on the occasion of official visits to the palace, to the enforcement of a ceremonial requiring him to take off his shoes before entering the royal presence, and to sit on the floor before the King. When Sir Douglas Forsyth was sent upon a mission to Mandalay in 1875, he was instructed to use his own discretion with regard to following past precedent, but not to allow a mere question of form to prevent the success of his negotiations. He accordingly took off his sword and shoes in the accustomed manner before entering the palace, and seated himself on the floor with his feet tucked in behind him, in the posture of a supplicant before the King. On the conclusion of his mission, however, he raised in his report the question of continuing to submit to a ceremonial so degrading to a British Envoy. In consequence of this the Burman Government were told as tactfully as possible that the British Resident must in future be treated in a manner suitable to his high rank, and the Resident at Mandalay was instructed not to take off his shoes nor sit on the floor when next received in audience by the King. Mindon, however, tacitly refused to comply with the British Request, with the result that from that time to the final withdrawal of the British Representatives from Mandalay in October 1879, no British Resident was ever again received in audience, and all business had to be conducted through the Burmese Minister. This suspension of direct personal intercourse was naturally inimical to British influence. Though it was clearly necessary to terminate the degrading ceremony, it seems to have been a mistake for the Government to have put a stop to it before they were prepared to insist both on a suitable form of reception, and on full privilege of access to the King, being secured to their Representative. It was a weak policy, because it led us into a not altogether creditable *impasse* for the last three years of Mindon's reign; and, when Thibaw succeeded him, the opportunity of insisting on an improved status of diplomatic intercourse was lost.

Death of King Mindon, 1878.

In September 1878 King Mindon died and was succeeded by his fourth son Thibaw, his two eldest sons, the Nyaungyan and Nyaungok Princes taking refuge with the British Resident, and afterwards, at the request of the Burmese Government, being removed to Calcutta. It was at first hoped that the new King would pay more respect to British demands, but it soon became evident that things had, if possible, changed for the worse.

Thibaw inaugurates his reign with a massacre of his relations.

Thibaw started his reign by a bloody massacre of about eighty of his relations, in order to make his seat on the throne more secure, and an attempt was even made on the two Princes under British protection in Calcutta. Indignities, which need not be enumerated, began to be heaped on British subjects, a British mail boat on the Irrawaddy was seized, the Burmese garrisons in the river forts were increased, and it was generally clear that the violent party then in power desired a rupture with the British Government.

The Indian Government now made a display of strength on the British Frontier, both to maintain peace within our own territory and to support the Resident in his somewhat critical position. At the same time they impressed on the British Government the necessity of addressing an ultimatum to the Burmese King, demanding a change in his policy towards the British. Owing, however, to our being engaged at this time with the Zulu war and the Afghan campaign, the British Cabinet decided that troops could not be spared to enforce our demands in Burma, and consequently no further steps were taken in the matter.

The respite thus given to Thibaw, and the news of British reverses in Zululand, were the cause of further atrocities, which culminated in a plot to massacre the British Resident and his guard. This design had, however, only reached its preliminary stage when it was discovered by the British, and, as a result, the Government ordered the withdrawal of the officers, escort, and records from the Residency. Notice thereof was duly given to the Burmese Ministers and to all British subjects, and the withdrawal was quietly effected on 7th October 1879, without the occurrence of any untoward incident.

About this time an unfortunate circumstance occurred, the consequences of which the Burmese attributed to the British. In May 1880 the Nyaungok Prince left Calcutta secretly, and, entering Upper Burma with a few adherents, made a feeble attempt to raise a rebellion. The attempt failed, and, being found under arms in British Territory, the Prince was apprehended and sent back to Calcutta, but the Mandalay Ministers accused the British Government of connivance and of a breach of its obligations to keep him in safe custody. The Government repudiated any such obligation. Subsequently a formal request for the extradition of the Prince and his followers on a charge of dacoity was also refused, on the ground that international law and custom forbade the delivery of political offenders. The Burmese Government followed this up with a claim for compensation assessed at Rs. 55,800 for damage done during the Prince's incursions. The claim was rejected, the Burmese being informed that for any injury caused by acts, independent of the insurrection, by persons who were in British Territory, resort could be had to the civil courts. It was felt, however, by the Government that the Prince's escapade was a very awkward circumstance, and that it very materially weakened the British position, for the Burmese undoubtedly believed that the British were to blame for the whole affair.

The attitude of King Thibaw's Government now grew more hostile. Unprovoked attacks were twice made on British mail steamers on the Irrawaddy, and demands for redress were replied to in so curt and discourteous a manner, that the Government of India recommended the renunciation of all treaty engagements with the Court of Ava. The British Cabinet, however, being now engaged in war with the Boers, within a few months of the termination of the Zulu and Afghan campaigns, were unable to accept the policy urged by the Indian Government, and deprecated the precipitation of a crisis.

Meanwhile the relations between the Government of India and the Court of Ava were at a deadlock. Upper Burma became completely disorganized, and bands of armed robbers roamed about at will, and at times even raided into British territory. Commercial progress was retarded and trade intercourse interfered with by the King following the policy of his predecessor in creating monopolies; and in other matters also the attitude assumed by the Burmese Government continued to be unmistakably unfriendly. The hostilities gradually became more marked, and it was stimulated by the intrigues and machinations of certain foreigners.

Burmese Mission to Europe.

This policy of hostility in May 1883 led the Court of Ava to despatch a Mission to Europe, for the purpose of seeking alliances with foreign powers and of arranging political and commercial agreements which could not but conflict very seriously with established British interests. So long as the Kingdom of Ava occupied an isolated position, its overt unfriendliness could be treated with extreme forbearance by the Government of India; but when once the external policy of the Burmese began to exhibit symptoms of desiring to prosecute designs which might result in the establishment of preponderating foreign influence at the Court of Ava it became impossible for the British Cabinet any longer to view the situation without anxiety.

It should be stated that a treaty had been under negotiation between Burma and France in 1873, but had never been completed, as the French Agent sent to Burma for this purpose had taken upon himself the responsibility of entering into fresh clauses of so objectionable a nature that promises were given by the French to the British Government that it would not be ratified. On the arrival of the Burmese Embassy at Paris in 1883, they desired to renew negotiations regarding this unratified treaty of 1873. In the diplomatic conversations held during the ensuing summer between Lord Lyons, the British Ambassador, and the French Minister for Foreign Affairs, no opportunities were lost of impressing on the French Government the objections entertained by the British Cabinet to the conclusion of any but a purely commercial agreement with King Thibaw, and it was understood that the British authorities desired that facilities should not be given to the Burmese for the purchase of arms. It was also pointed out that owing to the geographical position of Upper Burma, and of British India's political relations with that country, the affairs of the Kingdom of Ava were of the utmost concern to the British Government, whereas to the French they could only be of secondary interest.

In April 1884, M. Ferry, Minister for Foreign Affairs, assured Lord Lyons that any treaties resulting from the negotiations would be of an entirely commercial character, and that no facilities would be afforded the Burmese for the purchase of arms, as the French Government were determined not to facilitate the introduction of military stores into Tonkin. In May 1884, M. Ferry was again informed that the British Government would naturally entertain the most serious objections to any special alliance or political understanding between Upper Burma and any other foreign power. In the course of an interview in July 1884, during which Lord Lyons handed M. Ferry a paper *pro memoria,* embodying the position taken up by the British Government, the French Foreign Minister observed that it was very difficult to draw any distinct line between commercial and political functions. The present intention of the French Government, he avowed, was to station only a Consul at Mandalay; but the title given to such agent would after all be a matter of little consequence, as whatever title he bore he would have to deal with general questions between the two countries. Finally, M. Ferry gave a distinct assurance that the French Government had no intention of forming an alliance of any special political character with Burma.

Trouble on the Manipur frontier.

Troubles had meanwhile been brewing on the boundary between the British protected State of Manipur and Upper Burma. In consequence of certain disturbances which had occurred on this frontier, and of doubts regarding the exact frontier line, the Government of India, early in 1881, determined to depute a commission to mark out the boundary. The Court of Ava were informed of this intention and invited to depute representatives to be present at the demarcation, but in reply they stated that a fresh demarcation was unnecessary, and that they would refuse to abide by any ruling made by the British on the subject.

The British Commissioners therefore proceeded to mark out the frontier alone, and finding an armed Burmese post in a village which proved to be in British territory, they requested the Burman local authorities to have it withdrawn. For two years the Burmese Government sent repeated threats that they would destroy the new boundary marks, but nothing was done till May 1884, when a peremptory letter was received from Ava to the effect that if the new frontier line was not altered, the boundary marks and Kongkal outpost would be destroyed. In answer to this letter, the Indian Government instructed the Maharaja of Manipur to resist any such attempt on the part of the Burmese, and sent a detachment of infantry to his support. In consequence of this prompt action the Burmans allowed the matter to drop.

Completion of Franco-Burman Treaty.

In January 1885 M. Jules Ferry informed Lord Lyons that the treaty which has been for over eighteen months in negotiation in Paris, between the French Government and the Burmese Embassy, had at length been signed on 15th January, that it contained no political or military stipulations, but was merely a treaty stipulating for rights of residence, intercourse, commerce, most-favoured-nation treatment, and so forth.

The intentions of France were, however, afterwards apparent from a letter, also dated 15th January 1885 (the day the treaty had been signed), which came into the hands of the Chief Commissioner of British Burma towards the end of July 1885. It was from the French Prime Minister to the Burmese Minister for Foreign Affairs, and contained the following passage :—

> With respect to transport through the province of Tonkin to Burma, of arms of various kinds, ammunition, and military stores generally, amicable arrangements will be come to with the Burmese Government for the passage of the same when peace and order prevail in Tonkin, and the officers stationed there are satisfied that it is proper and that there is no danger.

There is no necessity for considering this Franco-Burmese Treaty in detail. It is sufficient to remark that King Thibaw's government were evidently bent on welcoming to the upper valley of the Irrawaddy foreign influence which could not fail at some future time to trouble the tranquillity of British Burma, and to engender complications extending beyond the British Frontier.

The law of the Senate and the Chamber of Deputies authorizing the President of the French Republic to ratify the Franco-Burmese Convention of 5th January was not passed till the 24th November 1885. It was published in the *Journal Official* of 26th November the very day that the Burmese Minister were begging an armistice from the British General at Ava.

It may be here remarked that this Franco-Burmese Treaty, and the attitude displayed by the French Government during the negotiations, rendered absolutely impossible, on the conclusion of the third Burmese war, any question of deposing King Thibaw in favour of any other scion of the Burman Royal House. The attitude of the French Government, and the intrigues of M. Haas, who reached Mandalay in May 1885, as Consul of France, though not the actual *casus belli*, may, therefore, be looked upon as the direct and chief cause of the annexation of Upper Burma to the British Indian Empire, and of the extinction of the Kingdom of Ava. An international treaty existing between France and Burma would have been binding on a Burmese King, but its operation ceased *ipso facto* when Burma became part of the British Empire. Annexation, under these circumstances, was the only way of completely removing possible causes of friction between France and Britain in this particular matter.

Chief reason for annexing Burma.

By the end of 1883 Thibaw's misrule had become so great, and dacoity so prevalent, that large numbers of inhabitants of Upper Burma crossed the frontier to obtain the advantages of British protection. The Kingdom of Ava had by this time sunk to a condition of anarchy, and the King did not dare venture beyond the inner enclosure of his palace. The greater part of the feudatory Shan States, forming nearly half of the eastern part of the kingdom, had been for about three years in open rebellion, and in the early part of 1884 a serious

Anarchy in Ava.

revolt also took place in the northern districts peopled by the Kachin hill tribes, which carried fire and sword half-way down to Mandalay. In addition, rumours were current that the Myingun Prince had escaped from Pondicherry, and made his way to Bangkok, whence he expected to accomplish Thibaw's downfall. Some of the Burman Ministers now told the King they believed the prisoners in the jails were conspiring against him, and advised him to execute them, in order to prevent them escaping and joining the cause of the Myingun Prince. In consequence of this, on the 22nd September 1884, an indiscriminate massacre was begun of all the prisoners in Mandalay, in which nearly 300 men, women, and children lost their lives.

The day after the massacre the corpses were carted out of the city and were thrown in heaps of four and five together, into shallow graves. While these atrocities were being perpetrated, high festival was held within the palace, and theatrical and other performances were given night after night, to distract the attention of the people from the horrors that were being continually committed around them.

Trade had for the moment become paralysed. In October 1884, the Rangoon Chamber of Commerce memorialised the Government of India to interfere immediately in Upper Burma, and either annex the Kingdom of Ava, or constitute it a protected State under some other ruler than Thibaw, the former course for choice. But it was obviously not in accordance with the settled policy of the Government of India to interfere with the internal administration of a neighbouring State, or to annex that country, merely because commerce therewith was not increasing so rapidly as British Chambers of Commerce might wish.

While these matters were receiving the consideration of the Indian Government, the town of Bhamo, situated about 200 miles north of Mandalay, and the centre of trade with Western China, was captured and sacked by Chinese marauders on 8th December 1884. Fortunately there was no reason to believe that this seizure was instigated by the Chinese Government, as this would have introduced a still further complication into the already existing tangle of affairs. In any circumstances, however, it meant the strangulation of the

Chinese raid Bhamo.

trade between Rangoon and Bhamo until the country around the latter town was once more in a settled state. Between Mandalay and the frontier the country was overrun with numerous and powerful bands of dacoits. No troops could be sent against them as all the rabble soldiery was required for the operations towards Bhamo. The Governor of Magwe was murdered by one gang, while the Governor of Salemyo was attacked in open court by another, and narrowly escaped with his life. To avoid attacks and international questions the commanders of the British mail steamers were desired by rural Governors to anchor their vessels in the river under steam at night, instead of following the usual course of mooring alongside the bank.

Of all these various matters the Government of India had full cognizance. They were also aware of the sensible alteration which the conclusion of the Franco-Burmese Treaty of 15th January 1885 made in the political situation, and they could not but be apprehensive that the presence of M. Haas as Consul of France at Mandalay was likely to increase their difficulties in dealing with the Court of Ava. Hence they were of opinion that something should be done to restore British influence at Mandalay.

The situation was surrounded with difficulties, the satisfactory solution of which was far from easy. It was not considered desirable to insist upon the reception of a British Agent at Mandalay. After the withdrawal of the Resident in 1879, the Burmese Government had been informed that any overtures for revision of existing relations, or for the return of a political officer, must proceed from them. If, despite the altered circumstances, negotiations with either or both of these objects had been opened by the Government of India, this would have amounted to a cancellation of their intimation of 1879, and might easily have been construed in Mandalay as a sign of timidity, or even of actual weakness, on the part of the British. It could hardly be anticipated that a British Agent would be suitably received and properly treated, save under pressure of an authoritative demand, supported by a display of armed force; and for action of this nature the season was inopportune. Again, if any secret political alliance, involving ulterior designs inconsistent with British interests, had been concluded between France and Ava, the reception and courteous treatment of a British Agent, while not necessarily re-establishing British influence, would have the effect of embarrassing the British position if more direct measures of interference became unavoidable. In these circumstances the Government of India were unable to recommend to the British Cabinet any specific course of action. They could only watch the affairs of Ava with special care and anxiety, in the hope that before long some satisfactory solution of the difficulty might present itself. And such did present itself most opportunely and satisfactorily, within six months from the time when this resolution of the Government was taken in March 1885. So desirous were the Government of India to avoid irritating the susceptibilities of King Thibaw and his Ministers that they did not even send a letter of remonstrance regarding the September massacres, as was proposed by Mr. (afterwards Sir Charles) Bernard, the Chief Commissioner of Burma. There was no proof that British subjects were sufferers in the course of the barbarities; and it was thought doubtful that a letter of protest would have any useful result, even if it pointed out that, by keeping away from Burma other claimants to the throne of Ava, the Government of India were assisting in maintaining Thibaw in undisturbed possession of the crown.

Rangoon Chamber of Commerce appeal to have Burma made a Crown colony.

The declaration of this policy of temporary non-interference created much discontent in commercial circles, and the Rangoon Chamber of Commerce addressed a circular letter to the various Chambers of Commerce in Great Britain, practically desiring them to bring pressure to bear on the British Cabinet. British Burma's geographical position, its ethnographical condition, its natural wealth, and the undeniable fact that public works and internal development were starved owing to more than one-third of the revenue raised in Burma being appropriated by India, were all raised as arguments for cutting British Burma adrift from the Indian Empire and constituting it a Crown colony. Their appeal closed with the words:—

> Were British Burma a colony independent of India, not only would more have been done by this time to develope its own resources, but a firmer policy in connection with the petty kings beyond British territory would have done much to extend British trade through a large part of Indo-China, and would have made Rangoon one of the largest trade centres in the world.

This agitation for the constitution of British Burma as a Crown colony would have undoubtedly been pushed with vigour, but for the favourable trend affairs took later on in the year 1885.

The British Government, while concurring in the opinion that the state of affairs in Ava did not justify armed intervention, considered that both for commercial and political reasons, diplomatic representations should be resumed at Mandalay. Under the Yandabo Treaty of 1826, the Court of Ava were bound to receive a British Resident with an armed escort of fifty men; and they were not cognizant of any communication having been made in 1879 which need act as a bar to the adoption of this measure whenever convenient. The time and the manner of resuming direct representation were, however, left to the discretion of the Government of India.

The apprehensions entertained with regard to the activity of the French Consul at Mandalay in obtaining "concessions" of various sorts, and in generally creating a commercial and political position for France quite incompatible with the previously existing predominating British interests, were almost immediately verified. Before the arrival of M. Haas, the Consul of France, at Mandalay, a French engineer named M. Bonvillein was reported to be negotiating for a lease of the whole of the ruby mines at Mogok and Kyatpyin for fifteen years, at an annual rental of three lakhs of rupees.

M. Haas.

M. Haas, who arrived at Mandalay in May 1885, had not been there a couple of months before abundant evidence was forthcoming of the strong position which he and other French Agents were endeavouring to establish for themselves with a view to acquiring a predominating influence in Ava, which might be utilized at some future time in joining hands with the French possessions on the upper reaches of the Red River. His first efforts were towards the establishment of a French bank, the running of a French flotilla on the Irrawaddy, the working of the ruby mines, and the opening out of a trade route from Mandalay through the Shan States to Upper Tonkin. His main idea was to grant loans to the King, and, in return, to obtain industrial concessions, on the ground that, even if Britain should be ultimately driven to annex the country, actual concessions to French subjects would be respected,

In pursuance of this policy he urged upon the Court of Ava the necessity of avoiding any collision with the British Government; and he also advised them to ask for a Resident, as otherwise they ran the great risk of having one forced upon them on terms they would not like.

This temporizing was declined in favour of a continuation of the policy of procrastination, for the more wilful and ignorant of the King's advisers believed that if the tension with Russia had led to actual war the British would have lost India, and the Kingdom of Burma would once more have extended to the Bay of Bengal. It was the intention of the Burmese Government to pick a quarrel with the British as soon as they were fully occupied with troubles elsewhere. M. Haas pointed out the folly of such a course before the Court of Ava had strengthened their position by forming alliances with other European nations. He pressed the Ministers to profit by the present attitude of the Government of India towards Ava in forming treaties with France, Italy, and Germany, and to get each of these countries to proclaim Ava as neutral territory. In pursuance of this astute advice, one of the Ministers who spoke French fluently was accordingly despatched once more to Europe during the second half of July 1885.

Finding the Ministers reluctant to follow his views, M. Haas, early in July, endeavoured to work upon the King through the Buddhist Archbishop, who had frequent personal interviews with Thibaw, during which he discoursed on the advantages to be derived from a close and intimate alliance with France. M. Haas offered to work with the Burmese Ministers in organizing the finances, and the general administration of the country; he promised the maintenance of the integrity of Ava, and gave assurances that when Tonkin became tranquil the Burmese would have free passage for anything they required.

So far as concerned preliminary contracts for concessions of a valuable nature, M. Haas' machinations were successful. By the middle of July terms had been arranged for the construction of a French railway in Upper Burma, and for the establishment of a bank in Ava, and the contracts had been sent to Paris for formal completion by the French Government. If finally ratified and carried out, these agreements would have given the French practically full control over the principal sources of revenue in Ava, and over the only route open for traffic from British ports to Western China. The consequences would have been disastrous to British trade, and to the interests of British Burma. If once firmly established in Ava, the French would, no doubt, have tried to induce other European nations to neutralize Ava, and have the Mandalay river declared, like the Danube, open to vessels of all nationalities.

As the proposed arrangements were still in an embryo state, there was yet time to take steps either at Paris or Mandalay to prevent their conclusion, and the startling discovery of the letter of 15th January 1885 from M. Jules Ferry to the Prime Minister of Ava, thoroughly opened the eyes of the Government of India and the British Cabinet to the unfriendliness of France and the hostility of Ava. The Government of India recommended that the reception and proper treatment of a British Resident at Mandalay, to whose advice in all matters of foreign policy the Court of Ava should submit, ought to be insisted on; and that if those terms were refused, measures of coercion should be adopted.

In an interview at the Foreign Office in London on 7th August, Lord Salisbury informed M. Waddington, the French Ambassador, of the information he had received regarding a proposed concession to French capitalists, which would include the control over the post office, railways, steam navigation, and various branches of revenue; and he pointed out that, if such an undertaking were attempted to be carried to any practical issue, the necessary consequence would be that the British Government would have to intervene and materially restrict the liberty and power of the King of Burma. M. Waddington replied that he had no knowledge of the proposed concessions, but promised to make enquiries and communicate again on the subject.

Before the end of September M. Waddington was authorized to inform Lord Salisbury that the French Government knew absolutely nothing of the alleged agreements, and that they had given no kind of authority for making them. If made at all, they must have been made at the instance of some speculative company. Early in October M. Haas was *mis en disponibilité pour raison de santé,* and his machinations and intrigues in Mandalay were at an end. While these diplomatic representations were being conducted an occurrence took place, most opportunely, in August 1885, which demanded even more prompt and decided action, while at the same time it had the unquestionable advantage of fixing the quarrel with the King of Ava on an issue with which the French Government could not possibly admit themselves to be mixed up.

One of the chief industries in Upper Burma is the timber trade, and in this there was much capital invested by various Lower Burma companies and by individuals. These traders being for the most part British subjects, their position and interests in Upper Burma were guarded by the influence of the British Government at the Court of Ava, and the rights conceded to them were in accordance with the treaties between the two Governments. In the summer of 1885 the actions of the Bombay-Burma Trading Corporation were called into question by the Burmese Government and an arbitrary fine of twenty-three lakhs of rupees was imposed upon it. It must be here noted that the imposition of this enormous fine was proved to be partly due to the desire of the Burmese Government to force British influence out of the country, and to substitute it by French influence. The fine was one that the Corporation could not pay, and in default of immediate payment all their forest leases were to be cancelled, and their property seized and confiscated by the Government.

The Bombay-Burma Trading Corporation.

As regards the imposition of the fine there is no doubt that the Burmese had some causes of complaint against the Bombay-Burma Trading Company, but these were not commensurate with the fine imposed. Under existing circumstances the imposition of a fine which would expel large British influences from Upper Burma, to make room for French influence, had a grave political significance, so much so that the case was immediately taken up by the British Government.

It should be observed that the rupture that now took place between the two Governments did not occur because the British Government considered the fine unjust, but because the Burmese refused to allow them to enquire into its justness.

As soon as the matter had been reported by the Corporation to the Government of India, an intimation was given to the Burmese

Court that the British Government insisted on British subjects receiving a fair trial, and requested that the order for the payment of the fine should be suspended until the matter had been fully and impartially investigated. An offer was also made to appoint a judicial officer of experience as arbitrator.

In answer to this communication, the Burmese questioned the right of the Government of India to raise the subject, and refused point-blank to agree to any arbitration, or to suspend enforcement of the fine.

With the unanimous consent of his colleagues, therefore, and the full approval of Lord Salisbury's Cabinet, the Viceroy, Lord Dufferin, at once authorized the Chief Commissioner of Burma to despatch an ultimatum[1] to King Thibaw, demanding the acceptance of certain definite proposals for the settlement of existing disputes, and warning them that in the event of the proposals not being accepted the Government of India would take the matter into their own hands.

British Ultimatum.

The terms of this ultimatum, despatched on the 22nd October, were—

1. The suitable reception of a Resident with full access to the King.
2. The entire suspension of proceedings against the Bombay-Burma Trading Corporation until the arrival of the Resident.
3. The acceptance of a permanent Resident with a suitable guard for his protection.

The Court of Ava were further warned that they would be expected in future to regulate their external affairs in accordance with the advice of the Government of India, and to grant proper facilities for the development of British trade with Western China, through Bhamo.

Simultaneously with the despatch of the ultimatum, troops were moved over from India to Burma in sufficient numbers to convince the Court of Ava that the British Government were in earnest.

The ultimatum was despatched by a special steamer, the *Ashley Eden*, to Mandalay, so as to reach there about the 30th

[1] See Appendix.

October, and it was intimated that, if not interfered with, she would remain there till the 5th November in order to bring back the King's reply. She was to leave Mandalay without fail on the morning of the 6th ; and if she brought no satisfactory reply to Rangoon by the 10th, the British Government would proceed to take such further action as seemed fit.

The British plan of campaign was already cut and dried. Major-General Prendergast had been appointed to command the field force, a political officer had been selected, and four civil officers warned to accompany the army and arrange for pacifying the country through the native officials under the orders of the Military Commandants.

The Burmese Government, on the other hand, were entirely unprepared for war, and never realized that the British would really proceed to extremities.

The reply to the ultimatum was duly received on the 9th November, and was tantamount to a refusal or evasion of the three terms. It declined to discuss the case against the Corporation, and said that if the British wished to re-establish a Resident, he would "be permitted to come and go as in former times." As for external affairs, they intended to manage these for themselves, intimating boldly that "friendly relations with France, Italy, and other States have been, are being, and will be maintained" ; while with regard to the opening up of trade with Western China, they stated that "commerce will be assisted in conformity with the customs of the country."

Simultaneously with this announcement, King Thibaw on 7th November issued a proclamation throughout his dominions, calling upon all his officials and subjects to expel the British, who threatened war and intended to destroy the religion and national customs of the Burmese. The proclamation further announced the King's intention of taking the field in person, of exterminating the British, and annexing their territory.

War declared.

On 10th November the Viceroy telegraphed to the Secretary of State, proposing to at once begin hostilities. Next day the reply was received :—"Please instruct General Prendergast to advance on Mandalay at once" ; and the third Burmese war was begun.

Had action been delayed, a situation most prejudicial to the interests of Britain would have been created in Burma, and one with which it might have been difficult to deal. As it was, the decree of the French Senate on 24th November, 1885, authorizing the ratification of the Franco-Burmese Convention (which might possibly have caused complications) was promulgated too late to save King Thibaw from downfall. It was not until the extreme limit of forbearance had been reached that the declaration of war took place, and under the circumstances there was no other course left open. Nor, in view of the attitude of France, was anything short of annexation possible, for the Nyaungyan Prince, the only member of the royal house fit to be raised to the status of ruler of a protected State, was now dead.

CHAPTER X.

BRITISH PREPARATIONS FOR THE WAR.

THE following extracts from letters and telegrams show the preparations which were made for the expedition, previous to the date on which General Prendergast received his orders to advance on Mandalay.

Extract from a telegram from the Chief Commissioner, British Burma, to Foreign Secretary, Simla, detailing the precautions taken for the safety of Europeans in Upper Burma.

As to European and British residents, a special steamer goes up single-handed, passes mail steamer which carries ultimatum, and warns Europeans and British subjects at certain riverside stations. I have authorized Flotilla Company to keep off Mandalay, at Government expense, a steamer with banked fires to bring away refugees. I have left to discretion of Mr. Andrino [1] when to come away and how to warn others. His judgment and courage may be trusted. Letter imparts special warning to officials, soldiery, and others against injury to Europeans and British subjects trading in Upper Burma. Our official letter to you, dated 16th October, submits my views as to measures advisable. If King Thibaw is dethroned, I trust troops may move on Burma quickly. I have published fact that corvette *Turquoise* is returning hither. If extra troops had partly arrived, I should have more hope of pacific result from ultimatum. At present case stands thus: if older Ministers prevail, ultimatum will be unconditionally accepted; if Teindah Minister retains power, we may expect refusal, followed by outrages. I believe most, perhaps all, Europeans will get away safely if flight is necessary. I am grateful to Viceroy for giving me explicitly terms of ultimatum. My letters will explain how I guard against our precautions for safety of refugees forming ground for claim for repayment of losses from public treasury.

Orders issued for despatch of 10,000 men to Rangoon.

The Viceroy approved of the precautions taken for the delivery of the ultimatum and safety of British subjects, and added in a telegram, dated 22nd October 1885, that "orders have been given for the despatch of 10,000 men to Rangoon." Of course the Burmese Government

[1] Consul-General for Italy at Mandalay.

received the news that troops were preparing to advance in event of an unsatisfactory reply being sent to the ultimatum; this apparently in no way influenced the reply, but it is probable that the absence of outrage on Europeans was partly due to it. Two or three were thrown into jail, but though the community was threatened and passed a most anxious time, there was no violent action of any kind directed against them as a class.

Great credit was due to Mr. Andrino, the Italian Consul, at Mandalay, for his courageous behaviour in this trying time; owing to his advice and example the majority of the European population remained in Mandalay, and their immunity from violence is attributed in a great measure to the influence which Mr. Andrino exerted at the Court.

It appeared that there were two parties in the Burmese Court–the war party, headed by the *Teindah Mingyi* Minister and the Queen Soupialat, and the 'surrender' party, headed by the *Kinwun Mingyi*. The Queen had great influence in the Court and insisted vehemently on resisting the English at any cost. It was said that on one occasion, when the *Kinwun Mingyi* was advocating peace negotiations, the Queen in a fit of indignation offered him her dress to wear at home, while she went out to fight the 'Kullahs' (a contemptuous term for strangers).

The *Kinwun Mingyi* had great influence in the country and exerted it to protect the European community. It is certain that he protected the captains and crews of the two Irrawaddy Flotilla ships, who were at Mandalay when the ultimatum was delivered by Captain Cooper of the *Ashley Eden*. He also procured the release of Captain Redman of the S. S. *Okpho*, who was captured and dragged about in a cart in Mandalay in the blazing sun without any clothes on: the perpetrators of this outrage were captured and punished soon after the arrival of General Prendergast's expedition at Mandalay. The *Kinwun Mingyi* was the only Minister who subsequently was not deported for encouraging dacoity and rebellion in the province.

The following telegram was sent to our Chargé d'Affaires in China:—

In consequence of recent occurrences in Upper Burma, Burmese Government have been called upon to accept certain terms, failing which British force

will march on Mandalay, and it is possible that Burma may be annexed. Do you think such a result would arouse any feeling in China? I presume there is no probability of remonstrance.

Reply telegram from Chargé d'Affaires, Pekin, to Viceroy.

If Burmese appeal to China as tributary state, China may remonstrate and will probably object to annexation. So far Yamen has said nothing, though I have written to Ministers this day, who had certainly heard of proposed expedition. Explanation volunteered here might encourage interference.

Telegram from Chief Commissioner, British Burma, Rangoon, to the Foreign Secretary,—dated Viceroy's Camp, the 26th October 1885.

Civil officers for expedition.

I am arranging to send with expeditionary force four civil officers conversant with Burmese, one of whom would be available for General Prendergast to leave with the Commandant of each fort which he may take and garrison as he passes on; the civil officer would then arrange for pacifying the country through the existing native officials. He would be under orders of the local Commandant. I would give them written orders after consulting General Prendergast. I have warned four young officers for his duty; each will have with him two of our Burmese officials. I solicit permission to arrange on these lines when necessity comes. Nothing would be done without General Prendergast's assent, but I had better select men.

Colonel Sladen, Chief Political.

If Colonel Sladen is to go as chief civil officer, he should leave Akyab by next steamer, which will reach this on 6th November. May I order him down? He would understand that he went as civil officer under General Prendergast's orders, and not as separate envoy.

Telegram from Chief Commissioner, British Burma, Rangoon, to the Foreign Secretary,—dated Viceroy's Camp, the 28th October 1885.

I submit reply on four topics referred by your telegram of 27th: first, I think Sladen is best and most competent man for expedition as chief civil officer under command of General. I should gladly go myself, but am perhaps wanted here to promote objects of expedition. Sladen is first-rate Burmese speaker. I am poor. If Viceroy prefers my going, I would gladly go, leaving Sladen in command here. I would send with expedition four or five young civil officers, with small Burmese staff.

Instructions to political officers.

Instructions to Sladen would be that after troops have once crossed frontier, no offer of submission can be accepted or can affect movement of troops. Mandalay must be occupied and Thibaw dethroned, if ultimatum is not unconditionally accepted by date named therein. To civil officers, including Sladen, instructions would be that one with his staff should remain in every fort or other place taken or garrisoned by expedition. Such officer would, under order of Commandant, get hold of local Governors and officials, and through them administer and pacify country, giving assurances that Thibaw would not remain in power. I would give them printed Burmese proclamations to distribute. Secondly, if it is decided to annex, I would go myself to Mandalay as soon as city is taken by our troops, and submit detailed scheme.

Future requirements for administration.

I should try to retain services of good native Governors, but should require about fifteen European civil officers and twelve European police officers at outset. I would take them all from Lower Burma at first, as they must know language, filling their places here by juniors. I can find two or three good uncovenanted men of experience for Assistant Commissioners. I should perhaps take one or two Cooper's Hill Engineers for civil duty in Lower Burma. I would employ Burmans to fill some vacancies. I should ask for six civil officers of two to five years' standing from India, six police officers of same standing. Among civil officers would be two Burma civilians, Snow and Morrieson, sent to Bombay. Rest might be military men or civilians from Punjab Commission, who might volunteer. We do not want bad bargains or senior men, who must have difficulty in learning language. We cannot put civilians from outside above men of their own standing here. I should ask leave to extend Sladen's services for two or three years, and I should want one senior civilian for position of either Commissioner of Dakaiti Commissioner. I would prefer a Punjabi, either Ibbetson, Roe, Purser, or Thorburn. I know these men only by repute, but I cannot take a man who has failed to get beyond his fellows elsewhere. I should try to arrange economical staff, as Upper Burma would not pay at first. I should want 200 Punjabis or Gurkhas for mounted police. Ponies and saddles would be provided here. I should want two topographical survey parties, one of which I would take from here. Engineers I could provide out of our redundant staff, but I should like to have Brandreth of Roorki College for temporary Chief Engineer in Upper Burma. He could succeed as sole Chief Engineer when Smyth goes home in spring.

I should ask leave to begin surveying for railway to Mandalay at once. The railway would be a great pacificator. I would prefer State railways, but a well-known and wealthy Burman merchant in London would get up company for lines to Mandalay and Bhamo. In case Government cannot provide money he would take over our open lines.

Proposals in event of non-annexation.

Thirdly and fourthly, in event of non-annexation, whether Thibaw remains or new Prince succeeds, I advise, not that a treaty be made, but that a carefully worded document be drawn up, setting forth that the Viceroy places or retains upon the throne of Burma Prince so and so in the position of a feudatory of British India. He and his successors, according to national custom, will be allowed to remain on the throne so long as they adhere to the position, duties and responsibilities of a British feudatory. Among other things they must . . . then would follow clauses about external relations, employment of foreigners, number of troops, disarmament of river forts, procuring of arms through British Resident only. Resident and armed guard, power to keep British force at Mandalay and Bhamo, if Viceroy desires, absolute freedom of trade by land and river towards seaboard, towards China, and towards Shan States, abolition of duties beyond 5 per cent., system of collection of duties to be under sanction of Resident, Mixed Court, extradition, promoting railways to Mandalay and Bhamo, and giving land therefor in sovereignty to British Residents, access to King, Resident's right to advise, Resident's right to appoint political officers to other places, freedom for political officers to travel and enquire throughout the kingdom, relations with Shan dependent States to be specially subject to Resident's supervision, no important contracts with British subjects or foreigners to be made without consent of Resident, reservation to Viceroy of full power to act regarding East and West Karenni, good government, avoidance of barbarous executions and practices, general clause providing that Viceroy's decision shall govern doubtful points; document would then recite that these are the only terms on which British can consonantly with safety and prosperity of the two countries allow continuance of separate state. Prince so and so and his Chief Ministers have understood this, and have accepted the terms, knowing that on serious breach thereof the Viceroy will be at liberty to dethrone the Prince, or alter the form of Government, or annex the country, and they have set their signatures to the English and Burmese copies of this document in token of their submission and acceptance. English version to prevail over Burmese version in case of doubt; former treaties to be abrogated. I think this is the only safe and prompt way of setting a new Prince or retaining Thibaw on Mandalay throne.

Any negotiations for a new treaty would be endless. I will prepare draft of detailed document and submit. I would keep at Mandalay, until matters are quite settled, an armed gun-boat and also a despatch boat; also, one wing Europeans, one battalion native infantry, and 150 mounted native infantry, with one mountain battery. I would arrange for selection site, levelling part of Mandalay wall and erecting barracks and small fort, the first thing after reaching Mandalay. If plan of having document ready for acceptance by Ava Prince, as above, is approved, Sladen could best arrange preliminaries.

I would go up to Mandalay and see to ratification and absolute understanding of terms on which Prince is placed or retained on throne; but if

Viceroy is pleased to trust the matter to Sladen, he would bear burden of work, and if he does well would merit recognition. In 1867 he really did work of treaty, but Chief Commissioner went up afterwards to ratify and Sladen's good work was little acknowledged. If Burma gives unconditional submission to ultimatum before 10th, I would send Sladen with two civil assistants and escort of small force stated above, with exception mounted infantry. I would instruct him to present document to Thibaw's Government for acceptance and ratification, and with intimation that the Chief Commissioner would come up in twenty days to witness ratification. Sladen would not discuss any modification of document, but he would at once enquire into and settle Bombay-Burma dispute after document was accepted and ratified. He would retain escort until matters had settled down eventually. He would retain for Residency guard one company Europeans, two companies Indian infantry, and an armed gun-boat, *Irrawaddy* or *Tigris*. If Burma sends evasive or incomplete reply by date named, then text of ultimatum says that any other reply than unconditional acceptance of three first demands and general acquiescene in two other stipulations, will be regarded as refusal. On this basis we should act, and troops would go forward to Mandalay.

On the selection of a Prince to rule Burma as a feudatory state in case that policy was determined on, the following appears in a telegram, from the Chief Commissioner to the Foreign Secretary, dated the 28th October 1885 :—

Between Nyaung-oke Prince and Myingun I incline to former, because the latter is, and must be, allied with France and Frenchmen. We know that he is intriguing with them up to present moment. When an opportunity came, he would attempt to repeat intriguing if on the Ava throne. I do not believe he could do mischief in Ava or in Shan States, whilst we are at peace with France, so long as feudatory supported by us is on throne. When we have railway from Toungoo through Shan States to Bhamo, those states will be bound to us. I admit the former Prince is not clever, but he would owe life and everything to British Government. He would be docile, and with Resident's support and guidance he might succeed.

I should prefer late Nyaungyan's infant son as candidate to Myingun. We could secure good government by a Regency under Resident, and have country in fair order by time young Prince came of age. I think this plan is worth considering. I know nothing of either of the older candidates except by hearsay.

Telegram from Foreign Secretary, to the Chief Commissioner, British Burma, dated the 30th October 1885.

Your telegram, 28th. If troops advance on Mandalay, Sladen will be Political Officer, but chief political as well as chief military authority will rest with General Prendergast, who should correspond direct with Government of India, Foreign Department, repeating all telegrams to you and sending you copies of all letters. You can send with Sladen any civil officers required.

Secondly.—If Burma is annexed, Viceroy approves your going yourself to Mandalay after occupation by British troops. Meanwhile arrangements are being made to get ready officers and mounted police required by you.

Thirdly and fourthly.—Please send by telegram draft of detailed document proposed. You will be informed directly it is settled whether country is to be annexed or not.

Finally.—If Burmese Government accept terms, Sladen should go up with two civil assistants as proposed.

Telegram from Chief Commissioner, British Burma, to the Foreign Secretary, dated 31st October 1885.

If the Burmese Government accept ultimatum unconditionally, I would despatch swift steamer to Mandalay, saying that Sladen as Envoy was coming with a small protecting force to explain details of terms which Viceroy requires Upper Burma to accept. I would add in letter that those detailed terms were not open to discussion, but must be accepted as they stood. Meanwhile to keep part of expeditionary force ready until terms of document were fully accepted.

Sladen would receive instructions to say that ten days were given for acceptance and ratification of document, and that, if not accepted within that time, he should order the troops up.

For my part I think we shall get either refusal or evasive reply, or else no reply to ultimatum. In either of these cases force advances forward and Thibaw is dethroned.

MILITARY PREPARATIONS.

On the 21st October 1885, orders were issued for the troops named below to proceed to the ports of embarkation (Calcutta and Madras). The details of the expeditionary force is shown in the following extract from General Orders, dated Simla, 30th October 1885 :—

Strength of the Force.

Naval Brigade from Her Majesty's ships on the stations.

2 Mountain Batteries, Native (with coolie equipment).

1 Field Battery (officers, non-commissioned officers, and gunners only).
2 Garrison Batteries.
1 Mountain Battery, British (with mules).
3 Regiments, British Infantry.
7 Regiments, Native Infantry, including one of Pioneers.
6 Companies, Sappers and Miners.

Detail.

Divisional Troops.

Q-1 Royal Artillery.
9-1 Cinque Ports Division (Mountain), R.A.
3-1 Scottish Division, R.A.
4-1 North Irish Division, R.A.
No. 4 Punjab Mountain Battery, P.F.F.
No. 1 Bombay Mountain Battery.
Nos. 4 and 5 Companies, Bengal Sappers and Miners.
B, D, and H Companies, Madras Sappers and Miners.
No. 2 Company, Bombay Sappers and Miners.
1st Madras Pioneers.

First Brigade.

2nd Battalion, King's Liverpool Regiment.
2nd (Queen's Own) Bengal Infantry.
11th Bengal Infantry.

Second Brigade.

1st Battalion, Royal Welsh Fusiliers.
21st Madras Infantry.
25th " "

Third Brigade.

2nd Battalion, Hampshire Regiment.
12th Madras Infantry.
23rd " "

Staff.

Major-General H. N. D. Prendergast, C.B., V.C., R.E. Commanding.
Colonel H. M. Bengough, *h.p.* . . . Assistant Adjutant and Quartermaster-General.
Major J. G. R. D. MacNeil, Madras Infantry.
Major W. P. Symons, South Wales Borderers.
Major C. W. Walker, 19th Madras Infantry.
Captain R. L. Milne, Liverpool Regiment.
} Deputy Assistant Adjutant and Quartermaster-Generals.
Colonel W. Carey, R.A. . . . . Commanding Royal Artillery.
Colonel G. E. L. S. Sanford, R.E. . . Commanding Royal Engineers.

Medical Department.

Deputy Surgeon-General J. M. Donnelly, M.D., Indian Medical Service. Principal Medical Officer.

1st Brigade.

Colonel F. B. Norman, C.B., B.S.C. . . Commanding.
Captain V. A. Schalch, 11th Bengal Infantry. Brigade-Major.

2nd Brigade.

Colonel H. H. Foord, 23rd Madras Infantry	Commanding.
Captain R. A. P. Clements, S. W. B. .	Brigade-Major.

3rd Brigade.

Brig.-General G. S. White, C.B., V.C., *h.p.* .	Commanding.
Major G. Simpson, 11th Madras Infantry. .	Brigade-Major.

Variation in constitution of Infantry Brigades.

Owing to the non-receipt of the above-quoted General Order by the General Officer Commanding Expeditionary Force, variation occurred in the detail of the three Infantry Brigades, which were constituted as under—

1st Infantry Brigade.

Brigadier-General H. H. Foord, Commanding.
2nd Battalion, King's Liverpool Regiment.
21st Madras Infantry.
25th " "

2nd Infantry Brigade.

Brigadier-General G. S. White, C.B., V.C., *h.p.*, Commanding.
2nd Battalion, Hampshire Regiment.
12th Madras Infantry.
23rd " "

3rd Infantry Brigade.

Brigadier-General F. B. Norman, C.B., B.S.C., Commanding.
1st Battalion, Royal Welsh Fusiliers.
2nd (Queen's Own) Bengal Infantry.
11th Bengal Infantry.

Colonel F. B. Norman, C.B., B.S.C., and Colonel H. H. Foord, M.S.C., nominated above to command Brigades, were given the temporary rank of Brigadier-General (2nd Class) whilst commanding brigades in the force ordered to Burma.

A Reserve Brigade was warned for service from the Bombay Presidency.

The detail of the Naval Brigade, Burma Expeditionary Force, 1885.

Name of vessel in which serving.	Name of Her Majesty's ship to which they belonged.	Name of Commanding Officer.	Number of 64-pr.	Number of 25-pr.	Number of 9-pr.	Number and nature of other guns.	Machine Guns.		Number of officer.	Number of men.		Remarks.
							Nordenfelt.	Gardner.		Seamen.	Mariners.	
Palow ..	Turquoise ..	Captain R. Woodward, (Commanding Brigade).	2 R.M.L.	4 R.M.L.	1 R.M.L.	1·7-pr.	1	1	8	99	23	
Pulu ..	Bacchanta ..	Commander C. J. Barlow, (2nd-in-Command).	..	8 R.M.L.	..	..	2	1	15	138	27	
Irrawaddy ..	Woodlark ..	Commander W. L. Clutterbuck.	..	..	4 R.M.L.	2·20-pr., R.B.L.	4	4	5	43	7	
Kathleen ..	Turquoise ..	Lieutenant F. P. French, to 19th December 1885, then Mr. Sayres, Gunner.	..	..	..	2·12-pr., R.M.L.	..	1	3	12	4	After 19th December 1885 crew consisted of 1 officer, 7 seamen.
Tigris ..	Sphinx ..	Lieutenant A. T. Carter ..	..	..	..	..	4	4	3	24	4	
Pegu ..	Turquoise ..	Lieutenant F. P. French ..	..	..	..	1·7-pr., R.M.L.	..	1	2	12	4	After 19th December 1885.
Ngawoon ..	I. M. Survey ..	Commander Carpenter, R. N.	..	..	..	..	..	..	3 of R.N.	Indian	Marine.	A barge with one 64-pr., R.M.L., was lent to *Ngawoon*, when necessary.
Sitting ..	Woodlark ..	A 1st Class petty officer ..	..	..	..	..	1	..	..	5	..	
Naval Explosive Party.	Mariner ..	Commander J. Durnford ..	..	..	..	..	..	..	1	14	..	

Mounted Infantry.

In addition to the troops already detailed, at the urgent request of General Prendergast, Major E. C. Brown, Royal Scots Fusiliers, was ordered to form a mixed mounted corps to go with the expedition.

It was raised locally and was composed as follows :—

	Officers.	Rank and File.
Royal Scots Fusiliers	1	30
Rangoon Volunteers	1	14
Police	2	50

They were mounted on Burmese ponies. The Europeans were armed with carbines and artillery bayonets, the Burmans with hog spears and *dâhs* (Burmese swords).

The Chief Commissioner of Burma, having been warned to make preparations for the expedition, stated in a telegram to the Military Department, dated Rangoon, 20th October 1885 :—

For despatch of troops up the river, partly from Rangoon, and partly from Prome Terminus, to frontier, and thence onward, we can hire ample steamers and flats (of the Irrawaddy Flotilla Company) at rates of existing contract; their rates are high, but cannot be changed now.

In another telegram, dated 22nd October, he stated that the contract rates were Rs. 45 per ton for steamers and Rs. 15 per ton for flats, giving an average rate of Rs. 32,000 per steamer and two flats per month.

The amount of superficial space allowed for troops in river steamers by the Transport Regulations was—

For British Troops .. .. $6' \times 2' = 12$ square feet.
,, Native ,, ... $6' \times 1\frac{1}{2}' = 9$,, ,,

But it was evident that the duration of the occupation of these steamers might be prolonged for a considerable time; consequently the accommodation proposed in a memorandum issued from the Intelligence Branch, Quartermaster-General's Department, was adopted, *viz.*, a river steamer and two flats for the troops carried by an ocean steamer. This gave, roughly speaking, twenty square feet apiece to British and ten to fifteen square feet apiece to native troops.

Colonel Bengough, Assistant Adjutant and Quarter Master General to the Force, in his report of this accommodation said:—

This allowance was found none too much even under the unusually favourable conditions that obtained, as regards the absence of severe fighting, serious sickness, or long delays; had it been otherwise, the want of surplus space and spare steamers would have been a serious cause of anxiety.

In Mr. Bernard's telegram to the Military Department, dated 22nd October, he stated that the Irrawaddy Flotilla Company could collect the transport required for the proposed expedition at Rangoon with ten days' notice, and that most of it could be ready in five days. He also stated that the fleet would take five days to reach Thayetmyo from Rangoon. Thayetmyo was some eighteen miles from the frontier.

Assembly of troops.

The Bengal and Madras troops assembled at Calcutta and Madras between 28th October and 5th November 1885. Appended is a return of their respective embarkation and disembarkation—

Bengal Troops.

Corps.	Strength.				Embarked at Calcutta.	Arrived at Rangoon.
	Officers.	Warrant Officers.	Native Officers.	Non-Commissioned Officers and men.		
11th Bengal Infantry	10	..	17	667	1st November..	5th November.
1st Battalion, Royal Welsh Fusiliers, and details.	18	3	..	727	2nd	6th „
	..	9	..	2		
2nd (Queen's Own) Bengal Infantry	8	1	..	575	2nd „ ..	6th „
2nd Battalion, Liverpool Regiment	21	5	..	700	3rd „ ..	7th „
3-1 Scottish Division, Royal Artillery.	3	1	..	112	3rd „ ..	7th „
9-1 Cinque Ports Division, Royal Artillery.	3	1	..	101 British, 140 Native.		
Hazara Mountain Battery ..	3	..	..	90	6th „ ..	10th „
No. 1 Bombay Mountain Battery ..	4	..	..	90		
Nos. 4 and 5 Companies, Bengal Sappers and Miners.	6	..	4	17 British N.-C. O's., 227 Native N.-C. O's. and men.		
Details	2	..	..	....		
Coolie Corps	4	11	..	....	9th „ ..	14th „

Madras Troops.

Corps or Department.	Strength. Officers.	Warrant Officers.	Native Officers.	Non-Commissioned Officers and men.	Embarked at Madras.	Arrived at Rangoon.
Head-Quarters Staff	12	3	..	7		
2nd Battalion, Hampshire Regiment	20	4	..	738	3rd November	7th November.
Details	..	2	3	7		
4-1 North Irish Division, Royal Artillery.	6	1	..	115		
Q-1 Royal Artillery	5	1	..	89	3rd ,, ..	8th ,,
Details	8	3	33	5 N.-C. O's.		
Head-Quarters, 1st Brigade ..	3	..	..	....		
21st Madras Infantry	9	..	13	749	4th ,, ..	10th ,,
Details	5	2	..	5 N.-C. O's.		
Head-Quarters, 2nd Brigade ..	3	..	..	....		
12th Madras Infantry	10	..	13	720	3rd ,, ..	8th ,,
Details	9	4	..	....		
A., C., D. & H. Companies, Madras Sappers and Miners.	8	..	8	British N.-C. O's. 12, Native N.-C. O's. and men 489.	4th ,, ..	10th ,,
Details	5	..	..	1 N.-C. O.		
1st Madras Pioneers	7	..	14	608	4th ,, ..	10th ,,
Details	2	....	....	....		
23rd Madras Infantry	10	..	15	765	5th ,, ..	11th ,,
Details	13	2	..	7		
25th Madras Infantry	9	..	14	751	5th ,, ..	11th ,,
Details	4	..	..	2		

Detail of river fleet and dates of arrival at Thayetmyo.

The following table shows the fleet of river steamers engaged, the distribution of the expeditionary forces on the various steamers, and the date of each ship's arrival at and departure from Thayetmyo :—

No.	Transports.	Troops, etc.	Left Rangoon.	Arrived at Thayetmyo.	Left Thayetmyo.
1	Steamer *Thambyadine* ..	General Officer Commanding and Head-Quarters Staff.	10-11-85	13-11-85	15-11-85
2	" *Burma*	The Hampshire Regiment ..	11-11-85	16-11-85	16-11-85
	Flats Nos. 17 and 42 ..	Brigadier-General, and Head-Quarters, 2nd Brigade.			
3	Steamer *Yankeentaung* ..	The Liverpool Regiment ..	9-11-85	14-11-85	15-11-85
	Flats Nos. 19 and 55 ..	Telegraph Department, and stores on flat No. 19.			
4	Steamer *Aloung Pya* ..	Royal Welsh Fusiliers ..	8-11-85	14-11-85	15-11-85
	Flats Nos. 21 and 45 ..				
5	Steamer *Shintsawboo* ..	1st Madras Pioneers ..	10-11-85	14-11-85	15-11-85
	Flats Nos. 56 and 57 ..	12th Madras Infantry ..			
6	Steamer *Shway Myo* ..	Bombay Mountain Battery ..	12-11-85	17-11-85	17-11-85
	Flats Nos. 26, 27 and 38 ..	6 Companies, Sappers and Miners			
7	Steamer *Irrawaddy* ..	21st Madras Infantry ..	11-11-85	16-11-85	16-11-85
	Flats Nos. 40 and 49 ..	25th " " .. Brigadier-General, and Head-Quarters, 1st Brigade.			
8	Steamer *Thooreah* ..	2nd Bengal Infantry ..	8-11-85	14-11-85	14-11-85
	Flats Nos. 18 and 50 ..	11th " " ..			
9	Steamer *Ashley Eden* ..	23rd Madras Infantry ..	13-11-85	17-11-85	17-11-85
	Flats Nos. 34 and 43 ..	Hazara Mountain Battery ..			
	Lighter 38 with telegraph stores	Telegraph cable			
	ROYAL ARTILLERY.				
	HEAVY SIEGE FLEET.				
10	Steamer *Annanda* ..	Two-thirds 4-1st Royal Artillery.	12-11-85	17-11-85	18-11-85
	Two barges, 4 guns. { Two 40-pounder, M. L. rifled guns. Two 6·3-inch R. howitzers.				
11	Steamer *Ataran*	Two-thirds 3-1st Royal Artillery	11-11-85	16-11-85	17-11-85
	Two barges, 4 guns (four 6·3 inch R. howitzers).				
12	Steamer *Yunnan*	One-third 4-1st Royal Artillery	13-11-85	16-11-85	17-11-85
	White Swan Barge. Heavy Battery. { Two 40-pounder M. L. rifled guns. Six 6·3-inch R. howitzers. Twelve 5·5" Royal Mortars. 250 rounds per piece.	One-third 3-1st Royal Artillery. Q-1st Royal Artillery.			

No.	Transports.	Troops, etc.	Left Rangoon.	Arrived at Thayetmyo.	Left Thayetmyo.
		ROYAL ARTILLERY—*contd.*			
		MOUNTAIN BATTERY.			
13	Steamer *Panthay*	9-1st Cinque Ports Division ..	10-11-85	15-11-85	15-11-85
	Flats Nos. 28 and 30 ..	12 horses and 240 mules.			
		1 Mountain Battery in *Sway Myo*.			
		1 Mountain Battery in *Ashley Eden*.			
		MISCELLANEOUS.			
14	Steamer *Palow*—one 64-pr. ..	Naval Brigade	11-11-85	16-11-85	16-11-85
	Flat No. 6 { In flat four 25-pr. field guns for land service. In bow one 9-pr. and one 7-pr.				
15	Steamer *Pulu*	Naval Brigade	14-11-85	16-11-85	16-11-85
	Flat No. 24.				
16	Steamer *Rangoon*	Floating Hospital ..	13-11-85	16-11-85	17-11-85
	Flat Nos. 41 and 44	1,110 bearers, etc.			
		General Hospital for Thayetmyo.			
		2 Field Hospitals, complete.			
17	Steamer *Panlang* ..	Travelling Hospital.			
18	" *Waikema*	" "			
19	" *Kah-byoo*	Commissariat and postal service	15-11-85	18-11-85	18-11-85
20	" *Talifoo*	Mounted Infantry.			
	Flats.				
21	Steamer *Mendoon*	Reserve Steamer	14-11-85	....	....
		(1,600 Transport coolies from Rangoon.)			
22	*Ngawoon*—one 64-pr. in barge	Naval Brigade, River Survey..	11-11-85	15-11-85	16-11-85
	Steam launches.				
	H. M. S. *Irrawaddy* .. }	Naval Brigade	28-10-85	5-11-85	14-11-85
	Steam Cutter *Kathleen* .. }				
23	*Doowoon*	....	....	13-11-85	19-11-85
24	*Kadoe*	Despatch boat.			

In addition to the above detail, military signallers were told off to each steamer; and thus communications were kept up along the whole fleet.

It will be observed from the dates given above that, as each sea steamer arrived at Rangoon, the troops were disembarked at once, re-embarked on the several river craft, and despatched towards the frontier up the Irrawaddy.

The distinctive features of the constitution of the force were :—

1*st.*—Its mixed composition, comprising a Naval Brigade, and troops from each of the three Presidential Armies.

2*nd.*—The absence of the Cavalry arm, and the prohibition to take chargers for mounted officers, except those of the British Mountain Battery.

This restriction was presumably based on the assumption that the operations would be confined to the river, and on the current belief that horses rapidly became unserviceable from the effects of climate in Burma. A squadron, 2nd Madras Light Cavalry, was, however, sent to join the force after the fall of Mandalay, and the remainder of the regiment was sent from India in February 1886.

3*rd.*—The exclusive employment of coolies for land transport, including the transport of the Hazara and Bombay Mountain Batteries.

It may be stated here that this system of transport was not found applicable to the movements of troops in the field, and it proved especially unsuitable for the transport of guns in the vicinity of an enemy.

4*th.*—The arrangements for the transport of the force, complete with equipment, ammunition, provisions, hospital, etc., up the Irrawaddy river, in the steamers and flats of the Irrawaddy Flotilla Company.

The numerical strength of the Expeditionary Force was as follows :—

British	3,029
Native	6,005
Fighting men	9,034
Followers	2,810
Total ..	11,844

Guns for land service, manned by Royal Artillery	12	25-prs.
	12	6·3″ howitzers.
	18	Mountain guns.
,, for river service, manned by Naval Brigade	25	As detailed above.
Total	67	pieces.

Machine guns for river service	Nordenfelts .. 12	Total .. 24
	Gardners .. 12	

The organized Burmese army in October 1885 was estimated to number at most 20,000 men, and probably did not exceed 15,000.

Strength of Burmese army.

Their river forts were one on either bank of the river at Minhla, some fifty miles from the frontier; two on the left bank and one on the right, at the bend of the river at Ava, twelve miles below Mandalay; and one or two on the shore at Mandalay itself; beside these, there were temporary entrenchments made at Sinbaungwé twenty miles from the frontier, at Nyaungu near Pagan, and at Myingyan. They had five gun-boats, all out of repair; twelve steamers fit to ply on the river; and some ten steam launches. These boats and forts were armed with several smooth-bore cast-iron guns, in the use of which the Burmese were totally unskilled. Serviceable ammunition too was wanting.

The following is the text of the instructions given to General Prendergast by the Viceroy:—

General Prendergast's instructions from Viceroy.

You are doubtless aware of the general nature of the ultimatum lately sent to the Burmese Government. If the terms offered in that ultimatum are refused, or if the answer is evasive, you will be informed by the Chief Commissioner. You must then hold yourself in readiness to advance on Mandalay in accordance with any plan of operations prescribed by the Commander-in-Chief. But the actual order to cross the frontier will be sent to you from hence hereafter. From the time that you enter the enemy's territory, you will be vested with supreme political, as well as military authority. Colonel Sladen will be placed under your orders as political officer, and will be accompanied by some junior officers of the Burmese Commission.

With regard to political matters, you should correspond direct with the Government of India in the Foreign Department, repeating all telegrams immediately to the Chief Commissioner, and sending him a copy of all letters simultaneously with the despatch of the original. You will understand that after you cross the frontier no offer of submission can be accepted, or can affect the movement of the troops. Mandalay must be occupied and Thibaw dethroned. You should announce this definitely to the Burmese authorities and population. You will be informed hereafter whether Upper Burma is to be annexed. If so, the Chief Commissioner will go to Mandalay and assume civil control. Meanwhile it seems desirable that you should leave, in any important fort or other place taken and garrisoned by you, a civil officer, who should, under the orders of the Commandant, enter into communication with the local Burmese officials, and through them pacify and administer the country, giving assurances that Thibaw will not remain in power.

These instructions are subject to modification at your discretion in points of detail; but you should communicate freely by telegraph with the Government of India, and you should, so far as the circumstances of the case allow, submit to the Government for approval any measure involving important political consequences.

I trust that you will make full use of Colonel Sladen's services, his experience and knowledge of Burmese affairs being very exceptional. I hope also that you will work in communication with the Chief Commissioner, and that you will meet his wishes whenever practicable.

The immediate objects of the expedition are the occupation of Mandalay and the dethronement of King Thibaw; and it is extremely desirable that these objects should be attained rather by the display than the use of force. An unopposed occupation of Mandalay would be more satisfactory, and more acceptable to the Government, than any number of victorious engagements in the field.

You will, therefore, be careful to avoid, as far as possible, all conflict with the population at large, and you will do everything in your power to secure without bloodshed their acquiescence in any administrative or political changes which may be found necessary. At the same time you are to understand that the above-mentioned considerations shall not be allowed to hamper you in taking the measures which may be requisite, from a military point of view, for the security of the troops under your command and the definite success of the expedition. I hope the foregoing instructions will suffice to make you acquainted with the general objects and wishes of the Government of India; but if you desire more detailed explanation on any point, refer to me by telegraph.

A telegram containing further instructions was sent to General Prendergast on 8th November by the Adjutant General in India; it ran as follows:—

General Prendergast's instructions from Adjutant General in India.

The political object of the Burma Expeditionary Force which you have been appointed to command is to occupy Mandalay and dethrone King Thibaw, avoiding unnecessary conflict with the people. With that object in view it has been decided that the river Irrawaddy should be used for line of advance on Mandalay, and all the requisite materials have been provided for the force detailed from India, sufficient it is considered for the occupation of Mandalay and such places on the line of communication as you may deem necessary; and cooly transport to the extent of 3,000 men for any land movement, either during the advance or after arrival at Mandalay in the immediate vicinity, or cutting off the line of retreat of Thibaw. Should you, however, find, on arrival at Mandalay, that further land operations are necessary which require additional transport, arrangements will be made locally in Burma for such increase as may be required for the land operations to be undertaken. Report at the same time to Government your proposed plan of operations, the main object being rapidity of movement, and an early termination of the war. You may also consider it desirable to occupy Pyinmana, about twenty-four miles in advance of our frontier from the direction of Toungoo, but the Commander-in-Chief is adverse to movements by land, with a view to insufficient force, and therefore does not deem it desirable for you to undertake any forward movement from Pyinmana, but to content yourself with the moral effect derived from the occupation of that place. Should you, after consultation with Chief Commissioner and General Buck (Commanding British Burma Division), consider such movement necessary, the troops now stationed in Burma have been placed at your disposal, and a fourth or reserve brigade has been detailed for despatch from India, in case additional troops are required.

Mr. Bernard telegraphs on 4th November with reference to an advance by land from Toungoo—

Proposals regarding occupation of Ningyan by column from Toungoo.

I am quite clear that an advance on Mandalay from Toungoo is not desirable till capital is taken; then light column would march across from Pyinmana by Yamethin to Irrawaddy. Reasons against double invasion are carriage difficulty, length of land journey, and fact that prompt and more final blow can be struck along the Irrawaddy. Though this is my decided opinion, still General Buck and I advise that a strong small force be prepared to march and occupy Pyinmana, a large town 24 miles beyond our frontier: work could be done by British Burma permanent garrison, with perhaps one corps from expeditionary force.

Our idea is to cross the frontier towards Pyinmana directly we hear of Minhla being taken; if General Prendergast approves, I hope this may be allowed. I trust General Buck may be allowed to command Toungoo column; he has a first-rate staff officer in Colonel Protheroe.

General Prendergast commanded the whole of the troops in Burma. The two officers next in seniority to him were Major-General Buck, Commanding British Burma Division, and Brigadier-General Norman, C.B., Commanding 3rd Brigade.

Though the information to hand about the interior of Upper Burma was very scant, yet full and accurate descriptions and sketches of the river Irrawaddy and the forts on its banks were available.

In addition to this, the accurate local knowledge of the river possessed by the officers of the Irrawaddy Flotilla Company, who had all been for more than a year navigating the river between Mandalay and Rangoon, was of the greatest assistance to the expedition.

It will be observed from the foregoing preparations for the campaign that the object of the expedition was a *coup* to paralyse national resistance in Upper Burma by the capture of Mandalay and the deportation of King Thibaw, rather than a regular invasion. The question of the future of the country had been discussed, but no definite decision had been arrived at. The *coup* was eminently successful. General Prendergast crossed the frontier on 15th November 1885, and on 28th November the King and the city of Mandalay were in his power.

CHAPTER XI.

DESCRIPTION OF THE SCENE OF OPERATIONS.

IT will here be convenient to describe the physical features of Upper Burma, as affecting military operations.

The country has been aptly described as a vast military obstacle.

Upper Burma and the Shan States dependent on it comprise roughly 140,000 square miles, of which about half belong to Upper Burma proper. On the west and south the country is bounded by States belonging to, or under the influence of the British Government, *viz.*, Assam, Manipur, Chittagong, Arakan, Lower Burma, and Karenni; on the south-east it is bounded by Siam; on the east and north the boundaries were not very definite; in some places independent states intervened between Burma and China, in others the actual influence of the two Governments overlapped, so that the border States paid tribute to both.

The country is watered by the Irrawaddy, the Salween, the Mékong or Cambodia river, and the upper reaches of the Sittang.

The Irrawaddy runs through some 450 miles of Upper Burma, which it almost bisects. Its main tributaries are—on the right bank the rivers Mu, Chindwin, and Yaw; on the left bank the Taping, Shweli, Myitngé, and Yin. The river Sittang is itself only navigable for steam launches of small draught during the rains, and it has no considerable tributaries.

To give an idea of the physical features of Upper Burma, it is convenient to treat of the country under the three following headings—

(1) low-lying alluvial tracts, which are well watered;
(2) sandy and, comparatively speaking, dry tracts;
(3) hilly and jungly tracts.

Under the first heading come—

the country near the mouths of the Taping and Shweli;
the country round Mandalay and Kyauksé on the lower waters of the Myitngé and its tributary the Panlaung;

the country on the banks of the Chindwin ;
the country round Taungdwingyi in the basin of the river Yin ;
the country round Salin Myo and Sinbyugyun north of Minbu ;
the valley of the Sittang.

Under the second heading come—

the country between the Irrawaddy, the Mu, the Chindwin, and the hills which bound the Yaw valley, between latitudes 21° and 23° ;
the country between the river Panlaung and the Irrawaddy.

Under the third heading come—

the country north of Mandalay and east of the Irrawaddy ;
the country west of the Irrawaddy and north of latitude 23° ;
the Yaw country ;
the country between Minbu and Thayetmyo ;
the line of the watershed between the Sittang and Irrawaddy.
the district round the extinct volcano of Pôpa.

(1) Alluvial tracts.

The low-lying alluvial tracts are extensively irrigated and cultivated with rice crops. From February to May, inclusive, they are hard and dry, and are traversable in any direction ; for the rest of the year they are either under cultivation or else they become swamps, and are only just practicable for troops to move in. Occasionally there were practicable tracts along the banks of irrigation canals ; failing these, very slow progress could be made with transport animals, and so much extra labour was entailed in helping them along that only very short marches could be got over in seven or eight hours. In the rains local traffic was carried on in small dug-out boats along the irrigation canals, where these existed ; otherwise it practically ceased. The tracks made by wheeled traffic were, generally speaking, practicable from November till May inclusive and closed for the rest cf the year.

These tracts, being fertile, were thickly populated ; the villages varied in size from 20 to 200 houses, and were numerous everywhere. Occasionally long straggling villages and small towns occurred, with from 200 to 1,000 houses. These latter were generally found on ground slightly raised above the level of the surrounding swamps, and in groves of palm trees with dense thorny undergrowth, while the former were more compact and, as often as not, on the same level as, and surrounded on all sides by, the swamps. Trees and patches of jungle abounded everywhere and generally confined the view to a few hundred yards. The jungle undergrowth was generally dense and impenetrable on account of matted thorns and creepers.

In these districts the supplies always available were rice and paddy, slaughter-cattle, vegetables, and green forage.

Great difficulty was experienced in keeping the troops supplied with boots, which became perished in the mud and water, and fell to pieces after a few weeks' wear. Without boots neither Europeans nor Natives could move off the beaten tracts on account of the thorns.

The climate was healthy from January to May; though the heat was excessive (105° and 106° in the monasteries and huts in April and May), yet the atmosphere then was dry, and the troops were able to carry on active operations. The worst time of the year for active operations was the three weeks after the rains commenced, at the end of May or the beginning of June. The atmosphere was then moist, and the maximum heat in the shade gradually descended from 106° to 97° and 98°; Natives and Europeans alike suffered from heat-apoplexy, and active operations were impracticable; during the remainder of the rains the heat was oppressive, but it was rarely so severe as when they first broke. September and October, when the rains ceased, were especially unhealthy.

Though the nature of these tracts was utterly unsuited for cavalry performing their recognized *rôle*, nevertheless they were of great use during the dry season; they could move more rapidly than the Burmese, and could surprise gangs of dacoits where infantry were powerless. They could keep flying dacoits in sight, when infantry would lose sight and touch of them in a few hundred yards; and they could always catch a few men to give information.

(2) Sandy tracts.

The sandy and, comparatively speaking, dry tracts always enclosed stretches of swampy cultivation, but, except for these patches, were practicable throughout the year. The rainfall was very scanty and in places was altogether wanting. The larger and more prosperous villages occurred near patches of cultivation or where salt was found; small and poverty-stricken villages occurred at intervals all over the country. The vegetation consisted of thorny scrub jungle in bushes or patches; the inhabitants subsisted on *jowari* crops and *Palmyra palm* sugar; occasional fertile tracts of sandy soil supported tomatoes, gram, wheat, and other crops.

The cross country tracks were generally deep with sand and were rather heavy, but in consequence kept in better repair than any other form of untended road. Occasional low dry hills occurred, also clothed with thorny scrub jungle.

The heat was great in April, May, and June, but the atmosphere remained dry. Local supplies were very scanty, and in the district the only forage procurable was often *jowari* stalks or curby.

(3) Hilly and jungly tracts.

The hilly tracts were the refuge of the dacoits when harried by our troops; there they were in dense terai jungle, in which pursuit was impossible; the tracks were narrow and tortuous and admirably adapted for ambuscades. Except by the regular tracks there were hardly any means of approach; the jungle malaria to which the Burmese are acclimatised was fatal to our troops, and the dacoits, knowing this, felt doubly secure; at best a column could only penetrate the jungle and move on.

The villages were small and far between, they were generally compact and surrounded by dense impenetrable jungle. Supplies for troops were scanty, but forage was always procurable, either in the shape of grass or bamboo shoots.

The paths were either just broad enough for a cart or very narrow, and where they led through jungle, that part of it which fringed the road was often so overgrown with brambles and creepers that it was quite impenetrable. A good deal of the dry grass and underwood is usually burned in March, after which, till the rains have well set in, the jungle proper is fairly open.

Very little was known of the nature of the country in the semi-independent states, except that it was generally hilly country, approachable by passes, which a few resolute men could defend for some time. The Shan hills to the east were known to be of plateau formation and comparatively open, scantily stocked with provisions, except in favoured localities. The foot of the plateau was fringed with a belt of terai jungle, and the passes up to it were steep and not negotiable by wheeled transport.

In none of the dependent states was the population dense nor were supplies procurable in any quantity.

As regards communications throughout the country, the great waterway of the Irrawaddy is navigable for steamers from the extreme north to the extreme south of the country.

Communications.

Its main tributary, the Chindwin, is navigable for smaller steamers and launches up to the confines of Manipur.

The Myitngé is navigable for launches up to the foot of the Shan hills.

Government manned two or three steamers on the Irrawaddy with the Indian marine, and had subsidised the Irrawaddy Flotilla Company, so that, as far as the requirements of the field force were concerned, transport on this river was unlimited; and the steam transport on the others was sufficient for the purpose of supplying the troops and of keeping up communications. It was capable of development on emergencies.

The following lateral branches of the Irrawaddy were navigable by country boats, which were everywhere procurable:—the Taping, the Shweli, the Madaya, the Panlaung, the irrigation canals of the Kyauksé district, and the Yin river on the east or left banks; and the rivers Mu, Yaw, Salin, Môn, and Man on the right bank.

The river Sittang was navigable for steam launches in the rain, to Sinthewa near Pyinmana.

Unmade cart tracks led from village to village in every direction all over the country; in the sandy tracts they were open all the year round, but in the alluvial districts they were closed, as a rule, from June to November. Footpaths and pack tracks led into, and through, all the inhabited parts of the country.

No roads or tracks were good or adapted to military requirements; previous to our occupation of the country they were rarely made or tended, and in no cases were they metalled; no wheeled conveyances, except the country carts, could traverse them, and the progress of these rarely exceeded two miles an hour. Columns could never advance along cart tracks on a broader front than infantry fours, and, along pack tracks, than single file; their direction was tortuous, and, either owing to the jungle or the surrounding swamps, it was exceedingly difficult to keep up communication between the units of a long and, from its formation, necessarily straggling, column on the march.

The nature of the sandy and alluvial tracts was eminently adapted to visual signalling owing to the constant recurrence of small hills of 200 to 700 feet above the plain. It was rare for posts to be unable to establish signal stations, and columns on the march could generally during the day communicate with one or other of the stations on these little hills. In the hill tracts, however, the jungle was generally dense and the view from the crests very limited. In these districts, too, it was often very difficult to get the natives to undertake to carry messages, as they could be so easily surprised and captured in the jungles by dacoits. Except during the hot months of April and May the light was generally favourable for visual signalling. During the above-mentioned months a thick haze lay over the whole country and only lifted for a day now and again.

Signalling.

The supplies procurable in any district through which a column was moving were never to be relied on; at best they were of limited quantity, and were especially so at that time, owing to the unsettled state of the country, and the active or passive hostility of the inhabitants. Each column that marched had to go fully provisioned for the time it was to keep the field. Except in parts of the sandy tracts, water was universally obtainable at short intervals, either from shallow wells in constant use or from running streams. In some parts of the sandy tracts the only available water was often found to be that in a few muddy tanks near villages; and in other parts, notably between the alluvial tracts of Kyauksé and Pyinmana, all the water was brackish.

A great saving in transport was due to the excellent accommodation available everywhere in monasteries (*Hpongyi Kyaungs*) and rest-houses (*Zayats*). The monasteries are capacious buildings of wood (generally teak), raised on piles, and occupied by a few monks; surrounding the monasteries are open rest-houses, with good roofs and floors, also on piles. These monasteries and shrines, though revered by the people and rarely molested by dacoits, are not desecrated when used as resting-places by troops or travellers, and

Burmese under arms always use them for this purpose. They are numerous all over the country, and, except in very out-of-the-way parts of Upper Burma, in a 10-mile march some three or four of them are met, capable of giving shelter to 200 or 300 men. In the dry weather it was no hardship for men to bivouac, as large trees, with thick foliage, were plentiful everywhere.

CHAPTER XII.

THE CAPTURE OF MANDALAY.

As has already been detailed, the Expeditionary Force arrived at Rangoon between the 5th and 11th November, and immediately proceeded up the river to Thayetmyo. Major-General Prendergast received his orders to advance on Mandalay on the 14th November 1885, and hostilities began that day, by the armed steamers *Irrawaddy* and *Kathleen* crossing the frontier, engaging the Burman batteries near Nyaungbinmaw, and, after a smart skirmish, capturing a King's ship. The ship was sent down to Thayetmyo in charge of the *Kathleen*, while the *Irrawaddy* brought down the two flats which she had been towing at the time of her capture. One of these had been prepared for sinking in the river, and had rows of posts, each ten feet high by six inches square, let into the deck and sharpened into points which must inevitably have destroyed any shallow-bottomed river steamer that ran against them. When the ship was first shelled, the crew jumped overboard and fled, accompanied by Commotto, one of two Italian adventurers (Commotto and Molinari) who had become hirelings of the King. To Commotto had been allotted the task of blocking the river near the frontier, which he was on his way to accomplish, while Molinari was charged with strengthening the fortifications below Mandalay. From the papers left on the steamer by Commotto information was obtained as to the King's military preparations, which corroborated the news given by the last two Irrawaddy Flotilla Company's ships which had run the gauntlet of the forts in their latest trip down stream.

On the 15th November the expedition crossed the frontier, the ships falling in to the following order, which was maintained throughout the advance:—

Order of sailing in squadron.	Distinguishing number.	Steamers.	Corps.	
1	—	H. M. S. *Irrawaddy* and *Kathleen*.	Naval Brigade.	
—	1	*Thambyadine* ..	General Officer Commanding and Head-quarters Staff.	
2	15	*Pulu* .. .. Flat No. 24.. ..	Naval Brigade.	
3	14	*Palow* .. .. Flat No. 6	" "	
4	12	*Yunnan* .. .. *White Swan* Barges ..	Q-1st Cinque Ports, Royal Artillery, one-third of 3-1st Royal Artillery, and one-third of 4-1st Royal Artillery.	
5	13	*Panthay*	9-1st Royal Artillery, Mountain Battery.	
6	6	*Shway Myo*	Queen's Own Sappers and Miners, Bombay.	
		Flats Nos. 26, 27, and 38	Mountain Battery.	
7	2	*Burma* .. .. Flats Nos. 17 and 42 ..	Hampshire Regiment, Head-Quarters, 2nd Brigade.	2nd Brigade.
8	5	*Shintsawboo*	1st Madras Pioneers.	2nd Brigade.
		Flats Nos. 56 and 57	12th Madras Infantry.	2nd Brigade.
9	9	*Ashley Eden*	23rd " "	2nd Brigade.
		Flats Nos. 34 and 43 .. Lighter 38 ..	Hazara Mountain Battery, Telegraph Stores.	
10	17	*Panlang*	Travelling Hospital.	
11	10	*Ananda*	2-3rds of 4-1st Royal Artillery.	
12	3	*Yankeentoun* ..	Liverpool Regiment ..	1st Brigade.
		Flats Nos. 19 and 55 ..	Telegraph Department ..	1st Brigade.
13	7	*Irrawaddy* ..	21st Madras Infantry ..	1st Brigade.
		Flats Nos. 40 and 49 ..	25th Madras Infantry ..	1st Brigade.
14	18	*Waikema*	(Head-Quarters, 1st Brigade) .. Travelling Hospital ..	1st Brigade.
15	11	*Ataran* .. .. (2 Barges, 4 guns) ..	Two-thirds of 3-1st Royal Artillery.	
16	4	*Aloung Pya* .. .. Flats Nos. 21 and 25 ..	Royal Welsh Fusiliers ..	3rd Brigade.
17	8	*Thooreah*	2nd B. N. I.	3rd Brigade.
		Flats Nos. 18 and 50 ..	11th "	3rd Brigade.
18	20	*Talifoo* .. .. Flats	Mounted Infantry ..	3rd Brigade.
19	16	*Rangoon* .. .. Flats Nos. 41 and 44 ..	Floating Hospital.	
20	21	*Mendoon*	Reserve steamer. Coolies and coal.	
	19	*Kah-byoo*	Commissariat and Postal service.	
	22	*Ngawoon*	River survey.	
	23	*Doowoon*		
	24	*Kadoe*	Despatch boat.	

The river steamers had the advantage of being worked by Captains who all had considerable experience in the navigation of the river, which is difficult and intricate owing to the constant shifting of the channel. The Flotilla Company maintained pilot stations at short intervals along the bank, but in these troubled times the Burmese would not allow the pilots to join the fleet, so the river had to be surveyed and buoyed out by the Naval Brigade. In fact the advance was a naval operation, conducted by the Naval Brigade, and on them fell all the work of reconnoitring and guarding the fleet against surprise by water. The heavy guns were mounted on barges for river service and accompanied the Naval Brigade as escort to the fleet; the remaining steamers and flats were transports for troops and stores, and were not fighting units. The escort headed the column of ships, to clear the river in front, to prevent any attack by water from reaching the transports, and to silence the guns of any positions on the banks before the transports had to pass them. When the guns of the escort were not sufficient for this, troops were to be disembarked and land operations were to be undertaken.

Necessity of rapid action.

It should be noted that the whole success of this advance on Mandalay depended on the rapidity with which it could be carried out. The only advance on the capital was this 300 miles of water-way, and it was known that this was easily defensible by small numbers with but short notice, as the channel could quickly be obstructed and the river barred to the advance of a hostile fleet. If at any point on its route the expedition had been stopped in this way, the British discomfiture would have been complete, and a fresh expedition would have been necessitated, as no provision had been made for land transport of any kind. All this had, however, been calculated on, and the collapse of the resistance to the British advance was solely due to the rapidity with which all preparations were made and plans carried out.

On the 16th November the Burmese stockades erected at Nyaungbinmaw and Sinbaungwé were carried without any serious resistance.

On the following day a simultaneous attack was made on the strong forts of Minhla and Gwegyaun which faced each other on opposite sides of the river. It was expected that the latter fort, which was much the stronger position of the two, would be resolutely held, but on the approach of our troops the garrison fled and the position was captured with a loss on our side of only two men wounded.

Gwegyaung was a particularly strong redoubt, designed and built by the Italian, Barbieri; it had a command of 250 feet over the river and was provided with a broad deep ditch having masonry scarp and counter-scarp. Two tiers of guns bore on the reach of the river towards Malun, and another battery was constructed to fire westwards towards Minhla; the east front was weaker and was commanded by high ground to the east of it. From the gorge wall on the north the ground fell precipitously. The redoubt was furnished with casemated barracks and magazines, and was in good order; there were twenty-one guns, stores of ordnance, and a garrison of 1,700 men. The project for attack prepared by Major-General Prendergast in 1883 was carried out under his own eye with the most complete success. Our troops landed three hours' march from the fort itself and made for its east front; the enemy were completely surprised at the sudden approach of the British and made a precipitate retreat, leaving the frontier defence on which King Thibaw had set his trust in the hands of the British.

The brigade employed on the opposite side of the river consisting of the 2nd and 11th Bengal Infantry and the 12th Madras Infantry, had a more arduous task to perform, and encountered considerable opposition in the attack on the village and fort of Minhla. The former was a place of some size, stretching along the river bank south of the fort, and surrounded by a bamboo stockade; the latter was a square stone structure, its walls about 25 feet in height, entered on the side facing the river by a narrow arch, and having on the west a double ramp which approached the ramparts with a slope of about 25 degrees. The troops for the attack were landed at Malun, a large village about four miles down the river, and on approaching the village of Minhla the advance was received by a smart fire from the enemy concealed in thick jungle. The 11th Bengal Infantry, however, pushed on rapidly, and, supported by the 2nd, quickly carried the stockade and entered the village. The attack was now directed on the house of the *Wun*, which was within another stockaded enclosure, and, in spite of a vigorous resistance, the Burmans were driven from point to point and the position captured. The fort alone remained, and it was approached by an encircling movement, the 11th Infantry making for the left or north side of the ramp, while the 2nd, extending to the right, cut off the line of retreat to the river, and at the same time approached the southern side of the ramp. During the whole advance the troops were subjected to a heavy fire from the jungle and from the fort, but, advancing steadily, the ramp was carried by a final rush from both sides, and the garrison, flying into the casemates of the fort or out of the east gate, offered no further resistance.

Capture of Minhla.

In the day's fighting Lieutenant Drury, 11th Bengal Infantry, was killed and four officers of the 12th Madras Infantry were wounded, while of the rank and file, three were killed and twenty-three wounded.

The Burmese casualties were heavy. They carried away many of their dead, but 170 were buried by the British, and 276 prisoners were taken. The town of Minhla was burnt down, being accidentally set fire to by a shell, but the fort was strengthened and garrisoned by the British. This was the only place where anything like stubborn resistance was offered to the British advance, and with its fall the opposition of the Burmese army was practically at an end.

Mr. Phayre, who had been Assistant Resident at Mandalay until October 1897, was left at Minhla as civil officer. The people and the priests appeared to willingly accept the new situation, though the high officials could not be expected to submit till they knew that Mandalay had fallen. At Magwé on the 20th, the two Italians already mentioned surrendered themselves as prisoners of war.

On 22nd November shots were exchanged with the batteries just above Pagan, but the enemy soon abandoned their works, which were dismantled by the British. At Pagan another military post was established, with a civil officer to initiate the work of administration. At Pakôkku, which was passed on the 24th, about 1,000 troops from Mandalay had been posted, but they ran away on the British approach.

The same afternoon Myingyan, a large and important town near the mouth of the Chindwin river, was reached, where a large Burmese force was reported to be holding the forts. While the big guns

Capture of Myingyan.

were engaging the batteries on the river bank, a body of about 2,000 men was descried on rising ground some distance inland. These turned out to be the reserve of the Burmese army, but they took no part in the fight that day, and before operations could be resumed next morning they had disappeared.

This easy capture of Myingyan, where 6,000 picked troops are said to have been sent, practically decided the campaign; it was afterwards ascertained that if the British had met with a check here the Burmese intended to hold out at Ava and Sagaing, and compel the expeditionary force to undertake siege operations.

A garrison and a civil officer were left at this place.

Many Burmese, who had previously fled from the town, while it was in the hands of Thibaw's troops, came in to welcome the British arrival, and the head *hpongyi* said the town had been an abode of misery while the Burmese soldiery were there.

On the 26th November, Yandabo, the extreme limit of the advance of the British troops during the first Burmese war, was passed; and on that afternoon, near the village of Nagzun, the King's State barge arrived with a flag of truce, bringing envoys to open negotiations for peace.

Peace overtures.

Coming on board without their shoes the envoys delivered a letter from the Burmese Prime Minister to General Prendergast.[1] Beginning naively with the statement that the Burmese Government were under the impression that the former friendly conditions would still prevail and that they therefore could not believe that the British would make war against Upper Burma, the letter stated that the King of Burma was ready to grant all that was demanded in the ultimatum; that he desired the cessation of hostilities and offered to enter into a treaty. Under the instructions upon which he was acting, General Prendergast could only reply that no armistice could be granted, but that if King Thibaw surrendered himself, his army, and his capital, and if the European residents in Mandalay were all found uninjured in life and property, the King's life would be spared and his family respected. A reply to this was demanded before 4 A.M., on the following morning. Meanwhile the fleet continued to advance, and

[1] See Appendix.

was anchored for the night off the village of Kyauktalôn, about seven miles below Ava. As no answer was forthcoming the fleet moved on at daybreak, and orders were issued for the attack on Ava. About half past ten, when the proposed landing-place was in view, the State barge was seen putting out with a flag of truce. The same envoys this time brought a telegram from the King conceding unconditionally all the demands made on the previous day, ordering the ministers conducting the military operations at Sagaing and Ava not on any account to fire on the British, and directing them to keep all the troops quiet. At Ava Fort some 8,000 troops, only about two-thirds of whom were in possession of fire-arms, the rest being armed with spears, swords, and *dahs*, were collected to oppose the British advance. General Prendergast insisted on this portion of the army laying down their arms, but the commander of the forces, who was senior in rank to either of the envoys, refused to do so without a direct order from the King.

The fleet thereupon continued their advance up the river and took up their positions for shelling the forts. This manœuvre caused some delay owing to the channel of the river being barred, and by the time all was ready for the attack the Royal Mandate had arrived and the Burmese General professed his readiness to surrender. Most unfortunately only some 550 of the rifles were then obtained, for, as soon as the King's orders for the surrender became known, large numbers of the soldiers went off in all directions before British troops could be landed to ensure the disarmament of the whole force. The forts at Sagaing and Thambayadaing on the right bank of the river above Ava likewise surrendered without a blow, and were disarmed, though here again only about 400 rifles were collected. From Ava fort twenty-eight guns were carried off as trophies, while thirty-two were destroyed at Sagaing and fourteen at Thambayadaing.

The practical humanity of the proceedings at Ava is open to criticism, as though three strong forts were captured and some thousands of soldiery were disbanded without a blow being struck, yet this very soldiery were thus turned loose, armed and unconquered, on the country, and undoubtedly became the backbone of the dacoity by means of which large tracts of country were devastated and many valuable lives lost.

Had troops, however, been landed, and operations undertaken to ensure the surrender being made complete, General Prendergast would have exceeded his instructions. In these he was enjoined to avoid all unnecessary conflict with the Burmese, his sole object being the capture of Mandalay and the King's person; consequently to avoid all chance of a conflict, the troops lay off Ava, while the forts were being surrendered. Eventually one regiment landed in front of the fort on the left bank, to take over the arms which were laid down, but meanwhile the Burmese garrisons were streaming off unmolested from the back of all three forts.

With the exception of the troops landed to complete the destruction of the forts, the fleet now proceeded to Mandalay, which was reached at 10 A.M. on the 28th November. Crowds of Burmese watched the arrival of the force from the banks, and appeared only too pleased to obey the Royal Mandate that had been issued, prohibiting any opposition to the landing. Information was at once obtained that the King had been in his palace up to nine o'clock, and that the city was quiet.

Capture of Mandalay.

The arrival of the British force was immediately notified to the Prime Minister, and intimation given that, in accordance with the terms of the previous day's communication received at Ava, the immediate surrender of the capital and the King was expected. He was further informed that unless a reply was received by noon, the troops would land and be employed as circumstances might demand. As it was not till after midday that the *Kinwun Mingi's* reply was received, the troops were landed at 1-30 P.M.

The royal city of Mandalay is situated about three or four miles to the east of the Irrawaddy, with which there is connection through the outer town along four main roads (still known as A, B, C, and D roads) running due east from the river. The first brigade, under General Foord, marched by "A" road, and secured the southern and eastern gates of the city. The third brigade, under General Norman, marched along "C" road, and secured the western and northern city gates, and the west and north gates of the palace enclosure. The second brigade, under General White, accompanied by Colonel Sladen, proceeded by "C" road, entered the city by the south gate, and secured the south and east gates of the palace enclosure.

At the five main gates of the city, from which bridges led over the broad moat surrounding the city wall, the guards were disarmed and allowed to return to their homes, being replaced by British and Native troops.

Knowing the road, Colonel Sladen proceeded with guides ahead of the troops, to the palace enclosure, to meet the Prime Minister. The Minister met him at the main entrance of the enclosure and asked him to accompany him alone into the King's presence, and not on any account to let the troops enter. Leaving a note for General Prendergast, asking that the troops should not be allowed inside the palace before again hearing from him, Colonel Sladen entered the *Hlutdaw*, or Great Council Chamber, and was shortly afterwards received by the King. With very little preamble the King surrendered himself and his kingdom, and it was arranged that he should consider himself a prisoner, and formally surrender to General Prendergast on the following day. Colonel Sladen then left the palace, and the Hampshire Regiment, the 1st Madras Pioneers, and the Hazara Mountain Battery were left under the command of Brigadier-General White to guard the royal enclosure for the night, the rest of the troops returning to the transports.

King Thibaw surrenders himself.

The following morning General Prendergast proceeded to the palace and formally received the surrender, and the King, accompanied by his two Queens and the Queen Mother, was escorted to the river by Brigadier-General Norman. The procession consisted of 23rd Madras Infantry, leading; the 9-1st (Cinque Ports) Royal Artillery; then the King and his suite; while the Royal Welsh Fusiliers closed the rear. Nothing amounting to a demonstration was made, and there was no attempt at a rescue, and at a quarter past six the King and his retinue were safely placed on board the steamer *Thooreah*. The *Thooreah* left for Rangoon the next morning, escorted by two companies of the Liverpool Regiment under Colonel LeMesurier. Without again putting his foot on Burmese soil, Thibaw was transferred with his two Queens to an ocean steamer at Rangoon on 10th December, and was taken *viâ* Madras to Ratnagiri fort on the Bombay coast, where he still remains a prisoner of State. The Queen Mother was sent to Tavoy, in Lower Burma.

Thus, within three weeks of the declaration of war, the King was a prisoner, Mandalay was in our hands, and we held the line of river from Mandalay to our frontier. That is to say the instructions given to the expedition had been carried out, and all that now remained for it was to maintain itself in its position till further orders were received.

The British casualties during the advance were :—

Killed	.. ..	1 officer and 3 sepoys.
Drowned	.. ..	2 European rank and file.
		2 Native " " "
Wounded	.. ..	4 officers, 22 native rank and file.

No accurate estimate of the Burmese loss was possible, but it could only have been slight, and cannot have exceeded 250 all told.

CHAPTER XIII.

SUBSEQUENT OPERATIONS TO 31ST DECEMBER 1885.

UNFORTUNATELY the success with which the campaign had been opened could not be followed up by decisive action. Changes of ministry at home,[1] and the unsettled state of politics, prevented the Government from at once entering into the subject and deciding the future of Upper Burma without delay, and consequently no definite instructions could be issued. The most that the army of occupation could do was to secure its line of communication, and support whatever authority it could establish ; this unfortunately was for the time restricted to the country in range of its rifles.

Then followed a period of great individual activity on the part of the troops, but no actual progress could be made, as their object was merely to maintain themselves where they were. They were numerically quite inadequate to invade or rather occupy the 140,000 square miles of country, comprised in the territories recently governed by King Thibaw, even if they had been given such an objective, and consequently their efforts to establish order in their immediate vicinity were extremely local in effect, and beyond the range of their rifles the disorder which arose on the collapse of the government fomented without restraint. The success of the first *coup* completely paralysed all national resistance, and if it had been followed up at once by the occupation of the country and the re-establishment of law and order, it seems probable that the third Burmese war would have been, comparatively speaking, inexpensive and bloodless. As it was, except in the very small strip of country occupied by our troops, adventurous Burmese had several months to establish their influence, organize

[1] The several Prime Ministers were—

1. Marquis of Salisbury, Conservative, June 24th, 1885.
2. Mr. Gladstone, Liberal, February 6th, 1886.
3. Marquis of Salisbury, Conservative, August 1886.

Thus, in little over one year three Ministries were overthrown. These events, together with elections and party politics, fully engrossed the attention of Government during this period.

districts, and spread far and wide the determination to resist all interference on the part of the British. By the time Mandalay was occupied no local resistance was organized, and if the administration of the country had recommenced at once, well supported by force, it would have been impossible for local organizations to have assumed the considerable proportions which they did when allowed to remain unmolested from their very birth. Eventually when the future administration was decided on in March 1886, various collateral circumstances prevented its being vigorously undertaken till the commencement of the cold weather of the same year. During the time which thus elapsed trade was paralysed, the country was being devastated by dacoits, and the men who were to resist the enforcement of our rule were receiving a practical training in the use of arms and in the application of those tactics which rendered their gangs, at home in their native swamps and jungles, so unapproachable by disciplined troops. When the suppression of these disturbances was undertaken it not only entailed loss of valuable lives, but also vast expenditure. The organizations against us had remained unmolested for so long and had such a hold on the people that military measures alone could make head against them, and thousands of the pick of the manhood of the country were killed before the resistance to authority could be overcome.

Proclamations issued to the Burmese.

On the 1st December a proclamation was issued notifying King Thibaw's surrender, dethronement, and deportation, and intimating that until the will of Her Majesty the Queen-Empress was known, the civil and military administration of the country was vested in General Prendergast, who desired to carry on the government with the aid of such of the Ministers, Governors, and other officers of State, at present in office, as agreed to remain and perform loyal service to the British Government. This provisional *Hlutdaw*, or Council of State, included two *Mingyi* or Ministers of State, four *Atwinwun* or Privy Councillors, and seven *Wundauk* or Under Secretaries. Special notification was made that the *hpongyi*, or religious body, would be protected, and allowed to carry on their religious duties unhindered, and that all religious buildings and their precincts would be preserved, while Buddhism would remain the national religion and would be respected. Provided they were quiet and peaceable, all were to remain unmolested; and were to be permitted to engage in their national sports and to follow the customs of the country. The Governors of districts, judges, town magistrates, village headmen, and the officers performing miscellaneous military-police duties, were provisionally and temporarily retained on condition that they should faithfully discharge their duties under the orders of the British civil officers, and should do their utmost to suppress crime, allay public anxiety, and pacify the towns and villages under their charge. Dacoits, robbers, and vagrants were to be arrested and sent to the British civil officer. All the members of the *Hlutdaw* agreed to these terms, and were consequently retained in office.

The administration of the country being thus temporarily vested in the State Council of Burmese Ministers and Officials, under the presidency of Colonel Sladen, and under the orders of General Prendergast, their first act was to proclaim a general disarmament of the civil population. None except Members of Council and its staff were allowed to possess other arms than the common *dah*, in ordinary use for all domestic, agricultural, and forest purposes, unless they received special passes; the inhabitants of Mandalay and its suburbs were called upon to deliver up at once any muskets, swords, spears and the like in their possession; any one found disobeying this order was to be seized, and would be liable to be shot. Many arms were given up, but nothing like all of them.

As soon as the Burmese realised that their old Government had ceased to exist, disorder and dacoity prevailed everywhere in Mandalay and its suburbs; strong pickets had to be posted in and around it, and strong patrols were marched through the streets during the whole night. As this abnormal state of affairs in the city and suburbs subsided, patrols and reconnaissance were pushed out further from the city, and every effort was made to secure quiet in the immediate neighbourhood.

Situation of the Field Force.

The extension of the troops into fresh country during the ensuing months was not done so much with a view to occupying more country as to improving their strategical position, though there can be no doubt that by doing so their responsibilities were considerably increased; the very fact of establishing a post in a town or village placed a large number of Burmese of the surrounding country under our protection, and to them it was due that we should not only maintain a semblance of order amongst them themselves, but that we should keep off dacoits from outside. For the force to maintain itself in its position it was only necessary to prevent any dacoit movement from assuming dangerous proportions, and to keep open the lines of communication; but its duty to the inhabitants of the country could not be left unperformed, and this so enhanced the work which the troops were called on to perform that they were incessantly taking the field. The strength of the posts established varied from thirty and fifty men in small connecting posts to 250 and 300 men in the larger and more important ones.

Soon after the fall of Mandalay two columns were sent out to patrol and reconnoitre the country in the immediate vicinity of the capital, but owing to provision not having been made for the expeditionary force to undertake land operations, not much in this way was possible at that time. It will be remembered that, save for a coolie corps, 3,000 strong, the Expeditionary Force was entirely without land transport; this was a great clog on all operations undertaken. Without transport not only could moveable columns not be despatched, but posts, if established, could not be supplied with provisions. The coolie transport was tried with the columns detailed to patrol the neighbourhood of Mandalay early in December, and it failed completely. In equipping a column rationed for seven days four coolies were required to carry the rations, etc., of every five coolies required by the troops. On the march the narrowness of the paths necessitated the advance being made in single file. In December the paths were very muddy, and the coolies, who numbered three times the fighting strength of the columns equipped for seven days, straggled out so much that it became impossible to keep up communications between the front and rear of the force. It was also impossible to adequately escort and protect the coolies in the close country, where they were liable to be ambuscaded at any minute. To do this the whole of the fighting force would have had to be extended at

Difficulties of transport.

intervals along the line. Some of the coolies too, especially those from the Madras Presidency, were old and feeble, and quite unable to carry the light loads to which they were detailed.

The Assistant Adjutant and Quartermaster General of the Field Force says in a report—

A coolie's nominal load is 40 lbs., but when carrying a blanket, and say seven days' rations for himself, his transport powers are practically exhausted, and in any case there is always inconvenience in dividing baggage into the necessary small loads. Besides this, when in large numbers, they are liable to spread epidemic diseases, and their sanitation and discipline are alike troublesome. The above objections are minimised, or disappear when coolies are worked by stages, exchanging loads at each stage, as during the Ashanti Expedition, 1873-74.

The experience gained by the first moveable columns showed that a great reduction in the scale of baggage was practicable, and that for future operations it was imperative that columns should not be entirely dependent on coolie transport; to this end it was necessary that every effort should be made to obtain and equip pack-animals. During December some 100 royal elephants and 300 ponies from the Manipur Cavalry in Mandalay were brought into the Transport Department of the Field Force, but of these half the elephants were without mahouts or only half trained, and half of the ponies were unserviceable. In addition to these, ponies were purchased in Upper and Lower Burma as fast as they were brought in.

The Expeditionary Force in its equipment being devoid of animal transport, it was also devoid of gear, so gunny-cloth pads were made for the elephants, and the ponies' backs were covered with a rough gear on the same principle as that used in the Punjab. Inefficient as it was, this improvised transport was found to be a great boon, and enabled moveable columns to march unencumbered with coolies.

On the 10th December the Head-Quarters of the Burma Field Force were established in the palace; and on the 15th Mr. Bernard, Chief Commissioner of British Burma arrived with a small staff from Rangoon in order to concert administrative measures till the final policy of the British Government could be declared.

Field hospitals were established and the sick were despatched to the base hospital at Thayetmyo.

During the advance up the river there had been a slight outbreak of cholera as follows:—

European Troops	..	..	5 cases, 3 fatal.
Native Troops	..	..	33 „ 5 „
Followers ..	..	..	14 „ 5 „

Otherwise the health of the troops was good.

The cholera epidemic lasted till the beginning of January; the total number of cases which occurred is shown below:—

	Number attacked.	Number died.
British Troops ..	35	28 or 1 in 1·25 attacked.
Native Troops ..	115	49 or 1 in 2·35 „
Followers	121	77 or 1 in 1·57 „
Total ..	271	154

Throughout the whole of December armed parties were scouring the country round Mandalay in search of Thibaw's disbanded soldiery and of men in possession of arms; moveable columns were operating against the bands of dacoits, often large in number, formed of the runaway troops; while the garrisons left at Minhla, Pagan, Myingyan, Ava, and Sagaing were all busily engaged in operating against the dacoits infesting these districts, and in endeavouring to assist the civil officers left at the three first-named stations in introducing law and order. The military situation remained unchanged. There was no organized resistance to authority, but bands of dacoits overran the country in all directions. The telegraph line to the frontier was constantly interfered with, and the wires cut again as soon as repaired.

In the middle of December General Prendergast received information that the Chinese were massing troops on their frontier, with a view to the seizure of Bhamo. He accordingly decided to occupy Bhamo immediately, and embarked with a force of 1,000 men for that place on the 18th December, occupying Shwebo, a town of great political importance, *en route*.

The Bhamo Expedition.

The expedition was composed as follows :—

Steamship *Pulu*, with two flats.—Field Force Head-Quarters, Naval Brigade, *Turquoise* detachment and 37 Mounted Infantry.

Steamship *Kah-byoo*—Field Force Head-Quarters and gun-barge.

Steamship *Pallow*, with two flats.—Brigadier-General Norman, C.B., and Staff, half Battalion, Royal Welsh Fusiliers, Hazara Mountain Battery, 290 coolies, six mortars, with detachment of thirty officers and sixty gunners, 4–1st North Irish Division, Royal Artillery (half Battery).

Steamship *Okpho*, with two flats.—Head-Quarters and half Battalion, 25th Madras Infantry, one Company, Bengal Sappers, Commissariat Ordnance Stores, and 335 coolies.

Steamship *Colonel Fytche*, with two flats.—Hospital and fifty coolies.

Steamship *Ananda*.—Survey party under Commander Carpenter, Royal Navy.

Paddle launch *Pegu* } *Turquoise* detachment.
Steam launch *Berta* }

The distance from Mandalay to Bhamo by river is 250 miles, and in the low water season the navigation is very difficult. The country on both banks of the Irrawaddy was said to be in a state of anarchy. The vessels employed for the expedition were such as drew less than two and a half feet of water.

The advance was conducted the same way as was the advance on Mandalay. No opposition was met with, and on the 28th December Bhamo was occupied, and the whole of the Irrawaddy from north to south of Upper Burma was now in the hands of the British.

Although an important emporium of trade with Yunnan, Bhamo was only a small town of about 5,000 inhabitants. No Chinese troops were found in the vicinity, except the usual small garrison at Tengyueh beyond the frontier, and there appeared no reason to anticipate hostile operations on the part of the Chinese.

After being about a week at Bhamo, General Prendergast, returned to Mandalay, leaving Brigadier-General Norman behind, in charge of a strong force, and also a civil officer to oragnize administration with the help of the military.

This occupation of Bhamo was an operation of considerable importance, as it not only completed the execution of the original scheme, by which we became masters of the situation in Upper Burma, but it also brought us in contact with the Chinese Empire. The boundary between Upper Burma and China lies about fifty miles from Bhamo to the north-east.

Disturbances at Bhamo by the Chinese.

The possession of Bhamo has always been rather coveted by the Chinese, as it would give them a footing on the Irrawaddy. It has been captured and recaptured by the Chinese and Burmese in their several wars, but the Chinese permanent boundary has never been placed south of it. Recently there had been a so-called Chinese occupation of Bhamo, but on enquiry it was found that the Viceroy of Yunnan and his subordinates had nothing to do with it; that it was purely a local disturbance unbacked by any Chinese official authority. It came about thus—when the place was attacked by Kachin marauders from the surrounding hills, the Burmese Governor employed a number of Chinese to defend the town; they were promised a certain sum for their services, and when they did not receive it these Chinese collected some of their friends and looted and burned the whole place.

It will be seen from the chapter on the Settlement of the Claims of the Chinese Government over Burma[1] that the Chinese were very anxious for Bhamo to be handed over to them, but they were unable to support their claim on any substantial grounds. Bhamo was occupied before these negotiations had arrived at an advanced stage, and considerable uneasiness was felt in Yünnan as to the upshot of the Burmese war. It appears that shortly after the first occupation of Bhamo by General Prendergast, Chinese troops to the extent of some 2,500 under Brigadier-Generals Ting and Chu were concentrated on their frontier. They were employed in putting the frontier in a state of defence and intriguing with the neighbouring hill tribes to secure their hostility to the British. It is observable that the Chinese confined themselves to defensive precautions, and committed no aggressive acts of hostility, while on our side all acts which might tend to bring us in contact with the Chinese were carefully avoided. The Bhamo garrison and the troops

[1] See Appendix.

in the command, as well as the Political Officers, limited their actions to establishing themselves in the selected localities. Between Bhamo and the Chinese Frontier the hills are inhabited by independent tribes of Kachins who are marauders by nature and inclination, and, except as marauders, they gave little or no trouble so long as their autonomy was respected. To the west and north-west are Shan States and with these negotiations were undertaken, from which it soon became manifest that the most influential ruler, the Wuntho *Sawbwa*, would resent any interference on our part, and was in danger of becoming actively hostile. For the present, however, all conflict with these tribes was avoided and all negotiations with the Chinese were carried on in a friendly spirit.

About the 19th December an expedition was sent up the Chindwin river, whence news had been received of the murder of three of the Bombay–Burma Trading Corporation's employés. This force was ordered to join hands with another column operating from Manipur.

Outbreaks in Lower Burma.

The lawlessness and disorder prevailing in Upper Burma had meanwhile communicated itself partially to Lower Burma. In the Shwegyin district the *Mayan Kyaung Hpongyi*, a Shan priest, raised a following of about 500 men. Troops from Rangoon and Toungoo managed to scatter this little force, but it was long before the smaller bands thus raised were completely suppressed and the priest captured.

Prize.

When Mandalay fell into our hands a Prize Committee was appointed to collect money, valuables, and other property of the King and the late Government. The cash and the amount realised by sale of properties amounted to some nine lakhs.[1] General Prendergast applied that this sum might be distributed to the troops as prize money, and his application was strongly recommended to Government by the Commander-in-Chief. As Mandalay was not captured by assault, but had been taken over by General Prendergast with the government of the country, it was ruled that the royal money and properties belonged to the revenue of the country and, as such, could not be distributed amongst the troops of the expedition. Consequently, a grant of money was

[1] Of this nine lakhs, eight lakhs were from the palace property.

made by Government to be distributed as a gratuity[1] amongst the troops in lieu of prize money; and the treasure and property which was taken possession of on the advance to and occupation of Mandalay was ordered to be handed over to the civil authorities, to be credited to the State in the usual manner.

The following is a return of the ordnance captured by the Expeditionary Force:—

Place.	Iron.		Brass or bronze.	Wall pieces.	Brass mortars.	Total.	Remarks.
	Smooth-bore.	Rifled.					
Nyaungbinmaw	8	..	..	..	..	8	Destroyed by Commander Durnford, R.N.
Gwegyaungkamyo ..	12	..	6	3	..	21	Collected and destroyed by Royal Engineers.
Minhla	16	..	6	2	..	24	Four on board *Panthay*; remainder on board flat alongside *Thooreah*.
Nyaung-u (Pagan) ..	5	..	2	4	..	11	To be collected by Lieutenant Stuart, Bombay Mountain Battery.
Myingyan	21	..	..	..	..	21	Destroyed by Naval Brigade, except three embarked in S. S. *Doowoon*.
Pakôkku	7	..	..	..	..	7	Destroyed by Naval Brigade.
King's steamer (November 26th).	6	..	..	..	..	6	
Ava Redoubt	3	..	..	..	..	3	Embarked in S. S. *Aloung Pyah* and *Thooreah* for Rangoon.
„ Fort and palace ..	25	..	..	..	..	25	
„ lines	21	..	..	..	..	21	
Sagain	11	..	3	5	..	19	Embarked in S. S. *Burma* for Rangoon.
Thabyadan	12	..	7·8	3	..	23	Embarked in S. S. *Ashley Eden* and *Ataran*.
Mandalay Palace	994	8	158	369	17	1,546	Part sent to Rangoon Arsenal; remainder variously disposed of.
„ Gun Factory ..	2	..	3	..	..	5	
„ river bank ..	7	..	..	..	..	7	
Salemyo	6	..	..	..	..	6	
Bhamo	11	..	2	..	..	13	
Pyinmana	..	..	15	..	..	15	Captured by Somersetshire Light Infantry with Toungoo column.
Myingyan	..	1	..	..	..	15	Discovered after occupation of Myingyan.
GRAND TOTAL ..	..	..	..	..	..	1,782	

	Rs.
1 To the Military forces	2,51,410
Naval forces	24,456
Total ..	2,75,866

The distribution of the Expeditionary Force on the 28th December 1885 was as follows :—

At Bhamo.

Head-Quarters.

Naval Brigade { S. S. *Pulu*, S. S. *Ananda*, S. S. *Pegu* } *Turquoise* and *Bacchante* detachments.

Half Battery, 4–1st North Irish Division, Royal Artillery.

Thirty-seven Mounted Infantry.

Half Battalion, Royal Welsh Fusiliers (Head-Quarters).

Hazara Mountain Battery.

One company, Bengal Sappers.

Half Battalion, 25th Madras Infantry (Head-Quarters).

At Mandalay.

2–1st Royal Artillery (*en route* to Rangoon).

9–1st Cinque Port, Royal Artillery (one division to Mingyan, Pagan, Minhla, and back).

3–1st Scottish Division, Royal Artillery.

One-half of 4–1st North Irish Division, Royal Artillery.

Two companies, Royal Welsh Fusiliers (two companies at Shwebo).

Hampshire Regiment (2 officers and 100 men at Sagain; 1 officer and 60 men to the Chindwin river; 1 officer and 60 men to Myingyan, Pagan, Minhla, and back).

2nd Madras Light Cavalry, 70 sabres (1 officer and 60 sabres to Myingyan, Pagan, Minhla, and back; 1 officer and 30 sabres to Singu and back).

Three companies, Madras Sappers and Miners.

1st Madras Pioneers (1 officer and 60 men to Myingyan, Pagan, Minhla, and back).

12th Madras Infantry.

21st Madras Infantry (1 officer and 100 men telegraph escort to Minhla).

23rd Madras Light Infantry (1 officer and 100 men at Sagain; 2 officers and 60 men to Chindwin river).

25th Madras Infantry, half Battalion (at Amarapura).

At Ava.

H. M. S. *Irrawaddy* with *Woodlark* detachment.

At Myingyan.

Steam launch *Kathleen* with *Turquoise* detachment.

Two companies, Liverpool Regiment.

Two guns, Bombay Mountain Battery.

One company, Bengal Sappers.

Four companies, 11th Bengal Infantry.

At Minhla.

Two companies, Liverpool Regiment.

Two guns, Bombay Mountain Battery.

Six companies, 2nd Bengal Infantry (Head-Quarters).

At Thayetmyo.

One company, 2nd Bengal Infantry.

At Allanmyo.

One company, 2nd Bengal Infantry.

The original distribution of the Field Force in three brigades ceased to exist except in name immediately after the army reached Mandalay, as, owing to the nature of the operations undertaken and the paucity of the troops, detachments had to be detailed according to the most urgent requirements of the moment.

On the 28th December Brigadier-General Foord was ordered back to India, as his brigade was completely broken up.

CHAPTER XIV.

DACOITS.

ON THE 1st January, 1886, on the advice of the Chief Commissioner, Lord Dufferin issued a proclamation to the effect that the territories formerly governed by King Thibaw had become part of the British dominions, and would, during Her Majesty's pleasure, be administered by such officers as the Viceroy might from time to time appoint.

The immediate objects of General Prendergast's expedition had thus been thoroughly and almost bloodlessly accomplished. But it was well known that this was merely the preliminary towards the serious work of pacification which had now to be faced and carried through. The new territory that had just been incorporated into the British dominions had an area of about 140,000 miles, and a population estimated at about three and a half millions. A considerable part of this vast expanse was impenetrable jungle, and even in the least sparsely populated districts there were no roads or bridges. During the rainy season the difficulties of communication were much increased by the sudden rise of the rivers and streams, which intersected the country in all directions. Large tracts of country often remained under water for weeks at a time.

The Burman character.

Though not a warlike race, the Burmese had a traditional and hereditary love of desultory fighting, raiding, gang robbery, and the like and their inordinate national vanity preserved vivid recollections of the time when they were a conquering race, driving the Shans, Kachins, and Assamese into the hills. Villages had long standing feuds with other villages, and the gangs of robbers mixed up in these were recruited from time to time by the young bloods from the villages concerned. After a time such young men went back to their usual occupations, but those who liked the hard lawless life under a dacoit *boh* could easily take to it permanently as partisans of one or other of the professional bandits who were usually in open revolt against the sovereign. This had been the case under all the Burmese Kings, and King Thibaw had proved himself to be below the average of Burmese sovereigns in administrative capacity.

These various difficulties arising from the nature of the country, the character of the people, and the existing political situation, were rather increased than lessened by the suddenness of Thibaw's overthrow. When the plan of campaign, settled years before in Simla, had been almost bloodlessly carried out in a fortnight, it was found that the raw and undisciplined levies hastily called out to oppose our advance, had dissolved and spread themselves over the country in small lawless bands. The very ease with which Mandalay was taken and the King deposed tended greatly to retard the work of permanent pacification. Had there been anything like a national army, its overthrow might have cost much bloodshed at the outset; but once its opposition had been overcome, this would have swept away the main difficulties and left a free stage for the introduction of a better organized system of administration, so that troops, treasure and time would eventually have been saved.

Aware of these peculiar difficulties, conscious of the state of anarchy which existed under Thibaw's rule, and guided by the experiences gained in Pegu a generation before, the Government of India quite understood the gravity of the situation and the magnitude of the task before them in undertaking the pacification of the new territories. It was felt that the necessary measures could only be satisfactorily concerted on the spot in communication with those having local knowledge and experience; hence the Viceroy, and the Commander-in-Chief, Sir F. Roberts, took the earliest opportunity of proceeding to Burma in order to draw up schemes for the future administration of the country, and for the further military operations still requisite before a stable form of government could be established.

Until further measures could be thus decided on, British civil officers supported by troops, were in command of each of the five districts of Mandalay, Myingyan, Pagan, Minhla and Pyinmana, and were working in direct subordination to the Chief Commissioner and without reference to the *Hlutdaw*. The civil and ordinary criminal jurisdiction was in the hands of these civil officers, except where troops were stationed or were operating, when, the country being still under military occupation, the Provost-Marshal's officers exercised some jurisdiction.

Outside of these five districts the rest of the country was nominally governed by the *Hlutdaw* or State Council, presided over by Colonel Sladen; but it was soon apparent that the authority of the *Hlutdaw* had gone with the power which had formerly upheld it, that with the fall of Mandalay the machinery of the Burmese Government in the districts had collapsed, and that, though outwardly the people were friendly, yet the members of the royal family, the official classes, and the disbanded soldiery were strongly opposed to our rule and were doing all in their power to persuade the populace to resist us and prevent its establishment. In some places the ordinary local officials succeeded in enforcing partial order, but the country at large was in a state of anarchy and disorganization.

It must be borne in mind that the Government of the country was at present only provisional, as it had not been decided by the British Government what policy to pursue with regard to the future administration. The Expeditionary Force was totally inadequate to occupy the whole country, and there were only five civil officers, who at best could only deal with their districts as far as the troops could co-operate with them. Our own action of forcibly taking away the King and of breaking up his army of itself completely undermined the power of the *Hlutdaw*; so that what actually occurred was a complete collapse of all central authority, and this could not be re-asserted till an executive was re-established throughout the country.

Dacoits.

When the local authorities found that they were not supported or controlled by any central authority from Mandalay, they either commenced to rule their districts themselves or decamped and sought protection in the British stations. As was natural, there was considerable competition amongst these upstart rulers, and each one set about strengthening his position and extending his influence as far as possible. Professional dacoits were in great demand to form the nucleus of their bands; their usual *rôle* was to send round orders to different villages to provide a certain number of guns and a certain number of men who were to rendezvous at a named spot. This order was generally accompanied by a demand for money. The men thus collected were the dacoit bands, and the villages that had refused to comply with the orders were taken as their objective. It often happened that one dacoit *boh*, or leader, would summon a village that had supplied men or arms to another *boh* ; these occasions were constantly the prelude to a feud between the two bands. It was very rare that two neighbouring dacoit bands were on friendly terms with each other. The light in which they regarded our troops was as opposition bands starting opposition *bohs* in their districts.

These dacoit *bohs* exercised a complete terrorism. The village that refused to help them, or the village that assisted any other band, whether British or Burmese, was burned and plundered on the first opportunity ; and they maintained their authority against that of the British by exerting this terrorism on the country, rather than by fighting the troops. A band of from 200 to 4,000 would collect with a certain object, and when attacked by a few of our troops they would melt away ; they had little or no intention of fighting us. If they were lucky and killed one or two soldiers, their prestige increased ; if they were unlucky and lost several men, those men were considered fools for not getting out of the way of the soldiers, and the remainder re-assembled again when summoned, not the least demoralised. Of course the villagers themselves would give us no assistance as a rule ; 1st, because they dare not ; 2nd, because the bands opposed to us were composed of themselves, their friends, and relations ; 3rd, because they had no particular wish to be rid of their leader, who generally ruled with discretion and moderation where he was supported and not thwarted. It was found, too, that assistance could not with justice be even accepted if proffered by villagers who did not live within easy striking distance of an established military post, as, unless subsequently protected, they were at the mercy of the dacoits.

General procedure of dacoits.

The general procedure of a band of dacoits is to approach the village to be dacoited soon after dark ; they commence firing off their guns when they get close ; if the people bolt, they ransack the village and then burn it; if their shots are replied to, they either make off, or set the village on fire by throwing disks of burning oiled rope on to the houses; the people then seize their valuables to make off with them and are looted by the dacoits as they go. Dacoits do not, as a rule, attack villagers whom they find alert or awake, hence the custom holds in villages of, from time to time during the night, firing off guns in the air; when there is any disturbance in a village at night all the inhabitants rattle the bamboos of their houses to show they are awake. Every village surrounds itself with impenetrable hedges of prickly pear or with matted rows of dry brambles and thorns, which are not negotiable by assault, and behind which look-out crow's nests are placed at intervals. Any village that was thriving or worth dacoiting could be told at once by the appearance of its defences; but this was no guide to British troops as to its politics, since for a long time the most thriving villages were the head-quarters of the different gangs of dacoits. As regards the atrocities committed by the dacoits, there were many instances of the most barbarous and inhuman practices, but these were exceptional cases for the extortion of evidence or to find where treasure was buried; on these occasions they spared neither age nor sex. Occasionally men were crucified alive, but there was evidence to show that in the majority of cases the victim of crucifixion was killed first.

Pretenders with the dacoits.

The Burmese as a race and individually have the deepest admiration and affection for a king, and any dacoit who could either establish his claims to being called a king, or could obtain a prince of the royal blood either to maintain as a puppet king of his district, or who would accept his allegiance, thereby greatly enhanced his power. Consequently, the survivors of the palace massacres of 1878 were in great demand, and when found were immediately appropriated by the dacoit *bohs*. In the bands headed by these princes all the court ceremony was maintained, ministers were appointed, 'royal orders' were issued according to Burmese custom, scratched on palmyra leaves, and proclamations were promulgated stamped with the royal peacock seal; the houses the princes lived in were called palaces and their dacoit bands called 'royal armies.'

It was found that operations carried on against bands of dacoits were of no avail unless the dispersion of the dacoits was followed up by the occupation of the district. The dacoit bands never stood up to fight our troops, and, consequently, were rarely defeated; they would disperse on the approach of a column, and, as soon as it had passed by, they would assemble again. Consequently, after the first few months, operations were only undertaken by columns sent out from the various posts to disperse the gangs in their immediate neighbourhood. It was necessary for the success of any expedition that its attack should partake of the nature of a surprise; the dacoits had wonderful means of obtaining information as to the moves and projected movements of troops, and it happened oftener than not that a column sent to operate against a band found it already dispersed of its own accord. It was fruitless searching for the dacoits, because it was the villagers themselves who had recently been under arms as such. Unless a band was reached before it dispersed, it was quite impossible to operate against it or its component parts; and in a populous or jungly district the biggest band would completely melt away in twenty minutes. For these expeditions it was necessary to have the columns as mobile and light as possible; pack transport was indispensable. It was found that in the close country and on the narrow paths, columns of over 200 men were cumbersome and unwieldy, and that 200 men were sufficient for the work they had to do; consequently, it was very rare that a column exceeded that strength.

Experience of the country as a field of operations.

Usual strength of columns operating against dacoits.

As the dacoits so rarely stood, and when attacked disappeared so quickly, columns composed entirely of infantry operated at a great disadvantage. They would have to march for five or six hours, pushing on as fast as they could and making straight for the position, knowing that if they rested for a moment they would lose touch with the dacoits at once. To follow them up for long was impossible, as they spread out in all directions, were lightly clad, fresh, and could generally keep out of sight in the jungles and villages; even if infantry left their posts unobserved, any spies on the way could outstrip them and give information of their approach. Hence the unsatisfactory results of infantry engagements.

Cavalry and mounted infantry, on the other hand, were able to surprise gangs of dacoits by their rapid movements, and when surprised they could keep touch with them as they fled.

As regards the unsuitability of the country for cavalry operations, this was in a great measure nullified by the nature of the enemy and of the operations undertaken against them. The positions in which dacoits made their temporary stands were so selected and arranged that escape from them was in no way obstructed; they only prepared those sides for defence from which they expected an attack. Being threatened with a turning movement, they at once withdrew. It thus happened that any position which mounted men could approach was not tenable as a position against them. The only positions unassailable by cavalry were those in dense jungle or among the hills, and that only because they were unapproachable.

The dacoits had no drill, and in retreat, as a fighting body, their disorganization was complete. Hence, from the commencement, a cavalry action partook of the nature of the pursuit of a disorganized enemy, and as long as two or three mounted men could keep together the pursuit could be continued. In Burma there are no horses, and the ponies of the country average about 12 hands 1 inch; consequently, the appearance of men mounted on 15-hand horses was imposing, and when the dacoits had once felt their power of pursuit they lived in abject fear of them; they talked of them as the "great-horse devils," and, if possible, they would fly long before the cavalry were close enough (200 yards) to suffer from the effect of their fire.

The moral effect of artillery was great, but the range was generally very limited. A gun brought into action against a band of dacoits would often save the infantry from attacking, but with the object of punishing them this was a doubtful advantage.

During the winter the climate was found to be fairly healthy except in special places; but the hard marching and exposure told heavily on the troops. The nature of the operations to be undertaken demanded incessant forced marches and night marches, rarely of shorter duration than seven hours, and often exceeding twelve. In the swampy country very short distances could be covered in these times, and the fatigue was enormously enhanced by the difficulties in getting the transport along. It was rare for the garrison of any post to remain inactive long; the dacoit bands were always increasing and threatening, and, as soon as troops had rested from dispersing one band, they were taken out after another.

The *Hlutdaw* and dacoits.

On several occasions papers and other proofs incriminating the ministers of the *Hlutdaw* were found in the dacoit camps; this was only natural, as a good deal of their power and income during the ex-King's reign was derived from the protection they afforded to some of the dacoit *bohs*. Consequently, it was found that while these ministers were ostensibly assisting the civil power at Mandalay, the dacoits in the districts were supported by their influence and supplied by them with all the latest information. As these facts were discovered it was considered necessary to deport successively the *Teindah Mingyi*, the *Shwe Hlan Boh* (Cavalry Commander-in-Chief) and the *Hlaythinatwinwun* (Admiral of the Fleet).

Every effort was made to induce the dacoit *bohs* to come in to our officials, but with very limited success. A few former district officials however tendered their allegiance, and were in nearly every instance re-established in their former posts.

Orders incriminal proceedings.

Though Upper Burma was now annexed to the British dominions, it had not yet been incorporated with British India; hence Indian codes did not apply. The civil officers were instructed, however, to proceed in criminal cases on the lines of the Indian codes, except that dacoity or gang robbery might be punishable with death, that flogging was to be administered in place of imprisonment on petty offenders physically fit to undergo such punishment, and that no appeal lay from criminal sentences. Rebels in arms captured on the field were liable to be shot, but the death penalty was not to be enforced by civil officers without a proper trial.

CHAPTER XV.

OPERATIONS FROM 1ST JANUARY TO 31ST MARCH 1886.

DURING January, February, and March, frequent small engagements with dacoits occurred, a brief account of which will now be given.

During January posts were formed at Tigyaing on the Irrawaddy, below Katha, at Ava (Sagain Fort), and at Myotha, and the following expeditions took place: 7th to 13th—To Madaya, Kangyi, etc., by columns under command of Captain Dorward, R.E., Lieutenant-Colonel Budgen, R.A., and Major Collins, 2nd Hants Regiment. From Mandalay a column proceeded to Zibingyi to rescue, if possible, a European who had fallen into the hands of the Minzaing Prince's adherents. The expedition failed in its object, but found at Zibingyi the dead body of the European, who had evidently been murdered shortly before the arrival of the force, and dispersed the gang which had committed the murder. 6th to 15th—March of Lieutenant Keary, 1st Pioneers, with a small force of infantry from Myingyan to Mandalay, repairing the telegraph wire. 25th—Return of Major Warner's column to Mandalay from Kyauksé, where they had four skirmishes with the insurgents. 28th—Return to Mandalay of Chindwin river expedition, which had left Mandalay on the 17th ultimo. This expedition reached Kindat on the 4th January, when it found that the Europeans for whose protection it had been sent were safe. The following affairs also occurred during the month: 2nd January—Affair with dacoits at Nyaungu near Pagan. Lieutenant O'Meara, R.E., wounded. 9th—Attack on officers at Sagaing wherein Surgeon Heath lost his life; Lieutenant Armstrong, 2nd Hants Regiment, who was dangerously wounded, subsequently dying of his wounds on 29th. 10th—Affair at Obu near Sagaing, when a mixed force under Lieutenant-Colonel Gordon, 23rd Madras Light Infantry, attacked and dispersed a gang of dacoits. 11th—Affair at Kyauktalôn, where Captain Hewson, R.A., and several passengers from two steamers landed and protected the village from attack by a band of dacoits. 12th—Action at Kandu, twenty miles south of Shwebo, between a force from Shwebo, commanded by Lieutenant-Colonel Simpson, and some of the Prince Maung Hmat's adherents, who were defeated and dispersed. 16th—Affair near Pagan between a detachment under Major Stead, 11th Bengal Infantry, and some dacoits. 19th—Skirmish near Myotha between party under Captain Macdonald, 2nd Hants Regiment, and dacoits. 26th—Affair on Mu river at village of Nyaunggain about eighteen miles west of Shwebo, in which Major Williamson, Royal Welsh Fusiliers, attacked and dispersed a large party of the followers of Prince Maung Hmat and Hla-u, killing fifty-three of their number. He was subsequently attacked on the same day at his camp in the village of Séaim close by, but drove off the enemy, who disappeared, leaving a brass gun, some standards, and many arms and spears. 29th—Skirmish at Myotha; dacoits dispersed by a party under Captain Preston, who killed five of their number and captured two golden umbrellas and several *jingals* and muskets.

State of the province in January 1886.

At the end of January the state of the province was briefly as follows: The districts of Minhla, Pagan, Myingyan, and Pyinmana, administered by British civil officers, were fairly quiet. In Bhamo and its neighbourhood the country was quiet. Mandalay town and city was quiet; but in the districts round about Mandalay, which were still managed by the *Hlutdaw*, presided over by the Chief Political Officer, the country was much disturbed, and no progress had been made in pacification beyond the range of the rifles of the troops.

During February posts were formed at Alôn on the Chindwin, at Kyauksé, and at Yankintaung, while on the Eastern Frontier Colonel Dicken advanced from Pyinmana on the 13th, occupying Yamethin without opposition on the 18th, and establishing a chain of road-posts between the above specified places.

The following affairs took place in different parts of the country. On the 1st February Colonel Johnstone, Political Agent, Manipur, attacked and routed rebels at Pottah, twenty miles from Manipur. On the 2nd, Major Williamson, Royal Welsh Fusiliers, commanding at Shwebo, attacked Tabaing, a walled town thirty miles from that place, held by Maung Hmat and the dacoit leader Hla-u. Enemy driven out and barracks or huts capable of containing 2,000 men burned; enemy's loss not ascertained. On the 3rd, Captain Macdonald, 2nd Hants Regiment, commanding Ava post, had a skirmish with dacoits at Tada-u seven miles south-east of Ava; four of the enemy killed. 8th—Moveable column under Major Aitkin, R.A., proceeded from Mandalay to Thabengaing and Tada-u, two dacoit villages, both of which were burned. On the 13th, Lieutenant Dobbie and sixty sepoys of the 26th Madras Infantry repulsed attack of 200 dacoits on Taungdwingyi, killing twelve and wounding thirty. On the 19th, Captain Macdonald, 2nd Hants Regiment, commanding the outposts at Ava, dispersed a gang of dacoits, killing six and capturing several prisoners, and recovering some stolen property. 19th and 20th—Major Warner, 2nd Madras Lancers, at Kyauksé, attacked and dispersed the followers of the Minzaing Prince at Ywakainggyi, Yéwun, and Hanbyinbo, killing and wounding sixty-nine of the enemy and capturing five guns. The Minzaing Prince escaped to Kinlé. On the 19th, Lieutenants Fendall, R.A., and Dobbie, 26th Madras Infantry, from Taungdwingyi, attacked and destroyed the dacoit villages of Talopbin and Magyigôn, dispersing bands of dacoits found at each; enemy's loss—fifteen killed. On the 20th they burned two more villages for harbouring dacoits, and returned to Taungdwingyi on the 21st. On the 19th to the 22nd a reconnaissance was pushed from Bhamo to Sinbo and the party returned, having gained much valuable information, without opposition. On the 23rd there was a skirmish with some dacoits between Taungtha and Wélaung in the Myingyan district. On the 25th, Popa village, a haunt of dacoits, was destroyed by a party under Lieutenant Seton, 2nd Liverpool Regiment, twenty-five of the enemy being killed and thirty wounded. On the 27th, a column under Major Symons, Deputy Assistant Adjutant and Quartermaster General, scoured the north and west of Sagaing district and destroyed the head-quarters of the dacoits at Sadaung and Kyamengyi, recovering some stolen property. On the same day Lieutenant-Colonel Anderson, 3rd Madras Light Infantry, with a small force from Yamethin, dispersed a gathering of rebels under U Paung and other chiefs. On the 28th Lieutenant Seton of the 2nd Liverpool Regiment had a further skirmish with dacoits at Sagyin near Popa, and on the same day Major Stead, 11th Bengal Infantry, attacked and routed a large body of rebel followers of the Minzaing Prince at Taungthamyo. The enemy fell back to a position on the Natôgyi road and joined a gang of dacoits in a walled pagoda, out of which they were turned by the bayonet, enemy's loss—seven killed and many wounded.

During March 1886 posts were established at Mahlaing, Minthe, and Hlaingdet, and the following expeditions were carried out:—

11th, reconnaissance by a detachment of 2nd Brigade from Bhamo to Sinbo and Mogaung. No opposition was made to the advance of the party, and some valuable information was obtained. 8th, Major Bradshaw, 2nd Somerset Light Infantry, with a mixed force from Yamethin, attacked and drove about 500 rebels out of Engyingan, a village about seven miles north-west of Yamethin; enemy's loss—about forty killed and wounded. On the 10th and 11th Major Warner, 2nd Madras Lancers, dispersed two dacoit bands in neighbourhood of Kyauksé, killing and wounding about twelve of the enemy. On the 11th Lieutenant Armitage, 2nd Liverpool Regiment, with a party from Natôgyi, surprised at Palangôn village a party of rebels, headed by a chief who had been wounded in a recent fight with Major Stead's column on the 28th ultimo. The gang made a stand while their leader escaped, and then retired, leaving ten killed and a number of carts and cattle. On the 14th Lieutenant Fendall, R.A., with two guns, 3–1, Southern Division, R.A., fifty-six rifles, Royal Scots Fusiliers, and fifty-two rifles, 26th Madras Infantry, marched from Taungdwingyi through Yaungbinwet to Yamethin, which place he reached on 22nd, and after accompanying a reconnaissance under Lieutenant-Colonel Anderson, 3rd Madras Light Infantry, from Yamethin to Yanaung, returned to Taungdwingyi, reaching that place on the 5th April. On the 18th the cavalry of Colonel LeMessurier's force surprised and cut up a body of 400 rebels under the Kyin-myin-daing Prince close to Yindawmyo on the Mahlaing–Yamethin road—sixty of the enemy were killed, twenty wounded, and thirteen taken prisoners. On the 19th Lieutenant-Colonel Ommaney, 11th Bengal Infantry, pursued dacoits who had burned Zigat, near Pagan, killing three and taking six prisoners and two guns. On the 21st Captain Barnet, R.E., in command of a party from Mandalay, had a skirmish with dacoits at Khettpin village on an island north of Sheinmaga; enemy's loss one killed and fifteen prisoners. On the same day Colonel Dicken attacked and dispersed a party of rebels under the ex-*Léwun* of Pyinmana at Kinywa, nine miles east of Thanegon, and subsequently burned Kinywa. On the 22nd Lieutenant Dobbie, 26th Madras Infantry, left Taungdwingyi with a small force of thirty rifles, Royal Scots Fusiliers, and forty-three rifles, 26th Madras Infantry, and after visiting Tabingôn, Kalashin, and Thugyaung, surprised a body of dacoits at Magyigôn, who immediately dispersed and escaped to thick jungle; enemy's loss—three killed and two wounded, six prisoners. Magyigôn was searched, and, as it was clear that the village was a haunt of dacoits, it was destroyed. The column returned to Taungdwingyi on the 2nd April. On the 24th Major Braddon, 2nd Hants Regiment, commanding at Sagaing, attacked and dispersed some 600 dacoits who had taken up a position in pagodas near the village of Yéthit, killing about eighteen of their number. During this month preparations were made for storing Commissariat supplies at all posts in Upper Burma for the consumption of the troops during the rainy season, when the roads are almost impassable.

Reconstruction of Burma Command.

On the 15th February His Excellency the Viceroy, accompanied by the Commander-in-Chief in India, visited Mandalay, the result of this visit being a reconstruction of the command in Burma as follows, namely, that Upper and Lower Burma were constituted into one command under General Prendergast, with head-quarters at Rangoon, while the troops in Upper Burma were divided into two brigades, under Brigadier-General White, and Brigadier-General Norman, with head-quarters at Mandalay and Bhamo respectively. As troops had been drawn from all three presidencies of India, the military administration of Burma was, for the time being, placed under the Commander-in-Chief, to obviate the difficulty of the relative rank of Sir Herbert Macpherson, Commander-in-Chief of Madras, and Sir H. Prendergast.

The main points the Viceroy had to consider were whether the new dominions should form a protected state under the Indian Government, or be annexed outright, and brought directly under British administration. As the result of his deliberations he sent a telegram to the Secretary of State advocating annexation, and in his minute, dated Mandalay, 17th February 1886 (*vide* Appendix), he set forth at length his reasons for this decision and his proposals for the future administration of the country. There were four methods proposed for re-establishing order in Upper Burma :—

(1) To constitute it into a "buffer" State.
(2) To maintain it as a fully protected State with native dynasty and native officials, guided by a British Resident.
(3) To nominate one of the young princes as King, and to administer the State with British Officers till he should come of age.
(4) Annexation.

In the minute each of the former three measures was discussed and rejected and the fourth measure was justified ; consequently it was resolved to incorporate Upper Burma in British India, and this was effected by command of Her Majesty with reference to the Statute 21 and 22 Vic., cap. 106.

The attempt to restore order and to govern through the *Hlutdaw* was proving a complete failure, so it was decided to abolish that council, and to retain only a few trustworthy ministers as advisers to the Chief Commissioner in matters connected with the late government. The *Hlutdaw* was accordingly abolished on the 3rd March 1886.

After it had been decided to incorporate Upper Burma with the Indian Empire and the British Government, it was found necessary to substitute for the arbitrary powers of the Viceroy an order in Council under anno 33 Vic. cap. 3, sec. 1, extending that section to the whole of Upper Burma except the Shan States. It thus became a scheduled district removed from the operation of the Statute law applying to the rest of the Indian Empire, and so enabled the local administration of Burma to frame simple regulations with the approval of the Government of India, suitable to cope with the actual state of affairs. These regulations differed from Acts in being issued by the Governor-General in Council, instead of being passed by the Legislative Council of the Government of India, but in their effect there was no practical difference between the two. Mr. Bernard, Chief Commissioner of British Burma, was placed in charge of the whole of Burma, which was consolidated into a Chief Commissionership in September 1886; while Mr. Hodgkinson, one of the Commissioners acted as his assistant in charge of Lower Burma. The Shan States were to be treated as feudatory or tributary States, without attempting to bring them under any direct administrative control.

CHAPTER XVI.

OPERATIONS FROM 1ST APRIL TO 31ST JULY 1886.

ON THE 31st March 1886 General Prendergast vacated the command of the forces in Burma, and the Upper and Lower Burma brigades were again separated. Brigadier-General G. S. White was given command of the Upper Burma Field Force divided into two brigades with head-quarters at Mandalay and Bhamo. In addition to this there were two independent commands; one with head-quarters at Pyinmana, and the other with head-quarters at Taungdwingyi.

At this time, without attempting to dictate subordinate military arrangements from Calcutta and Simla, the Government of India urged the desirability of first thoroughly dominating the central area close to the main arteries of communication, and thence gradually extending administration and jurisdiction according to the means at disposal and the opportunities occurring. The despatch of spasmodic and disconnected expeditions into tracts which could not be at once permanently occupied and protected was deprecated. Such a method of procedure could only disquiet and compromise peaceable and well-disposed villages, because, if they showed themselves at all friendly to the military detachments visiting them, this only exposed them to subsequent ill-treatment and plunder at the hands of rebels and dacoits as soon as the British had left. The difficulties and dangers to health unavoidable during the hot months of April and May were also humanely pointed out and recommendations were made to move the troops about as little as possible during the hottest time of the year, and to canton them in as healthy localities as possible during the approaching rainy season, even though this might for the moment retard the progress of operations.

System of operations recommended by Government of India.

In accordance with these recommendations, British authority was first confined to the tracts bordering the Irrawaddy, to the country around Mandalay and Bhamo, and to the southern frontier districts of Minhla and Pyinmana. Military posts were distributed in various localities, and small moveable columns were organized, capable of moving in whatever direction occasion required. When in Mandalay, Sir F. Roberts had laid down a minimum strength for each post and column, and the wisdom of these arrangements was proved by the fact that no post was ever forced.

State of Upper Burma on 1st April 1906.

At the beginning of April 1886, although there was no organized Burmese army in the field, and therefore no particular objective requiring the concentration of large bodies of troops, yet the country generally was being overrun by armed bands. Five scions of the royal line were pushing their claims to the throne in different localities. The Myinzaing Prince, a son of Mindôn, held the Natteik pass into the Shan hills, and harried the plains lying to the south-east of Mandalay; while a pretender calling himself the Kyinyin Prince was troubling the districts to the south of that, as far as the Toungoo frontier. At Chaungwa, in the Ava district, the Chaungwa Princes Yan Naing and Yan Baing, whose father was massacred in 1879 by Thibaw, were endeavouring to assert themselves; while Prince Maung Hmat Gyi, a son of the heir-apparent killed in 1866, had a large following in the Shwebo and Yeu districts, north-east of Mandalay. Numerous dacoit leaders had become nominal supporters of these pretenders, plundering villages and levying blackmail in their names. Some of the dacoit *bohs* even went the length of themselves becoming pretenders to the throne. Bo Shwe, who had been harrying the Min and Minhla districts for the last twelve or thirteen years, boldly proclaimed himself king of Minbu, and appointed a Governor of the river. The most influential of the other dacoit leaders at this time were—Nga Hlau, who had for years harried the districts between the Irrawaddy and the Mu river, north-west of Mandalay; the Thondatin Thugyi, Maung Min Po, in the Pindali district; U Paung in Meiktila; and Buddha Yaza in Pyinmana. The Myinzaing Prince even offered a reward of 2,000 rupees for the head of Sir Charles Bernard, the Chief Commissioner, and threatened to burn the palace of Mandalay.

Incendiarism had become rife. Early in April several fires occurred in the more crowded suburbs of Mandalay city, and other fires broke out in the city itself about the middle of the month, at which date the Burmese new year happened to fall in 1886. About 800 houses within the city, and between 2,000 and 2,500 in the suburbs, were thus destroyed, chiefly by some thirty adherents of the Myingun Prince, who made an organized outbreak and rushed one of the two police stations. The citizens appeared to be demoralized for the moment, the shops and bazaars were closed, and business generally was at a standstill. From April onwards large bodies of armed men harrassed the whole of the districts around the capital and all the principal towns, and before the close of the rainy season it had become very apparent that it was necessary to considerably strengthen the troops in Burma. Hardly a day passed without a skirmish taking place in some part of the country; and the guerilla system of warfare gave great advantage to the rebels and dacoits.

Incendiarism at Mandalay.

General White soon found that for the pacification of the country and the suppression of dacoity or other armed resistance, it was necessary to closely occupy the country by establishing strong military posts in each of the various districts, of sufficient strength to maintain order in their immediate neighbourhood and to afford contingents for flying columns to skirmish against rebel bands. It was only when they saw the troops and felt they could rely on their protection that villagers could be expected to give information or assistance against the rebel bands and dacoit gangs. It was only thus that military ascendancy and prestige could be secured, the main lines of communication by land and water protected, civil authority and administration established, and the population encouraged to render assistance. In addition to posts along the Irrawaddy, others were established along the route from Mandalay to Toungoo, and from Toungoo across the hills to Thayetmyo. The central part of Upper Burma was thus enclosed in a roughly triangular series of strongholds, forming bases from which the further military operations were undertaken. Near the eastern base line a railway was being constructed from Toungoo to Mandalay,

General White's dispositions.

with great success and rapidity, in spite of unusual difficulties and dangers.

Public Works in 1886.

The expenditure on Public Works was intended to be limited at first to barracks, obligatory military roads, and telegraph repairs and construction; but the great importance of continuing the Rangoon-Toungoo railway line to Mandalay was recognized and urged both on political and military grounds. The Secretary of State suggested that, for the present, it might be more advantageous to make good roads, passable at all seasons, between the various civil and military stations. The arguments placed before the Government of India by Sir Charles Bernard were, however, so convincing that sanction was given to commence construction in the autumn of 1886. It was successfully urged by him that a trunk road would be costly and unremunerative, that the expense of moving troops and supplies would be five times as great by road as by rail, while the time occupied would be ten times as long, and that, in short, the railway would be far more effectual in pacifying the country, in promoting trade, and in strengthening the position, whether viewed from a military, a political, or an administrative standpoint.

State of affairs in Lower Burma.

The position in Lower Burma had meanwhile become such as to cause much uneasiness. Partly through the emissaries of the royal Princes pretending to the throne, and partly in sympathy with the lawless feeling prevalent within the newly annexed territories, dacoity sprang up to an alarming degree throughout the older province. Troops had therefore to be poured into Lower, as well as into Upper Burma. In the summer of 1886 there were 17,022 troops in Upper Burma, distributed in forty-three posts, and 7,162 in Lower Burma, occupying no less than forty-seven posts on the Sittang river and in the delta of the Irrawaddy.

Strength of British Force in Burma.

Everything resembling patriotic sentiment in the Burmese had become united with the inherent strain of brutality and lawlessness running through the national character; and this combination of innate forces found its expression in the bands of armed men infesting the jungles all over the new province. It was certainly not patriotism pure and simple, while it was equally certainly not merely dacoity in the true meaning of that word ; but it was armed resistance to British administration, and as such it had to be put down with a heavy hand. Lurking in jungle recesses almost impenetrable for regular troops, these armed bands were seldom to be met with in the open field. As a matter of course they were entirely dependent on villagers for food and other contributions, their demands for which they enforced with such barbarities as burning and devastating villages, slaughtering headmen, and crucifying or otherwise executing men suspected of giving information to the British.

Difficulties of suppressing the rebellion.

The enormous difficulties of contending with widespread revolt, rebellion, and crime of this sort can be easily imagined. It was necessary to attack the root of the evil by constantly harassing the armed bands so as to keep them in a continual state of apprehension, isolate them, cut them off from villages in which they had friends or relatives, and deprive them of their secret supporters.

It will be noticed that so far the British had been unsuccessful in capturing any of the chiefs who were fighting against them. These men never exposed themselves in action and were the first to make off at the slightest sign of danger. The country people were still afraid to give information which would lead to their capture, and did all in their power to assist in their escape. They had excellent information of the British movements, and even if our troops accidentally got near to them, they could always easily effect their escape on fast ponies, while their adherents scattered, to re-unite on a future day after the departure of the British.

It was evident that the only remedy was an unrelenting pursuit of the chiefs at such a pace as to tire them out and eventually effect their death or capture, but this course was at present impracticable owing to the time of the year and the flooded state of the country.

Between the 1st April and the 31st July a hundred small engagements were fought. An account of them in detail will be dull reading, but will nevertheless be now given, in order to show the strength of the resistance offered to our rule throughout the 100,000 square miles from Kindat to Pyinmana. Wherever there was an objective, that objective was sought out and mastered, with the one exception of the western portion of the Minbu district, where the climate proved so unhealthy that it was found necessary to suspend operations and withdraw the force. One division (two guns) of Royal Artillery returned from the effort to meet Boh Shwe with only one-eighth of gunners and drivers effective, the remainder of their strength being on the sick list; other corps were in much the same state.

There appeared to be an idea, at this time, that the widespread anarchy and rebellion were traceable to the civil and military administration of Upper Burma, and were of recent birth, and that the loss of officers and men in their suppression could have been avoided. The details of the actions, however, totally disprove the second charge, and show that the loss was unprecedently small when compared with the efforts called for.

Comparison of the pacification of Pegu in 1853-56, and that of Upper Burma.

It is interesting to compare the state of Upper Burma at this time with the state of Pegu after its annexation.

Pegu was annexed on 20th October 1852; Captain Phayre reported on the 2nd August 1853 that the whole of the country east of the Irrawaddy was entirely unsubdued. In September 1853 things were reported to be no better. A projected expedition against Tapun had to be abandoned, as it was not possible to hold the place. It was decided that only posts on the river could be held. It was not till the beginning of 1855 that Gaing Gyi's power was broken, and he was never caught. Our troops suffered defeats up to the third year of our occupation.

In contradistinction to the idea in 1853 that only posts on the Irrawaddy could be held, the force occupying Upper Burma in 1886 had struck inland and occupied the country at the foot of the Shan hills, a distance, in some places, of 120 miles from that river.

In Pegu a large portion of the population were in active alliance with us; in Upper Burma this result had not as yet been arrived at. The area of Pegu is but 26,000 square miles; that of Upper Burma is about 100,000. The population of the former is one-third of that of the latter.

Had the Burma field force remained stockaded on the banks of the Irrawaddy, there would not have been the daily reports of actions, and their consequent casualties, but dacoity and insurrection would have grown and would have remained unprobed; it seems, indeed, that the energy with which the probe was applied, was mistaken in some quarters for the origin of the disease.

The following is the detailed account of the 100 engagements, above referred to, which occurred between 18th April and 31st July 1886.

On the 1st April the road-post at Thayatgôn on the Pyinmana-Yamethin road was attacked by dacoits early in the morning. The dacoits were driven off without casualties on our side. On the 3rd, Colonel Dicken, Commanding Pyinmana Column, hearing that Hlaingdet was threatened by the Minzaing Prince with 3,000 followers, started at once from Yamethin for that place with a force as per margin. The party made a forced march and reached Hlaingdet on the afternoon of the 4th, and hearing that the rebels were in force at Kyah Tun, about a mile to the north, moved out on the morning of the 5th, strength as per margin, to attack them. The enemy was found in force at Za-un, Colonel Dicken attacked and drove them out of their position, returning to Hlaingdet the same day. Enemy's loss, twelve killed and a good many wounded. Casualties on our side, Lieutenant Peacock, 2nd Somersetshire Light Infantry, slightly wounded. An accidental fire at Hlaingdet on this day burned down half the town.

8-1, London Division Royal Artillery	..	2 guns.
Somersetshire Light Infantry	78	rifles.
3rd Palamcottah Light Infantry	80	"
Mounted Infantry ..	.. 11	"

2nd Liverpool Regiment	.. 40	rifles.
2nd Somersetshire Light Infantry	73	"
Mounted Infantry ..	.. 15	"
3rd Palamcottah Light Infantry	70	"
11th Bengal Infantry	.. 47	"
2nd Madras Lancers	.. 13	sabres.

On the same date Captain O. S. Smyth, Royal Artillery, with a force as per margin, moved out from Shwebo to attack Prince Maung Hmat, who, with several followers, was reported to have established himself at Uyin, twenty miles from Myotha, on the Mu river. The enemy was found on the 7th, near Chimkakgyin, in a position on the bank of the Mu, about 600 strong, with four standards, and was at once attacked and dispersed. Loss of insurgents unknown; our casualties *nil*. Prince Maung Hmat, as usual, escaped, and the force returned to Shwebo.

9-1, Cinque Ports Division, Royal Artillery	..	2 guns.
Royal Welsh Fusiliers	.. 100	rifles.
12th Madras Infantry	.. 40	"
2nd Madras Lancers	.. 13	sabres.

On the 4th, Major Warner, 2nd Madras Lancers, commanding at Kyauksé, with a force as per margin, left that station on a reconnaissance, and passing through Mingundaing, Kinayé, Shébawjun, Yewun, and Zalé returned to Kyauksé, on the 9th instant. The country was found to be very unsettled and dacoities frequent, and a few gatherings of dacoits were dispersed without loss on our side. As the result of this reconnaissance, Major Warner strongly recommended the permanent occupation of Yewun.

9-1, Cinque Ports Division, Royal Artillery ..	.. 2 guns.
Madras Lancers ..	.. 21 lances.
Royal Welsh Fusiliers	.. 28 rifles.
2nd Hants Regiment	.. 15 ..
23rd Wallajahbad Light Infantry	.. 60 ..

On the 5th, Migyaungdet, a village on the right bank of the Myitngé, about fifteen miles from Mandalay, was occupied by troops and held as a post. On the same date Lieutenant Vallentin, Somersetshire Light Infantry, with twenty rifles, 2nd Somersetshire Light Infantry, and thirty rifles, Palamcottah Light Infantry, attacked and destroyed the dacoit villages of Libôk and Shwemyo, about sixteen miles to the north-east of Pyinmana.

On the 8th, Major Bradshaw, commanding at Yamethin, attacked some insurgents near Theingon, two and a half miles east of that place. Six of the enemy were killed. Casualties on our side,—one private, 2nd Somersetshire Light Infantry, severely wounded.

On the same date Colonel Dicken, returning to Yamethin from Hlaingdet, proceeded by Shwényaungbu (about ten miles from the former place), which had been partially destroyed by U Paung, to Nankwé, a dacoit village which had been occupied by the ex-*Léwun* of Pyinmana, but was evacuated shortly before the arrival of the troops. The village and its defences were destroyed, and the troops returned to Yamethin on the 11th April.

On the same date (8th), a convoy, escorted by a naick and six privates of the Palamcottah Light Infantry, was attacked by dacoits near Thayetpin, on the Pyinmana-Yamethin road. The naick was killed, one private wounded, and seven carts looted, the remainder being rescued by a party from Thayetpin. On this date, a military post was established at Ye-u, about fifteen miles north-west of Shwebo, under the command of Lieutenant-Colonel Watson, 21st Madras Infantry.

On the 9th, orders were issued, in view of the approaching rains, for all inland posts to be stored at once with six months' commissariat supplies, river posts being filled up with four months' stock.

On the 11th, Major Braddon, 2nd Hants, with a party as per margin, proceeded from Sagaing *viâ* Ywathitgyi, to Sadaung, reported to be occupied by dacoits; the village was surrounded; ten of the enemy were killed, and ten brought in as prisoners by the cavalry.

2nd Hants Regiment	..	50 rifles.
2nd Madras Lancers	..	32 lancers.
3rd Wallajahbad Light Infantry		50 rifles.

On the 12th, Pakôkku was attacked by a force of rebels, estimated at 1,500, who were beaten off by Subadar Najab Khán, in command of fifty rifles of the 11th Bengal Infantry stationed there; three of the insurgents were killed, and many wounded.

On the same date Captain Wace, Royal Artillery, with a force as per margin, advanced from Bhamo against the Karwan *Sawbwá*, in the Kachin hills. He was opposed by the Kachins, and, after overcoming several obstacles, and proceeding beyond a Kara village a few miles from Mansi, had to retire, owing to the want of carriage for his wounded (eleven men), without accomplishing the object of the expedition, namely the occupation, and, if necessary, destruction of Karwan.

Hazara Mountain Battery	..	2 guns.
Royal Welsh Fusiliers	..	43 rifles.
Mountain Infantry	..	8 „
Bengal Sappers and Miners	..	38 „
26th Punjab Infantry	..	36 „

On the 15th the military post at Yankintaung, near Mandalay, was attacked by about 300 Burmans, who were beaten off with a loss of some twelve killed; our loss was one naick killed and two sepoys wounded. On this night also a patrol of the 26th Punjab Infantry was attacked in Mandalay suburb at 11 P.M. by a gang of dacoits, about fifty strong. Patrol fired and killed two; British casualties *nil*.

On the 16th, Major Bradshaw, 2nd Somersetshire Light Infantry, with a force as per margin, proceeded to Thayetpin and Baw-hlaing, to clear the surrounding country of dacoits. On the 17th he drove them out of Kyauk Sayitkôn and burned it. On this day a large

Somersetshire Light Infantry	..	60 rifles.
3rd Palamcottah Light Infantry		106 „
Mounted Infantry	..	13 „

band of dacoits attacked and captured Nayagan, a village three miles to the south of Ava, dispersing the Burmese Police, about 100 in number, stationed there, eleven of whom were captured and murdered.

On the 17th Major Wade, 2nd Liverpool Regiment, proceeded on a reconniassance from Mahlaing to Welaung. He had a skirmish with dacoits near Kyaukpôn, killing six, but failed to surround them.

9-1, Cinque Ports Division, Royal Infantry	..	1 gun.
2nd Madras Lancers	..	25 lances.
Royal Welsh Fusiliers	..	24 rifles.
2nd Hants Regiment	..	20 „
23rd Wallajahbad Light Infantry		60 „

On the 18th, Major Warner, 2nd Madras Lancers, commanding at Kyauksé, with the troops as per margin, attacked and dispersed a gathering of 500 Shans, Burmese, and (Panthay ?) Chinese dacoits at Hanbyinbo, near Kyauksé. On the same date, Major Aitken, Royal Artillery, with 180 men and a gun, attacked a party of Burmese, about 1,000 strong, under Boh Pyangyi, one of the Prince Maung Hmat's adherents, at Kinu, about fourteen miles north of Shwebo ; on the artillery opening fire the enemy retreated and were pursued, about eighty of them being killed ; no casualties on our side.

On the same date, a party of twenty sepoys, 11th Bengal Infantry, under command of Jamadar Rammudhar Awusti, left Hlaingdet, with orders to proceed to Meiktila and escort stores thence to Hlaingdet. At 9 P.M. that day it was reported at the latter place that they had been attacked and surrounded by dacoits ; at 11 P.M., Lieutenant Forbes, 11th Bengal Infantry, with twenty rifles, 2nd Liverpool Regiment, and thirty rifles, 11th Bengal Infantry, was sent from Hlaingdet to their assistance. It appears that on the 18th the Jamadar's party was attacked by dacoits at Minhla, about nine miles from Hlaingdet, but beat them off and proceeded as far as Kôndaung, when they were surrounded that night by a considerable number, some say 2,000 or 3,000, the attack being kept up till daybreak, when, Lieutenant Forbes's reinforcement arriving, the insurgents retreated into the jungle. The whole party then proceeded to Meiktila. The return journey was commenced on the 20th, and Lieutenant Forbes being anxious to have his wounded attended to, pushed on till dark, when he camped out in the open. They were fired at all night, and on the morning of the 21st, being about six miles from Hlaingdet, they continued their march and were met by large numbers of the enemy, who had blocked the road and lined the jungle on both sides. The detachment, 2nd Liverpools, was skirmishing in front; Lieutenant Forbes followed with twenty sepoys in support, and the remaining thirty sepoys were in rear with the carts. Lieutenant Forbes had just ordered the support to lie down, when he fell, shot through the heart. The escort fought their way through the enemy until clear of the jungle, when the dacoits left them alone. They reached Hlaingdet at 9-30 A.M., bringing in their wounded, the body of the late Lieutenant Forbes, and the whole of the convoy intact. The casualties on our side were—18th, at Minhla, three privates, 11th Bengal Infantry, wounded; at Kôndaung, 18th and 19th, four privates, 11th Bengal Infantry, wounded; on 21st, killed, Lieutenant Forbes, wounded none. Enemy's loss estimated thus,—at Minhla, three killed; at Kôndaung, seventy killed; on night of 20th and morning of 21st, fifty killed; number of the wounded unknown.

On the 19th, a gang of dacoits, said to be 150 in number, attacked the *Wun's* house in Shwebo, released the prisoners from lock-up, and burned down some thirty or forty houses in the town, escaping before a force from the cantonment got down to the scene of their operations. The *Wun's* men in charge of the prisoners made no resistance. On the morning of the same day, about 4 A.M., the camp at Kyaukmyaung was attacked by a gang estimated at 250 strong. Lieutenant Hudson, 12th Madras Infantry, beat them off; no casualties on our side. Enemy's loss, three killed and several wounded.

On the 20th, Lieutenant Tripp, 2nd Liverpool Regiment, commanding post at Natôgyi, proceeded with fifteen rifles, 2nd Liverpool Regiment, and twenty rifles, 11th Bengal Infantry, to Gwé Gwé, a village nine miles north-west of Natôgyi, said to be occupied by dacoits. Arrived there at dawn, surrounded the village, taking the people quite by surprise; a few shots were fired at the troops, and then the dacoits fled, escaping into the thick jungle; ten of their number were killed. No casualties on our side.

On the 21st, Captain Dundas, 2nd Liverpool Regiment, being at that time in command of a small mixed force at Meiktila, heard that the Kemmendine Prince, with 300 followers, was at Miah. He at once proceeded after them and was conducted by a Burman by circuitous route to cut off the party from the Bosodaung hills. After going some distance, they came in sight of several mounted men, about a mile and a half away. Captain Dundas, Lieutenant Eliott, Royal Artillery, and six sowars, 2nd Madras Lancers, at once gave chase and suddenly came on the whole force, about 300 mounted and 1,000 or more on foot, retiring over a fairly open country. The party rode through the infantry, who flung away their arms and dispersed in all directions, and made for the mounted men, pursuing them for three or four miles, killing twelve and wounding several others. Their horses being dead beat, the fugitives drew away from their pursuers, and the prince escaped. Lieutenant Elliott captured an armed *Hpongyi*. Only one other prisoner was taken.

On the 24th, Captain C. A. R. Sage, 18th Bengal Infantry, commanding at Alôn, with seventy-eight rifles, 18th Bengal Infantry, proceeded from that village to Kanthit, about ten miles distant, and attacked a gang of 300 to 400 dacoits, who had taken up a position in a monastery under the leadership of Nga Pau and Nga Kunzi. The dacoits were driven out and retreated, with a loss of two killed and four prisoners. No casualties on our side.

On the 25th, Major Warner, 2nd Madras Lancers, commanding at Kyauksé, moved out from that station, with a force as per margin, towards Zalé to attack a force collected in the neighbouring jungle.

9-1, Cinque Ports Division, Royal Artillery	2 guns.
Royal Welsh Fusiliers ..	21 rifles.
2nd Hants Regiment ..	20 "
23rd Wallajahbad Light Infantry	60 "
2nd Madras Lancers ..	20 lances.

The enemy was turned out of the position they had taken up and dispersed: loss unknown. On the same day, Major Egerton, 2nd Liverpool Regiment, commanding at Hlaingdet, attacked and dispersed a gang of rebels, about 500 strong, who had taken up a position in Thamusagôn, a village about five miles from Hlaingdet. Enemys' loss,—killed two, wounded six. Casualties on our side *nil*.

On the 26th the bridge over the Myittha Chaung, about three miles from Ava, was burned by dacoits from the villages in its neighbourhood. A detachment under Major Collins, 2nd Hants Regiment, moved at once from Ava, but was too late to find the dacoits or save the bridge. On the same day, the military post of Myinmu, at the entrance to the Mu river, was attacked, and several houses burned. Captain Badgeley, Royal Engineers, and one follower were severely wounded; the dacoits were beaten off.

On the 27th, Colonel A. D. Parsons, Commandant, 2nd Madras Lancers, proceeded with fifty-three lances, 2nd Madras Lancers, and fifty of the 25th Madras Infantry, under Lieutenant Burrows, to Tadaingshé, a village about twelve miles south-east of Mandalay, which they surrounded, and where they captured seventy-two prisoners, all dacoits,—six dacoits killed and wounded when attempting to escape; on our side one horse wounded. This was a very important capture of dacoits: of the prisoners, four were executed, over forty sentenced to imprisonment for various terms, and about twenty were released after full enquiry. On the same day Lieutenant Claud Hamilton, 18th Bengal Infantry, commanding at Yetagyo, proceeded with twenty-five rifles, 18th Bengal Infantry, and fifty friendly Burmans, to Shwémyo, a village about four miles north-west therefrom, to attack a gang of 150 dacoits, whom they drove out, killing five and taking five prisoners. Casualties on our side *nil.*

On the 1st May, Captain Macdonald, 2nd Hants Regiment, commanding at Myinthi, reported that at 1 o'clock that day, the village of Yegamo near Myinthi, was burned by about fifty mounted dacoits. He went out with twenty-five soldiers, and drove them off, killing five of their number. On the same date Subadar Lall Bahadar, 11th Bengal Infantry, commanding a detachment of his regiment at Sametkyôn, Myingyan district, pursued a band of fifty-nine dacoits, who had plundered the village of Zigôn. The dacoits made a stand at Zigôn, but were dislodged and ran away, losing three of their number, two of whom were headmen, killed, and two wounded. The villagers' property, nine carts, and twenty-one bullocks, were recovered.

3rd.—Lieutenant Holloway, 2nd Madras Lancers, proceeded with a party from Ava to the village of Thaungadôn, seven miles distant, where he defeated and dispersed a band of dacoits, killing five and taking ten prisoners.

4th.—Lieutenant Burrows, with a small force surrounded and surprised the village of Sowtôn, about twelve miles due south of

Mandalay, arresting twenty-eight men, who were identified as dacoits and several of whom had been present at the massacre of the Burmese policemen at Neyagan. The prisoners were made over to the civil power. No resistance was made by the villagers. On this date Subadar Bulleeraj Singh, 2nd Queen's own Bengal Light Infantry, with sixty rifles, left Sagu, in the Minhla district, for Napé. On the 5th instant he was joined at Kyunbya by the Deputy Commissioner, Mr. Phayre, with thirty rifles of the newly-raised Punjab Police. The following is the Subadar's account of the affair at Padeng on the 6th and following days:—

The force marched to Padeng, distant from Kyunbya twenty-four miles, and occupied a *Hpongyi Kyaung* near it, after slight resistance; the party halted on the 7th to allow of the baggage coming up: on the 8th Mr. Phayre ordered a march to Napé, but on drawing in the picquets preparatory to starting, a heavy fire was opened by the rebels from three sides, which was continued to 8 A.M., when Mr. Phayre took ten sepoys and ten Punjab Police, and entered the village, advancing towards the enemy. The rebels, on seeing him, fired a volley, and he fell wounded in the arm and stomach. Jamadar Surrubjeet Singh, with two men, tried to raise him, when the rebels fired a second volley, wounding a police sepoy and again hitting Mr. Phayre, this time in the chest, and killing him. The police then retired, and the Jamadar, being left alone, had to fall back, leaving Mr. Phayre's body on the ground. The Subadar subsequently sent thirty sepoys to recover Mr. Phayre's body, but it had been removed by the rebels, into whose hands his carbine, revolver, and watch fell. The firing continued all day on the 8th, and, on the 9th, being unable to communicate with head-quarters, and finding that ammunition was running short, the Subadar retired to Sagu.

5th.—At 5 A.M., the post at Mingin on the Chindwin river was attacked by about 100 dacoits, who were easily beaten off. Enemy's loss,—one man killed; number of wounded unknown. Casualties on our side,—two men wounded. On the same date a force as per margin, under command of Lieutenant Angelo, 23rd Wallajahbad Light Infantry, left Mandalay at noon for the opposite (western) bank of the Irrawaddy, and proceeded to Sadaung,

2nd Madras Lancers	..	25 lances.
2nd Hants Regiment	..	30 rifles.
Police Levy	..	100 ,,

where it was reported there was a large gathering of insurgents. Arriving there on the 6th it was found that the enemy had decamped. On the morning of the 7th, it being ascertained that the enemy was halted in the jungle a few miles off, the cavalry and some Hampshire Mounted Infantry were sent in pursuit, and found them in camp one mile to the west of Thazin, a village four miles from Sadaung. The enemy was completely surprised and bolted, the cavalry and mounted infantry pursuing for about three miles and killing sixty-six including three *bohs*. No casualties on our side.

10th.—Lieutenant Walton, 2nd Battalion, Royal Scots Fusiliers, with twenty men of his battalion, attacked a party of dacoits, about ten miles to the west of Imbetkôn, on the wet weather track, about twenty miles south of Yamethin; he burned their stockade and returned to Imbetkôn, which in his absence had been attacked by sixty dacoits, who carried off twelve bullocks and two cart-drivers belonging to his party. On the same date, Major Jenkins, civil officer, proceeding to Pyinmana with a few sepoys from Thayetpin and Nyaunggyin posts, and some friendly Burmans, attacked and dispersed a gang of dacoits over 100 strong, about two miles off the road between Yamethin and Bawhlaing. Three dacoits killed and several wounded.

On the same date, a small party of sepoys of the 18th Bengal Infantry were sent with the *Myook* of Mingin to disperse some dacoits reported to be at Patholôn. The party returned the same evening, having accomplished their task, killing three of the enemy and fifteen killed capturing three prisoners. On the same date, Lieutenant Claud Hamilton, 18th Bengal Infantry, reconnoitring from Yetagyo with thirty men, was attacked within a mile of the post by 300 dacoits, who were beaten off with a loss of fifteen killed and several wounded. Casualties on our side,—five wounded. On the same date, the native officer commanding the post at Myitche, opposite Pagan, pursued some dacoits who had plundered the neighbouring village of Naungbin; four of their number were killed and all the stolen property recovered. On the same date, Captain Smyth, Royal Artillery, routed an outpost of 600 insurgents, about thirty-two miles from Shwebo, driving them across the Mu and killing several, and subsequently dispersing the main body of 2,000 collected at Korthundi. The Prince (Maung Hmat) fled with a few followers.

15th.—Post at Myitche attacked at daylight by a large band of insurgents, estimated at 2,000; enemy driven off. Casualties on their side,—nine dead bodies found, six wounded and taken prisoners: many were seen to be carried off. Casualties on our side *nil*.

16th.—Lieutenants Higgins, 21st Madras Infantry, and Gough, 1st Battalion, Royal Welsh Fusiliers, with a few lances, 2nd Madras Lancers, and some mounted police, proceeded with the civil officer to Tezé near Ye-u, where they met Mr. Calogrœdy, who informed them that a party of insurgents, about 800 strong, had occupied Tingotgyi, four miles east of Tezé. The friendly Burmese, supported by the cavalry and mounted police, surprised and rushed Tingotgyi, and the dacoits, retiring into the open, were repeatedly charged and ridden through by the cavalry and police, and were thoroughly routed. Enemy's loss,—about 100 killed, including one *boh* and thirty-eight severely wounded, twelve prisoners. Our casualties—Lieutenant Gough, slightly wounded in the hand, one policeman also slightly wounded. On the same date Lieutenant Peacock, 2nd Battalion, Somersetshire Light Infantry, drove some of the followers of Buddha Yaza from the village of Pyingyi, about twenty-two miles south-west of Yamethin, with a loss of eleven wounded. Casualties on our side,—one man wounded.

17th.—Major Brown, 18th Bengal Infantry, with 100 men of his regiment marched from Mingin and drove a gang of dacoits, said to be 300 strong, from two villages, Minyan and Ingyindaung. Casualties on our side *nil*. On side of dacoits,—two wounded.

19th.—A force as per margin under command of Lieutenant-Colonel Fitzgerald, 26th Punjab Infantry, left Bhamo with orders to proceed to Karwan, the head-quarters of the Ponkan *Sawbwá*, stated to be about nineteen miles from Bhamo in the Kachin hills. The village was to be occupied, and, in the event of the *Sawbwá* refusing to submit to certain terms to be imposed on him by Major Cooke, the Political Officer with the force, his house was to be destroyed.

Hazara Mountain Battery ..	2 guns.
Royal Welsh Fusiliers ..	119 rifles.
4th Company, Bengal Sappers and Miners	80 "
26th Punjab Infantry ..	168 "

The troops proceeded as far as Pan-Yaung, overcoming all opposition. On the 24th, on the representation of the Political Officer to the effect that the *Sawbwá* had been sufficiently punished, that he had just heard that Karwan was within the Chinese frontier and that an attack on it might give rise to serious political difficulties with China, and that its capture would involve the previous destruction of two intervening villages, which was unadvisable, it was decided to advance no further; the force accordingly halted at Pan-Yaung for a few days and returned to Bhamo on the 28th. Enemy's loss during the advance and return,—ten killed, number of wounded unknown. Casualties on our side,—eight wounded.

20th.—Major Stead, 11th Bengal Infantry, with a flying column, defeated and dispersed about 1,000 insurgents, near Pakhangyi. Enemy's loss,—eight killed; no casualties on our side. On the same day a new post was established at Yewun, near Kyauksé, with a force as per margin. Slight opposition was made to the occupation of the post, one lancer being wounded by the *Thugyi* of South Yewun, who was himself wounded and taken prisoner.

9-1, Cinque Ports Division, Royal Artillery	..	1 gun.
2nd Madras Lancers	..	12 lances.
Somersetshire Light Infantry	..	50 rifles.
Queen's Own Sappers and Miners		50 ,,
23rd Wallajahbad Light Infantry		50 ,,

21st.—A party of fifty rifles under command of Lieutenant Fraser, 18th Bengal Infantry, proceeded from Mingin in a launch to a place between the villages of Htamaing and U, about fourteen miles down the river, where 150 dacoits were said to have erected a stockade. Owing to defective information they came on the enemy unexpectedly, before daylight, on the top of a hill instead of in the plain below. Enemy's loss,—two killed; two leather *jingals* and some *dahs* seized. Casualties on our side *nil*. On the same day Buddha Yaza, with 700 followers, attacked the post of Yanaung to the north of Yamethin, but was repulsed with a loss of twelve men killed.

22nd.—The Officer Commanding at Ava proceeded with a small force to Kyaukkawgyi and attacked and drove off some dacoits who had taken up a position on the Taungdaw range. Enemy lost one man killed, two prisoners taken. No casualties on our side.

The Officer Commanding Minbu reported on this date that Captain Channer, 2nd Bengal Infantry, met a column from Thayetmyo hotly engaged with about 300 dacoits under Bo Shwe at Taindah. Captain Channer co-operated with the Thayetmyo detachment and drove off Bo Shwe, killing twelve of his party and taking two prisoners.

The whole of Minhla district was reported to be in a very disturbed state, nearly all the officials being in open rebellion or disaffected.

24th.—Lieutenant Elliott, 2nd Liverpool Regiment, with sixty rifles, proceeding from Singu (Pagan district) on the morning of this day, was met at Singam by 800 rebels, and after a long fight routed them, killing thirteen of their number. No casualties our side.

On the 25th Captain Sage, 18th Bengal Infantry, commanding at Alôn, with eighty-two rifles, 18th Bengal Infantry, attacked a large gang, estimated at over 600 dacoits, led by four *bohs*, at the village of Padu, on the west bank of the Chindwin, driving them out of the village and dispersing them. Casualties on our side,—one sepoy slightly wounded. The enemy lost one man killed, and their standards were captured.

26th.—Captain Hastings, 25th Madras Infantry, commanding at Katha, proceeded with 100 men to Petsut, about eleven miles west of Katha, and attacked and captured a stockade held by 450 Shans, Kachins, and Burmese from Monhyin, Mawlu, and Manlé. The stockade was rushed from three points, and the enemy escaped, leaving six dead; several were wounded and were seen being carried off. No casualties on our side.

27th.—Major Wade, 2nd Liverpool Regiment, with a force as per margin, left Meiktila at 1 A.M. this day and proceeded to the village of Myogyigaung, about nine miles to the north-east, where he routed and dispersed a large collection of rebels, estimated at 1,000 strong, killing and wounding some seventy or eighty of their number. On the same day Lieutenant Fryer, 18th Bengal Infantry, proceeded up the Chindwin to U and destroyed a position taken up by dacoits at that village. No casualties on our side. Enemy's loss,—one man killed, one wounded.

Bombay Mountain Battery	..	2 guns.
2nd Madras Lancers	..	20 lances.
2nd Liverpool Regiment	..	10 rifles.
27th Punjab Infantry	..	60 „

On the same day Major Stead, 11th Bengal Infantry, in command of a small flying column on the west bank of the Irrawaddy, attacked and dispersed a gathering of rebels under the *ex-Wun* of Myingyan, at the village of Pangôn, ten miles from his camp at Myaing. Casualties on our side—one trooper, 2nd Madras Lancers, wounded; on the enemy's side,—four killed.

28th.—On this day Jamadar Brij Lall Singh, 2nd Bengal Infantry, with forty sepoys from Minhla, attacked a gathering of rebels twenty miles south-west of Malun, killing twelve and wounding several; no casualties on our side. On the same day, in concert with Brij Lall Singh, Jemadar Kanhye Pattack, 2nd Bengal Infantry, crossed from Sinbaungwe and attacked retreating enemy, killing five.

29th.—Lieutenant Huggins, 21st Madras Infantry, with a party of eighty-one rifles of his regiment, in company with the district officer and some police, attacked and destroyed the dacoit village of Kyundawgôn, about twenty miles north-west of Yeu; little resistance was made by the enemy, who deserted the village on our approach.

1st June.—A convoy of twenty-three carts, escorted by one naick and ten rifles, 26th Madras Infantry, proceeding from Minhla to Taungdwingyi, when passing through a jungle between Thityagauk and Kokogwa, was attacked by about sixty dacoits. The sepoys behaved very well, having quickly got together and fired volleys into the dacoits, who ran away, some nine or ten of their number being seen to drop. On the same date Lieutenant Churchill, Royal Scots Fusiliers, with a party of twenty-eight rifles, Royal Scots Fusiliers, attacked a gang of dacoits who were in the strongly-stockaded village of Thaikyansan in the Taungdwingyi district; after a prolonged resistance the position was carried at the point of the bayonet, the dacoits fighting well to the last. Eighty-five dacoits were killed and wounded. Casualties on our side—Lieutenant Churchill, wounded severely.

2nd.—Major Wade of the 2nd Liverpool Regiment, with a force as per margin, proceeded from Meiktila to Wundwin to disperse a band of rebels reported to be collected in the neighbourhood of that village, which is about twenty miles north-

2nd Liverpool Regiment	..	40 rifles.
27th Native Infantry	..	110 ,,
Bombay Mountain Battery	..	2 guns.
2nd Madras Lancers	..	5 lances.

east of Meiktila. They found the advance party of Maung Gyi's force in some *Kyaungs* to the north and east of the village, but these retired on approach of our troops, who camped at Wundwin, marching on the 4th to Aingda, a village about seven miles west, where the Kemmendine Prince and the Shwé-dah *Boh* were said to be located. Aingda was occupied by the enemy, who, however, retired when the force advanced on the village. No casualties and no loss to the enemy reported.

5th.—Lieutenant Delamain, 5th Bombay Light Infantry, with ten lances, 2nd Madras Lancers, and fifty rifles, 5th Bombay Light Infantry, accompanied by the Deputy Commissioner and a mounted force of friendly Burmans, attacked the village of Parabyan near Ladaw, sixteen miles south of Shwebo, held by about 200 dacoits, who, after firing a few shots, fled across a marsh to the east of the village, in which several were killed. No casualties on our side.

7th.—The village of Lamaing, about seventeen miles north-east of Mandalay, was occupied, and arrangements made for establishing a permanent military post there. The following garrison was detailed for the post, which was an important one, being close to the Shan frontier,—Captain J. E. Preston, 12th Madras Infantry, with 150 rifles, 12th Madras Infantry.

8th.—Lieutenant Hodson, 23rd Wallajahbad Light Infantry, with a force as per margin, was attacked on the night of this date by a band of rebels and dacoits under the leadership of Hla-U at Wadaw village, a few miles to the east of Alôn. The enemy forced the sentry and managed to reach the rest-houses occupied by the detachment before they were beaten off. Casualties on our side—eight sepoys of the 5th Bombay Light Infantry, and one sepoy and one follower, 23rd Wallajahbad Light Infantry, wounded. Enemy's loss not known.

23rd Wallajahbad Light Infantry,	38 rifles.
5th Bombay Light Infantry ..	50 „

Lieutenant-Colonel Toker, Commandant, 18th Bengal Infantry, with 152 rifles of that regiment, on his way up the Chindwin from Mingin to Kindat, attacked and drove the enemy out of Balet, a village on the right bank of the river, about forty miles from Mingin, and destroyed the stockade and *Myothugyi's* house. Casualties on our side—one sepoy slightly wounded. The enemy lost three killed; number of wounded unknown.

12th.—Captain Dunsford, 2nd (Queen's Own) Bengal Light Infantry, commanding at Salin, having received information that rebels were collecting to the north and west of the town with the view of attacking it, moved out with twenty rifles, 2nd Battalion, Liverpool Regiment, and twenty rifles, 2nd Bengal Light Infantry for five miles to the north, where a large body of the enemy was seen on the left flank, moving on Salin. Captain Dunsford changed direction to the left, and attacked and drove this party out of a position they had taken up, when they retired to a high hill and pagoda, two miles south of Salin. The hill was carried without casualty; a brisk fire was then exchanged with the pagoda, which was presently rushed and taken by our troops, led by Captain Dunsford and Lieutenant Wynyard, 2nd Liverpool Regiment. Casualties on our side—killed, Captain Dunsford, shot through the head in the final rush, and one private, 2nd Liverpool Regiment; wounded Lance-Corporal Lever, Lance-Sergeant Fox, both of Liverpool Regiment, two sepoys, 2nd Queen's Own Bengal Light Infantry. Enemy's loss not stated.

3-1, South Irish Division, R.A. ..	2 guns.
Royal Scots Fusiliers ..	50 rifles.
26th Madras Infantry ..	75 „

Lieutenant Dobbie, 26th Madras Infantry, with a force as per margin, left Taungdwingyi to reinforce the police stations at Satthawa and Gonnyindan, which were threatened by dacoits, and afterwards to attack the villages of Piongywa and Yahni. Lieutenant Dobbie reached the police stations on the 13th, and on the 14th attacked and dispersed a band of 200 insurgents at the village of Chaungywa, which they had just fired. The dacoits at Piongywa and Yahni, on hearing of his approach, fled, having previously successfully resisted an attack made on them by Lieutenant Parsons, Assistant Commissioner, from Kadingatha, a village in the north of the Miade township.

On the same date Lieutenant C. H. Clay, 43rd Gurkha Light Infantry, with 100 rifles, occupied Sé, a village a few miles to the south-east of Pagan. Slight opposition was offered, the party being fired on by a gang of about eighty dacoits, who, however, were easily driven off. Sé was afterward established as a military post.

On the same day Lieutenant Huggins, 21st Madras Infantry, with the force as per margin, proceeded from Yeu to Tezé, a village a few miles to the north-west, which was threatened by dacoits. The party found the village occupied by a large collection of dacoits, who were promptly driven out, ninety-two being killed, amongst whom were four *bohs*, and thirty-one, including six *bohs*, taken prisoners. Several standards, muskets, and *dahs* were taken, and the insurgents thoroughly dispersed.

Royal Welsh Fusiliers	.. 21 rifles.
21st Madras Infantry	..100 ,,
2nd Madras Lancers	.. 8 lances.
Mounted Police	.. 12 men.
Foot ,,	.. 52 ,,

15th.—Lieutenants Huggins, 21st Madras Infantry, and Gough, Royal Welsh Fusiliers, with a few cavalry, accompanied the civil officer and some mounted police from Yeu to Tezé, where they heard that 800 dacoits under *Boh* Nga Taw had occupied Tintotgyi (a village four miles to the east of Tezé), and intended attacking Tezé that night. The above officers, therefore, taking with them about 500 friendly Burmans from Tezé and Toktalok, at once proceeded to Tintogyi and surprised the dacoits, killing about eighty of their number and capturing twelve prisoners, amongst whom was the leader of the gang, Nga Taw.

17th.—In consequence of the mails from Kyaukmyaung to Shwebo having been looted on the 16th, parties of cavalry and mounted infantry went out from both the above places, and searched three villages supposed to be implicated in this business. About thirty prisoners were taken; five carts, full of loot, were found in the jungle and destroyed, and the dacoit village of Atchi was burned.

19th.—Captain C. A. R. Sage, 18th Bengal Infantry, commanding at Alôn, with the force as per margin, attacked Hla-U's band of dacoits near Magyiôk, Hla-U's village, and drove them from a position they had taken up on the banks of a neighbouring *nullah*. The dacoits dispersed, and Captain Sage destroyed the village of Magyiôk, which was evidently a dacoit village. It was rumoured that Hla-U was wounded in this affair, a rumour which was subsequently confirmed. No casualties on our side. Enemy's loss unknown.

18th Bengal Infantry	.. 30 rifles.
23rd Wallajahbad Light Infantry,	20 ,,
25th Bombay Light Infantry	.. 41 ,,
Military Levy ..	.. 25 ,,

On the same day Major J. A. D. Gordon, 2nd Queen's Own Bengal Light Infantry, in command of a flying column from Minbu, marched from Padein to Napé, which he occupied after having driven the enemy from a position on a hill to the west of the village. Major Gordon's fighting force consisted of the troops as per margin. The enemy's force was estimated at from 500 to 700. The rebels made a prolonged resistance, and held the infantry in check until the guns were brought into action at 200 yards distance. After firing thirty rounds the enemy's fire slackened, when the position was charged, and carried, the enemy retreating with their dead and wounded. Our casualties were,—Royal Artillery, killed: one battery *syce*; wounded severely, four non-commissioned officers and rank and file; slightly, two rank and file. 2nd Liverpool Regiment: killed, three rank and file; wounded slightly, Lieutenant E. P. Williams; severely, six rank and file. 2nd Queen's Own Bengal Light Infantry: killed, two rank and file; wounded, eight rank and file. Bengal Sappers and Miners: wounded, two rank and file.

7-1, North Irish Division, R. A.	2	guns.
2nd Liverpool Regiment ..	53	rifles.
2nd Bengal Light Infantry ..	95	"
Sappers and Miners ..	7	"

23rd.—Captain J. Grant, 25th Bombay Light Infantry, having been sent from Yewun, with 120 rifles, to intercept a reported movement of the Minzaing Prince, crossed the Panlaung at Myittha and marched to Taligôn, about three miles to the south. While halted, he was attacked by a party of rebels, who were driven off by Captain Wilbraham and a party of the Somersetshire Light Infantry, and retreated to Kumé, about four miles south of Taligôn; Captain Grant followed them and drove them from some outer monastery buildings into a walled enclosure surrounding a pagoda. Here they made an obstinate resistance for about an hour, when the place was carried with the bayonet. Four *jingals* and some ammunition were taken. The position was occupied for the night, and, as no further gatherings of rebels were found round Kumé, the force returned next day to Yewun. The casualties on our side were,—one Lance-Corporal killed; Captain Wilbraham, (since dead), and seven men, wounded. Enemy's loss unknown.

On the same date Captain C. S. Shephard, Deputy Assistant Adjutant and Quarter Master General, accompanied by Mr. Scott as civil officer, with fifty rifles and four lances, 2nd Madras Lancers, proceeded from Meiktila to Thaphan, a village which was reported threatened by dacoits; on arrival at Thaphan they were informed that the dacoits were at Kambé, five miles to the north; they then proceeded to Kambé and attacked the dacoits, who fled out of a *Hpongyi Kyaung*, about 200 yards from the village, at their approach. Casualties,—one dacoit killed and four taken prisoners; none on our side.

24th.—Lieutenant H. T. Shubrick, 2nd Somersetshire Light Infantry, proceeded with two guns and thirty men from Pyinmana to Theagôn, a military post on the Pyinmana-Yamethin road, about six miles from the former station, with orders to search certain villages in its vicinity which were known to be the haunts of dacoits. After destroying several villages near Theagôn on the 26th, Lieutenant Shubrick occupied the hamlet of Quingyi, where, while halted for breakfast, he was attacked on all sides by dacoits and killed, being struck in the neck by a bullet. The dacoits were eventually driven off, and the force returned to Pyinmana under command of Lieutenant Coxhead, Royal Artillery, with Lieutenant Shubrick's body. Casualties on our side,—one officer killed as above, two Burman police wounded, two elephants wounded. Enemy's loss unknown.

27th.—The Lamaing post, commanded by Captain J. E. Preston, 12th Madras Infantry, was attacked at night by a party of Shan dacoits, some of whom got inside the work and wounded Captain Preston: after some fighting the enemy were driven out. Casualties on our side,—killed, Jemadar Gopal Singh, 12th Madras Infantry, and one sepoy; wounded, Captain J. E. Preston, and four privates, 12th Madras Infantry.

29th.—Lieutenant Ayerst, 5th Bombay Light Infantry, with twenty rifles, 5th Bombay Light Infantry, when returning to his post at Sheinmaga in boats, after surveying near Mingon Pagoda, was fired at from the village of Pôgôn and its pagoda. He at once landed, and after a fight of about three-quarters of an hour, succeeded in driving the enemy (about 100 dacoits) from the pagoda and village; on returning to his boats, however, he was again fired at. Loss of the enemy not known, though several were seen to drop; casualties on our side,—wounded Lieutenant Ayerst, slightly; Subadar Shaikh Cassim, slightly; two rank and file, slightly.

3rd July.—Lieutenant Dobbie, 26th Madras Infantry, who had left Taungdwingyi on the 26th June, in pursuit of dacoit bands, proceeded from Magyicho with twenty-four rifles, Royal Scots Fusiliers, and forty-five rifles, 26th Madras Infantry, and surprised and dispersed Ngawin Yaung's gang, destroying their stronghold in the jungles, three miles east of Satthwa, and capturing the whole of their property, including many arms and much ammunition. No casualties on our side; enemy's loss unknown. On the same date Major Sorrell, Royal Artillery, commanding a force which had been sent from Yamethin on the 1st instant, attacked and destroyed Buddha Yaza's stockade at Lizan, in the forests to the west of Imbetkon. He pursued the enemy on the 4th and 5th, but had to return to Yamethin owing to sickness and want of rations. Buddha Yaza and his followers were dispersed, and their place of rendezvous burned. Casualties on our side,—one private, Somersetshire Light Infantry, dangerously wounded. Enemy's loss unknown.

On the morning of the 4th, Jemadar Imam Khan, of the 26th Madras Infantry, in command of a party of thirty rifles, 26th Madras Infantry, proceeding on escort duty from Taungdwingyi to Minhla, was attacked at Thityagauk by 200 dacoits, of whom seventy were Shans. Having had previous intimation of the probability of an attack, the Jemadar had made his dispositions, and after an hour's fighting the dacoits were driven off, with a loss of sixteen killed and thirty-three wounded. No casualties on our side.

On the same day, Lieutenant Gough, Royal Welsh Fusiliers, who had been sent from Yeu with a small force to disperse some dacoits in the neighbourhood of Tezè, came upon a band at the village of Lekse. The dacoits fled on the approach of our troops; the cavalry and mounted infantry killed twelve of their number. No casualties on our side.

7th.—Colonel Le Mesurier, commanding at Myingyan, attacked and carried a position on Petkyudaung, six miles south-east of Natôgyi and about twenty miles due east of Myingyan, held by the rebels. The attacking column was about 200 strong. The enemy fled on the advance of the troops, making slight show of opposition.

Their defences on the hill were destroyed, and the force returned to Myingyan. Lieutenant Gayer, 21st Madras Infantry, who had been sent to the village of Paya with 100 men, to co-operate with Colonel LeMesurier and cut off the retreat of the enemy, was attacked by the rebels on the 6th instant, the day before Colonel LeMesurier delivered his attack, and compelled to fall back on Myingyan, with a loss of one Burman policeman killed, one private, 21st Madras Infantry, and two followers, slightly wounded. Two boxes of Snider ammunition in charge of the police were lost here, the animals carrying them being frightened by the firing, and bolting into the jungle.

8th.—Captain A. A. Pearson, Deputy Assistant Adjutant and Quarter Master General, 3rd brigade, with forty rifles, under Lieutenant Boileau, 27th Bengal Infantry, proceeded on this date from Meiktila to Ywathit, a village about twelve miles distant, to disperse a gathering of dacoits. They, however, heard of his approach and scattered before his arrival at the village; three prisoners and a few arms were taken.

9th.—Lieutenant-Colonel Baber, 3rd Palamcottah Light Infantry, with a small force, proceeded from Pyinmana to Wahnagôn, a village about ten miles to the south-west, which was occupied by a guard of seventy-five rifles, 1st Bombay Grenadiers, and was reported to be hard pressed by dacoits. The detachment arrived at Wahnagôn, about 1 P.M., to find that the *Myoôk* and guard had two hours previously evacuated the village, which was in flames. Lieutenant-Colonel Baber attacked and drove off the dacoits, who were stated to be about 700 in number, and returned to Pyinmana *viâ* Ehla, a post about ten miles to the south of that station, and where the surrounding country was apparently quiet.

11th.—Jemadar Imamuddin Khan, 18th Bengal Infantry, proceeded up the Chindwin from Kindat with fifty rifles, 18th Bengal Infantry, and attacked some rebels in a stockade about eight miles from the station. He killed four, and took eight prisoners. No casualties reported on our side. On this date a party of about 120 dacoits was found entrenched about 600 yards from the military post at Se, Pagan district. They were at once dispersed by the detachment of 43rd Gurkha Light Infantry under Lieutenant Clay. No casualties on our side; two of the enemy were wounded.

15th.—Lieutenant King, 1st Battalion, Royal Welsh Fusiliers, in command of a small column from Shwebo, attacked and after two hours' fighting dispersed a body of dacoits about 800 strong, who had occupied the walled town of Yatha. Enemy's loss,—twenty-six killed. Casualties on our side, one sepoy, military police, severely, and two sepoys, 5th Bombay Light Infantry, slightly wounded. This was a very dashing affair. The town of Yatha was protected with a heavy embankment, well-provided with firing places, and defended with abatis and other obstacles; and the garrison, a strong one, held out until the place was carried by the bayonet.

17th.—Lieutenant-Colonel Baker, 2nd Hants Regiment, with a force as per margin, proceeded from Lamaing and destroyed the Shan villages of Kyabin, Nyaungbintha, and Zibyubin, the inhabitants of which had recently attacked our military post at Lamaing. Considerable opposition was met with: the villages, and road leading to them, were in dense jungle, which greatly favoured our opponents. The dacoits kept up a continual fire on the force without exposing themselves, our men having to fire at the puffs of smoke, and the smoke hanging in these forests to such an extent as to obscure the view. After the destruction of the above villages, the troops returned to Lamaing. Casualties on our side,—killed, one private, 5th Bombay Light Infantry; died of his wounds, one *bhistie*, 12th Madras Infantry; wounded, one sergeant, 2nd Hants Regiment; nine rank and file, 5th Bombay Light Infantry. Enemy's loss unknown, but two dead bodies were found outside the village of Zibyubin.

9-1, Cinque Ports Division, R.A.	1 gun.
2nd Hants Regiment ..	50 rifles.
5th Bombay Light Infantry ..	50 „
43rd Assam Light Infantry ..	100 „
12th Madras Infantry ..	50 „

21st.—Major Lynch, 1st Bombay Grenadiers, with a force consisting of 150 men and two guns, moved out from Pyinmana and destroyed the villages of Yebaya, Indinetha, and Kanhla, all occupied by rebels, who made considerable opposition before they were driven off. Casualties on our side,—two British soldiers killed and one wounded, two privates, 1st Bombay Grenadiers, wounded; enemy's loss unknown. Having performed this duty, the troops returned to camp.

23rd.—Major Sorrell, Royal Artillery, with two guns and 218 men from Pyinmana, attacked about 700 dacoits and rebels who had again collected in the village of Gyinlo, driving them out of it, and subsequently out of the village of Sanyadôn, three miles further on. Our casualties,—three sepoys wounded. Enemy's loss,—four killed, five prisoners. On the same day Lieutenant Huggins, 21st Madras Infantry, with a small force, attacked and dispersed an outpost of the dacoit leader Hla-U at Pagan Lekti, a few miles from Yeu, killing five of their number.

24th.—Lieutenant Rainey, 1st Madras Pioneers, commanding at Myitche, opposite to Pagan, dislodged several dacoits from positions they had taken up in Jugdu and at a pagoda. Enemy's loss,—three dead bodies found, three *jingals*, some guns, two ponies, and five prisoners. No casualties on our side.

26th.—On this date Lieutenant-Colonel Toker accompanied by the Deputy Commissioner, Chindwin district, and a party of troops from Kindat, arrived at Thaungdut, where the Sawbwa was disposed to be friendly, but stated he was quite capable of protecting his own territory, and expressed a hope that no post of British troops would be formed at his town.

On this date Mr. Munford, Assistant Superintendent of Police, with 114 mounted police and friendlies, supported by a small force under Lieutenant Huggins, 21st Madras Infantry, surprised a gang of about 500 dacoits, who were engaged in burning the village of Kanbya, about sixteen miles south-west of Yeu, and killed over 150 of them. No casualties on our side. Subsequently, the force occupied the dacoit leader Hla-U's village Magyiôk about twenty miles south of Yeu, near which two *Bohs* were killed and one taken prisoner by the Burmese police. Hla-U escaped into thick jungle, where it was impracticable to follow him with troops with any prospect of success; the force therefore returned to Yeu.

28th.—Major Collins, 2nd Hants Regiment, with 100 men, proceeded in the I.G.S. *Irrawaddy* and four launches to the island of Aingdaing, above Sheinmaga, on which it was reported large numbers of dacoits resided, and from which several dacoities were said to have been recently committed. The island was surrounded by the launches, and the troops landed and searched the villages. No resistance was made. Most of the male inhabitants appeared to be away, and, as from the enquiries of the civil officer there appeared to be no doubt that the villages of Shwégyatyan and Aingdaing were engaged in dacoity and the reception of stolen goods, they were destroyed. Eight prisoners were taken. The island and the west bank of the river were searched for war-boats or such as were likely to be used for dacoity, of which four were found and brought back to Mandalay.

Major J. A. D. Gordon, 2nd Queen's Own Bengal Light Infantry, with part of the garrison of Salin, in the Minbu district, attacked and dislodged from their positions two large bands of rebels which were threatening Salin, but he was not strong enough to break them up and disperse them, and accordingly applied for re-inforcements which were duly sent to him.

On the same date Major Dudley Persse, 2nd Somersetshire Light Infantry, commanding at Ava, and Lieutenant Campbell, 25th Madras Infantry, commanding at Myinthi, made a successful combined attack on the notorious dacoit village Magyi, in the Ava district, surprising the inhabitants, who made resistance, and killing thirteen rebels, amongst whom were three chiefs. Two dacoit leaders and thirty-three others were taken prisoners. Casualties on our side,—one trooper, Madras Lancers, wounded.

30th.—Major Lynch, 1st Bombay Grenadiers, with 150 men and two guns, proceeded to Kanhla, four miles from Pyinmana and found it re-occupied by the rebels since the last occasion of its being attacked on the 21st. The village and stockade were destroyed, no opposition being offered, beyond a few shots fired at the rear-guard on the return to Pyinmana. No casualties.

31st.—Major J. A. D. Gordon, commanding at Salin, described himself as surrounded by, and engaged with, the enemy night and day, since the morning of the 30th; ammunition running short and suburbs of the town burned down. On this day reinforcements of fifty rifles, 2nd Hants, and 100 rifles, Native Infantry, under command of Captain Atkinson, 2nd Hants Regiment, arrived at Salin and drove off the rebels with great slaughter, their bodies being taken away in cart-loads. Casualties on our side,—killed; Captain Atkinson, 2nd Hants Regiment, commanding relieving force. Enemy's loss unknown.

Of these hundred engagements the military operations of special interest were—

(1) the Pônkan expeditions from Bhamo;

(2) the withdrawal of the Napé garrison, and the relief of Salin in the Minbu command;

(3) the death of Mr. Phayre, Deputy Commissioner, of Minhla.

Further details of the Pônkan Expedition will be found in the chapter on the Kachins. A note on headings (2) and (3) is given below.

THE WITHDRAWAL OF THE NAPE GARRISON AND THE RELIEF OF SALIN IN THE MINBU COMMAND.

Napé is situated in the *terai jungle* at the foot of the Arakan Yoma hills, some thirty-five miles due west of Minbu. Previous to the 19th June 1886 it had been the head-quarters of the noted rebel leader Boh Shwé; but on that date it was occupied by a force under Major Gordon, 2nd Bengal Infantry, as it was found necessary to give a blow to the great local prestige which Boh Shwé had derived from the unfortunate death of Mr. Phayre, the Deputy Commissioner of the district.

The following account is extracted from the History of the 6th Brigade by General Low:—

Reports, however, soon commenced of great sickness amongst the garrison: the sick were relieved, but the men who took their places got sick in their turn, and eventually Napé became so unhealthy that it was found impossible to keep troops there, and the post had to be abandoned.

On arrival of Brigadier-General Low, C.B., at Minbu, on 24th July, to direct the movements for the withdrawal from Napé, there were sick in the Minbu Hospital—

2 European officers.	138 Native soldiers.
56 ,, soldiers.	38 Followers.

The large majority of these had contracted fever at Napé, and the sick at that place were reported to be altogether about 150 men.

A force of 100 native infantry left Minbu on the 28th July with an ambulance column of dandies and stretchers carried by Burmans, and carts with food, and safely reached Napé on the 31st July. The withdrawal commenced on the 2nd August, and the column arrived safely at Minbu with the following sick—

51, Liverpool Regiment.	73, Native Infantry.
10, Royal Artillery.	31, Followers.

It must here be noticed that of the effective men that marched in from Napé, almost all were afterwards invalided to India, and, speaking generally, the attempt to occupy that place during the rains cost not less than 500 men in invalids.

While the retirement from Napé was proceeding, the post of Salin was attacked by large numbers of dacoits under Ottama *Hpongyi*, who had been joined by a portion of Boh Shwé's men. The only available troops at the time, and till the retirement from Napé was completed, were some troops returning from an expedition to Pin in the interior, on the east side of the river. This force was due at the post of Singu on the east bank of the Irrawaddy, about twenty miles below Pagan, on the 29th July. The steamer *Sir William Peel* was sent up from Minbu to Singu to take the troops on board and land 100 of them at Sinbyugyun, where, being joined by fifty Native Infantry from Yenangyaung, they were directed to move on Salin.

This was done, and Salin was relieved, Captain Atkinson of the Hampshire Regiment who commanded the column being killed just as success was achieved.

The abandoning of the post of Napé, which was occupied with a view to diminishing the prestige of Boh Shwé, was under the circumstances a most undesirable move, but it will be seen from the above remarks in General Low's History that the deadliness of the climate rendered it imperative. The Chief Commissioner, referring to this, says :—

We have had to withdraw post from Napé in Boh Shwé's country, by reason of extreme sickness among garrison. This is regrettable, but unavoidable. We shall occupy again when season improves.

It was only with the greatest difficulty that it could be relieved when it was. With two large gangs of dacoits in the field, Boh Shwé's near Napé and Ottama's near Salin, and 234 sick in hospital at Minbu, it became a very hard task to provide a sufficient garrison for Minbu, and a sufficient escort for the 134 sick to be withdrawn from Napé. As it was, 100 Native Infantry were all that could be spared. In addition to these difficulties, the Burmese had such an aversion to being taken out to Napé, that, to avoid accompanying the relieving column as cart-drivers and bearers, all those who were not placed under military guard ran away from Minbu into the surrounding *jungles*. The difficulties of the situation were further enhanced by the investiture of Salin by Ottama's gang, and the immediate need for its relief. General Low, however, made the best use of the very limited means at his disposal, and made a complete success of both operations.

Salin was situated about ten miles from the banks of the Irrawaddy, on an alluvial plain, and was one of the many old walled towns which are to be found dotted about the country. It was about 1,100 yards long by 650 broad, but the walls, which must originally have been about twenty feet high and twenty-five feet thick, were old and in several places broken down. On the north-eastern and southern sides thickly populated suburbs had sprung up, extending from one to two miles. At the time when the town was occupied by a detachment of the field force the numerous trees and luxuriant vegetation in these suburbs formed a dense *jungle* up to its very walls. The object of Ottama *Hpongyi* was to burn the old city inside the walls, as Boh Shwé had promised to ally himself with him if he succeeded in doing so. The small garrison of fifty-three rifles, Liverpool Regiment, and eighty-three rifles, 2nd Bengal Infantry, lined the old walls as far as possible and devoted themselves to keeping the dacoits out; a few dacoits did once effect an entrance through a gap, but they were all captured. The *jungle* and trees of the suburbs were so dense that no signalling could be established, and out of the four Burmese messengers who were slipped over the walls during the nights, only one escaped with his message. The dacoits were able to keep out of sight so close up to the walls that, when the detachment of the Hampshire Regiment came to the relief, Captain Atkinson was shot forty yards from the walls by a *jingal* in position between himself and the besieged garrison. The siege had lasted three days. As soon as the garrison was relieved all the troops turned out and drove off the enemy, inflicting severe loss on them; but no accurate estimate of their casualties could be obtained, as they carried as many as they could away in carts.

Another great difficulty which presented itself at Minbu at this time was the disposal of the sick. The allowance for the station hospital was only eighteen beds, and now there were 119 European and 211 native soldiers sick, besides sixty-nine followers. The previous long lists of sick had almost exhausted the stock of medicine, and tried the powers of the very limited hospital staff to the uttermost, and for the work they did in this very trying time the greatest credit is due to them.

THE DEATH OF MR. PHAYRE, DEPUTY COMMISSIONER OF MINHLA.

The great importance attached to the death of Mr. Phayre at the hands of Boh Shwé's gang was due to the fact that it established Boh Shwé's prestige in the district; and that from this time till Brigadier-General Low had repeatedly beaten his gangs whenever they showed themselves, Minbu was one of the most unsettled districts in Upper Burma. At the time when Mr. Phayre was killed, Boh Shwé, for whose head Rs. 1,000 was offered, had offered Rs. 500 for Mr. Phayre's head, and out of this he made great capital amongst his adherents.

The following is the official account of Mr. Phayre's death—

On the 4th of May 1886, a party of two Native officers and fifty sepoys was despatched by the Officer Commanding at Minbu to establish a military post at Napé in the Minhla district, where the rebels, under the noted leader, Boh Shwé, were reported to be collecting. On the following day, Mr. Phayre, the Deputy Commissioner, started from Minbu with about fifty of the newly organized police, intending to go to a place called Pylôngyaw North, where there were then thirty sepoys in an entrenched position, and where all was quiet; his purpose being to visit the villages in that direction, and distribute the new police. He afterwards changed his original plan, and joined the military party *en route* to Napé. Arriving at Padein, they found the place occupied by the insurgents, who held a strong position in a walled pagoda. Mr. Phayre, after driving in the enemy's advance guard, established himself on the evening of the 7th in another pagoda, 200 yards from that occupied by the rebels. His party was fired into all that night, during which Boh Shwé received large reinforcements. On the 8th Mr. Phayre, against the advice of the Native officers, taking with him ten sepoys and ten police, attempted to carry the enemy's post by direct attack. They were within twenty yards of the pagoda, when Mr. Phayre fell, struck by three bullets. The sepoys and police advanced to his assistance, but, owing to the heavy fire, were obliged to retire, leaving the body, which was carried off before reinforcements came up. The report that the detachment ran short of ammunition proves to be incorrect. The number of the enemy was estimated at 700. Mr. Phayre's body was subsequently recovered at Padein, unmutilated.

Mr. Phayre joined the detachment for Napé without the knowledge or consent of the Officer Commanding at Minbu. If his intention of sharing in the operations of the detachment had been known, the Officer Commanding would not have permitted him to go unaccompanied by a British officer in charge of the troops. His death is much regretted by the Government of India, and is a serious loss to Sir Charles Bernard and the Administration of Upper Burma. He was a brave and able officer, and had done exceptionally good work in the Minhla district.

The following is an extract from a circular from the Upper Burma Secretariat bearing on this subject—

Mr. Phayre died most gallantly; he has done excellent service, and the Chief Commissioner can only mourn his loss. But he deems it right to circulate this notice of the circumstance to you in order that you may be cautioned to avoid the mistake of—

(1) going against large bodies of dacoits or rebels with insufficient force;

(2) leading or sending on duty of this kind, or posting in the interior, bodies of half-trained military police. In fairness to these men, in accordance with the Chief Commissioner's order, and for the good of the country, they must be kept at head-quarters or at military posts where they can be properly trained until they are fit to meet an enemy, who usually attack or stand only when they greatly outnumber our men;

(3) taking command of sepoys when any officer (European or Native) is present with the force, or over-ruling the responsible military officer in command on a matter concerning the movement of the troops.

Of course emergency may happen when the responsible military officer is wounded, or otherwise incapable of acting, and it may be right for the civil officer on the spot practically to take command. When a panic occurs among a section of a force and no other officer is near, a civil officer may interpose with advantage. But it is not the duty of a civil officer to lead troops in action when any commissioned or competent non-commissioned officer is present; nor should a civil officer go in the front of a military force in action, unless it be clearly his duty to be there, either in order to guide the troops or to keep native guides up to their duty, or to prevent avoidable bloodshed by parleying with villagers or with the enemy.

The Chief Commissioner is glad to know that the civil officers serving in Upper Burma are gallant Englishmen who would court, rather than flinch from, personal danger. But he wishes to remind you that it is not ordinarily your duty to be at the head of troops or of military police in action against

insurgents and dacoits. The evil done to the Administration and to the district by the death of an officer in Mr. Phayre's position in an action with dacoits is great, and the risk of causing such evil ought not to be lightly incurred.

CHAPTER XVII.

GENERAL SITUATION IN JULY 1886.

EARLY in 1886 it was recognized that troops alone could not suffice for the work of pacification, but that the special difficulties in Burma would be overcome rather by the vigorous administration of civil government, and by the creation of an efficient police, than by the employment of military detachments scattered over the face of the country. Reinforcements of troops were at any time obtainable from India, but the available reserve of efficient police was much more limited. As the Burmese character is averse to discipline, and as the old Burmese police were incapable of coping with the dacoits and rebel bands, no time was lost in issuing orders for enlisting, training, and sending over to Burma a large body of police recruited from the warlike races of the Punjab and the North-West Provinces of India. In addition to 2,000 volunteers from the Indian police, and to the ordinary native police force of Lower Burma, 6,530 trained recruits were sent to Upper and Lower Burma during the rainy season of 1886; so that, with the 24,184 troops already in that country, the total of troops and military police for service throughout the whole province rose to 32,720.

Formation of Military Police.

It will not be out of place to remark here that the Irrawaddy Flotilla Company, which had rendered such great assistance in the advance on Mandalay, did even more for the country after the annexation than before. They put on express steamers, without cargo flats, to run once a week between Rangoon and Mandalay, and improved communication between Mandalay and Bhamo by running regular weekly steamers. They also instituted short services between Mandalay and important stations up and down the Irrawaddy, and began to ply regularly on the Chindwin river. For these new lines the company received no subsidy, though they obtained a large amount of Government work. Every steamer carried a small guard of troops or disciplined police for protection. A large flotilla of Government steamers had to be placed on the rivers to facilitate the movements of troops, to prevent the crossing of armed bands of rebels or dacoits, to keep down river piracy, and to generally patrol the rivers; but the assistance received from the commercial flotilla was invaluable.

It will be remembered that when General White took over command of the troops in Upper Burma on 31st March 1886, his force was divided into two brigades, with head-quarters at Mandalay and Bhamo respectively, and two independent commands at Pyinmana and Taungdwingyi. In June the Pyinmana command was constituted into a third brigade, and this organization of the Upper Burma Field Force held good till the commencement of the winter campaign in October, when the whole distribution was re-organized.

First reinforcements.

In the spring of 1886 the Upper Burma Field Force was reinforced by the Somersetshire Light Infantry, the 26th Punjab Infantry, the 5th and 23rd Bombay Infantry, and the 43rd Assam Light Infantry (now the 7th Gurkhas), bringing the total up to 14,000 fighting men of all arms. Subsequently further reinforcements were sent—the 3rd Gurkhas, 16th Madras Infantry, and 23rd Bombay Infantry. These reinforcements were absolutely necessary to assist the existing garrisons to maintain themselves in the positions they then held, and to lessen the work they would be called on to peform during the ensuing trying months. The troops were all hutted, the posts fortified and made easily defensible, and strict orders were issued that none but absolutely essential operations against dacoits were to be undertaken. The objects of these precautions were to minimise the evil effects of the climate and to economise the resources of the troops, so that they might take the field for a winter campaign in the greatest possible state of efficiency.

Casualties.

It is here interesting to note that in spite of all precautions taken, between the 17th November 1885, when the expedition first crossed the frontier, and the 31st October 1886, the field force, averaging some 13,000 men, was deprived of the services of 3,053 fighting men of all ranks by the ravages of disease. Of these, eleven officers and 919 European and Native rank and file had died, and seventy-six officers and 1,956 European and Native rank and file were invalided to India; amongst the latter are included some wounded officers and men. The fatal casualties in action during the same period were officers eleven, European and Native rank and file eighty. Thus, the total loss to the Field Force prior to the commencement of the winter campaign was 3,144, or rather more than 20 per cent. of the greatest number of troops at any one time in the field. The diseases claiming the most victims were malarial fever, dysentery, cholera, and heat apoplexy. The malarial fever was most malignant during the rains, especially in the localities of Bhamo, Katha, Napé, and Thabyebin.

In spite of the additional troops sent to Burma in the spring of 1886, raising the total to 14,000, it was evident that this number was barely adequate to perform the duties which they were called on to do.

The Quarter Master General commenting on General White's description of the military position on 17th July 1886, stated as follows:—

It is manifest from the disposition given by General White that, although there are some 14,000 troops in Upper Burma, there is not a man too much; indeed, it seems to the Commander-in-Chief that many of the districts are but weakly held.

Although it may not be advisable to send mor^ men at this season of the year to Burma, Sir Frederick Roberts would strongly advise reinforcements being prepared and transport provided, so that they might reach Rangoon by the 15th October, by which time it seems certain that General White's present force will be weakened by the ordinary casualties of war and climate.

In the opinion of His Excellency it will be desirable to bring away all, or nearly all, of the regiments and batteries sent to Burma last October, and the Commander-in-Chief would propose that the relieving regiments, or as many as General White may think necessary, be despatched from India so as to reach Rangoon by the 15th October. In carrying this out, the relieved regiments could remain in Burma during the winter months, unless any of them should be so sickly as to require being moved at an earlier date.

This arrangement would add considerably to General White's force, and with the addition of the three regiments of cavalry he has applied for to be sent to him next November, he should be able to take the initiative throughout all the disturbed districts.

Sir Frederick Roberts thinks General White shows a wise discretion in avoiding complication with the Shans, and trusts it may be found altogether unnecessary to use force against them; but if such a course is unavoidable, it is better that such operations should be postponed until the people in the plains have been brought to order.

It is evident to the Commander-in-Chief that, in addition to operations in Upper Burma, it will be necessary to open out the country between Manipur and Kindat, and His Excellency would suggest that this should be carried out as an entirely distinct operation under the orders of the General Officer Commanding the Eastern Frontier District; General White has his hands full and should not be required to do more.

If the above suggestion is accepted by the Government of India, the General Officer Commanding Eastern Frontier District will be communicated with in regard to the number of men to be employed, the best season of the year for the operation, the most suitable class of transport for the work, and such other arrangements as may be considered necessary, all of which will require careful consideration beforehand.

General White's report above referred to is subjoined *in toto.*

From MAJOR-GENERAL G. S. WHITE, V.C., C.B., *Commanding Burma Field Force, to the Quarter Master General in India, Simla,—dated Mandalay, the* 17*th July* 1886.

In reply to your deferred telegram of the 12th July, I have the honour to submit the following report of the military position in Upper Burma, and the military plans now being carried out and proposed for the future with a view to the pacification of the country.

(*a*) *The Military position in Upper Burma.*

2. The Field Force is divided into three brigades. The First Brigade, commanded by Brigadier-General Low, C.B., Bengal Army, has its head-quarters at Mandalay; the Second Brigade, commanded by Brigadier-General Griffith, Madras Army, at Bhamo; the Third Brigade, commanded by Brigadier-General Anderson, Bombay Army, at Pyinmana. In addition to these three brigades, the garrison of Taungdwingyi, furnished originally by troops from Lower Burma Command, has reported direct to Field Force Head-quarters.

3. Crossing the old frontier in the Sittang valley, the district held by the Third Brigade is first reached. The principal garrisons are—Pyinmana, Yamethin, Yindaw, Hlaingdet, Meiktila, and Mahlaing, with several smaller communication posts now in process of redistribution. These garrisons occupy

the country from Pyinmana to Hlaingdet on the extreme east, and then cross the continent of Upper Burma to the valley of the Irrawaddy at Mahlaing.

The strength of the Brigade is :—

One battery, Royal Artillery (elephant).[1] 31 Cavalry.
One division,[2] Royal Artillery (mule). 556 British Infantry.
1,524 Native Infantry.

As the Pyinmana and Yamethin districts have been much disturbed, reinforcements have been ordered and are now on their way to join the Third Brigade. They consist of two companies, 1st Bombay Grenadiers, from Toungoo and the 16th Madras Native Infantry from India. The latter is included in the reinforcement of three battalions referred to further on as *en route*.

4. Following the eastern margin of our occupation, *viz.*, the line of the Shan Hills north of Meiktila and Hlaingdet, there is a tract of country we have not yet occupied. The most important point is Wundwin, which will be garrisoned in a few weeks.

5. In the occupation of the country more remote from Mandalay, it has been found advisable, for more immediate communication and support, to organize the garrisons into district groups under one command.

North of the unoccupied tract referred to in the last paragraph lies the Kyauksé district of the First or Mandalay Brigade. It consists of four garrisons or posts, *viz.* :—Kyauksé, Yéwun, Kinywa and Taloksu, the last-named being a communication post which connects Kyauksé district with the Myit Myitngé river, and by it and the Irrawaddy, with Mandalay. The collective strength of these garrisons is—

One division, Royal Artillery (Mountain). 219 British Infantry, and
30 Cavalry. 608 Native Infantry.

6. The valley of the Myitngé is garrisoned by three posts—

Paleik (included in the Ava district), Migyaundet, and Kywetnahpa.

The two latter are held by levies under the Chief Commissioner.

7. To return to the old frontier, in the Irrawaddy valley, we first meet with the post of Taungdwingyi, some distance inland from the left bank.

This post has been referred to in paragraph 2. Its strength is—

One division, Royal Artillery.[2] 149 British Infantry.
189 Native Infantry.

8. Following the Irrawaddy upwards the district commands of the 1st Brigade have their head-quarters at—Minbu, Pagan, Myingyan, Ava, Sagaing, Mandalay, Shwebo, Tabayen, and the Chindwin valley.

[1] With mountain equipment.
[2] Of a battery.

9. It will be seen that the first, or Mandalay, Brigade is out of all proportion to the other two; but this division of the commands is the most convenient for communication and correspondence.

10. The districts named in paragraph 8 have many outposts, the commanders of which are under the immediate orders of the officers commanding the named district.

11. Minbu has outposts at—Sinbaunggwé, Minhla, Salin, Sinbyugyun, Yenangyaung, Sagu, Napé. The strength of these garrisons was by last return—

1 division, Royal Artillery. 224 British Infantry.
709 Native Infantry.

12. Still proceeding up-stream, Pagan district comes next. It has outposts at—Pôpa, Singu, Myitche, Sé, and Pakokku The aggregate strength of these districts was by last return—

2 divisions, Royal Artillery. 214 British Infantry.
514 Native Infantry.

13. The district of Myingyan has outposts at—Natôgyi, Sametkyun, Taungtha, Yetagyo. The strength was—

1 division, Royal Artillery. 229 British Infantry.
22 Madras Cavalry. 567 Native Infantry.

14. The Ava district has posts at—Ava, Chaungwa, Myinthi, Myotha, Paleik. These posts all report direct to the Brigadier-General at Mandalay. The strength is as follows:—

	Cavalry.	British Infantry.	Native Infantry.
Ava	28	53	73
Chaungwa ..	..	..	152
Myinthi	..	..	64
Myotha	..	46	86
Paleik	..	..	140

15. The Saigain district has posts at—

	Cavalry.	British Infantry.	Native Infantry.
Saigain	..	108	90
Myinmu	..	..	129
Sheinmaga ..	..	..	128

Chaungu and Samun are also held by levies under the Chief Commissioner.

16. The Mandalay district has outposts at—Yankintaung, Lamaing, Madaya, and Taunggyi (Taungni ?). The aggregate strength of Mandalay and these outposts was by last return—

⅔rds of a garrison battery. 153 Madras Lancers.
1 division,[1] mountain battery. 726 British Infantry.
3,224 Native Infantry.

[1] Of a battery.

17. The Shwebo district has two garrisons—Shwebo, Kyaukmyaung. The latter is on the Irrawaddy and is the Shwebo river-base of supply.

The aggregate garrisons are—

1 division,[1] Royal Artillery.	195 British Infantry.
16 Lancers.	196 Native Infantry.

18. The Tabayen district, between the rivers Mu and Chindwin, is held by a post at Yeu. The strength is—

15 Madras Lancers.	60 British Infantry.
	176 Native Infantry.

19. To complete the districts included in the 1st Brigade there still remains the—Chindwin valley. This includes posts at—Alôn, Mingin, and Kindat. Their aggregate strength is—

1 division, Royal Artillery.[1]	790 Native Infantry.

In addition to these regular troops, there are 375 of the Hindustani police levies now in the Chindwin valley. If the need arises, Alôn will be a suitable place for a detachment of British Infantry.

20. The Upper Irrawaddy is held by the 2nd Brigade, head-quarters at Bhamo. It has an outpost at Katha.

The garrisons of Bhamo and the out-station are—

½ garrison battery.	342 British Infantry.
1 mountain ,, (Hazara).	896 Native Infantry.

This garrison has been considerably reduced by sickness, and there are many of the above still sick. The neighbourhood is now quiet, and I propose to leave the garrison as it is. The smaller the force exposed to the influence of the malaria at this season, the more effectives there will be for work in the cold weather.

21. The total military force hitherto employed in Upper Burma has been about 14,000 men.

(b) *Plans then being carried out.*

22. The experience of the last few months has made it apparent that the most effective plan of establishing our rule in Upper Burma, and at the same time protecting and gaining touch of the villagers, is a close occupation of the disturbed districts by military posts.

23. That experience has further taught us how rapidly and secretly strong bodies of insurgents—numbering sometimes from 2,000 to 4,000 men—can be assembled in the neighbourhoods not protected by posts.

24. These bands are freebooters, pillaging wherever they go, but usually reserving the refinement of their cruelty for those who have taken

[1] Of a battery.

office under us or part with us. Flying columns arrive too late to save the village. The villagers having cause to recognise that we are too far off to protect them, lose confidence in our power and throw in their lot with the insurgents. They make terms with the leaders and baffle pursuit of those leaders by round-about guidance or systematic silence. In a country, itself one vast military obstacle, the seizure of the leaders of rebellion, though of paramount importance, thus becomes a source of greatest difficulty.

25. The widespread and continued resistance we have encountered was anticipated by few. The insurgents have cropped out in ever-varying districts and in considerable bands. Where the garrison of the local post, or a combined movement from several, has not been sufficient, the necessity has been hitherto met by sending troops from whatever reserve they could best be spared. This has necessitated much unsymmetrical distribution. On the arrival of the reinforcement (three battalions) now *en route*, flying columns will be formed on a larger scale. They will supplement the system of posts and form a stronger reserve in every district.

26. Up to the present, and for two or three months to come, the heavy loss consequent on exposure during the rains, and the danger of moving troops in an almost unknown country into unhealthy and infected districts, renders it not advisable to pursue this system at present, except in urgent cases, but the columns can be kept on the move with great advantage from October next.

27. To render these columns as mobile and as swift as possible, authority has been granted for the formation of a corps of mounted infantry, 825 strong. This corps, which will be composed of British and Native infantry in the proportion of one to two, will be organized in companies of seventy-five men each. These companies will be formed at the head-quarters of districts and will be attached to flying columns. There may be difficulty and delay in buying sufficient ponies, especially as the purchase of transport ponies is being pressed simultaneously. I hope, however, to succeed with both.

28. The operations of this campaign have falsified the supposition that cavalry is a useless arm in Upper Burma. Our experience has proved it the most effective. It has been stated in this report that it is of first importance to catch the leaders of rebellion. In a force without cavalry this is next to impossible; the *Bohs*, or chiefs, are nearly always mounted and the first to fly on the approach of our troops. Mounted Infantry on ponies cannot catch them. They have, however, the greatest dread of the cavalry. In a land where only ponies are bred, the cavalry horses seem monsters to the people, and the long reach and short shrift of the lance paralyse them with fear.

29. At this season of the year the country is not generally suitable for cavalry, but when the rains are over I would submit that three extra

regiments of cavalry, complete in establishments of grass-cutters, ponies, etc., should be sent for service in Upper Burma. I would distribute them thus—one regiment between Pyinmana, Yamethin, and Meiktila; one regiment between Minbu and Pagan; one regiment between Myingyan, Ava, and Kyauksé.

There is a regiment at Mandalay, and I would detach three troops from it for service at Sagaing, Tabayeñ, and Shwebo.

These cavalry regiments should arrive by the end of November at Rangoon, and should be sent back to India by the 31st May next: March, April and May, when the *jowari* crop is cut and the country is the driest, are the months when cavalry can be used with the greatest effect, but they will do good service from December. With due care and a proper establishment of grass-cutters, I do not contemplate any abnormal loss of horses. The country produces everywhere abundance of the richest grasses.

(c) *The future plans proposed to be carried out.*

30. With regard to the operations in the future :—

The earliest expedition must be to occupy the Ruby Mines.

A Gurkha Regiment, the 43rd Assam Light Infantry, will be ordered on this duty.

31. It is also possible, I am afraid I may say probable, that an expedition will be necessary against the Wuntho *Sawbwa*, a powerful chief whose country lies to the west of Katha, and who has not given in his allegiance. This expedition would require—two mountain guns, one troop of cavalry, seventy-five Madras Infantry, 150 British and 300 native infantry.

It has generally been found that punitive expeditions not followed by occupation have little lasting effect. The occupation of Wuntho must, therefore, be contemplated and provided for.

32. The telegraph extension to Bhamo from Singu on left bank of Irrawaddy, opposite Kyaukmyaung, must also be covered in construction and guarded on completion. This will doubtless entail some military posts on the line of wire, where later experience may show that it cannot be effectually guarded by river patrols.

33. There is a large country between the Chindwin and the Mu, north of our post at Yeu, which must be opened up and occupied.

34. The turbulent Yaws, whose country lies to the west of the Pagan district, must be dominated and the district held. The country is a difficult one, and the column must be strong.

35. Until the country we now occupy to the west of the Shan Hills is more in hand, I advise against sending an expedition into the Shan country unless we go by invitation or under assurances of welcome and support. At

present the Shan States are nominally friendly, and our enemies in Burma cannot rely on asylum or assistance from them. If the Shans fight us, it would much increase our difficulties in the Yamethin and Kyauksé districts and would be a heavy call on the force in Upper Burma.

36. The foregoing expeditions will occupy a large force. It may be necessary to ask for reinforcements. The Chief Commissioner, however, has informed me that he hopes within the next three months to be able to relieve the regular troops with the levies and military police at many of the posts now held by the field force. This will give the Officer Commanding the field force more disposable troops, and I would submit to His Excellency the Commander-in-Chief that we observe how far this will enable the present force to carry out the operations referred to before asking for further reinforcements.

37. I have consulted the Chief Commissioner on the operations in the future, and he agrees with what I have written.

38. * * * * * *

39. The efforts that the troops have been called on to make in taking and maintaining their positions may be gauged by the fact that from April last to the 30th June, seventy-two affairs have been fought. The enemy is a contemptible one, but the disciplined few have often had to stand under trying circumstances against vast numbers. The record of those numbers may be exaggerated, but I have no reason to think it more apocryphal than is the custom of war in like cases. The casualties recorded below will show that it has not been altogether a promenade. The losses from disease, exposure, and fatigue are always the heaviest casualties in war, and this campaign has been no exception to the rule. Everything possible has been done to afford prompt relief and change to the sick.

Casualties.

	British.	Native.
Killed in action	16	26
Died of wounds...	14	15
Died of disease	135	134
Invalided	549	410
Wounded	87	119

In a letter to the Adjutant-General in India, dated 18th August 1886, General White further stated :—

With reference to the plans now being adopted by me for the maintenance and extension of our supremacy in Burma, I have the honour to state, for the information of His Excellency the Commander-in-Chief, that, in communication with the Chief Commissioner, I am arranging for the extension of our communications from Yéwun to Hlaingdet and Meiktila, thus connecting the Pyinmana–Myingyan line of posts with that from Mandalay through Kyauksé southwards and covering our frontier in that direction from attacks of Shan raiders.

I am carrying out a new disposition of troops which will provide small flying columns, distinct from the garrisons of the stations, at certain strategical points throughout the country, ready to move and act in any direction at a moment's notice. As the weather becomes cooler and the country dries up, these flying columns will be kept constantly on the move.

As the police levies (most of which are at present undrilled) become fit to take up their duties, it is proposed to gradually place them in some of the posts now occupied by troops, which will be withdrawn and concentrated in convenient places in support and reserve. The increase of our establishment of mounted infantry, when completed, will enable the officers commanding posts at which they are stationed to patrol the country much more effectually than with men on foot.

The police were formed on the same lines as the Assam frontier police and were, as has been already stated, to, as far as possible, relieve the troops from the many police duties they were called on to perform. It was necessary that all operations should be conducted in support of the civil power rather than as purely military operations and, in consequence, nearly all duties which the troops were called on to perform were in reality police duties.

It was, however, evident that till the garrison of Burma could, with safety, be greatly reduced and its present duties taken over by an efficient police, the power of the civil government must lie in the troops at its disposal; that considerable and increased exertions must be made before the entire executive could with safety be handed over to a few thousand police, and that these exertions must take the form of military operations against, and the complete suppression of, every band of dacoits in the country, and the improvement of all the communications.

PREPARATIONS FOR THE WINTER CAMPAIGN, 1886–87.

With a view to reducing the country to the required state of subjection as quickly as possible, the following preparations were made for a winter campaign. It was to commence as soon after the 1st October as the various parts of the country which had been flooded during the rains became practicable for all military operations.

Brigadier-General G. S. White, C.B., V.C., with the local rank of Major-General, was to command the whole of the Upper Burma Field Force under Lieutenant-General Sir Herbert Macpherson, K.C.B., K.C.S.I., V.C.

Reconstitution of commands and brigades.

This appointment is referred to in a letter from Major-General Sir T. D. Baker, K.C.B., Adjutant-General in India, to the Secretary to the Government of India, Military Department, dated Simla, the 4th August 1886, as follows :—

With reference to the letter addressed to you by the Quarter Master General in India, dated 30th July 1886, proposing that certain additional regiments should be sent to Burma in October next, I am directed by the Commander-in-Chief to state that, as the force in Upper Burma will then be considerably augmented, and as it is very desirable, for obvious military reasons, that the extended operations which it will be necessary to carry on throughout Burma during the cold season should be under the command of one supreme General Officer, His Excellency considers that Lieutenant-General Sir Herbert Macpherson, K.C.B., K.C.S.I., V.C., Commander-in-Chief, Madras Army, should be directed to transfer his head-quarters to Burma temporarily, to arrive there about the 1st October 1886, and to remain until the conclusion of the operations.

I am directed to add that by this recommendation no reflection is intended to be cast on the manner in which Major-General White has carried out the duties of his command up to the present time. Indeed, the Commander-in-Chief feels assured that the Government of India will agree with him that Major-General White has done remarkably well under most difficult circumstances, and that he deserves great credit for the manner in which he is discharging the duties of his important command. But, as it is undesirable that the military operations about to be undertaken in Burma should be carried out under the system of divided command, the Commander-in-Chief makes the present recommendation, and hopes that it may meet with the concurrence of the Government of India.

It further appears to the Commander-in-Chief to be essential that, while operations in the field are being carried on, Sir Herbert Macpherson should act under the direct orders of Army Head-quarters and the Government of India.

Sir Herbert Macpherson would of course continue to exercise the command of the Madras Army while in Burma.

All these recommendations were approved of by the Government of India, and Sir Herbert Macpherson was directed to transfer the Madras Army Head-quarters to Burma.

The redistribution of the brigades in Burma was as follows:— Upper Burma was divided into eight military districts, six of which were constituted brigades, and two were independent commands. The troops were commanded as follows:—

Brigades.

1st *Brigade*—Head-quarters, Mandalay,—by Brigadier-General C. T. East.

2nd *Brigade*—Head-quarters, Bhamo,—by Brigadier-General Griffith.

3rd *Brigade*—Head-quarters, Pyinmana,—by Brigadier-General W. S. A. Lockhart, C.B.

4th *Brigade*—Head-quarters, Myingyan,—by Brigadier-General H. S. Anderson.

5th *Brigade*—Head-quarters, Shwebo,—by Brigadier-General R. C. Stewart, A.D.C.

6th *Brigade*—Head-quarters, Minbu,—by Brigadier-General R. C. Low, A.D.C.

Independent Commands.

The Chindwin Independent Command, Head-quarters Alôn,—by Lieutenant-Colonel A. C. Toker.

The Taungdwingyi Independent Command, Head-quarters Taungdwingyi.

This latter command was garrisoned by troops from the Lower Burma Division.

Sir H. Macpherson's instructions.

The following Instructions from His Excellency the Commander-in-Chief in India, dated 27th August 1886, were forwarded by the Adjutant-General in India to His Excellency Sir Herbert Macpherson, K.C.B., K.C.S.I., V.C., Commander-in-Chief, Madras Army:—

With reference to Military Department letter No. 954-A.S., dated 7th August 1886, appointing you to the command of the troops in Upper and Lower Burma, I am directed by His Excellency the Commander-in-Chief in India to inform you that this has been done with the object of placing the troops in both these provinces under one Commander, who will thus be in a position to carry out vigorous and combined offensive operations throughout the several disturbed districts.

2. To enable you to carry out the required operations, the Government has sanctioned a considerable increase to the force now in Upper Burma, and has appointed three additional Brigadier-Generals, one of Cavalry and two of Infantry, each with a staff of a Brigade-Major and a Deputy Assistant Quarter Master General. You will thus have under your immediate command in Burma two Major-Generals commanding divisions and six Brigadier-Generals, with a force amounting to about 31,000 men.

3. It is understood that you propose to leave Madras for Burma on the 2nd September. On arrival at Rangoon you should make all arrangements for the reception and despatch of the troops from India to Upper Burma, and then proceed yourself to Mandalay, where, in communication with Sir Charles Bernard and Major-General White, whose local experience will be of the greatest assistance to you, you will arrange all preliminary details for the cold-weather operations. The time at your disposal for this service may be said to be from about 15th November next to the middle or end of April 1887, and I am to impress upon Your Excellency the great importance of all preparations being vigorously pushed forward on your arrival at Mandalay, in order that the troops may take the field as soon as the weather will admit of their doing so.

4. With regard to the nature of the operations to be undertaken, I am instructed to inform you that the Government of India desire to see dacoity completely stamped out, and the authority of the civil power firmly established throughout Burma.

5. In order to attain this object, the Commander-in-Chief considers that, instead of a few movements, with one or two comparatively large forces, it would be preferable to carry on a series of minor operations by a number of small flying columns, under carefully selected leaders, acting under the orders of the several Brigadier-Generals commanding. It is desirable that the aim of the Government of India should be carefully explained to these officers, and that the utmost latitude of movement should then be given to them. The strength of the columns must depend on the nature of the country, and the amount of opposition to be expected; but it is essential that each party should be able to move rapidly and to follow up the enemy, who always endeavour to escape into the *jungles* as soon as our troops approach the position they may have taken up.

6. As a general rule, His Excellency considers that each of the smaller columns might appropriately be composed of two mountain guns, about thirty mounted infantry, from 50 to 100 British infantry, and from 100 to 200 native infantry, with as many cavalry as can be made available, and that these should all work in unison from a number of different points, in order, if possible, to hem in the dacoits, and to ensure every part of the country

being visited. When any serious resistance is anticipated, or when the enemy have taken up a difficult position, it is most desirable that guns should be used before infantry are committed to the attack ; and whenever practicable the cavalry should be sent to a flank, and endeavour to fall upon the enemy and follow them up as they retreat from their stockades. The troops should make their presence felt everywhere, and should remain long enough in all the principal places to enable the civil power to establish the administration on a firm basis, and to give the people of the country a feeling of confidence in the stability of our rule, and relieve them from the fear of being harassed by dacoits.

7. Speaking generally, the operations should extend from our old frontier northwards to the Shan hills on the east and the Kabaw valley on the west, and movements will probably have to be made from Lower Burma on Napé and Taungdwingyi, and in a westerly direction from Minbu, Salin, Pagan, and Myingyan respectively. The Yaw country will have to be dominated and the district temporarily occupied, while further north a force will have to be sent up the Chindwin valley. In an easterly direction small columns should be despatched from the valley of the Irrawaddy towards Yamethin and Pyinmana, and a strong force to the Ruby Mines. A convenient base for the latter expedition will, it is understood, be found at Kyanhnyat on the Irrawaddy, about 100 miles above Mandalay. Posts will have to be established between the base and the mines, and every care taken that the communication is kept open throughout. Operations will also have to be undertaken about Bhamo, so as to ensure our complete supremacy in that part.

8. Hereafter a large force may possibly have to be sent into the Shan country, but the Commander-in-Chief considers it very desirable that for the present operations should be confined to the plains of Burma ; a settlement with the Shan tribes does not appear to be pressing, and it is not advisable to get ourselves mixed up in the difficult mountains which surround Upper Burma on the north and east, until peace and order have been established throughout the lower country.

9. The reinforcements and reliefs from India will be arriving at Rangoon shortly after Your Excellency's head-quarters have been established in Burma. For some reasons Sir Frederick Roberts would wish that the date of their arrival could have been deferred, as the month of October is more or less sickly, and, unless the season is exceptionally dry, extended movements may be difficult before the middle or end of November ; but on account of the heavy monsoon weather which may be expected in the Bay of Bengal between the middle of October and the end of the year, it is considered advisable that sea voyages should be completed by the 10th October, and it

is also thought that the presence of these additional troops in Burma may help in some degree to settle the country.

10. His Excellency feels sure that it is needless to request that the utmost attention be paid to the comfort and health of the troops, and that they should not be subjected to any unnecessary exposure until the operations commence. All available shelter at Rangoon, Shwegyin, Toungoo, Thayetmyo, Allanmyo, etc., should be made use of in the first instance, and until you may consider it advisable for the troops to take the field.

11. While Your Excellency is temporarily in Burma, the ordinary duties of the Madras Command will be conducted in the same manner as if you were on tour; but, as regards the military operations in Burma, you will act under the direct orders of the Commander-in-Chief and the Government of India, and will forward your reports to Army Head-quarters in India.

12. Your Excellency will take with you to Burma such officers of your head-quarter staff as you may consider necessary.

13. The several Brigadier-Generals proceeding from India to Burma have been directed to arrive at Rangoon on or before the 15th proximo, and have been informed that orders from Your Excellency regarding their destination will await them on arrival at Rangoon.

14. Sir Frederick Roberts has every confidence in your ability to carry to a successful issue the important duty for which you have been selected by the Government of India, and His Excellency feels certain that the operations under your direction will be conducted with vigour, energy, and expedition.

The troops for relief and the relieving troops were both to be in Burma at the same time and three additional regiments of native cavalry, with other reinforcements, were also to be sent before 20th October 1886.

On the 1st July 1886 the present strength of the field force was 13,260 men; on the 1st of December, when all the reliefs and reinforcements had arrived, the present strength was 23,656 men, *i.e.*, making deduction for troops sent to operate in the semi-independent states, generally speaking one man to every three and a half square miles of the country to be actually occupied. It will be remembered that previous to 1st March 1886 no operations were undertaken against semi-independent states, and the army of occupation averaged some 11,000 men, about one man to every seven square miles.

The following programme shows the additional troops sent to Burma for the winter campaign of 1886-87.

CORPS.	Port and date of embarkation.	Date of disembarkation at Rangoon.
7th Bengal Cavalry	Calcutta, 10th and 23rd September and 5th October 1886.	15th and 28th September and 10th October 1886.
No. 9-1 (Mountain) Northern Division, Royal Artillery, with Portion of No. 2 Company, Bengal Sappers and Miners.	Calcutta, 11th September 1886.	16th September 1886.
1st and 5th Bengal Infantry ..	Calcutta, 20th September 1886.	25th September 1886.
No. 1-1 (Mountain) Eastern Division, Royal Artillery, with portion of No. 2 Company, Bengal Sappers and Miners.	Calcutta, 24th September 1886.	29th September 1886.
2nd Battalion, Royal West Surrey Regiment.	Calcutta, 3rd October 1886.	8th October 1886.
1st Battalion, South Yorkshire Regiment.	....	....
1st Madras Lancers	Madras, 17th, 19th, 21st, and 22nd September 1886.	22nd, 24th, 26th, and 27th September 1886.
3rd Hyderabad Contingent Cavalry	Madras, 30th September, 1st, 3rd, and 4th October 1886.	4th, 5th, 8th, and 9th October 1886.
17th Madras Infantry and 3rd Hyderabad Contingent Infantry.	Madras, 15th September 1886.	20th September 1886.
1st Battalion, Rifle Brigade .. } 2nd Battalion, Royal Munster Fusiliers. }	Madras, 28th September 1886.	3rd October 1886
1st Bombay Lancers	Bombay, 21st and 22nd September 1886.	1st and 2nd October 1886.
27th Bombay Infantry	Karachi, 5th October 1886.	17th October 1886.

Total 2 (European) mountain batteries. Total 4 (native) companies of sappers.
" 24 (native) regiments, cavalry. " 5 (native) infantry battalions.
" 4 (European) infantry battalions.

At the same time one European mountain battery and one regiment, native cavalry, were returned to India.

Total strength of Field Force on 20th October.

The total strength of the troops in Burma on 20th October 1886 was as follows:—

Detail.	Upper Burma.		Lower Burma.	
	British Officers.	Native Officers, British and Native Non-Commissioned Officers and men.	British Officers.	Native Officers, British and Native Non-Commissioned Officers and men.
Royal Artillery	31	583	4	104
Infantry	171	6,516	29	1,641
Total British Troops ..	202	7,099	33	1,745
Artillery	8	452	..	..
Cavalry	33	2,002	..	..
Infantry, and Sappers and Miners.	190	15,143	52	4,694
Total Native Troops ..	231	17,597	52	4,694
Grand Total ..	433	24,696	85	6,439

To facilitate the movements of troops, tracks from 40 to 100 feet wide were cut through the *jungle* along all main approaches. Permanent telegraph lines, supplemented by the field telegraph, were pushed out to all important posts, and systems of visual signalling were elaborated in each brigade.

Arrangements were also made for the navigation of the smaller rivers,—the Shweli, the Myitngé, the Panlaung, and Mu. As none of the existing steam launches were capacious enough to transport troops, orders were given for—two stern-wheelers to carry 150 men and fifty ponies, and to have a raised tower for a machine-gun; two launches, each to carry twenty men; and one composite stern-wheeler, iron frame, wooden skin, eighty feet long by sixteen feet beam, to carry one Gardner gun on raised platform, and guaranteed to tug a flat of her own size against the current of the Chindwin river.

Every exertion was made in purchasing and equipping pack transport, provisions were stored, and an efficient battalion of mounted infantry, 825 strong, was equipped and got ready for service.

The scheme for operations.

The general scheme on which the operations were to be conducted was that all established posts were divided into convenient groups. Each group was to be provided with sufficient troops of all arms to garrison all the posts simultaneously, while a flying column, composed of numbers and materials specially adapted to the peculiarities of the neighbouring country, was at all times to be ready equipped and available to take the field.

Special operations were to be undertaken against certain gangs of dacoits, and the general occupation of the country was to radiate from the already established posts. Whenever police were available, they were to relieve the troops in the occupation of the intermediate posts on lines of communication. The advance of the occupation was, as far as possible, to be effected by the establishment of successive lines of posts, with good communications between them all, and by constant and systematic patrols. Outside these lines of posts it was to be expected that the chief military operations would be undertaken, and inside them the civil officers, supported by the troops and police, were to direct their attention to the settlement of the country.

Measures for conciliating the people.

While measures were being concerted for putting down rebellion and dacoity with a strong hand, the necessity of directly and indirectly conciliating the people at large was not overlooked; hence punitive measures, such as the burning of villages harbouring or assisting rebels, were prohibited; an amnesty was offered to all who should voluntarily submit within a certain time; all imports and duties impending the free course of trade were abolished; the village system was adhered to, and the indigenous methods of administration were retained, so far as possible; demands for the collection of revenue were not pressed severely; and various means were taken to try and bring home to the people the fact that there was no intention of undermining or interfering with the Buddhist religion. Endeavours were also made to develop the rich natural resources of the country.

Agricultural interests, besides having for years back been hampered by dacoity, had suffered throughout the whole of the dry central zone from the state of disrepair into which irrigation works, dating from centuries back, had been allowed to fall. The ruby mines, jade mining, coal fields, oil wells, teak forests, and gold fields, were all valuable natural resources, whose exploitation would become of great importance as soon as the country began to be somewhat more settled.

As a means of pacification and of advance towards these desirable ends, the important step was taken of disarming the country. Begun in the Mandalay district, it was gradually, but without undue delay, extended throughout the whole of the fourteen districts of Upper Burma. All guns were called in from towns and villages, and were only distributed under proper safeguards. After being marked with distinctive marks and numbers, guns were only restored to licensees consisting of respectable men living in well-behaved villages and towns where there were at least five to ten licenses. Villages with well-kept *chevaux-de-frise,* bamboo stockades, and proper watch kept at the guard houses placed near the gates, were thought to be safer with ten or more guns in the hands of licensees than they were before [1]; whereas hamlets with only two or three guns would, under any circumstances, have been unable to offer strong resistance to dacoit attack, because experience showed that such small villages never attempted to defend themselves.

As soon as the mass of the people living in the towns and villages on the plains were deprived of their arms, it became no longer possible for rebels and dacoits to replace guns lost in action or given up on acceptance of amnesty. Insistence was at the same time made that villages whose position exposed them to attack should surround themselves with substantial stockades, and that a proper watch should be maintained there day and night. Wherever this proved ineffectual, and in outlying districts where military posts could not be established, small hamlets were grouped together to form a more easily defensible village, and villages were moved to more suitable sites. Inconvenience and a certain amount of hardship was inseparable from the latter measure; but as the

[1] This view was not afterwards held by Sir George White, *vide* his remarks on page 303.

houses in Burmese villages are only composed of posts, bamboos, and thatched grass, easily obtainable from the neighbouring *jungles*, the inevitable hardships were reduced to a minimum. Even in the royal city of Mandalay, the houses were mostly of the same flimsy and uncostly description, and were worth only about Rs. 50 apiece, although some were of course more valuable. The 6,000 houses located between the palace and the city walls of Mandalay were also subsequently cleared out on payment of compensation, and the householders thus ejected were granted building sites in the new town of Mandalay, while the old Shwémyodaw, or "Royal Golden City," was retained exclusively for the civil and military servants of Government, and transformed into Fort Dufferin.

CHAPTER XVIII.

THE WINTER CAMPAIGN 1886-87 AND SUBSEQUENT OPERATIONS TO MIDSUMMER 1888.

By the 1st October 1886 the preparations for the winter campaign were practically complete. Lieutenant-General Sir Herbert Macpherson had assumed direct command of the troops in Burma, the Field Force had been redistributed, and the troops to take part in the campaign were nearly all with their respective brigades or commands, only a few being still *en route.* Police battalions were being formed, to follow up the successes of the troops and relieve them of police duties, and the plans for the most important operations were only awaiting execution, when, on the 20th October, Sir Herbert Macpherson died of fever on the Indian Government ship *Irrawaddy* near Prome.

Death of Sir H. Macpherson.

This necessitated the immediate reconstruction of the command in Burma. On the 27th October the Governor-General in Council asked Sir F. Roberts, the Commander-in-Chief, to temporarily transfer his head-quarters to Burma, and assume command of the whole of the troops in that province. This transfer was consequently effected, and Sir Frederick Roberts arrived in Mandalay on the 17th November, remaining there till 12th February 1887.

Soon after his arrival Sir Frederick summarized the immediate objectives of the military operations, in order of importance, as follows :—

(*a*) To hunt down Boh Shwé and Ottoma, and to clear Western Minbu from their bands of dacoits.

(*b*) A similar result with regard to Hla-U in the *doab* of the Irrawaddy and Chindwin.

(*c*) A similar result with regard to the gangs infesting Yamethin and Pyinmana.

(*d*) The occupation of the Kanle and Pakangyi tract in the north-west of the Myingyan district, and the dispersion of the dacoits dominating it.

(*e*) The punishment of the rebels in vicinity of Katha, Sheinmaga, North Mandalay, Kyauksé, Welaung, Pôpa, Sé, Wundwin, and possibly of Bhamo.

(*f*) The permanent occupation of the Ruby Mines tract.

(*g*) The further exploration and pacification of the Chindwin valley.

(*h*) The establishment of the same control over the territory and *Sawbwa* of Wuntho as was exercised by the late King, including acknowledgment of the supremacy of the Indian Government, and the annual payment of tribute.

(*i*) The exploration and occupation, as far as necessary, of the Yaw country.

(*j*) The despatch of an expedition through a portion of the Shan States, with the object of cultivating friendly relations, establishing a police post and Resident at some suitable point, and arranging for the security of the new railway.

We will now proceed to deal with the way in which these various operations were carried out.

PURSUIT OF BOH SHWE.

An account has already been given of the evacuation of Napé in the presence of Boh Shwé's gang, and of the relief of Salin when besieged by Ottama *Hpongyi* in August 1886. From that date, owing to the unhealthiness of the climate, active operations were suspended against these powerful dacoits till a more favourable season of the year, the 15th December being decided on as the earliest date on which an expedition could start.

As a preliminary to more extensive operations in the interior active steps were first taken to clear the country on both banks of the Irrawaddy, and to stop piracy on the river itself by means of small moveable columns, co-operating with steam launches manned by crews of blue-jackets and armed with machine guns.

By the middle of December all was ready for a general advance westward. To prevent the bands of insurgents breaking back towards the old frontier, the southern cordon of Malun-Yenangyaung-Myothit was held by troops from Lower Burma; and as soon as the line Salin-Sidoktaya had been occupied to the north, a column under the immediate command of Brigadier-General Low was pushed forward in pursuit of Boh Shwé from Pyawbwe through Padein to Napé and Pa-aing, which place was occupied on the 16th December after only a slight resistance on the part of the enemy. On the 17th and 18th Boh Shwé was pursued up the Arakan hill from Pa-aing; his ponies, camp, tents, clothes, and records, etc., were captured, and the pursuit was only given up when the ground became impracticable. Boh Shwé was reported to have left Padein on the approach of the column, with 1,000 followers; this following was said to have been reduced to 450 by the time he reached Napé, and to only twenty-five by the end of the month. The casualties of the British column during these operations were :—

> Lieutenant Radclyffe, Rifle Brigade, severely wounded.
> One private, Rifle Brigade, killed.
> Four Non-Commissioned Officers and men wounded.
> Two privates, Hyderabad Contingent, wounded.

The pursuit of Boh Shwé and Ottama was continued with zest, but owing to the small numbers of followers that remained with them and to the wild nature of the hills to which they had flown, it was found very hard to get reliable news of the whereabouts of the enemy.

General Low, having visited the hill in which the dacoits were hiding, determined to try and follow them up with small columns. Six of these columns were formed, but owing to lack of intelligence they could do little more than keep the dacoits on the run, thus preventing them from reasserting their influence, or collecting large followings.

On the 30th January 1887, Captain Golightly, King's Royal Rifles, captured Boh Shwé's camp high up on the Arakan hills at a place called Pah; on the 8th February he found his advance guard strongly entrenched at Taung-chaung north-west of Padein; the gang, however, got off without casualties. On the 15th Golightly surprised the main camp and captured a large quantity of arms and property. Early in March Boh Shwé threatened the post of Sidoktaya, where Captain Golightly was encamped. Golightly accordingly advanced against him on the 9th March with some mounted infantry and thirty Gurkha police. Coming up with the dacoit at the junction of the Mu creek, he held him to his front with the dismounted infantry, while he sent the police against the left flank. The dacoits retired precipitately, and were pursued for four miles, with a loss of twenty-two killed and many wounded. After this action, Boh Shwé's band became so completely broken up that any systematic pursuit became quite impossible.

Boh Shwé's death.

During the summer of 1887, Boh Shwé remained a refugee in the Arakan Yomas on or near the old frontier line of Lower Burma. His influence had almost disappeared and very little was heard of him till October, when Major Harvey, South Wales Borderers, acting upon information received, made a forced march of fifty miles with a party of forty mounted infantry, South Wales Borderers, and thirty-one mounted infantry of the 7th Bombay Infantry. The camp was discovered and rushed on the 5th October, when Boh Shwé and ten of his followers were killed. The rest of the gang, estimated at 200, were completely scattered and never assembled again.

OPERATIONS AGAINST OTTAMA HPONGYI.

A column under Lieutenant Westlake, 1st Madras Lancers, was operating in the country between Minbu and Salin. His operations were chiefly directed against Ottama *Hpongyi*. He made several captures of dacoits, and by his energetic movements he prevented the gangs ever settling down in one place and collecting any considerable number of adherents; the rebel leader was thus reduced to the same straits as his rival Boh Shwé.

The chief successes which were scored by this column during February and March were—

On 12th February, thirty lancers, 1st Madras Lancers, surprised *Boh* Pe-gale's camp near Legaing, killing several dacoits, making twelve prisoners and capturing much ammunition and property.

On 19th February, in the bed of the river Môn, Lieutenant Westlake surprised and defeated with loss a gang led by Ottama himself, and a few days later he recovered six carts which the dacoits had looted from a convoy.

On 9th and 10th March, Lieutenant Westlake killed some dacoits and captured several more with their arms and ammunition at Zagswé.

A few days later a party of the 1st Madras Lancers defeated dacoits at Kyetspukkein, inflicting on them a complete defeat and a loss of fifty killed.

On the 14th March the scouts of the 1st Madras Lancers killed an important docoit leader named Ye-U, or the *Lephan Boh*, and several of his followers.

Minor bands of dacoits were harassing the districts round Sinbyugyun and Minhla. On the 10th March the officer commanding Sinbyugyun made an important capture of a *Boh* and nine followers, with their arms and ammunition. Several captures were made during these two months near Minhla, and on the 17th March a leader known as the *Hpongyi Boh* surrendered himself, with twenty-five followers, bringing in arms and ammunition.

THE OPERATIONS AGAINST HLA U.

Four columns were organized to proceed against Hla U, who had for some time been overrunning the country between the rivers Mu and Chindwin. The composition of these columns was as follows:—

I.—Under Captain R. P. Macdonald, 2nd Hampshire Regiment—

- 1 Troop, 7th Bengal Cavalry;
- 25 Rifles, Somersetshire Light Infantry;
- 27 British and Native Mounted Infantry;
- 94 Rifles, 5th Bombay Light Infantry;

to start from Myinmu, on the south.

II.—Under Major Symons, South Wales Borderers, Commandant, Mounted Infantry—

- 1 Troop, 7th Bengal Cavalry;
- 50 Rifles, Hampshire Regiment;
- 75 Rifles, Mounted Infantry { 25 Royal Munster Fusiliers; 50 23rd Bombay Light Infantry and 17th Madras Infantry;
- 100 Rifles, 5th Bombay Light Infantry;

to start from Magyizauk, on the east.

III.—Under Lieutenant-Colonel Middleton, 21st Madras Infantry—

- 2 Guns, 9-1 Cinque Ports, Royal Artillery;
- 1 Squadron, 3rd Cavalry, Hyderabad Contingent;
- 50 Rifles, South Yorkshire Regiment (King's Own Light Infantry);
- 100 Rifles, 21st Madras Infantry;

to start from Yeu, on the north.

IV.—Under Captain C. Sage, 18th Bengal Infantry—

1 Troop, 1st Bombay Lancers;

41 Rifles, Royal Munster Fusiliers;

80 Rifles, 1st Madras Pioneers;

to start from Alôn, on the west.

The pursuit of bands of dacoits, and the capture of their leaders in a roadless district abounding in hiding places, and surrounded by belts of jungle ten miles in depth, the approaches to which were known only to the dacoits themselves, was no easy task. Add to this the difficulty of obtaining information from inhabitants long held in terror under the relentless rule of the very leaders now to be hunted down, and whose punishment for information against them was crucifixion, and the difficulties which confronted these columns will be readily understood.

Before the operations were begun the column commanders were instructed to do their utmost to obtain information and to keep up constant communication with each other. They were told that they must always have enough supplies with them to enable them to keep the field for ten days at a time, and that their aim must be to drive the dacoits towards the Irrawaddy, and to prevent them escaping towards the north.

Operations began on the 15th November, and though no important engagement was fought, Hla U was kept constantly on the run, until, by the end of the year, his following had dwindled to vanishing point. Little more was heard of him during the beginning of 1887, but he again appeared committing small dacoities in the early part of April. His reign of terror was, however, near its end, and on the 19th April he was murdered in camp by one of his own adherents.

Death of Hla U.

THE OPERATIONS NEAR YAMETHIN AND PYINMANA.

The two districts of Yamethin and Pyinmana were entirely in the 3rd Brigade, and the operations there were conducted by Brigadier-General Lockhart, C.B. From the very commencement of the campaign in these districts till the arrival of reinforcements in October 1886 the paucity of men and the insufficiency of transport had crippled the commanders. Troops were unable to pursue and hunt down the rebels, as rations could not be carried for more than two or three days' supply. The enemy, therefore, invariably evacuated his position after a skirmish more or less stubborn, only to re-occupy it on the retirement of the troops. The density of the jungle in the Pyinmana district, and the want of mounted men to operate in the open country round Yamethin saved the rebels from any very heavy loss during their retreats. The people of the country early recognized the patent fact that the rebels were strong enough to levy and collect the taxes and impress men and labour whenever they wished to do so, and that the mere handful of British had invariably to retire after a hollow victory, often harassed by the rebels on their return march. Under these circumstances it was but natural that the inhabitants of these districts were unable to realize that the occupation of the country by the British would be permanent, or that resistance on their own part would be stamped out. They, therefore, for the most part stood aloof, watching events before throwing in their lot with either side, unless forced to do so. The rebels' method of rationing themselves was to sit down in some rich village or group of villages, and to remain there, unless disturbed, till provisions began to run short. They then either removed their camp to some similar spot, or sent out strong foraging parties of about 100 men to distant villages, and, attacking in the daytime when the men were in the fields, seized all they wanted. One of the first hopeful signs which followed on our successes was the satisfactory manner in which some hamlets defended themselves against this robbery. The rebellion in the Pyinmana district (in June) was well timed and planned. The long quiet which had been enjoyed there may have caused the rebels to hope that the British might be off their guard; and the advent of the monsoon, laying a large portion of the country under water, and converting the roads into quagmires, further aided them. The posts were but scantily manned, and all movements of troops and bringing up of supplies was of necessity very difficult, owing to the state of the country; and the dense jungle and almost impenetrable *kaing* grass bordering the roads of communication enabled the enemy to inflict loss upon and severely harass convoys and detached posts. Everything was then in their favour, and thus it was that until the much needed reinforcements arrived in October, the troops were virtually forced to act upon the defensive only.

Brigadier-General Lockhart, C.B., took over command of the brigade on 27h September, and he found the whole district, with the exception of the Yamethin township and the northern portion, in the hands of the rebels.

There were four centres of rebellion, *viz.*:—

On the east a gang established at Kinywa under the *ex-Laywun*.

On the south-west a gang under the *ex-Thanegon Thugyi* established at Chinzu (Pinzu ?).

On the south-west a gang under Buddha Yaza.

On the west and north-west under the Kemmendine Prince.

Owing to the thick forest growth, and difficult nature of the country throughout these districts, any concerted scheme for suppressing simultaneously the numerous bands of insurgents infesting this area was manifestly out of the question. General Lockhart's operations, therefore, took the form of attacking and following up the hostile gangs by means of detached and mobile columns.

His first object was to relieve Pyinmana of the pressure caused by the close proximity of the enemy, who were hemming this post in on three sides. This was effected by the despatch of several small parties to districts within striking distance of Pyinmana. The most successful of these expeditions was one under the command of the General himself which succeeded in surprising and capturing the Kemmendine Prince's camp, the Prince only narrowly escaping capture, and many of his followers being killed. The other parties were all more or less successful and the pressure on Pyinmana was at once reduced. The danger of the Yamethin road was, however, correspondingly increased; several convoys were attacked, and the General's next step was to clear this road and secure the safety of the numerous convoys bringing supplies to the various posts of the brigade. On 17th November Lieutenant-Colonel Elton, 16th Madras Infantry, with a force of 200 men dislodged the enemy from their rifle pits at Kanhla, but with a loss of Lieutenant Greenwood and one man killed, and one man wounded. On the 23rd Major Beale of the Queen's, with 150 of his regiment surprised and captured Buddha Yaza's camp, taking *Boh* Htum prisoner and seizing many arms. Buddha Yaza himself effected his escape.

On the 28th November two columns, one under Lieutenant-Colonel Butler and the other under Lieutenant H. H. Aspinall, routed the *Laywun* who was strongly entrenched at Kinywa.

As the result of these operations the enemy were driven off the trunk road, and the safety of convoys was assured.

On the 5th December Lieutenant-Colonel Elton marched with a force consisting of 119 men of the Queen's, twenty-five Somerset Light Infantry, 100 Biluch Light Infantry, and forty mounted infantry, for Yadan, his object being to engage Nga Hmat, who was reported to be threatening that district with 700 men. As soon as touch with the enemy was obtained they dispersed, and the whole surrounding jungle being searched without effect, the column returned.

Death of the Kemmendine Prince.

On the 1st January a party of mounted men under Lieutenant Lamport surprised the Kemmendine's bivouac, and in the action which ensued, the Kemmendine and several of his followers were killed, and fifteen taken prisoners.

Further small columns continued to be sent over the district, and, as a result of their operations, the more important rebel posts were captured and destroyed, Buddha Yaza, though not taken prisoner was driven as a fugitive into the fastnesses of the Yoma range, and on all sides there were strong indications of a collapse of the hostile organization.

THE OCCUPATION OF YAW AND KANLE, AND SUBSEQUENT OPERATIONS.

The country to the west of Myingyan, near which place the Chindwin river flows into the Irrawaddy, had for some time prior to November 1886 been in so unsettled a state that it became necessary to occupy this district with troops, in order to establish our authority and to protect trading interests. Orders were consequently issued for a column to advance on Pauk from Myitche, a post on the west bank of the Irrawaddy, forty miles below Myingyan, and about sixteen miles south of Pakokku. The continual occupation of Pauk was not contemplated, and the civil and military officers were enjoined to hold out no such prospect to the inhabitants.

A pretender named Shwe Gyo Byu had set himself up as Prince at Kanle, and was reported to have collected a large following.

Two other columns were, therefore, ordered to advance and combine in an attack on Kanle, one operating from the north-east and the other from the south-east. The former column was to start from Alôn, a post on the Chindwin, about forty miles above its junction with the Irrawaddy, and the latter from Pakokku. Owing to the amount of pack transport available being limited, all three columns were to carry a month's rations in carts, the Myitche column being provided with as much pack transport as possible, to facilitate any further advance into the hills to the west of Pauk.

The following is an account of the operations of these three columns:—

2 guns, 7-1 Northern Division, R. A.
145 rifles, 2nd Liverpool Regt.
116 lances, Madras Lancers.
41 rifles, Bengal Sappers and Miners.
207 rifles, 11th Bengal Infantry.

The Pauk column under Major Stead, 11th Bengal Infantry, consisting of the marginally named troops, left Myitche on the 2nd December 1886, and after slight resistance on the road, occupied Pauk on the 8th idem. Attention was then turned to the Yaw district, which was visited by the troops, and the headmen of which submitted to Major Stead. Thathein was occupied on the 4th January 1887, after a skirmish with some dacoits under Yakut at Sobya. A part of this column under Major Carrè, R. A., co-operated, as shown below, with the Pakokku column in the occupation of Minywa on the 12th February :—

2 guns, No. 1 Bombay Mountain Battery.
1 troop, 1st Bombay Lancers.
192 rifles, Royal Munster Fusiliers.
153 rifles, 23rd Bombay Light Infantry.
7 men, Bombay Sappers and Miners.

The Pakokku column, under command of Lieutenant-Colonel Gatacre, 23rd Bombay Light Infantry, left Pakokku on the 10th December 1886. At Kyauksauk, on the 11th, information was received that two bands of dacoits had been fighting some fifteen miles to the north, that one of them had advanced southwards and was encamped at Alégun, and that the other was in flight across the column's line of route. It was therefore decided to advance without delay on Myaing. On the 11th the Bombay Lancers, under Lieutenant-Colonel Heyland, were detached north, to Alégun, and the main body marched straight on Myaing, which they reached the same day without encountering any dacoits.

The cavalry arrived at Alégun soon after daybreak and effected a complete surprise ; the band, estimated at 700, were encamped inside a low stone wall surrounding several monasteries and pagodas in a clump of trees ; they were immediately routed, and were pursued upwards of a mile in fairly open country ; their loss was estimated at 200 ; *Bohs* Pothan and Tazee and eleven others were made prisoners, and a considerable number of arms and ponies were captured. Our casualties were Lieutenant-Colonel Heyland and a Duffadar, 1st Bombay Lancers, slightly wounded. The same day the cavalry rejoined the column head-quarters at Myaing.

The column remained at Myaing until the 19th, when, having established communication with the Chindwin force, an advance was made to Kanlé, which was found evacuated. The stockade was found to be strongly constructed ; it was evidently the Prince's intention to have established his head-quarters here, as several large houses were in process of building. The Prince on our advance had fled : an attempt was made to follow him up, but he escaped with a very small following into the hills, which are covered with dense jungle. Having destroyed the stockade, the column returned to Alégun on the 26th, a centre from which information as to the rebels was more easily obtainable.

On the 4th February Lieutenant-Colonel Gatacre's column met a detached party from the Pauk column under Major Carré, R.A., at Lebo. Lieutenant-Colonel Gatacre and Major Carré, in consultation, arranged for a combined attack on Minywa, where Yakut and his following had established themselves.

On the 10th February Major Carré accordingly left Pauk with the marginally-named troops. The route taken was through Watthet to Kyaungnet, and the column was twice attacked on the march by dacoits, who were repulsed with loss.

2 guns, 7—8 Northern Division, R. A.
62 rifles, Liverpool Regiment.
51 lances, 1st Madras Lancers.
100 rifles, 11th Bengal Infantry.

On the evening of the 11th the Pauk column halted at Kyaungnet, near which Lieutenant-Colonel Gatacre's force was assembled.

On the 12th February 1887, the combined attack was made on the stockaded village and pagoda of Minywa. Little opposition was met with, Yakut, with his principal chiefs, having fled the previous day.

Both columns separated again to make demonstrations through the district. The presence of our troops had the happiest effect, and the country appeared quite settled under British rule. The Pauk column eventually returned to Pauk, and the Pakokku column established itself at Myaing.

The Alôn column, under Lieutenant-Colonel Eyre, 1st Madras Pioneers, and consisting of the troops mentioned in the margin, left Sethu, opposite Alôn, on the 12th December, and arrived at Kanlé on the 20th idem, without adventure, effecting there a junction with the column from Pakokku. Lieutenant-Colonel Eyre's column then returned to Nyaunggôn; and near this place on Christmas Day Captain Hay, 1st Bombay Lancers, with the cavalry, dispersed a large gang of dacoits under Nga Poh Tôk, inflicting heavy loss.

2 guns, No. 1 Bombay M. B.
50 rifles, Royal Muns. Fus.
1 troop, 1st Bombay Lancers.
50 men, 1st Madras Pioneers.
20 „ Military Levy.
30 „ „ Police.

All these columns, until broken up, were employed in visiting villages in the neighbourhood of their camp, collecting arms and hunting small bands of dacoits.

Attack on Lingadaw post.

On the 10th April an important capture of the *ex-Wun* of Pakkangyi was made near the post of Lingadaw, which was held by Lieutenant Lincoln and a detachment of 23rd Bombay Light Infantry. On the night of the 11th a determined attack was made on the post at 1 A.M., by about 300 dacoits. Their object was evidently to rescue the prisoner. They attacked the post on three sides, on one of which a rush was made by about 100, with scaling ladders. This rush failed, and the dacoits were driven off after about three-quarters of an hour's fighting. The attack was led by Maung Kyaw-gaung, the chief officer of the Shwe Gyo Byu Prince's following; they lost about forty killed, and retreated westward into Yaw.

The result of these operations was that all the leaders of the rebellion had been defeated, and, finding it impossible to maintain themselves in the tracts occupied by the troops, retired into some remote parts of the Yaw hills, and were little heard of.

OPERATIONS TO THE NORTH AND EAST OF MANDALAY.

The country directly north and east of Mandalay was in the 1st Brigade, under the command of Brigadier-General East,

On the 1st October 1886 there were two posts to the north of Mandalay, *viz.*—Madaya and Lamaing, each with a small garrison of native infantry, while to the east of the capital were the three small posts of Yankintaung, Taungbô and Kywetnahpa.

These posts were all in the plains at the foot of the Shan Hills and commanded the approaches to them.

The plateau above Yankintaung, Taungbô, and Kywetnahpa was visited in January 1886 by a column which drove out the Minzaing Prince; he had not been able to return there himself, but it had ever since been a stronghold of his partizans. They had stopped all traffic between the plains and the Shan States, no passes remaining open. A great deal of the dacoity in the Kyauksé district emanated from this plateau, and the dense jungle under the hills in the vicinity of Lamaing and Madaya was infested by Dannu dacoits, who were constantly raiding on the neighbouring villages. Punitive expeditions had been sent into their jungles, and the garrisons of Madaya and Lamaing were incessantly making small excursions. The only effect of these was to cause temporary cessations of raiding.

The operations to be now undertaken were the occupation of the Singaung-Maymyo plateau to the east of Mandalay, and the opening up of the direct route north from Mandalay to the Ruby Mines.

The occupation of the Singaung-Maymyo plateau was entrusted to Colonel E. Stedman, commanding 3rd Gurkhas, with a column as given in the margin, the total number of rifles amounting to 400. The Sappers were to improve the very steep pass up the hills, which had a gradient of about 1 in 5, with many rocky steps.

3rd Gurkhas—
Colonel Stedman—
2 Britith Officers.
3 Native Officers.
145 Rifles.
Queen's Own Sappers and Miners—
Lieutenant Glanville, R.E.—
1 Native Officer.
55 Rifles.
Royal Engineers—
Lieutenant Petrie.
Lieutenant Sergeant—
1 Native Officer.
140 Rifles.
23rd W. Light Infantry—
Major Campbell—
2 Native Officers.
160 Rifles.

To facilitate the advance of the column, the sappers were sent twenty-four hours ahead, with Major Campbell and the 23rd Wallajahbad Light Infantry, to work on the worst parts of this pass. Major Campbell formed camp at Onngè at the foot of the hills on October 25th, and the day was spent in work on the pass and getting baggage and stores up to the top. Next morning Major Campbell, leaving eighty-five rifles at Onngé advanced on Zibingalé and Colonel Stedman left Taungbô to overtake him with the Gurkhas the same day.

Before he had advanced two miles, Major Campbell came across a defile blocked with felled trees and flanked by *sangars* held by dacoits. These he attacked and turned out, but with the loss of Lieutenant Glanville, R.E., and five privates, Native Infantry and Sappers, wounded. Colonel Stedman overtook Major Campbell after the affair was over. The following day camp was formed at Zibingalé, and the construction of the post started by Lieutenant Tanner, R.E. Two days later a column, under Colonel Stedman, visited Singaung (3,300 feet above the sea), being the first visit of our troops to the fine plateau on which it lies. A party of fifty dacoits under *Boh* Seh was driven off from Singaung without loss. Consequent on Colonel Stedman's reports it was resolved to send a column through Singaung along the Hsipaw route as far as Hsum Hsai, a town near the Shan frontier, where it was reported large convoys of traders were waiting for the country to quiet down, to enable them to get through to Mandalay.

3rd Gurkhas, 270 men.
Captain Dun, D. A. Q. M. G. Intelligence.
Captain Hobday, Survey of India.

This Hsum Hsai column left Zibingalé on 17th November 1886, strength as shown in margin, Colonel Stedman commanding. Mr. Thirkell White, C.S., Secretary for Upper Burma, accompanied the force as civil officer. The expedition was in every way successfully carried out. No enemy was encountered, and the villagers met our troops with the greatest friendliness. At Hsum Hsai there was some political difficulty in deciding which of several rivals should be supported there, but the chief dacoit leaders interviewed Colonel Stedman and Mr. White, and promised to remain quiet and to leave the country open to traders. When the force retired from Hsum Hsai posts were established at Maymyo and Singaung along this trade route (which leads *viâ* Hsipaw and Hsenwi to Yunnan), to ensure its safety from dacoity. The route to Maymyo decided on for occupation ran through Taungbô, Kywetnahpa, Zibingalé, Pyintha, and Singaung, and work was at once commenced on this road.

Operations near Lamaing.

A main pass to the Maymyo plateau runs east from the Lamaing, past the Dannu villages of Kyabin and Zibyubin; this pass was held by dacoits and was where they took refuge when at all hard pressed. They had been attacked here in July to retaliate for a night attack on the Lamaing post. It was determined to again punish these dacoits in November, and Captain Pulley, moving out against them with 200 rifles, 3rd Gurkhas, found them strongly entrenched in three stockades at Zibubin: one of the stockades enfiladed the road, and two were on his left flank concealed from view by thick jungle. The dacoits allowed him to pass the two flanking stockades before they opened fire. Captain Pulley then charged their position and drove them out, but, in doing this, was himself wounded in the arm. Six of his men and three followers were also wounded. He proceeded, however, to Taungaung, halted there the night, and then returned to Lamaing.

The result of these operations and the establishment of posts on the plateau was that the remaining organization of the Minzaing Prince's dacoit movement was completely broken up; the villages on the plateau settled down to trade and cultivation, the main trade routes to the northern Shan States were opened, and large convoys of Shan bullocks, with traders, immediately commenced passing up and down between Mandalay and the Shan States. The Dannu dacoits east of Lamaing were hemmed in, and having already experienced punishment, commenced to settle down quietly.

OPERATIONS IN THE KYAUKSE DISTRICT.

Hmyat Maung's gang.

After the death of the Minzaing Prince, the chief dacoit leader in the south of the Kyauksé was Hmyat Maung. He had established his strongholds at and near Hmawaing, in the densely jungle-clad hills west of the river Panlaung. There is a pass to the Shan plateau directly in rear of his position a few miles south of the Natteik pass, by means of which he opened communications with the petty Dannu States on the plateau, from whom he used to draw supplies when his position below became hemmed in and he could no longer depend on raiding for necessaries which he could not purchase. Hmyat Maung had spared no exertions to extend his influence, and had collected round him a considerable force led by several influential *Bohs*, and a large district was directly under his administration.

Early in December it was determined to attack the Hmawaing stronghold, and to effect this the co-operation of the 1st, 3rd and 4th Brigades was obtained. Major Aitken, Commanding 9-1 Cinque Ports Division, Royal Artillery, was placed in command of the column from the 1st Brigade, which was formed on December 11th at Kumé, the strength at his disposal being as per margin. With this column he was ordered to make a direct attack on Hmawaing stronghold from Kundaung. A small column under Lieutenant Elger, Somersetshire Light Infantry, advanced to Kinlé on the Natteik pass, in rear of the enemy's position, and the 3rd Brigade despatched a force from Hlaingdet into the upper valley of the Panlaung river, in case the rebels should endeavour to retire south.

Operations against it in December 1886.

1 division, 9-1 Cinque Ports, Royal Artillery.
50 rifles, Somerset Light Infantry.
120 rifles, 25th Bombay Light Infantry.

The column from the 4th Brigade (as per margin) assembled at Wundwin on the 9th December 1886, Captan Rose, 27th Punjab Infantry, in command. On that day information was received that the rebels were leaving Hmawaing and going west. To intercept them the mounted portion of the force was detached north under Lieutenant H. F. Williams, Royal Munster Fusiliers. The movement was successful, and the rebels were met and routed at Taunghu with a loss of two killed, and nine prisoners. Our loss was: one private, 23rd Bombay Light Infantry, killed. and one private, 1st Bombay Lancers, wounded. This force afterwards rejoined its own column at Hmawaing.

40 lances; 1st Bombay Lancers.
60 Mounted Infantry.
2 guns, No. 1 Bombay Mountain Battery.
60 rifles, Royal Munster Fusiliers.
20 rifles, Bombay Sappers and Miners.
140 rifles, 27th Punjab Infantry.

On the morning of the 11th December, Captain Rose's column left Wundwin, crossing the Samôn river at Palébyin; a Burman, who was captured and made to act as guide, stated that stockades had been erected on the road, trees felled, and pitfalls dug. After crossing the river the dense jungle which runs along the foot of the Shan Hills was entered. The guide was in the act of pointing out where some trees had been felled, when the enemy fired a volley, and he fell mortally wounded; a sepoy was also wounded. Advancing steadily through the thick jungle by a narrow pathway, with flanking parties ever on the alert, the column entered the village of Magyipaya, without resistance, at 1 P.M.

The village of Magyipaya is situated on open and level ground, with hills on three sides, which are covered with thick jungle and boulders. From these hills, especially the southern one, where a *jingal* battery was established, an incessant fire was kept up. The troops advancing soon drove the enemy out, and after destroying the village, retired. Directly the retirement commenced, the enemy following up opened fire, and at one time came so close that the guns came into action. Two rounds of case quieted the rebels for the time, but a desultory fire continued until the column got clear of the jungle near Palébyin. Our casualties were six men wounded.

On the following day, the 12th of December, Major Aitken's and Captain Rose's columns concentrated on Hmawaing. Both columns advanced through dense jungle, along narrow tracks, obstructed with bamboo spikes and pitfalls; Captain Rose's column met with no opposition, while Major Aitken's was fired on the whole way, its losses being two killed and eight wounded. Owing to the denseness of the jungle no enemy was seen. Hmawaing was occupied by both columns unopposed, and at 2 P.M., having destroyed the village, the troops retired, both columns proceeding to Kanswé. The enemy fired from the hills during the march. The next day the columns halted.

On the 14th, the village of Othnewé was destroyed and Captain Rose's force proceeded to attack Maungwet, about three miles from Kanswé. Two strongly fortified positions were found *en route*, the ground near them being formidably spiked. At 8 A.M. the village of Maungwet was occupied. It lies in a recess in the hills, and was undefended. Before picquets could be posted, the enemy commenced firing from the hills; their position was at once attacked, and they were driven out of a breastwork they had erected. On this occasion Lieutenant Reid, 27th Punjab Infantry, was severely wounded and three men were spiked. Large stores of grain were found here, but, for want of carriage, they had to be destroyed. After burning the village the force retired to Yozun.

The bands under Hmyat Maung having had their defences destroyed, and being considerably scattered, the columns were then broken up.

The loss to the enemy in this jungle fighting was naturally unknown; our losses were three men killed, and Lieutenant Reid, 27th Punjab Infantry, and eighteen men wounded.

Subsequent operations.

On January 4th, 1887, General East, commanding the 1st Brigade, proceeded to the Kyauksé district to decide on the spot what fresh steps should be taken for the pacification of this part of the country.

As the result of this visit, the number of troops in the district was increased, two new posts were formed at Thabyedaung and Ingôn, and instructions were given to Colonel Bance, commanding the Kyauksé district, to despatch flying columns and patrols in various directions, to destroy villages and crops, and, where possible, to remove stores of grain collected by the dacoits.

Several small columns were consequently kept on the move during January and February, but owing to the difficulties of the country, and the facility with which the dacoits could disappear when attacked, little success was met with.

Destruction of the Hmawaing stronghold.

In March Colonel Bance was ordered to assemble a column at Thabyedaung, for the purpose of advancing on Hmawaing in co-operation with another column from the 3rd Brigade. Accordingly, on the 21st March Colonel Bance marched to Gônywa and was joined the next morning by the troops of the 3rd Brigade under Major Ilderton, 2nd Royal West Surrey Regiment. The whole force was divided into three parties; the main column under his immediate command, consisting of two guns, I-1 Eastern Division, Royal Artillery (Lieutenant De Butts), two Gardners (Captain Airey, New South Wales Artillery), 74 rifles (Lieutenant Cox), Somersetshire Light Infantry; 40 rifles, 15th Madras Infantry; 50 rifles, 25th Bombay Light Infantry (Captain Nuthall), and 22 rifles, Mounted Infantry, under Lieutenant Stevens. The right party under Major Ilderton consisted of 50 rifles, 2nd Royal West Surrey Regiment, and 34 rifles, 27th Punjab Infantry. The left column under command of Captain Presgrave, 15th Madras Infantry, consisted of 30 rifles, Somersetshire Light Infantry (Lieutenant Johnstone), and 75 rifles, 15th Madras Infantry (Lieutenant Oswald). The troops commenced to advance at 6-30 A.M.

At 12 noon the main column gradually approached to within 100 yards of a stone barricade on Hmawaing height, firing shells during the advance. On arriving at this spot they were met by a heavy and continuous fire from *jingals* and guns, and Captain Airey, New South Wales Artillery, Lieutenant Cox, and a private, Somersetshire Light Infantry, were slightly wounded. Two shrapnel shells reversed were fired into the stockade, about fifty yards off: the 'cease fire' was sounded and the stockade rushed, the dacoits flying as the troops entered. From information from a wounded leader, *Boh* Tsine, it appeared that there had been about 250 men in the stockade. The flanking parties joined the main column and the force retired to Gônywa. Two *jingals*, several guns, pistols, and *dahs* were taken, and several bodies found in the stockade.

The dissolution of the gang.

Shortly after these operations Brigadier-General East, with a column from his own (the 1st) Brigade, marched to Myôgyi, the head-quarters of the chief of the Baw State, which lies on the edge of the Shan plateau east of Yéwun and north-east of Hmawaing. The *Ngwegunhmu* (Chief) of Baw had wavered in his allegiance between the British and the neighbouring dacoit chiefs, and was waiting safe in his own hills till affairs should develop themselves. His subjects, mostly Dannus, had from time to time taken advantage of the lawlessness which prevailed along the Baw border, and made some successful raids in the Kyauksé district. General East's column reached the capital without opposition, and was met by the Chief Minister of the State, the Chief himself having sought safety in flight. The State tendered its allegiance to the British and was fined Rs. 2,500 and deprived of 100 guns on account of dacoities recently committed. Thus Hmyat Maung's whole position had been thoroughly explored and opened out.

At this time Major Ilderton, 2nd Queen's, stationed at Wundwin, obtained a wonderful influence over the whole gang and inspired them with such confidence that the several leaders with their following came in and surrendered themselves to him. Hmyat Maung himself also came into Wundwin shortly afterwards and surrendered himself to Major Ilderton on the 9th May. The history of Hmyat Maung's gang is unique in the war; their able leader kept the whole of the gang together, supplying itself and holding its own against all comers but the British. His subordinate leaders were loyal to him and each other to the end; there was very little of the mutual quarrelling amongst them which so weakened other gangs, and there was very little desertion. When they were really beaten, and could no longer remain in their own country as dacoits, finding that they could trust in Major Ilderton, whom they only knew as an enemy, they all came in and surrendered to him. So complete was the surrender of this gang that shortly after Hmyat Maung had submitted, he took out Major Ilderton and Lieutenant Miller, of the same regiment, to show them his old positions, and to get them some shooting in the neighbouring hills.

Operations to the west of Kyauksé.

The settlement of the country to the west of Kyauksé and in the neighbourhood of Ava had already been partially effected previous to October 1886, but constant vigilance was necessary and many small dacoities continued to occur. The chief centres of dacoity were round Minzaing and Mingyi. To put a stop to these depredations three small columns were sent to the Minzaing district, and three to the country around Mingyi. The former three columns were under the command of Lieutenant-Colonel Cotton, Major Persse and Captain Renny, respectively, and their operations call for no further comment than to say that they left their respective posts of Myotha, and Chaungwa, on the 13th December, and, proceeding by various converging routes, met at Kane on the 22nd December, whence they returned to their stations, having successfully scoured the whole district.

The three columns for the Mingyi district were under the commands of Lieutenant Lloyd, Lieutenant Campbell, and an officer of the Somersetshire Light Infantry (name not mentioned) respectively, and began their advance on the 1st January 1887. The *Boh* who had been giving trouble in this neighbourhood was *Boh* Shweyan. Lieutenant Campbell surprised this man's camp on 1st January near Subagin, capturing eleven ponies, five guns, and many spears. Shweyan himself escaped with difficulty. He had infested this district since the first occupation of Kyauksé in January 1886, but he now disappeared, and the inhabitants settled down quietly.

OPERATIONS IN THE NEIGHBOURHOOD OF WELAUNG, SAMETKYON, SHANMANNGE AND POPA.

The 4th Brigade Command comprised the civil districts of Myingyan and Meiktila and was under the command of Brigadier-

General H. S. Anderson. The troops were distributed as follows:—about 800 at Myingyan, about 220 at Mahlaing, 250 at Meiktila, 160 at Wundwin, 100 at Natôgyi, 100 at Yetagyô, fifty-five at Samet-kyôn, and fifty at Taungtha. The measures adopted to dominate the country were the constant movement of flying columns, attacking any gatherings of rebels; and a regular system of patrols from village to village.

In October 1886, it was decided to send a column against a dacoit named *Boh* Yanuyaung, who had been infesting the hill of Pôpa, about forty miles south of Myingyan, and who had recently attacked the British post at Taungtha. Accordingly, on the 5th November a column, under command of Lieutenant-Colonel Heyland, 1st Bombay Lancers, marched from Myingyan on Taungtha. Brigadier-General Low, C.B., Commanding 6th Brigade, sent a force from Pagan to co-operate, and troops were likewise despatched from Mahlaing to Shabadaung, sixteen miles south-west of that station, in case the rebels should endeavour to escape in that direction.

112 Lances, 1st Bombay Lancers.
100 Rifles, R. M. Fusiliers.
150 " 17th Madras Infantry.

Lieutennat-Colonel Heyland's column marched from Taungtha on the 7th November. Owing to continuous heavy rain from that date until the 11th no signalling could be arranged with the other columns, and the inclement weather delayed their arrival at their respective posts. After visiting several villages Lieutenant-Colonel Heyland selected Welaung as the most favourable for a post. From this place, extensive patrolling was carried on by cavalry and infantry detachments, the former visiting villages twenty miles from the post; and several villages were destroyed.

Every endeavour was made to communicate with the other columns by heliograph but without effect. The mist was so heavy and dense after the recent rain that messages could not be read. Leaving a garrison at Welaung, the rest of Colonel Heyland's force marched on the 21st November towards Myingyan, the cavalry making a detour to the westward to Dhattaw on the Irrawaddy. Although reports of rebels were received, they always escaped into the dense *jungle*, and none were seen. The troops arrived at Myingyan on the 24th November. The bands of rebels around Pôpa were for the time completely broken up.

In November a combined movement of troops of the 1st and 5th Brigades took place against the rebels infesting the country between the Mu and Chindwin rivers. The General Officer Commanding 1st Brigade requested the post at Sametkyôn to be instructed to keep a look-out to intercept dacoits should they attempt to cross the Irrawaddy river. This force consequently patrolled the river banks and thoroughly searched the islands in the Irrawaddy, and though no rebels were captured, not a single rebel leader was able to cross the river.

50 Royal Munster Fusiliers
55 17th Madras Infantry
50 23rd Bo. Light Infantry
} Sametkyôn Garrison.

Information was received by telegram on the 11th of December that Major Roberts, Liverpool Regiment, in command of column in the Pin district, had had 'severe fighting,' and he requested a force might be sent to operate against the rebel chief Tok Kyaw. This leader was a man of influence, who resided at Shanmanngé, a village about twenty miles from Meiktila. He ruled the district and collected the revenue in his own interest, but had, it is believed, not committed himself openly against the British. On the 13th December a force under Lieutenant-Colonel Woodward, Royal Munster Fusiliers, arrived at the village of Tsido, eight miles from Shanmanngé, and communications were entered into with Tok Kyaw.

The Shanmanngé Moveable Column.

40 Lances, 1st Bombay Lancers.
45 Rifles, Liverpool Regiment.
35 „ Royal Munster Fusiliers.
38 „ 17th Madras Infantry.

The civil authorities stated that hasty entrenchments and obstacles had been erected by Tok Kyaw's orders on the road to Shanmanngé, and as he failed to surrender, Lieutenant-Colonel Woodward advanced. After proceeding about five miles, the enemy opened fire from behind their entrenchments on the advancing column. Major Egerton, commanding the leading company—the Liverpools—replied, and advancing to the attack, rushed the position, the enemy running down into the *nullah* at the back of their defences. The Royal Munster Fusiliers and detachment 17th Madras Infantry at the same time drove the enemy out of their position on the left. The casualties on our side were—wounded: one Sergeant and four Privates, Liverpool Regiment; two Privates, Royal Munster Fusiliers; one of the latter died of his wounds.

Thirty-seven dead bodies of the enemy were counted on the ground. The force continued its advance, and on arriving at Shanmanngé occupied the village. The following day the village was destroyed, and the column returned to Tsido.

Lieutenant-Colonel Woodward reported on the 23rd that all the country was in the hands of the rebels, and that, until the bands were broken, it was most undesirable for him to proceed. On receipt of this intelligence a column was at once despatched from Meiktila under Lieutenant Wallace, 27th Punjab Infantry, reaching Shanmanngé on the 24th December, and Brigadier-General Anderson arrived from Myingyan at Tsido on the 26th idem. The next day Lieutenant-Colonel Woodward advanced in the direction of Pin, the Brigadier-General proceeding at the same time to Shanmanngé. On that morning a small force under Lieutenant Wallace surprised Tok Kyaw at Thebingôn, capturing his camp; the enemy fled, leaving three dead. The cavalry started in pursuit, but, owing to the time lost in getting through the village, both gates having been fastened, the enemy were not overtaken. No more opposition was met with, and Colonel Woodward, having advanced as far as Sulegôn, fourteen miles from Shwebandaw, near Pin, whence he detached Major Egerton's company to join Major Robert's force, marched his column back to Welaung.

2 guns, No. 1 Bombay Mountain Battery.
25 Lances, 1st Bombay Lancers.
50 Mounted Infantry.
60 Rifles, 27th Punjab Infantry.

Difficulties of Column Commanders.

The two principal difficulties which the Commanders of the various columns experienced at this time were lack of reliable information, and want of civil officers who could talk or even understand Burmese.

Subsequent to the operations already mentioned, dashes were continually made from the various posts at the dacoits whenever heard of. On the 6th February a gang of about 100 dacoits attacked the village of Aing, five miles south of Meiktila. Lieutenant Williams, Royal Munster Fusiliers, hearing that they had proceeded to a village named Lipanchin, surrounded the village at daybreak and captured eleven of them with some ponies and ammunition.

On the 14th February about 800 dacoits made an unsuccessful night attack on the post of Welaung.

On the 8th March, a subadar, with twenty lances, 1st Madras Cavalry, covering forty miles in the day, pursued 100 dacoits, of whom he succeeded in killing fifty.

At Taungdwingyi there was a garrison of about 350 men under Major Sir Bartle Frere, Rifle Brigade. The troops were constantly engaged in co-operating with the 3rd Brigade and in suppressing local dacoity. On the 29th March a party of thirty lances and seventeen mounted infantry attacked a gang of 700 in a walled position and succeeded in putting the dacoits to flight and in killing about 150 of them.

THE OCCUPATION OF THE RUBY MINES.

Soon after the occupation of Mandalay, the attention of the dealers in gems, both in India and Europe, was turned to the acquisition of the far-famed Ruby Mines of Upper Burma. These mines, at the villages of Mogôk, Kyatpyin, and Kathé, were reported to be the most valuable ruby mines in the world. They are on a mountain range on the left bank of the Irrawaddy, at an elevation of about 5,000 feet. The approaches were over intermediate ranges by mountain tracks, crossing unbridged streams which became torrents during the rains. The distance from the Irrawaddy was estimated at sixty or seventy miles. No supplies were procurable on the road.

The villagers of Mogôk, Kathé, and Kyatpyin were in possession of the mines, and the headmen were reported to be rich and determined to spend money on the retention of the valuable property they had appropriated to themselves on the fall of the Alompra dynasty. They were invited to meet the British Commissioner of the division, and were told that every consideration would be accorded to the privileges that had been conceded to them under Thibaw; but that they must submit to British rules and regulations, the property in the mines being a royalty which escheated to us as successors of the deposed King.

Burmese characteristics.

It would seem but rational to assume that the people of Burma generally would have become aware of the ease with which the British force had possessed itself of Mandalay, accounted by the Burmans the centre of the universe—and that, recognizing the futility of detached resistance, they would have accepted the inevitable, and availed themselves of the very liberal terms which we were only too anxious to offer for their acceptance. Experience has, however, taught us that rational inference from established facts is the least trustworthy of all guides to the Burmans' actual line of conduct. This seems to be due chiefly to the height of their vanity and the depth of their credulity. These two national characteristics were our greatest difficulty in obtaining peaceful possession of the outlying districts. If the spirits were declared propitious, no flight of fancy was too lofty for the ambition of the Burman, and no fiction of our necessities too ridiculous for his credence. In 1886, fifty Burmans armed with *dahs* set up a pseudo-king, mounted him on an elephant, and advanced to capture Mandalay; in 1887 the people, a few miles from Mandalay, believed we were hemmed in there by a Russian army.

But to return to the expedition to Mogôk. The Chiefs of the Ruby Mine confederation were no exception to the rule of Burman arrogance, and, confident in the inaccessibility of their position, they stood aloof and made preparations to oppose our advance.

Operations.

The first point to determine was the river base from which the expedition was to start. Kyanhnyat was the point selected, as the route from it was over a level tract for a long way to the foot of the hills. Carts could be used over this tract, which extended for nearly forty miles, leaving but a short distance of hill to be worked by pack transport. When every pound of supply had to be taken with the force, every extra mile of country over which carts could ply became a consideration of the greatest weight.

60 Rifles, Hampshire Regiment.
132 ,, Queen's Own Madras Sappers and Miners.
100 Rifles, 23rd Gurkha Light Infantry.

Kyanhnyat was occupied on the 21st September by the marginally named force under Lieutenant-Colonel Skene, 43rd Gurkha Light Infantry, and a military pos was established there. Reconnaissances were then pushed out towards the hills; and Sagadaung, nearly forty miles from Kyanhnyat, was reached by Captain Barnet, R.E., on the 19th October. These reconnaissances were quickly followed by working parties of Gurkhas and Sappers, who, with great perseverance and labour, cut a way through dense bamboo jungle to Sagadaung. It was imperative to commence the work as early as possible in the colder months, and consequently the troops employed were subjected to the malarious influence rife in the *jungles* during October and November. One company of Madras Sappers became non-effective from sickness and was recalled to Mandalay, and even the Gurkhas from Assam were much weakened by fever.

On the 20th November, a party of the 43rd Gurkha Light Infantry, under Lieutenant-Colonel Skene, attacked and dispersed a body of Shans that had collected in force at Kyaukpyôn to oppose his advance. Two Gurkhas were wounded, and the enemy lost ten men killed, and some wounded. This was the first time the Shans had encountered Gurkhas, whose determined style of fighting completely overawed them. From henceforth there was no opposition of a resolute character to hinder the advance of the expedition. Sagadaung was occupied on the 30th November, and preparations made for the advance up the hills. All available transport was collected at that post and supplies were pushed on from Kyanhnyat. On the 5th December Brigadier-General Stewart arrived at Kyanhnyat to assume personally the direction of the expedition.

At that time the situation stood as follows:—At Sagadaung was collected the advanced party under Lieutenant-Colonel Skene, consisting of—

2	guns,	1-1 Eastern Division Royal Artillery.
96	Rifles,	South Yorkshire Regiment.
100	"	No. 2 Company, Bengal Sappers and Miners.
253	"	43rd Gurkha Light Infantry.

Detachments of the latter were holding stockaded posts at Taungywé, Kodan, and Webaung; additional cart transport had been brought from Shwebo, and 150 rifles, South Yorkshire Regiment, had arrived from the same place to strengthen the reserve.

With the addition of two Gardner guns and forty rifles of the 43rd Gurkha Light Infantry, the force above mentioned formed the column to advance towards Mogôk, and was concentrated at Sagadaung under Brigadier-General Stewart on the 17th December. Two days later this force advanced to Nabu, from whence Colonel Cubitt, V.C., commanding the 43rd Gurkha Light Infantry, was detached with a portion of the column on Ywazu. Here the main party joined him on the 20th, and the whole force commenced the ascent of the hills. On the 21st the column halted at Lwékaw; a fortified post was established there and the country towards Nampot reconnoitred.

The following morning a reconnaissance in force was directed on Nampot. The enemy's videttes were driven in, and his position, which had been evacuated, was occupied. It was an extremely strong one, with stockaded breastworks barring the road. On the 23rd the expedition reached Pyaunggaung (now Bernardmyo), situated at an elevation of 6,000 feet, and where the thermometer at 7 o'clock in the morning showed a reading of 26° Fahrenheit. On the following day the force advanced to Ingyauk, two miles further on. Here the road bifurcates, one branch leading direct to Mogôk, and the other to Kathé and Kyatpyin. The enemy was found to be holding stockades on both these roads, his main body being on the Mogôk branch. As the stockade held by the enemy on the Kyatpyin road flanked an advance along the Mogôk road, General Stewart decided to attack and dislodge him from it before moving towards Mogôk. Lieutenant-Colonel Skene, with thirty-three rifles of the South Yorkshire Regiment, and seventy-five of his own corps, was detailed for this duty, which was successfully carried out. Advancing through dense forest, and clambering up the steep gorge, they stormed the stockade at the summit, losing one man dangerously wounded. The enemy posted on the Mogôk road had commenced a desultory fire on the main body of our troops, but this had been easily silenced. On the return of Lieutenant-Colonel Skene's party it was too dark for further action and the force encamped at Ingyauk.

The next day, Christmas-day, the column halted, and the enemy's position was reconnoitred. A reinforcement of fifty rifles of the South Yorkshire Regiment arrived from Sagadaung, and a post was established at Ingyauk. On the 26th the main body advanced on the direct road to Mogôk against the enemy's stockade, while a party of 100 rifles of the Gurkha Light Infantry, under Captain Barrett, was detached to turn his position by moving round his right flank. This operation was successfully carried out. The enemy's position was found evacuated, and the detached party having rejoined the main body, the whole force continued its advance over the Taungmedaik pass, height 6,720 feet. A halt was made for the night at the village of Thipangaung.

Mogôk was occupied on the 27th December. The mercenaries employed by the inhabitants of the Ruby Mines district to oppose our advance, finding it easier and safer to turn upon their employers than to fulfil their engagement, had looted the town and dispersed. The villagers, feeling themselves compromised by their resistance, fled and hid themselves in the hills. Little by little, however, they gained confidence and returned to their normal occupation, with the exception of the Chiefs, who mistrusted our assurances and were afraid to come within reach of arrest.

To the south-east of the Ruby Mines district, and contiguous to it, lies the State of Mainglôn, which at this time was in a state of anarchy. Two rival claimants for the *Sawbwaship* had set themselves up—Kun Sine and Heng Nga Maung. With a view to re-establishing order and nominating one or the other as rightful *Sawbwa*, two columns were directed to proceed to Mainglôn—one under Lieutenant-Colonel Deshon, R.A., from Zagabin, thirty miles north-east of Mandalay, and the other from the Ruby Mines force. The latter party, consisting of 100 rifles, South Yorkshire Regiment, under Captain Earle, left Mogôk on the 9th January, and on approaching Mainglôn found it strongly stockaded and held by the partisans of both parties. After a slight skirmish, however, our troops carried the position. The column under Lieutenant-Colonel Deshon, consisting of two Gardner guns, seventy-five rifles, Somersetshire Light Infantry, and two companies, 17th Madras Infantry, reached Mainglôn on the 15th January, and Captain Earle's party returned to Mogôk. Lieutenant-Colonel Deshon's force remained at Mainglôn, while investigation was made into the rival claims of Heng Nga Maung, and Kun Sine. The latter was eventually declared our nominee, and Lieutenant-Colonel Deshon's force left for Zagabin on the 25th January.

Colonel Deshon's column.

Mogôk was visited by the Commander-in-Chief in India on 22nd January. The hills around appeared to offer sites at suitable elevations for a permanent hill station, and His Excellency ordered that they should be examined with a view to the selection of the most eligible position for a sanitarium. Pyaunggaung

(Bernardmyo) on the Sagadaung side of the Taungmedaik pass was selected; the head-quarters of the force were moved to it from Mogôk, and the hutting of the troops was at once commenced.

Disturbance in Mainglôn district.

Early in March 1887, Heng Nga Maung having gained the support of the neighbouring chief of Tawngpeng and of the Chaungwa Prince, now a fugitive in those parts, sought to create disturbances in the Mainglôn district. In order to support Kun Sine, our nominee, a party under Captain Earle, South Yorkshire Regiment, strength sixty rifles, South Yorkshire Regiment, eighty-five rifles, 43rd Gurkha Light Infantry and two Gardner guns, left Pyaunggaung (Bernardmyo) on the 11th March to disperse the adherents of Heng Nga Maung. This purpose was successfully carried out, and the party returned to Pyaunggaung on the 30th March.

The cantonment of Pyaunggaung was re-named Bernardmyo by order of the Viceroy, as a compliment to Sir Charles Bernard, the Chief Commissioner.

The result of the expedition was that the district became perfectly tranquil, industry in the mines was re-opened, and the prospects of a constant and prosperous trade were established.

OPERATIONS ON THE RIVER CHINDWIN.

The valley of the River Chindwin formed what was known as the Chindwin command. The district comprised in this command extended over three degrees of latitude, but this extreme length was compensated for by the excellent line of communications which the river afforded.

On the 15th October 1886 the forces of the command were distributed as follows: at Kindat 315 men, at Kalewa fifty-three men, at Mingin 212 men, at Alôn two guns and 168 men. The measures adopted for the domination of the Chindwin were limited to a great extent by the small number of troops compared with the vast size of the district. Above the Alôn district the hilly and wooded nature of the country on both sides of the river rendered the passage of troops extremely difficult, and, in many places impracticable; the roads, where they existed, were mere *jungle* tracks leading over steep hills which no laden pack animal could surmount, and through creeks which were impassable for a great portion of the year. In some parts, and notably between Mingin and Kindat, there were extensive forests where the absence of water prohibited the movements of troops.

Regular communication and the supply of stores for the troops could only be maintained by river, and the operations in the Upper Chindwin had thus to be chiefly confined to the river line.

The distances of the three larger posts, Alôn, Mingin, and Kindat, from the mouth of the Chindwin, are as follows:—

Mouth of river to Alôn	60 miles.
Alôn to Mingin	85 „
Migin to Kindat	92 „
TOTAL ..	237 „

The other posts held for any lengthened period were—

Paungbyin, about seventy miles above Kindat.

Kalewa, about forty miles above Mingin.

Yetagyo, about forty miles below Alôn.

The principal coercive measure adopted in the Upper Chindwin was the despatch of a force by river or land to attack and disperse any body of rebels directly news was received as to their whereabouts; flying columns of 100 or 150 men were on several occasions sent up the river on a large steamer with two 7-pounder guns, when information was received of the collection of any considerable body of dacoits; and, although the rebels never offered any opposition on these occasions, it was found that the expeditions invariably exercised a quieting influence on the country, causing the rebels in many cases to disperse, and re-assuring those villages that were either friendly to us or wavering.

In Alôn the chief measures were the posting of small parties in all troubled parts of the district, and constant visiting of all those portions of the sub-division that had harboured dacoits during the rainy season. Captain Sage was constantly on the move in the district with cavalry or mounted infantry, and patrolled on an average about fifteen miles daily; the results of these visits on the behaviour of the villagers were most marked, and Captain Sage's personal intercourse with the inhabitants had the best effects.

Patrolling was frequently carried out, especially by the mounted infantry at Kindat, who used to patrol three times a week. At Mingin this patrolling was carried out by the infantry parties alone, as the country being unsuited for mounted infantry, there were none in the post. On the first advance up the Chindwin the destruction and firing of the rebel stronghold of Balet and the use of the mountain guns had a great effect at the time. Masein, which had been preparing to resist us, capitulated on our approach, and we found the news had preceded us to Kindat, which was occupied without opposition.

Cultivation of friendly relations with independent Chiefs and others.

The pacification of the Chindwin was greatly facilitated by the cultivation of friendly relations with independent Chiefs by the civil authorities. Captain Raikes, the Deputy Commissioner, possessed great tact and knowledge of the Burman character and language, and his intercourse with the natives was minently successful. The *Sawbwas* of Thaungdut and Kalé, and he *Kyamaing* of the latter place, who had been appointed *Sawbwa*, *vice* his uncle the *ex-Sawbwa*, were friendly all through, and the latter sent 100 armed men to co-operate with us in the upper district, and assisted in the capture of the rebel of the Taungdwin district, calling himself Buddha Yaza. The *Shwe Hmus* of Masein and Matut were also friendly and gave contingents of armed men on the occasion noted above.

Disarmament of country.

The disarmament of the country was another measure taken for its pacification, but this could not be carried out on a large scale owing to the peculiar circumstances of the Chindwin. In the first place, there were not many arms in the country beyond those in the hands of the dacoits, and these could only be obtained by their capture or death. The civil authorities encouraged some of the friendly Chiefs as above noted to assist us with armed men, and it would have been contrary to the policy of the Government to disarm the followers of independent Chiefs like the *Sawbwas* of Thaungdut and Kalé. Then again to have entirely disarmed the villages on the right bank of the Upper Chindwin would have exposed them to the scant mercy of the wild Chins, who made constant raids on them every dry season.

Amongst further measures taken for the pacification of the district and for its domination, may be mentioned the making of roads, the establishment of the telegraph line, and the regular running of steamers on the river.

The following is an account of the operations from October to February 1887 :—

At Alôn, on the 19th October 1886, a column under Captain Sage, strength 106 rifles, *viz.*, 18th Bengal Infantry, twenty ; 25th Bombay Light Infantry, forty; and Military Levy, forty-five, marched *viâ* Chauk-Kah to Maletha to attack a body of dacoits in the *jungle* near Chauktat under *Bohs* Min-U, Nyo-O and the Pegu *Myingaung*. On the 20th Captain Sage with Lieutenant Loch and forty-five rifles, while making a detour, came upon the dacoit camp, and captured it after a short and sharp struggle. The Pegu *Myingaung's* nephew was killed, and several guns, ponies, carts, and cattle were captured. The casualties of the attacking force were one sepoy killed, and one severely wounded.

Rebellion in U district and murder of Mr. Gleeson.

On the 27th and 28th October, an unfortunate disaster occurred in the U district at the village of that name, which is situated on the right bank of the Chindwin, about fifteen miles above Mingin. Mr. Gleeson, Assistant Commissioner, had left Mingin on the 3rd of October, with an escort of twenty rifles, 18th Bengal Infantry, in the S.S. *Kyondo* to instal a new man in the office of *Shwe Hmu* at U. Mr. Gleeson had unbounded confidence in the Burmans, and on the 27th of October he appointed a number of Burmans in U to be police, and armed them with confiscated guns, which had been captured from dacoits. The senior havildar of the party, a very shrewd observant, had brought to Mr. Gleeson's notice on that day the suspicious fact that there was neither a woman nor an old man nor a child to be seen in the village—every person that met the eye was a strong able-bodied man—; and he begged him to allow two sepoys of the escort to sleep in a detached house in which he was living at some fifteen yards distance from the escort. Mr. Gleeson, however, would not do so, but laughed at what he called the old man's fears. He said that one sentry over his quarter was all that he required, and that if any attack were imminent, he would receive timely notice of it from the Burman police. He also instructed the havildar to warn the sentries that if any Burman were to come at any time in the night and give the word "*Paleik*," meaning "Police," he was to be admitted. Two sentries were accordingly posted, one over Mr. Gleeson's quarters and one over the escort.

At about midnight of the 27th–28th, some Burmans approached the latter sentry in the dark, and one man, giving the word "*Paliek*," had no sooner passed the sentry than he cut him down, and at the same time a general rush was made on the post by some 400 or 500 dacoits. A havildar, who jumped off the verandah of the guard house to rush to Mr. Gleeson's assistance, was immediately surrounded and cut down, being severely wounded in five places with *dahs*. Three sepoys were also wounded, in addition to the sentry who was killed, and Mr. Gleeson, being deserted by his Burman police, was cut down and killed with *dahs* as he ran from his house. The fifteen men who were left defended themselves during the whole of the night and the remainder of the next day. In the morning Naik Umrao Singh, with four sepoys, 18th Bengal Infantry, very gallantly volunteered to sally out and attack the village on the west side, whence the enemy were pouring in a galling fire from the cover of the houses, and he succeeded in driving the enemy out and burning down the village without loss. In the evening, finding their ammunition failing, the whole party retreated in the direction of Mingin, carrying all their baggage and kit with them, and were met at Chaungwa by a party which had come out to their relief under Major Rennick, 18th Bengal Infantry. Before leaving, the party had made a hastily improvised raft of plantain leaves, their only implements being the two havildars' sword bayonets, and had placed on it the corpses of Mr. Gleeson and the sepoy, the wounded men's kits, and the wounded havildar.

The raft was safely piloted down the river by sepoy Drigpal Singh, 18th Bengal Infantry, who volunteered for this dangerous service, and was several times shot at from the banks on his way down. Mr. Gleeson's body unfortunately became detached from the raft near Chaungwa, but was subsequently recovered at Pindin, many miles below Mingin, and buried at the latter place.

Major Rennick acted with much promptitude on the occasion, and the next day burnt several of the villages in the vicinity which were chiefly implicated, and imposed large fines upon others. The inhabitants of nineteen villages in the U district are said to have been implicated in this act of treachery. Eighteen dead bodies of the enemy were found when the scene of the encounter was visited the next day, and a great number must have been wounded. The three non-commissioned officers and sepoy Drigpal received the 3rd class of the Order of Merit for their gallantry on this occasion.

Punitive expedition.

During the month of October, the dacoits became very troublesome on the southern borders of the Payi district, and, gradually extending their influence northwards, they succeeded at last in inducing Pôh Tok, the *Myo-thúgyi* of Myogyi, to rebel. The latter had formerly owned fealty to the Kani Wun, who, on hearing of his intrigues with the dacoits, at once went over with only five followers to remonstrate with him, and his rashness led to his being treacherously murdered at Myogyi on the 4th of November 1886. On the 6th of November, in consequence of a rumour that the Kani Wún had been made a prisoner by Pôh Tok, a flying column of eighty-five rifles under Lieutenant Fryer, 18th Bengal Infantry, crossed the Chindwin and marched towards Myogyi with a view to release him.

The 1st Myogyi column.

After crossing the river, the road was found blocked in many places, and in some instances filled with abatis to a distance of 500 yards, which considerably impeded the advance. The next afternoon (7th) on Lieutenant Fryer's approaching Myogyi, he found it held by a large force of rebels who were strongly posted in pagodas. The dacoits opened a heavy fire on the attacking force, and Lieutenant Fryer, after replying with two volleys at a range of 200 yards, gave the order to charge. The enemy were driven out, only to open fire from another stockaded position 100 yards in rear of the first. Lieutenant Fryer, 18th Bengal Infantry, and one or two men were severely wounded in the first charge, and the former only stopped after losing much blood from the artery of the wrist, which had been severed. The command then devolved upon Lieutenant Hodson, 23rd Wallajahbad Light Infantry, who, well supported by Mr. Annesley, gallantly charged three successive positions, which were stubbornly held by the dacoits until our men were close upon them. The casualties on our side were Lieutenant Fryer, one sepoy, 18th Bengal Infantry, one private, 23rd Wallajahbad Light Infantry, and one transport driver severely wounded; one sepoy, 18th Bengal Infantry, and two privates, 23rd Wallajahbad Light Infantry, killed. The enemy's numbers were about 1,000, of whom about 300 were armed with muskets.

The column, having received information of the Kani Wun's murder, returned to Alôn.

2nd column to Myogyi.

The dacoits having again collected in large numbers at Myogyi under Pôh Tok a flying column under Lieutenant Tisdall, R. A., was sent from Alôn to disperse them on the 15th of November. The strength of the force was two guns and 150 men.

The column first encountered the dacoits when they were crossing the Kyaukmyit stream, at Pyanhle, where they were strongly entrenched. The dacoits were driven out of these defences after a short action, and the advance renewed; but, owing to the direct road being blocked at every hundred yards, a detour was made through scrub *jungle*, and the village approached from the south. As the dacoits had made no preparations to repel an attack from this direction, they retired without offering any further resistance. The casualties of the column in the action were one killed and seven wounded. The enemy suffered some loss, but the extent was unknown. The column remained nearly a week at Myogyi, destroying defences and clearing *jungle*, and then returned to Alôn.

In the beginning of December 1886, the Chins perpetrated several small raids in the neighbourhood of Kindat, and took away some villagers.

On the 8th December the rebel U Shwe Hmu (*Boh* Nga Bya) attacked and burnt Chaungwa in the U district. The inhabitants of this place had roused his ire by giving us boats and otherwise assisting us on the occasion of the murder of Mr. Gleeson.

Attack on Thambya.

On the 11th January an attempt was made to surround a body of rebels under Nga Bya who were known to be at Thambya, a village about six miles east of Taya, on the opposite side of the river. Three columns started at night with a view to making a simultaneous attack on the village from different sides by daybreak on the morning of the 12th. The columns all arrived near the village as intended, but the success of the plan was marred by a want of knowledge of the ground, which was extremely difficult, covered with *jungle* and intercepted by a deep creek. The dacoits fled on the first alarm, and owing to these difficulties succeeded in making good their escape. The expedition was not, however, without its results, as six men were captured, including *Boh* Nga Bya's *Hpungyi*, believed to be the instigator of the whole rebellion.

The further events that took place in the Chindwin valley between the 1st February and the end of March may be briefly summarized as follows :—

Operations subsequent to the 1st February 1887.

In the Alôn and Pagyi districts the work of disarmament was steadily carried on. *Thugyis* were called upon to collect and bring in all arms that were known to exist; where this method failed, the villages from which they had not been given up were carefully searched.

A column, from Alôn, under Lieutenant-Colonel Eyre, consisting of a company of the Royal Munster Fusiliers under Captain Chute, a detachment, 1st Madras Pioneers, and twenty-one mounted infantry of the Chindwin Police Battalion, crossed the Chindwin river on the 5th February, with the intention of proceeding against Nga Po, *Thugyi* of Thinkida. Nga Po sent some headmen to meet the column to explain that he had no wish to oppose the English, but that he could not come in till assured of protection, as his villages were exposed to the attacks of disaffected persons in the Yaw district. Under these circumstances, and owing to the difficulties of supply and transport, Lieutenant-Colonel Eyre returned to Alôn on the 14th February.

Lieutenant Custance, commanding Mounted Infantry, on the 14th March, surprised a party of dacoits at Kyadet, thirty-five miles south-west of Alôn, and killed *Boh* Kalain, the instigator of the Kain Wun's murder, capturing the father and brother of Pôh Tok, the actual murderer, and taking five guns. Owing to the number of dacoits reported to be in the district he was reinforced by fourteen men; and on the 16th March surprised and killed *Boh* Nga Poh, a noted leader in the Pagyi district.

Captain Sage, 18th Bengal Infantry, left Alôn on the 18th March with a small column and proceeded as far as Budalaing. He returned on the 22nd, reporting the country quiet.

Operations in the Taungdwin valley against Buddha Yaza.

Towards the end of February Buddha Yaza appeared in the Taungdwin valley with 300 followers from the Yaw country. On the 24th February eighteen rifles, 1st Madras Pioneers, from Taungdwin-gaung attacked him, but were obliged to fall back on their post, where they were shut in till the 27th February. The enemy occupied four commanding positions and cut off the garrison of the stockade from their water supply. A havildar, 18th Bengal Infantry, commanding a party of twenty men at Chaungwa, moved on the 27th February, to the relief of Taungdwin-gaung with eleven men, and attacking the northernmost of the four posts mentioned, which was held by 100 dacoits, drove them out of it and pursued them for a mile. His party now being joined by twenty from the stockade, the dacoits broke and fled.

On the 24th February Lieutenant Churchill, 1st Madras Pioneers, having heard of the rising in the Taungdwin valley, marched with a force of fifty-two rifles, 18th Bengal Infantry, and twenty rifles, 1st Madras Pioneers, from Mingin on Taungdwin-gaung Tinbit. On the morning of the 25th Buddha Yaza was suddenly discovered, holding a strong, apparently fortified, position, on the crest of a hill, with 600 followers. The only approach to the position was a path running through a fissure in the rock, the ground on either side being precipitous and covered with thick *jungle*, and the path only wide enough to admit of one man passing at a time. Lieutenant Churchill engaged the enemy for about half an hour and, seeing no chance of success, fell back. Our losses amounted to one man killed and six wounded. On the 27th February Major Browne, 18th Bengal Infantry, started for the Taungdwin valley with a small column from Mingin and marched through the district, but met with no resistance, and returned to Mingin on the 10th March.

The *Sawbwa* of Kalé captured Buddha Yaza early in March and sent him to Kindat; this caused the rising to subside at once.

A new military post was established at Payathon, and the strength of the post at Taungdwin-gaung was increased to fifty men.

On the 20th February 200 Chins, of the Kanhow tribe, attacked the British post of Auktaung in the Kubaw valley. The attack was repulsed and the Chiefs of the Kanhows killed.

THE OCCUPATION OF WUNTHO.

The *Sawbwa* of Wuntho, who, under the lax rule of King Thibaw had established himself in semi-independence, had hitherto failed to yield more than a mere verbal submission to British authority.

Although repeatedly called upon to come in person to meet the Commissioner of the Division and his civil officers, he had failed to do so, professing fear of arrest. Moreover, much of the raiding by dacoits in the territories of his neighbours who had submitted to the British was attributed by them to the connivance, if not to the influence, of this powerful *Sawbwa*. Further, he had failed to pay any instalment of revenue, which in Burma is the outward and visible sign of submission.

Ultimatum.

An ultimatum was therefore sent to him, and he was ordered to meet Mr. Burgess, Commissioner of the Northern Division, on a day named. In case of failure he was warned that the British forces would advance on Wuntho, and he would be treated as an enemy. At the same time every precaution was taken to make him reconsider his position, and to avoid hurrying him into resistance. He, however, failed to meet the Commissioner, and while Mr. Burgess was waiting at Manlé for the expiration of the time allowed him, authentic intelligence was received on the 13th January 1887 to the effect that the *Sawbwa* had fled from his capital, which was in a state of anarchy. An immediate advance of the British force at Manlé was consequently ordered.

Wuntho was situated west of the Bhamo district (2nd Brigade), north of the Shwebo district (5th Brigade), and east of the Upper Chindwin.

At the same time as the ultimatum was sent to the *Sawbwa*, preparations were made to send two columns against Wuntho, in the case of non-acceptance of the British terms. One column was to start from Katha in the north and the other from Shwebo in the south.

The Katha column was under the command of Brigadier-General Cox, and consisted of—

2 guns, Hazara Mountain Battery.	180 Rifles, 5th Bengal Infantry.
75 Rifles, Royal Welsh Fusiliers.	220 ,, 12th Kelat-i-Ghilzai Regiment.
56 Bengal Sappers and Miners.	
37 Rifles, 26th Punjab Infantry.	1 squadron, 7th Bengal Cavalry.

The Shwebo column, under the command of Lieutenant-Colonel Farrington, consisted of—

2 guns, 9-1 Cinque Ports Division, Royal Artillery.
173 Rifles, South Yorkshire Regiment (now the K. O. Y. L. I.).
103 ,, 1st Bengal Infantry.
140 ,, 12th Kelat-i-Ghilzai Regiment.
2 squadron, 3rd Cavalry, Hyderabad Contingent.

The Commanders of these two columns were ordered to keep up communication with each other by every possible means, and to enter Wuntho simultaneously on the 26th January. They were also instructed to show the greatest forbearance towards the people of the country, and to, if possible, come to a peaceful settlement. The actual military operations were in the hands of the Commanders, but Mr. Burgess, accompanying the Katha column, was responsible for the political part of the expedition.

It should be noted that the head-quarters of the 2nd Brigade had been moved, in November 1886, from Bhamo to Katha, in anticipation of an advance on Wuntho.

Two minor expeditions had also been made in the neighbourhood of Manlé towards the end of November, with a view to clearing the country for an advance on Wuntho. The first of these expeditions was the despatch of a force under the command of Lieutenant-Colonel Home, 5th Bengal Infantry, against the garrison of Mawlu, which was held in force by Nga Kyi, an adherent of the *Sawbwa's*. This place was successfully captured and a small garrison of Welsh Fusiliers left there.

The second operation mentioned above was the march of a force, under the command of Lieutenant-Colonel Creek, Royal Welsh Fusiliers, to the relief of Thila, about twelve miles north-west of Mawteik, a village belonging to the *Wun* of Mawteik, and which had been for some time beseiged by the *Sawbwa's* men. This expedition was also successful; favoured by a dense fog, the British advanced right up to the enemy's position without being seen, and succeeded in putting them to flight without loss.

Before the expiration of the ultimatum, the Katha column had been assembled at Manlé, ready to advance on Wuntho, in the case of such a move becoming necessary. On the 13th January, as soon as Mr. Burgess heard of the *Sawbwa's* flight from Wuntho, he asked for, and received permission, to proceed at once with the cavalry to that place, where he arrived on the 15th, without encountering any opposition *en route*. The next day reinforcements of infantry and guns followed him, and the whole of the Katha column arrived at Wuntho on the 19th January. The inhabitants were friendly, and appeared glad to welcome the British.

The Shwebo column began its march on the 3rd January and reached Wuntho on the 26th, as originally arranged. General Cox now took command of the combined force.

On 1st February, in consequence of a report received that the post of Nabetkyi had been attacked, a squadron of the Hyderabad contingent was sent to its assistance, under Captain Gubbins. This officer was attacked on the 3rd at 2 A.M., by 300 or 400 dacoits, but drove them off after an hour's fight, with a loss of two killed and two wounded.

On the 2nd February, the *Kinwun-Mingyi* (the chief Burmese official in Upper Burma) arrived at Wuntho and at once opened negotiations with the *Sawbwa*, who stated he would come in and discuss matters, provided only a small garrison was left in the town. It was consequently decided to agree to the *Sawbwa's* request, and a garrison of only seventy-five Welsh Fusiliers and thirty police was left, in a fortified position, in the town, while the Shwebo column was despatched to Kawlin, and the cavalry and infantry of the Katha column to Kaing-Chaung and Mawnaing, respectively, both of which places were about six miles from Wuntho, and outside of Wuntho territory. Shortly after the *Sawbwa* had been informed that these moves would be carried out, an order arrived from head-quarters, forbidding the removal of the troops, but General Cox having already given his word, decided that he could not go back on it. In spite of these concessions, great difficulty was experienced in inducing the *Sawbwa* to meet any British officers, but he at length agreed to meet Mr. Cloney, the *Kyundaung Myoôk*, at Mawkin on the 22nd February. The interview was proceeding most satisfactorily when Mr. Cloney's escort of police, whom he had left some distance behind, suddenly, through some misunderstanding, fired a few shots. Three Burmans were wounded and the interview closed abruptly, Mr. Cloney only just managing to make good his escape.

After this incident the *Sawbwa* was persistent in refusing to meet any British officer accompanied by an escort, and all hopes of having an interview disappeared. Eventually, however, terms were agreed upon, which included the payment of Rs. 50,000 by the *Sawbwa*, and the surrender of all arms, except 350 muskets. These terms were fully complied with by the 1st April, on which date the troops were withdrawn.

To guard the interest of those who had helped the British advance, military posts were established at Kawlin, Hluttaik and Mawlu, and the direct road to the Irrawaddy at Tigyaing was opened out.

Reduction of the garrison of Upper Burma.

On the 6th June 1887, General White, owing to the arrival of the Burma police and continuous pacification, recommended a gradual reduction of the Upper Burma garrison, starting with the withdrawal of the 18th Bengal Infantry to India. This step met with the approval of the Government of India, and it was subsequently arranged to withdraw, in addition, before the end of the cold weather of 1887-88, the following—

Two regiments of Cavalry.
A battalion of British Infantry.
A battery of Garrison Artillery.
Ten Native Infantry Regiments.

OPERATIONS OF THE LOWER BURMA DIVISION.

Although the Provinces which were formerly known by the name of British Burma were annexed to the British Empire by a proclamation of the Governor-General of India on the 30th June 1853, on the outbreak of the war with Upper Burma, in 1885, many parts of the country were but little known, and the natural lawlessness of the people and their love of dacoity, etc., was very far from having been overcome. As recently as 1882 and 1883 dacoities in the immediate vicinity of Rangoon itself were not unknown. It was only to be expected, therefore, that when, on the fall of King Thibaw in November 1885, the reign of robbery and violence set in in Upper Burma, this spirit of general lawlessness would spread also to our Burmese provinces, the population of which had not yet been able to shake off their traditions of the past. And this actually did occur. In the month of December 1885 large gangs of marauders collected in the Shwegyin and Pegu districts and commenced a series of outrages, burning and looting peaceful villages, and committing many atrocities. Raising the Peacock standard and announcing themselves as a part of the royal army of Thibaw, they succeeded in striking terror into the hearts of the people, and it became necessary to invoke the assistance of the military for their suppression.

Distribution of troops.

The total number of troops stationed in the province on the outbreak of hostilities was 5,319 of all arms. Of these 2,035 were Europeans and 3,284 natives. At Rangoon there were the 2nd Battalion of the Somersetshire Light Infantry, the 6-1st Southern Division, Royal Artillery, the 5th Madras Native Infantry, and a detachment of Madras Sappers and Miners. At Thayetmyo there were stationed a wing of the 2nd Battalion, Royal Scots Fusiliers, the 5-1st Southern Division and the 3-1st Mountain Battery South Irish Division, Royal Artillery, and the 26th Madras Infantry. At Toungoo there were a wing of the Royal Scots Fusiliers, the 8-1st London Brigade, Royal Artillery, and the 3rd Punjab Light Infantry. Moulmein was garrisoned by a wing of the 9th Madras Native Infantry, the head-quarters of the regiment being stationed at Port Blair.

Operations in aid of the civil power.

During December 1885 there were constant small disturbances in the districts of Pegu, Syriam, Shwegyin and Sittang, and the General Officer Commanding the British Burma Division had to send out continual minor expeditions in aid of the civil power against the numerous bands of insurgents infesting these districts. As time went on the contagion spread to other districts, and the presence of troops was constantly needed all over Lower Burma until th end of the winter of 1886-87. Without entering into details of these various skirmishes, it will suffice to say that they were in nearly every case successful, and that on no occasion were the British casualties at all heavy.

OPERATIONS IN 1887–88.

During the cold weather of 1887–88 great progress was made in the pacification of Upper Burma. The continual hunting of the various dacoit *Boh* had sensibly reduced their following, and, where, a year before, their numbers had to be reckoned by hundreds, they could now be counted by tens. The sustained action and dogged persistence of the British was having its inevitable result, and large tracts of country were now as free from trouble as the Lower Provinces. This result was, however, not effected without much toil and hardship. The story of the year is a record of endless marches by day and night, through dense jungle where the path could hardly be traced, along paths so thick in mud that the soles of men's boots were torn off as they marched, over sandy tracts devoid of water, over hills where there were no paths at all. Rarely was there the chance of an engagement to cheer the troops; stockades were found empty, villages deserted, camps evacuated, and yet everywhere there was the probability of a sudden ambush from every clump of trees or line of rocks, or at any turn of the road.

The principal operations of this open season were the expedition to Mogaung under Captain Triscott, and the operations in the Shan Hills. Both these expeditions are fully dealt with elsewhere—the former in the chapter on the Kachins, and the latter in that on the Shan States, so it will suffice here to say that the result of Captain Triscott's operations was the occupation of Mogaung and the establishment there of British authority, while Colonel Stedman and Mr. Hildebrand succeeded in rapidly pacifying the Shans and in putting a stop to the inter-tribal warfare which had up till then been so prevalent.

CHAPTER XIX.

REVIEW OF THE SITUATION IN UPPER BURMA IN 1888.

BEFORE proceeding to an account of the further operations in Burma it will be well to take a general view of the work that had already been accomplished.

By the end of the winter of 1886-87, as a result of the vigour with which the numerous operations had been carried out, the principal leaders of rebellion and dacoity had all either been accounted for, or were more or less fugitives; their bands had been hunted down and broken up, and were no longer formidable; while the system of patrolling and of small flying columns prevented their reassembling in any considerable numbers.

State of Upper Burma in March 1887.

The number of posts in Upper Burma had risen to 141, while seventeen civil districts had been formed and grouped into three divisions under Commissioners. The civil officers were still not able to move about their districts without escorts, but the tide of affairs was beginning to turn.

Sir Frederick Roberts had returned to India in February, leaving the Upper Burma Field Force under the command of Sir George White, and on the 1st April this force, which now consisted of 20,971 troops, was re-divided into four brigades.

Redistribution of the field force.

Of the six brigades which had existed during the winter months, the 1st and 3rd remained intact; the 2nd and 5th, amalgamated, formed the new 2nd; and the 4th and 6th, amalgamated, formed the new 4th. The head-quarters of these four new brigades were placed at points within easy communication by road and water, namely, 1st at Mandalay, 2nd at Shwebo, 3rd at Meiktila, 4th at Myingyan. The troops were concentrated at strategical points round the head-quarters of their respective brigades, whence flying columns could be sent in any required direction.

In addition to the four brigades, independent commands were established at Bhamo and Chindwin, the former watching the Chinese frontier and the latter the undeveloped country to the north-west, while a detached force at the Ruby Mines watched for any disturbing elements which might arise to the eastwards.

The following outposts were thrown out from the various brigades—

(a) a post at Maymyo from the 1st Brigade, and one at Fort Stedman from the 2nd Brigade, to watch the Shan States;

(b) a post at Pyingyaung from the 4th Brigade to watch the temper of the Chins bordering on the Yaw country;

(c) a post at Kawlin from the 2nd Brigade to watch the frontier of the Wuntho *Sawbwa*.

The garrison of Lower Burma was again formed into a separate force under Major-General Gordon, and consisted of 2,106 European and 4,088 native troops.

During the following year, 1887-88, the system of constantly patrolling the country, and of sending small flying columns to the more remote districts, was kept up, and satisfactory progress continued to be made in the work of pacification. Order was almost completely restored in Lower Burma, while in Upper Burma a large Military Police force of 13,244 officers and men had been organized, and the work of maintaining order, previously performed by the troops, was now efficiently carried out by these police, acting under the immediate control of the civil officers. On 1st April 1888 the purely military force was reduced to 16,602 and ceased to be on the footing of a field force, while the number of brigades was reduced to three. The total effective strength of troops and Military Police, however, rose from 31,830 to 34,712; for while the military garrison of Upper Burma was reduced by over 4,000 men the Military Police under civil administration rose by 8,400. Mention of this force of Military Police has already been made on another page, and it will not be out of place to give here a short account of their organization.

Organization of the Police.

The necessity of maintaining an armed force in Upper Burma having suggested the raising of military police to admit of the withdrawal of the main part of the regular forces, the sanction of the Government of India was obtained in March 1886 for the enlistment of—

2 Military Police Levies, consisting each of 561 officers and men;
2,300 Military Police, to be recruited from Northern India.

The formation of the former, consisting of volunteers from the regular Indian Army, was quickly carried out. The organization of the latter, composed for the most part of untrained men, was a matter of slower progress. The enlistment and training of Burmese as policemen was carried out simultaneously.

As the circumstances of our position in Upper Burma became better known, and the administration of a greater extent of territory became a necessity, it was evident that this police force would have to be considerably increased, and in March 1887 the Government of India sanctioned its strength to consist of 16,000 men; 9,000 being Military Police recruited from natives of India, and 7,000 to be Civil Police formed of Burmese. A military officer (General E. Stedman) was appointed to command the forces as Inspector-General, with another military officer as Deputy Inspector-General. The Military Police, as distinct from the civil part of the force, were divided into separate battalions of various strength. A military officer was selected to command each of these battalions, assisted by a second-in-command, also a soldier.

The organization of the Military Police and the establishment of Military Police posts, in place of posts held by troops, contributed greatly towards the progress of pacification. As soon as the pacification of any district was sufficiently advanced, the military posts were withdrawn and Military Police posts established there. These Military Police Battalions were organized like native regiments in all except the scale of commissioned officers. Their duties were almost entirely military, and subsequently, when the work of pacification was completed, several of them were transferred bodily to the Indian Army.

At first the minimum strength of any post was fixed at twenty-five men, but this was raised to forty, in order that when patrols of ten or more men were sent out, the force remaining behind would always be strong enough to hold the post against attacks, for experience showed that when troops were withdrawn there was a recrudescence of dacoity.

The district magistrate had control over both the Civil and Military Police in his district, and decided what posts were to be occupied, and what the strength of each should be. The general principle was that the most central posts should be occupied by fairly large bodies of Military Police, to each of which should be added a few Burmese constables to receive reports, investigate cases, and collect information. Between these protective Military Police posts intermediate posts were held by the Civil Police, consisting of the locally recruited Burmese. To enable long marches and prompt pursuits to be made, from eleven to twenty per cent. of the men in each Military Police battalion were mounted on small Burmese ponies.

Communications.

Another step which added greatly to the pacification of Upper Burma was the improvement of existing communications all over the province. The work on the Toungoo-Mandalay Railway was energetically carried on, and though in its unfinished state it was of no practical use to the troops during 1886-87, its pacifying effect in obtaining peaceful employment for several thousand labourers was very great.

Roads were constructed on all overland main lines of communication and the jungle clearing extended over 1,000 miles of old country tracks; these tracks were also temporarily repaired and bridged.

Where visual signalling was attended with difficulties, field telegraph was, as far as possible, laid down, and permanent lines were established between all the important centres.

During the campaign not a great deal of use was found in field defences, but the following extract from a report of the Royal Engineers is of interest:—

Field Defences.

Owing to the complete collapse of all regular resistance in the very beginning of the campaign against King Thibaw, hasty field defences were never used in Upper Burma.

In the subsequent operations against dacoits it was always found that a bold forward rush or simple turning movement was sufficient to drive the dacoits from their positions, and that here also the employment of field defences was unnecessary.

2. The military posts occupied all over the country afford therefore the only examples of hasty defences that were used. When a military post was formed the strength of the garrison was communicated to the Engineer, who generally designed a square or rectangular fort on the selected site with flanks at two opposite angles of sufficient size to contain conveniently the different buildings required to accommodate the proposed garrison.

3. In constructing the post a bamboo stockade was first put up all round. This could be done very quickly and cheaply by the Burmese, and it formed a good obstacle against assault or a hidden rush at night. The parapet was then proceeded with, the flanks on which the sentries were posted being completed first.

4. As the bamboo stockade is not strong enough to act as a revetment to the interior slope of the parapet, the latter was made the natural slope of the soil, and the space between it and the stockade filled in with thorns or prickly pear.

5. At 4½ feet high a horizontal bamboo was run along the stockade forming a rest on which the men could lay their rifles in firing. Below this bamboo the stockade was made of close work and above of open work, thus leaving intervals through which the rifles could be fired.

6. A very efficient obstacle was formed of bamboo spikes, the pointed ends being charred to harden and preserve them. These placed on the berm and in front of the ditch at irregular intervals become almost impassable at night, and on many occasions inflicted most severe wounds on people trying to cross them.

7. Transport animals were generally placed outside the post in a stockade enclosure, the sides of which were flanked from the parapet. As the garrisons at posts were from one cause and another constantly being varied, it became necessary to alter posts as soon as they were completed. As a rule, it was found sufficient to protect extensions with a bamboo stockade only, but in disturbed districts where an attack was likely the post was re-designed to suit the increased garrison.

8. In some cases it was possible to utilize pagoda walled enclosures as small strong positions for the garrison to rendezvous in if attacked. These positions, connected by bamboo stockades which they flanked, made very good and cheap defensive posts. In other cases brick buildings were available for use in the flanks of posts. These walls and buildings were rendered defensible in the usual way.

9. At some unhealthy places where it was desirable to reduce the garrison to the lowest limit, blockhouses were constructed to hold twenty men. These were designed and made up in Mandalay, and the materials, with Chinese carpenters to erect them, sent to the place in question.

The bamboo stockade had the great fault that it could be easily cut down by the Burman using his *dah*. The description of stockade used by the Burmans about Wuntho and Bhamo was, however, very difficult to cut down. This stockade, which is believed to have come originally from China, was really a very formidable obstacle, and was used by the Engineers whenever they could get Burmans who were accustomed to construct it. A description of the stockade at Tigyaing will explain the nature of these works

The stockade consisted of vertical timber posts at about four feet interval, and ten or eleven feet high, fixed firmly in the ground. On the outside was fixed bamboo matting to a height of six feet, horizontal intervals being left for split bamboo spikes, which were fixed afterwards. This bamboo matting was made by interlacing partially split female bamboos with smaller bamboo uprights. The bamboos were first cut one side lengthwise and then flattened out.

The matting was then fastened to the outside of the timber uprights, the top of it being about six feet from the ground. Above this height lengths of split bamboo were woven at irregular intervals, the tops of the vertical bamboos being pointed.

The matting having been tied on to the vertical timbers by strips of rattan, or skin of the green bamboo, the next operation was the fixing of the horizontal bamboos, which served the double purpose of strengthening the frame-work, and were also necessary for the attachment of the split bamboo spikes. The spikes were seven feet lengths of split female bamboo, pointed at both ends. They were wound round the inner of the two horizontal bamboos, and one end passed to the front above, and the other end under, the outer horizontal bamboo.

The spikes were very strongly woven round the inside horizontal bamboos, and outside to the front they interlaced thickly and increased greatly the efficiency of the stockade as an obstacle. Such a stockade could not be rushed, and scaling ladders placed on it would sink down till they rested on the upper horizontal bamboos, and the spikes would stick through between the rungs. There being, of course, a berm to form on, if men even got a footing on the bamboos of the matting they would still have a drop of six feet inside the stockade before they could fix bayonets. Outside the stockade, a distance of from eight to ten feet, was a bamboo fence of about the same height. This had first to be removed by cutting through the uprights and then forcing it down, the stockade itself then had to be forced, and this could only be done by burning a portion of it to effect an entrance. Some bundles of straw soaked in kerosine, thrown against the spikes and ignited, were the most rapid means for doing this.

CHAPTER XX.

THE WINTER CAMPAIGN OF 1888-89.

THE cold weather campaign of 1885-86 was marked by the fall of the Alompra dynasty and the occupation of the Burmese capital. During the operations of 1886—88 the country had been reduced to order, and all, or nearly all, internal troubles quashed. In the cold weather operations of 1888-89 we were called upon to shield our loyal subjects from the attacks of the border tribes on the north, east, and west; and having in the previous year shown that we were strong and prompt to punish rebellion within our borders, we now had to prove that we were ready and able to defend those who looked to us for protection, and to strike with a heavy hand against outside enemies.

The principal military operations of this period were—

(1) General Faunce's Expedition to the Chin Hills.

(2) The second Mogaung Expedition.

Operations against the Chins.

Owing to constant raids made by the various Chin tribes on the plains of Burma, two columns were sent into the Chin Hills under the supreme command of Brigadier-General Faunce. A post was established at Tokhlaing, afterwards called Fort White, from which various columns operated all through the winter months, with the result that the Chins were severely punished and 200 Burmese captives were recovered. At the end of the operations the garrison of Fort White and the lines of communications were formed into a second class district in place of the Chindwin which had been given up. Our losses in the expedition amounted to thirty-six killed and fifty-four wounded. A full account of the operations will be found in the chapter dealing with the Chins.

The Mogaung Expedition, 1888-89.

Further operations to bring the Kachins to submission and to punish them for numerous outrages becoming necessary, a column under the command of Captain O'Donnell proceeded to Mogaung in January

1889, and meted out severe punishment on the Lepeé, Ithi and Lataung tribes. From Mogaung the force proceeded to Sinbo and operated against the Masan tribe and Hlegyomaw dacoits with equal success. Further particulars of this expedition are given in the chapter on the Kachins.

Work of the Military Police.

The following information regarding the Military Police in Upper Burma during 1888–89 is extracted from the *Report on the Administration of Burma during* 1888–89 :—

During the greater part of the year the police of Upper and Lower Burma were administered as separate departments, the Upper Burma force, of which the larger portion consisted of military police enlisted in India, being under the control of Brigadier-General E. Stedman, C.B., and the Lower Burma force, composed for the most part of natives of the province, under the late Mr. T. D. Jameson. This territorial distribution of the police force was of a provisional nature, and was not intended to be permanent. Early in the year the administrations of other departments in Upper and Lower Burma previously separate had been amalgamated, and it was considered desirable to effect a similar union in the case of the Police Department. In October 1888 it was accordingly arranged that the police forces of Upper and Lower Burma should be united under one Inspector-General assisted by two Deputies—one for civil, the other for military police. * * * *

In Upper Burma during the past year the most important part of the work of the police was the extinction of organized gangs of dacoits. The military police was therefore the more important part of the police force. The constitution and organization of the force remained unchanged, but the strength was largely increased in the past year. At the end of 1887 the sanctioned strength was 17,515 of all ranks, and the actual strength 13,244. At the end of 1888 the sanctioned strength was 19,177 and the actual strength 17,880. The increase in the responsibilities falling on the force and in the area of the country brought under protection more than kept pace with the increase in strength. The greater number of the 4,000 men of the reserve battalions, whose enlistment was ordered by the Government of India in 1887, arrived early in the year under review, and were drafted to the several battalions. During the year proposals for the addition of five companies to the Mogaung levy for the protection of the Mogaung sub-division of the Bhamo district, and for the establishment of two levies, each to consist of six companies, for the Chin frontier and for the Shan States, were submitted to, and sanctioned by, the Supreme Government. Hitherto the force in the Mogaung subdivision was only sufficient to hold the town and the communications with the Irrawaddy, while the Chin frontier and the Yaw country had not been held at all, and the small garrison in the Shan States was provided by the regular troops. The men of the additional companies did not for the most part arrive in Burma till after the close of the year.

The military police force in Upper Burma at the end of the year 1888 included 3,937 Sikhs and 3,546 Punjabis of other classes, 7,766 Hindustanis, of whom 5,830 were Hindus and 1,936 Mahomedans, and 1,429 Gurkhas and other hillmen. As in the previous year, the force was distributed in battalions, one for each district in Upper Burma, one for the Kabaw valley, on the borders of Manipur, and one for the protection of the railway under construction from Toungoo to Mandalay. The Government of India were moved to sanction the addition of 16 officers in order that there might be a second-in-command for every battalion and one extra second-in-command, or assistant commandant, for Mandalay, Katha, Sagaing, the Upper Chindwin, and Minbu. For the Chin levy two and for the Shan States levy three subaltern officers were considered necessary, while the site of the Mogaung levy and its distribution over an extensive tract of country rendered it necessary to attach three junior officers to this battalion. The proposed addition of assistant commandants to the district battalions was sanctioned ; but it was considered that one English officer as second-in-command would suffice for each of the Shan and Chin frontier levies to which selected Native officers from the army have been attached as wing officers. * * * *

The number of posts held by the military police at the beginning of the year was 175 and at the end of the year 192. The concentration of the troops in a few principal stations, and their reduction in number, left the task of garrisoning the greater part of the country almost entirely to the military police.

The conduct of the military police was good. In action they behaved uniformly well, and instances of special gallantry were not uncommon. The force lost forty-six men killed in action and seventy-six wounded. Their conduct towards the people of the country was generally satisfactory. It is an indication of the good behaviour of the great mass of the men that there were only eighty-four cases in which military policemen were prosecuted on criminal charges. These charges include charges of negligently suffering prisoners to escape. On the average strength this is slightly more than ·5 per cent. Only thirty-one of the cases were against Burmans or the property of Burmans. Departmental offences numbered 232, or 1·5 per cent. of the average strength, and 131 men were dismissed.

There was a good deal of sickness among the military police, and the death-rate of the year (5·32 per cent.) was high. It is impossible to prevent the occurrence of sickness amongst a large body of men serving under strange conditions in a climate to which they are not accustomed, and it is impossible to abandon all the unhealthy posts, which are in some cases so situated as to render their maintenance necessary. It is probable that the comparative youth of the large portion of the recruits contributed to render them more liable to disease than would have been the case with older and more seasoned men.

The experiment of forming a Karen battalion was continued during the year, but only two companies were raised. The Karens are equipped and organized in the same way as the Indian Military Police. The head-quarters of the battalion is at Mandalay, detachments being sent out for service as required. They have proved themselves amenable to discipline and of great value in operations in the jungle, where they are able to move more easily than the Indian police. There is every reason to hope that the experiment will be entirely successful.

Termination of Major-General Sir G. White's command.

In 1887 the Government of India had accepted the proposed combination of the Upper Burma and British Burma Commands into one, but it was afterwards deemed inexpedient to bring that scheme into effect on the 1st April 1888, the date originally proposed, and the two commands remained separate until the 1st April 1889. On that day, however, Sir G. White handed over command of Upper Burma, and the entire force in Upper and Lower Burma was brought under the Commander-in-Chief, Madras Army, and called the Burma district.

This command was given to Major-General B. L. Gordon, C.B., R.A., and was distributed as follows :—

1	Mandalay District	Head-quarters, Mandalay.
	Bhamo Command	Head-quarters, Bhamo.
	Ruby Mines Command ..	Head-quarters, Bernardmyo.
	Shwebo Command	Head-quarters, Shwebo.
2	Myingyan District	Head-quarters. Myingyan.
	Chin Field Force	Northern Division.
	Chin Field Force	Southern Division.
	Chindwin Command ..	Head-quarters, Alôn.
3	Rangoon District	Head-quarters, Rangoon.
	Thayetmyo Command ..	Head-quarters, Thayetmyo.
	Meiktila Command ..	Head-quarters, Meiktila.

During the year, the troops in Upper Burma were reduced by 2,000, but this was overbalanced by the numbers of police which rose from 13,000 to 17,800. The total strength of troops and police in Upper Burma thus rose from 26,500 in April 1888 to 29,000 in

April 1889, while throughout the province it increased from 32,890 to 34,440. It must be remembered, however, that the area to be protected had increased very largely in the last year.

His Excellency the Commander-in-Chief records his appreciation of Sir G. White's work.

The Adjutant-General in India, addressing the Secretary to the Government of India on 18th July 1889, wrote as follows :—

* * * Sir Frederick Roberts desires to record his obligations to Major-General Sir George White. During the three and a half years of his employment in Burma, Sir George White has for two years held the chief command of the large force employed in the Upper Provinces, and His Excellency feels that it is due to the ability and discretion of this officer, and to the cordial relations which he has invariably maintained with successive Chief Commissioners, that the civil and military administrations have gone hand in hand, and that their united efforts have been rewarded with undeniable success.

The Secretary to the Government of India, Military Department, in reply wrote on the 27th August 1889 :—

As also His Excellency the Governor-General in Council.

* * * Sir George White has held the chief command in Burma, except during the intervals when Their Excellencies the Commander-in-Chief in India and the Commander-in-Chief of the Madras Army were present in person, from March 1886 until April 1889—a period characterized by almost continuous operations in the field, at first against the bands of insurgent dacoits which overran the country, and of late more especially against the frontier tribes to repel their incursions into Burma and their ravages upon the peaceful inhabitants of the country. The success of these operations, which have involved great labour and hardship on the troops, and the satisfactory progress made towards the pacification of the country, must be ascribed in a very large measure to the skill, judgment, and ability of Sir George White. The Governor-General in Council fully concurs in the high approbation expressed by the Commander-in-Chief of the Major-General ; His Excellency in Council also cordially endorses the Commander-in-Chief's praise of the ability and energy with which the several commanders acting under Sir George White have directed the detailed columns under their commands ; also His Excellency's approbation of the troops, officers, and men of all ranks alike, both British and Native, for the untiring and cheerful endurance displayed by them throughout those protracted and laborious operations. It will be the pleasing duty of the

Governor-General in Council to bring these valued services to the notice of Her Majesty's Government. The Governor-General in Council entirely concurs in the opinion expressed by Sir Frederick Roberts that the cordial relations maintained by Sir George White with the successive Chief Commissioners of Burma and the hearty co-operation of the civil and military administrations has conduced in a high degree to the success which has been achieved towards the pacification of that country.

Sir G. White's remarks on progress of affairs in Upper Burma.

Sir George White, in concluding his report made on giving over command, writes of the steps made towards the pacification of the country and the contrast between the rebellious lawlessness of the people in 1885 and their respect for authority and peacefulness in 1889 as follows:—

As I have had exceptional opportunities of watching the military operations in Upper Burma since their commencement in November 1885 until the present time, it may not be out of place if I conclude this report with a few remarks on the general aspect of affairs in that province and its progress towards peaceful and settled government. The narrative of events with which this report commences is, as I have already said, a story of continuous military activity. To those unacquainted with the previous military and political history of this, the newest, province of our Eastern Empire, that story may convey an idea of anarchy and lawlessness still rampant throughout its great area. But to those who know the stages through which Upper Burma has passed since our earliest attempts at establishing government, the progress made towards law and order seems most remarkable. It has been too much the view put before the public that we found Upper Burma a peaceful province, and that the dacoity and anarchy revealed later were the after-growth of our occupation. This was not the case. Years of weak, yet cruel, government, nominally by the king whom we displaced, but actually exercised by the corrupt officials of his court, had deprived the country of all government worthy of the name. Some of the strongest ministers were known to be the patrons of dacoits, from whose ill-gotten gains they did not scruple to swell their incomes. The dacoits on their part were glad to pay something to secure immunity from punishment in the rare cases in which they were brought up. The punishment which the dacoit chief had earned fell not rarely on the officer who had arrested him for his temerity and ignorance in interfering with an institution under the scarcely veiled protection of so strong an official as, say, the Toingda Mingyi. The people, thus left to themselves, fell back upon that panacea of more advanced communities—local government. The villagers grouped themselves together under the leadership of the strongest dacoit chief they could attract to their service for the protection of their own property and for the acquisition of that of their neighbours.

We had not been long in Mandalay before we found that, though its capture had been easy, yet the preparation of Upper Burma for the reception of civil government was likely to be a much tougher and more serious task than any one had anticipated; and it was not until we had forced our way to the Shan Hills on the east and to the Arakan Yomas on the west that we had any gauge of the vastness of the system of dacoity which it was our first duty to eradicate. The dacoit leader was in many cases rather the chief and defender of the people in his own immediate circle than the common enemy. Socially he was a hero, not an outcast; and the sympathy of the people was largely with him. As an instance of this, I may cite a case that occurred in the Ava district. A column had attacked a band of dacoits reported in this district and dispersed them, driving away the leader Shwè Yan. This disturbed the offensive and defensive arrangements of the villagers, whose chief he was. Greatly to the surprise of our officers, the villagers asked for a military post. This was the last request expected. The explanation given was that they would now be dacoited by the villagers upon whom they had previously preyed; in fact that, as we were the cause of their helplessness, they looked to us for defence. Dacoity was thus an institution of the country. The more enterprising enjoyed it as a pastime combining profit with distinction. A young Burman was not considered to have won his spurs until he had been out once or twice. There was thus at first not only the terrorism which, as we gained ground, became the chief weapon against us, but also a considerable amount of sympathy with, and admiration of, the calling. This made our task a most difficult one. To introduce the elements of civilized government, we had to protect the weak, in spite of themselves, against the strong.

Since that time the military force in Upper Burma has been reduced by four battalions of British infantry, four regiments of cavalry, and eighteen battalions of Native infantry. It may be said that the military police have to a large extent replaced these regular troops; but, on the other hand, it should be remembered that we have enormously extended the area of our occupation. Until the spring of 1887 we had not entered the Shan States. All this vast country is now under our rule and paying us tribute.

Until the spring of 1888 we had not attempted to administer the large country north of Sinbo, on the Upper Irrawaddy, which stretches on the north to the Kachin hills beyond Mogaung and to the Jade Mines on the west. We had not a soldier in the great Yaw country or along the Chin frontier until November 1888. We have now subdued the Kachins ninety miles beyond Bhamo. We have reduced Sawlapaw and his Red Karens to sub-mission on the south-east, and we have established ourselves right in the heart of the Chin hills to the west. All this has been done while reducing the garrison.

* * * The operations of last season were nearly all confined to the more remote districts, while the central and more important ones were generally undisturbed. Where disturbances did take place, they were transient outbreaks of dacoity, easily met and rapidly put down. Such periodical and local outbreaks must be expected for some years to come, but they are in very marked contrast to the anarchy which obtained in 1886–87. The operations of the three field forces to which I have alluded before were carried out beyond the borders of the country which we had occupied in 1886–87.

As a proof of the change that has been worked in what I may call Upper Burma proper, I would instance the present state of the district in which Brigadier-General Lockhart commanded in 1886-87. But two short years ago he was continuously engaged against strong and organized bands of dacoits. The railway has since been constructed through the heart of this district, and now connects Mandalay in undisturbed and peaceful communication with the sea. The bright forecast of Sir Charles Bernard as to its influence as a pacificator was more than realized even during its construction, and its success as a financial venture—a success which, it is patent, could only be secured in a peaceful country—is being verified daily by increasing traffic.

Although the general progress made towards happier relations between the people and the system of government introduced by us has been very satisfactory, yet a system of dacoity such as I have described takes long to eradicate thoroughly. The minor military expeditions during the past year sufficiently establish the national tendency of the Burmans to take up arms in season and out of season. It is this tendency that makes a general disarmament of the people so necessary. Arms left in a village for defence will in nine cases out of ten sooner or later fall into the hands of some enterprising dacoit leader, or be used by the villager himself for a little venture of his own in some neighbouring district. A Burman living in a district affording opportunities of dacoity looks upon a gun hanging idly in his hut for defence only as so much unemployed capital. Where there is no dacoity, arms are not required, and their absence is a safeguard against its reappearance.

It has been urged that a disarmed village is at the mercy of dacoits. Experience, however, shows how often the arms are the special prize of which the dacoits are in search, and how seldom they are used by the villagers to defend themselves. The dacoit leader when organising his forces makes his requisitions on the villagers for so many guns. The villagers often fear the consequences of refusal and become compromised. On the other hand, if villagers will help the authorities now constituted by giving the intelligence which is at their disposal, dacoity will be rapidly stamped out. A few hard cases may result from a general disarmament, but individual cases make bad law.

I have the high authority of the Marquis of Dufferin for saying that one of the pleasantest features of the earliest years of our administration in Upper Burma has been the happy relations which have existed between the civil and military officers employed on the great work of the pacification of that province. I cannot more fittingly conclude this report than by putting on record my most grateful recollections of the uniform consideration and cordial co-operation which I and the troops under me received in the first instance from Sir Charles Bernard, and afterwards from Sir Charles Crosthwaite, under whose straight, strong, and energetic administration the hold we have now firmly established on the country is rapidly developing, bringing with it increased security of life and property, and consequent happiness to the people, and adding to their material prosperity. The darkest chapters of the early history of British rule in Upper Burma were the legacy of the dynasty which we overthrew in 1885. Soldiers and civilians have since worked together for the common purpose of removing those evils and of giving the advantages of peace and a happier condition of life to the very interesting and attractive people of our newest province.

CHAPTER XXI.

OPERATIONS OF 1889-90-91.

Chin Lushai Expedition.

NOTWITHSTANDING the lessons taught to the Chins during the cold weather of 1888-89, their raids were continued during the following year. To punish them for these inroads, and also to explore and open out the small tract of country which alone now separated Upper Burma from India, it was decided to send columns from both Burma and Chittagong into the country of the Chins and Lushais.

Brigadier-General Symons was placed in command of the Burma Columns, while Colonel Tregear commanded the troops from Chittagong. As a result of these operations which are fully dealt with elsewhere--General Symons' in Chapter XXII and Colonel Tregear's in Volume IV—a marked impression was made on the natives by the junction of the British Forces from east and west, several Chin tribes formally submitted and restored their captives, much valuable survey work was completed, and a road practicable for baggage animals was constructed from Kan to Haka, Haka to Fort Tregear, and Fort Tregear to Chittagong.

The Tònhôn Expedition.

In the same season, 1889-90, an important series of operations was undertaken in the north-east of the State of Momeit where two rebels who had caused much disturbance were still at large.

The force operating in this district was under command of Major Blundell, and his orders were (1) to expel the rebels from the neighbourhood, (2) to punish the Kachins who had harboured them, and (3) to establish the power of the *Sawbwa* of Momeit in the outlying part of the state.

Neither of the rebels were captured, but the two last objects of the expedition were successfully carried out. A detailed account of the operations appears in Chapter XXIII.

The Pônkan Expedition, 1889-90.

The third expedition of importance during the open season of 1889-90 was the Pônkan Expedition, under the command of Brigadier-General G. B. Wolseley, C.B., A.D.C.

Two expeditions had been sent against the *Sawbwa* of Pônkan in 1886, but neither had succeeded in reaching Karwan, the village of the Chief of the most important tribe; and since that time constant reports of disturbances had reached Bhamo. It was therefore decided to send a force under General Wolseley against this troublesome neighbour with the object of breaking up the Pônkan tribe of Kachins, occupying the *Sawbwa's* capital, and destroying all hostile villages. This expedition, which was entirely successful, is also described in Chapter XXIII.

General situation at the end of 1890.

By the end of 1890 the work of pacification throughout Upper Burma was almost complete, and organized resistance to the British Government had collapsed. The system of replacing military posts by Military Police posts, as soon as a district became pacified, had been continued, with the result that whereas in 1887 there were 142 posts held by troops and fifty-six by police, by this time the figures had changed to forty-one and 192, respectively. A reduction in the strength of the garrison of Burma could, however, not yet be ventured upon, as much still remained to be done in the frontier districts, where dacoity and lawlessness were still rife.

Major-General Gordon made over charge of the Burma Command on 31st May 1890 to Brigadier-General Wolseley, who was relieved on the 26th October by Major-General R. C. Stewart, C.B. The troops at this time amounted to 18,763, while the Military Police numbered 16,506, representing a total effective strength of 35,269 men.

Operations against the Chins, 1890-91.

During the open season of 1890-91, it was found necessary to undertake further operations in the Chin Hills where the turbulent tribesmen were still giving endless trouble. Columns were despatched against the Northern Chins from Fort White, against the Southern Chins from Fort Haka, and against the independent tribes to the south from Yawdwin. As these operations are described in detail in the chapter dealing with the Chins it is only necessary to say here that, as a result of the work of the various columns, great progress was made in the pacification of the hill tracts and many more Burmese slaves were liberated.

THE WUNTHO EXPEDITION, 1891.

The State of Wuntho was classed as a Shan State, but was never at any time on the same footing as the true Shan States, and only escaped becoming an integral part of the Burmese Empire, like the neighbouring districts, through Burmese want of system. In 1891 it had a population of about 150,000 and an area of about 2,400 square miles. It was an independent state ruled by Maung Aung Myat, the son of the old *Sawbwa* who had abdicated in 1881. An expedition had been sent into Wuntho in 1887, an account of which has been given on another page, but, previous to 1891 it had never been actually hostile to the British. It had, however, been a constant source of annoyance, in that it was the resort of all bad characters from Burma.

In January 1891 a small column left Katha in search of two dacoits named Nga Hmat and Po Thein who had fled to this state. The former surrendered with a following of about forty men, but to get at the latter it was necessary to traverse a part of the country of the old *Sawbwa*, who had been passively hostile to the British ever since the annexation of Upper Burma.

Wuntho rebellion.

Probably hastened by the action of this column, and also, perhaps, by the advance of the railway into the country, a rebellion suddenly broke out at this time in both the north and south of Wuntho. Though no rumour of the approaching rising had reached the British authorities in the neighbourhood, it had undoubtedly been well organized beforehand. It began by the Sawbwa attacking Kawlin in the centre, while his father attacked the posts in the neighbourhood of Katha, and Maung San Nyan made for those round Tigyaing. The first news of any hostility that reached Mandalay was the information received on the 14th February to the effect that the Katha column's road was blocked and that some shots had been exchanged.

On the 16th February rebels from Wuntho broke into Kawlin, and set fire to several buildings, but were eventually driven out by the police. Reinforcements of police arrived the following day, and, early on the 19th, Lieutenant Nisbett arrived from Katha with 100 men, bringing the garrison up to 180. Other posts were meanwhile being attacked and, the situation growing most serious, reinforcements were hurriedly despatched from Shwebo and Mandalay.

Relief of Kawlin.

In the afternoon of the 19th the rebels made a second determined attack on Kawlin, dividing their force and assailing the town simultaneously from three sides. During the fight a small force of Mounted Military Police from Shwebo under Captain Keary, most opportunely arrived on the scene. Owing to the gallantry of this officer, who, taking in the situation at a glance, immediately assumed the rôle of cavalry and charged the dacoits, the enemy were driven off on all sides with heavy loss, and the town was relieved. The following day Captain Keary and Mr. Kenny cleared the surrounding country of the enemy, destroying Pegôn, the rallying-point for the rebels on the borders of Wuntho.

More troops now reached Kawlin, and on the 22nd, Captain Davies, Devonshire Regiment, with a force of about 400 men attacked and defeated a large force of the enemy who had taken up a strongly entrenched position at Kyaingkwintaung.

The success of this action and of an affair at Okkan, on the same day, in which Captain Hutchinson was mortally wounded, completely stamped out the rebellion in the south of the country within a week of its outbreak. The military operations were therefore practically over before the expeditionary force was in the field.

Meanwhile arrangements were being made in Mandalay for an expedition on a large scale to be despatched to Wuntho, under the supreme command of Brigadier-General G. B. Wolseley, C.B. Two columns were to operate against Southern and Northern Wuntho respectively, the base of the former to be at Tigyaing, and that of the latter at Katha.

The composition of the columns was as follows :—

Southern Column—under Major Smyth, D.S.O., R.A.

2 guns, No. 2 Mountain Battery.	200 men, Oxford Light Infantry.
100 men, Devonshire Regiment.	100 men, 11th Madras Infantry.
150 men, Duke of Cornwall's Light Infantry.	530 men, 28th Madras Infantry.
	50 men, Queen's Own Sappers and Miners.

Northern Column—under Lieutenant-Colonel Macgregor.

2 guns, No. 6 Mountain Battery.
100 men, Duke of Cornwall's Light Infantry.
200 men, Madras Infantry.
40 Mounted Infantry, 22nd Madras Infantry.
36 men, Queen's Own Sappers and Miners.
100 men, Karen Police Battalion.

Major Kitchener, Duke of Cornwall's Light Infantry, with two companies, 22nd Madras Infantry, formed the garrison at Tigyaing base, while 100 men, 11th Madras Infantry, were left at Katha.

In addition to the above troops the Military Police were placed at the disposal of the General Officer Commanding Wuntho Columns.

A third column was also ordered to work south from Mogaung under the command of Captain O'Donnell and was composed as follows :—

2 guns, No. 6 Mountain Battery.
100 men, Devonshire Regiment.
150 men, Mogaung Levy.

Objects of the expedition.

The primary object of the Southern Column was to relieve Kawlin, and concentrate there with a view to an advance on Wuntho and Pinlebu. That of the northern force was to protect Katha, and operate against rebels who had attacked Manton and other posts. The general objects of the campaign were to restore order in the country and to depose and, if possible, capture the *Sawbwa* and his father.

The Northern Column, after concentrating at Katha, advanced to Mawteik where they arrived on the 26th February. Leaving Mawteik the next day, Colonel Macgregor captured Banmauk after slight resistance, and with no loss on his side. The following morning a detachment under Lieutenant Caulfield was sent out to a village called Kyauktonlon where the *ex-Sawbwa* had taken up a strongly entrenched position. The village was successfully captured, but the *Sawbwa* unfortunately succeeded in making his escape. After this action no more opposition was offered to our troops during the campaign.

General Wolseley had meanwhile reached Pinlebu, where he had to wait the arrival of supplies, the advance of the column having been so rapid that only a few days' rations had been brought with the troops, it being arranged to send the remainder on as soon as sufficient transport had been organized. From Pinlebu the Southern Column marched to Mansi where they came up with the force under Colonel Macgregor. All was quiet in the neighbourhood and each day the tribesmen were bringing in their arms and surrendering.

Two columns were sent out from Mansi, in pursuit of the *Sawbwas*, one under Colonel Macgregor to open up communication with the Mogaung force, and the other under Captain Custance to Shwédwin where the *ex-Sawbwa* was supposed to be in hiding. The Northern Column met O'Donnell's force at Payani on the 30th March, without, however, effecting the capture of the young or the old *Sawbwa* who were now said to be in hiding at the Jade Mines.

Both columns then proceeded to Lôntôn on the Indawgyi lake, where they were joined on the 4th April by the General Officer Commanding and the remainder of the force from Mansi. On the 6th April Captain Custance returned from Shwédwin; he had found the inhabitants friendly, but could obtain no information about the *Sawbwa*.

After a few days' halt at Lôntôn, the two columns marched by converging routes to the Sanka Jade Mines where they arrived on the 15th. Here, as elsewhere, no reliable information could be obtained as to the whereabouts of either the *Sawbwa* or his father, beyond the fact that they had fled to the Chinese frontier. A last effort was made to cut them off by sending a small column to Labun, but from information received at that place it transpired that they had avoided all main tracks and were retiring *viâ* the Amber Mines, whither it was impossible to follow them.

A military post was established at the Jade Mines, and peace being now restored, the troops were withdrawn from Wuntho.

Result of the expedition.

Apart from the failure to capture the *Sawbwa*, General Wolseley's operations were successful throughout, resulting as they did in the complete pacification of the country, and in the opening out of the, up till then, little-known districts of the Jade Mines.

The British casualties throughout the expedition amounted to fifty-one killed and wounded.

With the termination of the Wuntho expedition the History of the Third Burmese War may be brought to a close.

End of the war.

No pretender, no rebel, or no dacoit *boh* having any considerable following was now to be found throughout what was formerly the Kingdom of Ava. All such leaders who had not surrendered or died, or else had not been killed or captured, were in hiding, deserted alike by their friends and adherents. The only remaining elements of disturbance were the wild tribes inhabiting the forest-clad hills of the northern frontier districts; in all other parts of the country District Officers could move about freely without escorts. In every case in which organized rebellion had been suppressed, terms had been offered to all except the principal leaders, and all over Burma large numbers of released or surrendered dacoits were now (under surveillance, but otherwise unmolested) engaging in peaceful pursuits. With regard to the frontier tribes internecine warfare in the Shan States had been stopped, and the paths of peace were leading the inhabitants to a prosperity hitherto unknown; Eastern Karenni had been brought under British protection and satisfactory arrangements made for its administration; on the north and north-west the Kachin tribes were learning that raiding and acts of violence were no longer to be permitted; while on the western border the Chin tribes had by similar punishment been brought to tender their submission, and were gradually settling down to a peaceful life.

These results had been obtained within five years of the annexation of Upper Burma, just half the time that had been required for the pacification of Lower Burma after the Second Burmese War.

BIBLIOGRAPHY.

Official History of the 3rd Burmese War.—Scott, 1900.

Gazetteer of Upper Burma.

Burma under British Rule, and Before.—John Nisbet, 1901.

PART IV.

THE CHINS, KACHINS AND SHANS.

CHAPTER XXII.

THE CHINS.

THE Chin Hills lie between latitude 24° and 21° 45′ and longitude 93° 20′ and 94° 5′, and form a parallelogram about 250 miles long and from 100 to 150 miles broad. They consist of a contorted mass of mountains intersected by deep valleys, and are utterly devoid of plains or tablelands. The approach from the Myittha valley is by rugged steep spurs covered with dense jungle and divided by deep narrow ravines. These hills are sparsely, if at all, inhabited, and lead up to the first ridge, which runs parallel to the Myittha river and about fifty miles west of it, with an average height of about 7,000 feet above sea level. Beyond this lie range upon range of almost bare hills, their sides dotted with villages and scored with terraced fields which have taken the place of the thin virgin forest. The main ranges run generally north and south, and vary in height from 5,000 to 9,000 feet. The most important are the Letha or Tang, the watershed between the Chindwin and Manipur rivers; the Imbukklang, which forms the divide for the waters of Upper Burma and Arakan; and the Rongklang, which occupies the same position for the southern hills, discharging on one side into the Myittha and on the other into the Boinu. The highest peak is the Liklang, about seventy miles south of Haka, which rises to nearly 10,000 feet. Others are Lunglen, the western point of the Chin-Manipur boundary, 6,531 feet; Katon, on the same frontier, 7,837 feet; Noakuvam, 8,500 feet; and Kul, which is known as Kennedy Peak, 8,860 feet. In the southern hills the chief heights are Rumklao, 8,231; Rongklang, 8,000; Boipa, 8,800; and many others ranging about 8,000 feet.

The country.

There are several rivers of fair size. The Manipur river, issuing from the Lontak lake, flows almost due south from Shuganu to Molbem, where it curves to the east and, passing below Falam, enters the Myittha a little below Sihaung. The Boinu rises in the

Yahow country and flows generally south into Arakan, where it enters the sea under the name of the Kaladan. Other rivers are the Tyao and the Tuivai, the largest tributary of the Barak. All these rivers are fordable except the Manipur, which can seldom be crossed below Kwanglui, and never before the month of February even as far north as Tunzan.

The climate, judged at an elevation of between 2,500 and 6,050 feet, is temperate, the shade thermometer but rarely rising about 80° or falling below 25°. During our occupation snow has seldom fallen and the natives speak of it as a very rare occurrence. In spite of the high altitude of our posts the climate has been found disappointing, for even in the winter there are numerous cases of malaria and other feverish complaints. The rains last from the end of May to the beginning of October, and during this season the roads are impracticable as a rule. The valleys are very unhealthy, especially Kale and Myittha, which are proverbial for malaria and blackwater fever.

The people.

The Chins are of Indo-Chinese origin, and it is probable that the Kukis of Manipur, the Lushais of Bengal and Assam, and the Chins themselves all originally lived in what we now know as Tibet, and are of one and the same stock. The chief characteristics of the Chin are slow speech, serious manner, pride of pedigree, love of drink, clan prejudices, avarice, distrust, thirst for revenge, impatience of control, and dirt. The Chins are well built, with strong limbs and good figures ; the average height of the men is about 5 feet 6 inches but many of them are only an inch or two under 6 feet. Drunkenness is their besetting sin, and they and their chiefs seize every occasion, whether it be one of joy or sorrow, council or welcome, as a pretext for a prolonged orgie. The liquor drunk is of two kinds, both home-made—one a kind of small beer ; the other a strong spirit.

The separate tribes recognized in the Chin Hills on our first advance into that country were the Soktes, Siyins, Tashôns, Hakas, Tlantlangs, and Yokwas. In the south of these were independent villages each with its own chief and recognizing no tribal system.

The Sokte tribe, which includes the Kanhow clan, is found on both sides of the Manipur river. This led to the people on the left bank being called Nwengals, from *nun*, a river, and *ngal*, across. This term has been brought into general use by us, and led to the Nwengals being considered a different tribe. This, however, is not the case and the name should disappear.

The latest (1906) details of the division of the various tribes, with their approximate numbers, is as follows :—

I.—*Northern Chins*—	
(1) Siyins	2,000
(2) Kanhows, (3) Soktes	10,000
II.—*Central Chins*—	
(1) Tashôns or Shunklas	28,000
(2) Whenohs	9,000
(3) Yahows	3,000
III.—*Southern Chins*—	
(1) Hakas	15,000
(2) Tlantlangs	5,000
(3) Yokwas, (4) Thettas, (5) Lungnos	3,000
IV.—*Chinmès* (*unadministered*)—	
(1) A group west of the Yomas.	
(2) The Wellaung group east of the Yomas.	
V.—*Chinboks* (*Pakkoku Chin Hills*).	

Of the northern Chins the Siyins are the most likely material for recruits ; they are active and intelligent, and would like to enter Government service.

Of the central Chins the Tashôns are the most numerous and are good coolies, but they have not got the fighting spirit to the same extent as the Siyins.

Of the southern Chins the Hakas are the best and are indeed the finest men of all the Chin tribes. They are, however, addicted to drink, and, as is the case with most Chins, this failing has dulled their wits.

As one goes south the stamp of man deteriorates, the Chinmès being found to have poor physique and few brains.

The number of languages spoken in the Chin Hills is confusing, and makes the question of guides a very difficult one. The languages recognized by Government are Siyin, Falam, Haka,

Manipuri, Pakkoku Chin Hills (Chinbok), and Chinmè; but this by no means includes all, as, owing to the constant inter-tribal feuds, the language in nearly every village has some peculiarity. The Chin is, in addition, uncommunicative when sober, and untruthful when drunk, so, even with the services of a guide who knows the language, it is difficult to extract much information from him.

There is no great variety of dress among the Chins and no particular colour or tartan to distinguish one tribe from another. A turban or cloth is worn round the head, a cloth round the loins, and a blanket or sheet is thrown over the shoulders. Latterly, however, the Chins have begun to adopt the Burmese style of dress.

The arms of the Chins are the same throughout all tribes, and consist of flint-lock "Tower" muskets, *dahs*, and spears. The *dahs* and spears differ slightly in pattern; but the difference is not a sign of the tribe to which the bearer belongs. Shields are carried by some, and others carry bows and arrows and pellet bows; but these are probably only used in *shikar*. Almost every free man has a gun, which he appears to keep in good order. Every village makes its own gun-powder, the saltpetre being obtained from dung; their bullets are roughly hammered lumps of iron or gun-metal. The Chinboks use poisoned arrows made by dipping the head in a decomposing fowl.

Some villages are defended by roughly constructed block-houses, but, as a rule, the tangled thicket which surrounds each village is its only defence. To defend a path, the Chins fell trees across it and plant *panjis* in or alongside the path. None of the southern villages are defended.

Chin methods of fighting.

When we first advanced into the hills the Chins fought in the open and from behind stockades, but they soon learnt what the power of quick-firing rifles was, and that they could not stand against the charge of British and Gurkha troops. They then tried fighting from covered-in trenches as at Tartan in 1889. This fight, though considered but a drawn battle from our own point of view, was regarded by the Chins as an overwhelming disaster to their arms; they frankly admitted that they were beaten and could never again stand face to face with the British.

The Chins, however, averred that, although fighting in the open and from behind stockaded positions were alike impossible, they could more than hold their own in guerilla warfare. In 1890, therefore, their tactics were to persistently hang round columns, firing from secure ambuscades, and to cut up stragglers on the lines of communication. At this time our columns used to consist of about 200 fighting men, and as a force of this strength required at least 200 coolies, and as the advance always had to be made in single file, the column, winding round the hills, would be at least a mile in length and was consequently exceedingly vulnerable to the new form of attack. The Chins saw their opportunity, and would fire first into the advance guard, then into the baggage, and again into the rear of the column. In these skirmishes, although we doubtless had more men in the field than the enemy, we really got the worst of it; for, whereas we scarcely ever hit a Chin, we ourselves had casualties nearly every time we moved out. Furthermore we did the Chins but little damage, for, hampered by our cooly corps, we could never move at night; the enemy, therefore, never lost sight of us, and always removed their cattle and property on our approach.

Owing to the difficulty of carrying sufficient supplies, we could never stay out more than ten days, and in this time could do but little harm to property, and could in no way stop cultivation. The Chins therefore laughed at us, and boasted that they could always keep out of the way of people who were "blind at night and who could never move off beaten paths."

The difficulty in Chinland is not due to the Chins but to the mountain in which they live. As a race the Chin is not courageous, but he is nevertheless an exasperating enemy, for he is content to silently stalk a column for days, watching his opportunity, and then suddenly, when least expected, a shot is fired, and word is passed along the line for the doctor.

The Chin almost invariably ambushes from below the path, and not, as one would expect, from above. The reason is sound. The spot has been carefully selected, and, after discharging his gun into the back of a man at such close range as to set fire to his clothes, the Chin slips off his rock and dives down the *khud*, not only out of sight, but out of all possible line of fire as well. We have, therefore, often given a Chin credit for doing a very plucky thing when in reality it was merely an impertinent action, and one which involved him in no danger whatever. Dangerous though the Chin is on the offensive, it was soon found that he quickly loses heart on the defensive, and that the real way to defeat him is to ambush him and cut off all cultivation. In the later expeditions, therefore, the plan of operations was to first destroy the rebel villages, and then, instead of hunting the rebel, with little chance of success, to place outposts on all the sites of the villages, and systematically ambush all paths and patches of cultivation. While villages had still to be attacked it was found almost impossible to avoid casualties ; it was impossible to avoid being ambushed. Flanking parties, however, minimized the danger, and to prevent the enemy slipping round the flankers and firing into the main body, it was found advisable for the main body and rear-guard, as well as the advance-guard, to have men on the flank. When Chins fired from ambush it was found best to rush them ; the Chin hates a rush, and when he knew that he would get one he paid less attention to his aim than to his way of escape, which would not have been the case had he known that his volley would cause a temporary check to the advance of the troops.

Grey dawn was the Chin's favourite time for attacking a camp, and all columns had to be particularly alert in the early morning, at which hour we constantly lost men who had carelessly wandered outside the picquets.

Double sentries were found advisable at night. A Chin is unrivalled in his cunning ; he would wriggle up to a sentry as noiselessly as a snake, and shoot him in the back at the distance of a few feet, trusting in his own speed and the darkness to make good his escape.

In 1889, murder and theft at night were so rife that, in addition to abattis and sentries and outlying picquets, a system of "tell-tales" was improvised, which consisted of numerous kerosine and other tins being connected with strings and strewn round the post. It was expected that the Chins would trip over the tins and so give warning to the sentries. The life of the "tell-tale" system, however, was short. Each dawn showed that the tins had disappeared, having been carried off under the noses of the sentries by the Chins, who wanted them for the sake of converting the solder into bullets.

The prisoners taken in the Chin raids appeared to have been well treated by their captors; but every attempt was made to evade their surrender, their retention being considered as necessary to the prestige of the tribe.

Villages.

The villages are built as a rule on terraces cut out of the hill, and are situated below the water-supply. The houses are all surrounded by fencing, and face inwards towards the narrow tracks which do duty for streets. The villages are surrounded by a dense tangled hedge of thorn bushes. The houses are built of fir planks, some of the planks being of great length and thickness. They are roofed with thatch, and raised from three to six feet from the ground. They consist of three rooms, the principal one, which is a half-closed verandah, being adorned with trophies of sport, skulls of animals, etc. The cattle are kept either under the house or at the side. Water is brought from the source higher up the hill by a conduit of hollowed out logs and bamboos.

Religion.

There is no order of priesthood among the Chins, and no religious belief or observances. They believe in *nats*, or spirits, and any misfortune is attributed to the displeasure of the *nat*, who must be propitiated by sacrifice. They also believe in omens, and consult them before undertaking anything of importance. They look to the stars for augury, and believe in a form of transmigration of the spirit.

Marriages and funerals.

Marriage with the Chins is a civil contract. After some preliminary feasts, with the customary amount of drunkenness, to settle the dowry, etc., the contracting parties and their friends meet, and the girl's parents declare that the man and girl are husband and wife.

The Chins bury their dead, instead of burning them as is the Chinbok custom. Great importance is attached to the remains being buried in or near the ancestral village. The Hakas, the Tashôns, and their tributaries bury inside their villages in deep vaults; the Siyins, Soktes, and Thados bury outside always, and the corpse is usually dried for a year before burial. Chiefs are not buried in the common cemetery, but, like the Kachins, on the side of the road leading to the village. Their graves are easily recognized by the number of stone pillars which stand round them.

Supplies.

There is very little cultivation in the Chin Hills, what there is being principally paddy, with occasional patches of maize, peas, and different kinds of beans. Oranges, sweet limes, and bananas are fairly plentiful. The most valuable live stock the Chin possesses is the mithun. Buffaloes and goats are sometimes met with. Milk is rare as the Chin never milks his cattle. Pigs abound but are probably unfit for European food.

Transport.

With regard to transport, the only mules in the country belong to the Police Battalion. There are a few bullocks but they make bad beasts of burden for the hills. Mules would be the best transport for an expedition, but difficulty would be found with regard to their forage, which would have to be brought from great distances. The Chins themselves are good coolies and carry loads of 150 lbs. if well packed.

An excellent system obtains in the Chin Hills whereby each village has to keep in repair a 4-foot mule track to the village next to it.

Administration.

With regard to the administration of the Chin Hills, at the present time the main power is vested in a Superintendent. Under him are three Assistant Superintendents, one at Tiddim in the north, one at Falam in the country of the Central Chins, and the third at Haka in the south. The jurisdiction of the last named extends to the Daidin-Tenshi line. In the unadministered tracts each village carries on desultory feuds with its neighbours, the weaker ones paying tribute to those of whom they are most afraid.

MILITARY OPERATIONS.

Early dealings with the Chins.

Up to the time of the 3rd Burmese War the difference between the Chins and Lushais was but little understood, and the various raids which these tribes made, all through the century, on the Chittagong, Arakan, and Assam borders were classed as Chin-Lushai raids. As they were probably more the work of the Lushais than the Chins, an account of them is given in the chapter on the former tribe in Volume IV. For the purposes of this chapter it will suffice to begin the history of our dealings with the Chins at the date of the annexation of Upper Burma. Previous to that time the Burmese and the Chins seem to have lived in perpetual enmity, the Chins regularly raiding the plains during the winter months, and the Burmese occasionally retaliating by sending abortive expeditions into the hills. After the pacification of Upper Burma it became necessary for us to put a stop to this state of affairs and to protect our new subjects from their turbulent neighbours.

1886-88.

The two years following the annexation of Upper Burma were spent by the British in exploring the country, suppressing local rebellions and stamping out dacoity. In due course attention was paid to the Kabaw valley, the Kale State, and the Yaw country, which were the western borders of the Burmese kingdom as we found it. The Kabaw valley was included in the Upper Chindwin district; the Kale state was under the control of the Deputy Commissioner of that district; and the Yaw tract was included in the Pagan and afterwards in the Pakkoku district.

Kubo valley.

The Kabaw, or Kubo valley, inhabited by Shans, and lying between the Shan States of Thaungdut (known in Manipur as Sumjok) in the north and Kale in the south, was occupied in 1886 by our troops who advanced from Manipur. The valley was administered by *Tamons* who occupied much the same position as *thugyis* in Burma. It was proposed at first to divide the valley between the *Sawbwas* of Kale and Thaungdut, or to make it over to Manipur. Both these proposals, however, fell through, as the *Sawbwa* of Kale did not attend the meeting which was convened on the 20th February 1887, and the inhabitants refused to be made over to Manipur, doubtless being influenced by the fact that, previous to 1834, they had from time to time been under Manipur rule and had by no means appreciated it. The people unanimously declared for British Government, and were finally included in the Upper Chindwin district, and the Kubo Valley Military Police Battalion (afterwards formed into the 1st Burma Rifles) was raised for their protection.

Kale valley.

The Kale valley at this time was ruled by a *Sawbwa*, but the state was paralyzed by the civil war which was being waged between two claimants for the *Sawbwaship*, an uncle, Maung Yit, and his nephew, Maung Pa Gyi. In 1886 the British found the old *Sawbwa* in power, but he had to be deposed owing to his corrupt government, and, on the 1st January 1887, his nephew was appointed in his stead. We had found the Kale State in a most unhappy condition, for the country, divided against itself, was continually fighting either on one side or the other, and the Siyin Chins, taking advantage of the confusion, had descended from the hills and committed a series of such barbarous raids that the valley was partially depopulated.

The Yaw country.

The Yaw country was first approached at the close of 1887, when four columns, starting from Pakkoku, Kalewa, Alon, and Salin, entered the tract, the primary object of the movement being to clear the country of dacoits and to give the civil officers an opportunity of learning and settling the country, and meeting the chiefs of the trans-border tribes.

There was at this time living in the Yaw country a man, styling himself Shwe Gyo Byu Mintha, who had succeeded in raising a rebellion in October 1887 on the confines of the Chindwin, Myingyan, and Pagan districts. In the operations which followed, Captain Bevile, Assistant Commissioner, and Major Kennedy were killed, and the pretender, being defeated, fled into the Yaw country.

The columns which operated in the Yaw country in the cold weather of 1887-88 dispersed the various dacoit gangs, and the Shwe Gyo Byu Prince fled to the Chin Hills. This season's work is important as comprising our first serious dealings with the Chins from Upper Burma, for although Captain Raikes (Deputy Commissioner of the Chindwin district) had met some Tashôn Chins at Indin in March 1887, and had warned them against their annual winter raids in the valley, they had not as yet been formally approached.

During the cold weather of 1887-88 Captain Raikes held a durbar of Siyin chiefs at Kalemyo and of Tashôn chiefs at Sihaung, during which he discussed various matters, including the question of a British exploring party proceeding through the Chin Hills to Chittagong. The durbars passed off satisfactorily and it was hoped that he had secured the chiefs' confidence and goodwill.

An attempt at negotiating with the Yokwa and Haka chiefs was not so successful. Of the three men sent up the hills to call the chiefs to the durbar, two were killed and the other only saved his life by escaping into the Arakan hill tracts.

A combination of circumstances now occurred which completely upset all our Chin frontier arrangements. The Shwe Gyo Byu Prince took up his residence in Tashôn territory, and the ex-*Sawbwa* of Kale escaped from Mandalay, where he had been sent when removed from the government, and joined him. The Tashôns, who had been made suspicious by the suggestion of the British to send an exploring party through their country, were persuaded to espouse the cause of the ex-*Sawbwa*, and to aid him in fighting against the British Government. Accordingly, on the 4th May, a large party of Tashôns descended suddenly on Indin and, seizing the young *Sawbwa* of Kale, carried him off to the foot of the hills, only releasing him on his promising to join the rebellion. Somewhat earlier the Siyins and Sagyilaings had raided in the Kubo valley, while the Yokwas, after our unsuccessful attempt at negotiations, had continued to raid the Yaw country. This was the position of affairs in July 1888, at a season when the nature of the climate prevented any active operations in the hills.

Tashôn rising.

OPERATIONS UNDER GENERAL FAUNCE, 1889–90.

Early in September raids recommenced, and the various tribes of the Baungshès,[1] namely, the Hakas, Tlantlangs, and Yokwas, entered into an alliance against the British. In view of the probability of a continuance of the raids, arrangements were made to place troops at Kalewa and Sihaung, and to establish a blockade to prevent the Chins from obtaining supplies from the plains. A force of about 470 men (350 Native Infantry, seventy Native Mounted Infantry, and fifty Madras Cavalry) under the personal command of Brigadier-General Faunce, was ordered to move up from Myingyan *viâ* Pakkoku and Pauk, while 300 Gurkhas, with Major Raikes, were sent up by way of Kalewa. It was arranged that Tilin, Gangaw, Kan, Sihaung, Kambale, and Indin should be held, and that, though no regular expedition into the hills should be undertaken, raiders should be pursued and punished. General White was particularly anxious that there should be an expedition

Expedition proposed.

[1] The name Baungshè is used here, as it is the name by which those tribes were known. It is, however, a mere nickname, derived from the Burmese words *paung*, to put on, and *she* in front, and is applied to all Chins who bind their hair over the forehead.

instead of a mere blockade, and had tried to get the approval of the Government of India to this step, pointing out to them that, in spite of the initial expense, it would be the cheapest course in the long run ; but up to this time the Government had withheld their consent.

The expectation that raids would recur was meanwhile justified. On the 17th October, Chippauk, four miles from Yazagyo post, was attacked, seven villagers being killed and forty-five carried off; on the 20th October, Chins attacked Kambale, three miles south of Kalemyo, and burnt the village ; on the 29th they attacked Kalemyo, burnt thirty-five houses, killed three villagers, and carried off forty.

In consequence of these raids, General White, on the 2nd November, telegraphed as under to the Quarter Master General in India.

Reference Government veto on Chin expedition and my No. 8491 of yesterday. Between 17th and 29th October no fewer than twelve people have been murdered and 122 carried off into slavery from our territory by Chins. I am very loath to occupy frontier with troops not furnished with transport to take offensive. Pure defence must fail in certain cases, and will never end the raiding. The great expense of supporting large bodies of troops on the frontier will consequently be continuous. I therefore earnestly invite Chief's support, while yet there is time, to raising 2,000 coolies in Assam, as proposed in my letter to Quarter Master General, No. 7453, dated Mandalay, 17th September, and would further ask that another Gurkha battalion, probably 44th, be placed at my disposal for offensive operations with arrangements already entered upon. With 2,000 coolies and 400 men of another Gurkha Regiment, I believe I can follow up the raiders to their own homes, and eventually save Government much money.

Meanwhile the Chins raided Indaw and killed the *Thugyi*.

On the 14th November General Faunce left for Pauk with the Southern Column, and on that day the Government of India consented to such operations as might be found possible being immediately undertaken against the Chins with transport locally procured.

The plan of campaign now decided on was to march first against Siyin (Koset) the head village of the Siyins, and from this centre to deal with the surrounding villages of the tribes ; the head-quarters of the force was consequently temporarily placed at Kambale. It was also decided that the Kanhows should be included in the punishment meted out to the Siyins.

On the 19th November Sir George White received information direct from the Military Department, Government of India, that his proposals with regard to the Chin operations had been sanctioned. Sir George White applied at once that the 44th Gurkhas, 400 strong, might move down to Kalemyo, bringing with them two 150-pound guns; that Colonel Macgregor should accompany this force, and that he should raise and bring with him a coolie corps 500 strong. Sir George White also proposed to bring two additional companies of the 42nd Gurkha Light Infantry from the Ruby Mines to the Chin border.

Sir G. White's proposals sanctioned.

On the 24th November the General Officer Commanding Assam reported that Colonel Macgregor could only take from Manipur a force of 250 rifles. This force he proposed should march in three detachments, Colonel Macgregor accompanying the first, and the guns marching with the second. These detachments left Manipur on the 26th and 29th November and the 4th December.

Tilin was, on the 22nd November, occupied by Captain Mason and sixty-nine rifles, 10th Madras Infantry; Gangaw by Colonel Leggett and 139 rifles, 10th Madras Infantry, and twenty-four mounted infantry of the same regiment, on the 25th November; and Kan, on the 27th, by Major Leader with 119 rifles, 10th Bengal Infantry, and 111 rifles, 10th Madras Infantry. Brigadier-General Faunce arrived at Kambale on the 3rd December, with fifty of the 1st Madras Lancers, and found there 159 of the 42nd Gurkha Light Infantry, two guns, No. 1 Bengal Mountain Battery, and forty-eight of No. 2 Company, Queen's Own Sappers and Miners. One hundred and fifty-six rifles, 42nd Gurkhas, were at Sihaung.

Border occupied by our troops.

The first encounter with the enemy took place on the 7th December, the Chins firing on a working-party sent to make a road between Kambale and Siyin. In this engagement, Lieutenant Palmer, R.E., was killed. After this, brushes with the enemy were continual.

On the 10th December Sihaung village and post were attacked by a force of about 1,000 Tashôns. The attacks were delivered simultaneously at 4 A.M. The enemy were, however, driven off with heavy loss, and were pursued to the foot of the hills, seven miles away, where they eventually succeeded in making good their escape. The same day, Soktes and Kanhows attacked the military post of

Kangyi, twenty miles north of Kalemyo, but were repulsed and pursued, our loss being one sepoy wounded. On the 25th the Chins again attacked a working-party but were driven off with loss. During December and January preparations for the advance into the hills were steadily pushed on. On the 4th February the village of Siyin was occupied without resistance, and by the beginning of March all villages belonging to the Siyins and Sagyilaings had been destroyed, and the head-quarters of the expeditionary force had been located at Tokhlaing, afterwards known as Fort White.

Capture of Siyin.

On the 8th March, after some fruitless negotiations, operations against the Soktes and Kanhows were undertaken, and continued until the 20th of the month. These operations were well planned and executed, and resulted in the destruction of eighteen villages, including Wunkathe, Saiyan, and Tiddim, the home of Kochin, at this time chief of the clan. The month of April was mostly taken up with negotiations with the Tashôns, and active operations were, for the time, suspended. The Chins, meanwhile, had begun to feel the loss of their villages, and various Siyin headmen came in, asking for permission to rebuild, a permission which could only be granted on the submission of the whole tribe.

On the 9th April the troops moved into Fort White.

It was now found that the Chins had rebuilt the villages of Sagyilain and Tartan, and expeditions were accordingly sent to destroy them. Major Shepherd on the 30th April marched to the former place with a force of 100 rifles, Norfolk Regiment, and 100 rifles, 42nd Gurkhas; the village was burnt, the Chins offering resistance by firing at long ranges.

Tartan was not so easily taken. On the 4th May, Major Shepherd marched against it with 65 rifles, Norfolk Regiment, and 60 of the 42nd Gurkhas. The enemy were found strongly entrenched in two stockades, and stood their ground until charged with the bayonet. One stockade was taken, but with the loss, on our side, of Lieutenant Michel and two men, Norfolk Regiment, killed; Captain Mayne, Norfolk Regiment, and Surgeon LeQuesne[1] severely

Action at Tartan.

[1] Surgeon LeQuesne afterward received the Victoria Cross, for conspicuous bravery while dressing Lieutenant Michel's wound.

wounded; and nine Gurkhas wounded. Owing to this heavy loss, the second stockade was not taken, though the men were eager to be allowed to make a second attack. The Chins had, however, received a severe lesson. On the 10th, Brigadier-General Symons, who had reached Fort White on the 4th May, took out a force of 150 men and destroyed both stockades, which were found unoccupied.

This was the last operation of the expedition.

Result of the campaign.

The Kanhows gave up their captives, and paid their fine between the 6th and 10th of May. Their spirit had, however, been rather scotched than killed, for they maintained a dogged demeanour, and continued to worry us whenever opportunity offered. A notable instance was on the 31st May when they made a night attack on the fort, which was, however, repulsed without loss on our side. The Tashôns were temporizing, and still refused to comply with our demands, which included the surrender of the Shwe Gyo Byu and his followers; but it was too late in the season to cross the Manipur river, so the expedition to the Tashôn capital had to be postponed.

The Yokwa and Haka Chins were as yet unvisited by our troops and had in no way suffered for raiding in the plains.

The campaign may be called successful in that it had caused the release of 200 captives, which was its principal object, and had meted out considerable punishment to the Siyins and Kanhows.

Our losses in the operations amounted to thirty-six killed and fifty-four wounded. The Chin Field Force was now broken up, and the troops restored to the ordinary peace footing. The garrison of Fort White and the lines of communication were formed into a second class command in place of the Chindwin, which had been given up, and the remainder of the troops were withdrawn.

The Yaw country.

Meanwhile a serious state of affairs had existed in the Yaw country, for the inhabitants broke out into rebellion, and, assisted by the southern Chins, espoused the cause of the Shwe Gyo Byu Prince. At first the rebels more than held their own, but troops were quickly sent from Pakkoku and down the Kale valley, and, after some sharp fighting, the rebellion was quashed and the inhabitants of Yaw disarmed.

THE CHIN-LUSHAI EXPEDITIONS, 1889-90.

Throughout the summer of 1889 the Political Officer kept up negotiations with the Soktes and Siyins, but though they surrendered a large number of Burman captives, they continued to give trouble by cutting the telegraph wires, ambushing convoys, and firing into the British posts. These facts, coupled with the advisability of thoroughly exploring and opening out the narrow strip of country which alone now divided British Burma from India, led to the undertaking, in the cold weather of 1889-90, of military operations from Burma and Chittagong into the country of the Chins and Lushais.

With regard to the Tashôns, they had throughout the summer showed a desire to be friendly, but had studiously evaded our demands for the surrender of the Burmese rebels. In August 1889, therefore, a proclamation was issued to them, informing them of our intention to send an expedition into their country, and telling them that we would refrain from punishing them for former misdeeds on the condition that they received our troops in a friendly way; paid a fine of Rs. 10,000, and a yearly tribute; and did their best to secure the surrender of the Siyins and Soktes. To make the terms easier for them the question of the surrender of the Shwe Gyo Byu Prince was waived.

Final orders for the advance of the troops from Burma and Chittagong were issued from head-quarters on the 5th September 1889 and the detailed objects of the campaign were set out as follows:—

1. To punitively visit certain tribes which had raided and committed depredations in British territory.
2. To subjugate tribes as yet neutral, but now by force of circumstances brought within the sphere of British dominion.
3. To explore the unknown country lying between Burma and Chittagong.
4. To establish, if necessary, certain posts in the regions visited, so as to ensure complete pacification and recognition of British power.

To carry out these objects, the troops working from the Burma side were divided into three portions as follows, the whole under the command of Brigadier-General W. P. Symons.

		Rifles.
I.—The Northern Column, to operate from Fort White under Colonel Skene, D.S.O., Commanding 42nd Gurkha Light Infantry.	1st Battalion, Cheshire Regiment ..	300
	42nd Gurkha Light Infantry ..	477
	No. 5 Company, Queen's Own Sappers and Miners.	95
	10th Bengal Infantry	400
	38th „ „	290
		1,622
II.—The Southern Column, to advance from Kan into the Baungshè Chin country under Brigadier-General W. P. Symons in person.	1st Battalion, King's Own Scottish Borderers.	500
	No. 1 Bengal Mountain Battery ..	84
	No. 6 Company, Queen's Own Sappers and Miners.	151
	2nd Battalion, 4th Gurkha Regiment ..	410
	2nd Madras Infantry	630
	Burma Company, Queen's Own Sappers and Miners.	94
		1,859

Grand total, 3,491 men with 117 officers.

III.—Garrisons to guard the western frontier of Burma, and to hold posts on the lines of communication, were found by the 10th, 33rd, and 38th Bengal Infantry and the 2nd Madras Infantry.

To the Northern column were assigned the duties of continuing and completing the subjugation and pacification of the Siyin, Sagyilaing, and Kanhow tribes of Chins, and of operating against the Tashôns in conjunction with the Southern Column.

The task of Brigadier-General Symons as Commander of the Southern Column was :—

First.—To drive a mule road through the heart of the Baungshè Chin country to Yôkwa and Haka, subjugating these tribes as he advanced, and obtaining the restoration of captives.

Second.—To advance in combination with the Northern column to the capital of the Tashôn Chins and compel their submission.

Third.—To advance west from Haka, and, in co-operation with the Chittagong Column, complete the opening of the road between Bengal and Burma, coercing the tribes, and obtaining submission to our authority on both sides of the line of advance.

Fourth.—To visit villages ; force the Chins to cease raiding and give up all captives ; to explore the Chin Hills in every direction as far as the limits of time and the working season would permit.

Fifth.—To establish the necessary posts to hold the country after the withdrawal of the main body of the troops.

No. 2 Company, Bengal Sappers and Miners.
3rd Bengal Infantry.
2nd Battalion, 2nd Gurkha Regiment.
28th Bombay Infantry (Pioneers).
Wing, 2-4th Gurkhas.

The troops operating from Chittagong, strength as per margin, were under the command of Colonel V. W. Tregear. A detailed account of the operations of this column, together with an account of a former expedition to Lushai from Chittagong in the previous year, an expedition undertaken principally to inflict punishment for the murder of Lieutenant Stewart while surveying in that country, will be found in Volume IV. Only passing reference will be made to the work of Colonel Tregear's column in the present chapter, which deals principally with the operations of the Burma Columns.

General Symons assumed command of the Burma Columns, Chin-Lushai Field Force on the 15th November 1889, and about this time the preparations for the expedition were in the following state :—

The Southern Column had concentrated at Pakokku for its march of 165 miles to Kan. On account of the unusually late rains the start of the expedition had been put off until the 23rd November. The Northern Column was ready at Fort White, and only awaited the arrival of its hill coolies. It had been decided to establish ten posts along the western portion of the Burma frontier for its protection against Chin raids. All the garrisons for these posts were sent up the Chindwin river to Kalewa. The late rains had flooded the Kale valley, and up to the end of November the country was impassable to anything but elephants. The energies of the officers, however, overcame all difficulties, and by the end of December these ten posts were constructed, occupied, and rationed.

Difficulties of transport.

To ration the Northern Column was no very difficult operation, as during the rains the Madras Sappers had converted the temporary track used by General Faunce into a good mule road, and rations were brought up to Kalewa by steamer, thence by country boat to Kalemyo, and from there by bullocks and mules to Fort White.

The rationing of Kan, however, the head-quarters of the Southern Column, was one of the greatest difficulties with which the General had to contend. Kan was 165 miles by road from Pakkoku, the main base, and on the 23rd of November, owing to the floods, carts could only travel sixty miles of this distance. A small river, the Myittha, connected Kan to Kalewa on the Chindwin, but it was very shallow and swift, full of rocks, and generally difficult of navigation. Owing to the difficulties of land transport, however, Lieutenant Holland, of the Indian Marine, explored the 136 miles of this river between Kan and Kalewa, and pronounced that it would be possible to send stores up by this route. This form of transport was accordingly adopted, and, under the supervision of Lieutenant Holland, was worked with conspicuous success until the end of January, when the river became too shallow for navigation. During February the transport officers had to meet a fresh difficulty in cattle-disease, which broke out with great virulence in the Kale and Myittha valleys, and through which the number of pack bullocks available was reduced by two-thirds.

The first troops of the Southern Column reached Kan on the 7th December, and the Sappers of the party began work on the road to Yokwa and Haka the next day.

Before the expedition started it was believed that the Southern Column would be able to reach Haka in at the most twelve days from Kan, and all calculations were made on this surmise. Such, however, were the unexpected difficulties of the country that, with the whole strength of the force devoted to making the road, sixty-four miles in length, it took the head of the column sixty-six days to get into Haka, while the mule road was not completed until the seventy-seventh day from commencing the work. This disappointing delay was not without its compensating advantages in dealing with the Chins. They expected us to make a quick advance, do some damage, and then retire. The steady persistent advance, together with the pains taken to get into touch with them, and to explain our objects and intentions, paralysed their efforts for resistance, and thus tribe after tribe submitted and yielded to our terms.

The same difficulty that met the Burma Column also greatly delayed Colonel Tregear, and he was unable to finish his road to

Haka till 13th April. This completion of the road from Burma to Bengal was the crowning success of the season's work. The junction of the two columns, however, occurred too late to allow of their undertaking any operations in concert, and the Chittagong Column returned to the west on the 16th April.

Beginning of hostilities.

The Chins first met with by the Southern Column were the Yokwas of the Baungshè tribe. From the outset it was resolved to try a lenient policy with the Southern Chins, who before these operations had not come into contact with us. After one poor attempt by the Yokwas at opposition to our advance on the 28th of December, near Taungtek, when they acknowledged to having had 500 men and 300 guns against us, and to having sustained a great defeat, they gave up all hope of keeping us out of their hills.

On the 8th January two Yokwa Chins came into camp, and from this date onwards we were never again out of touch with the tribes. The objects of our coming, and our terms, were carefully explained to these two men, and they were dismissed to repeat them to their chiefs, who formally surrendered shortly after.

The next day Lieutenant Foster and two other officers were strolling outside the camp when they were suddenly fired at by a few Thetta men in ambush, and Lieutenant Foster was shot dead. In consequence of this the nearest village, Lamtok, was burnt. Having dealt with the Yokwas, the column moved on Haka as soon as the mule path was sufficiently forward, arriving there on the 13th February. The same procedure as that adopted with the Yokwas obtained the full submission of the important Haka community; and the surrender of these two tribes was virtually equivalent to the submission of the whole Baungshè country.

Junction of Burma and Chittagong Columns.

Whilst waiting for the mule path to reach Haka, reconnaissances were made to the west to explore the country, obtain the submission of the Tlantlangs, get touch with the Chittagong Column, and assist them in their advance eastward. These objects were most satisfactorily obtained. On the 26th of February the advance parties of the Burma and Chittagong Columns met at Tao village, fifty-two miles west of Haka. The effect on the people of the junction of the two forces was so great that the heads of Lieutenant Stewart and the two men of the Leinster Regiment killed in the previous February near Rangamatia, together with several articles of property taken from the party, were given up directly they were demanded.

Meanwhile preparations were being pushed forward for a combined march on Falam, the capital of the Tashôn tribe. It was a matter of the first importance to ensure the success of this movement and the submission of this the most populous and influential of the Chin tribes, and it had consequently been decided that both columns should co-operate.

Malarial fever.

At this time, the end of February, sickness amongst the troops and carrier coolies had seriously weakened the strength of the Southern Column; so universal, indeed, was the sickness that it threatened at one time to frustrate all the plans of the campaign. Of the sixty-nine British Officers who served with the Southern Column only seven escaped malarial fever, while one died and twenty-six (two of whom afterwards succumbed) were invalided from this ailment alone. The following table shows the extent of the sickness among the troops.

Column.	Average strength during campaign.	Total admissions to hospital.	Deaths from disease.	Invalided.	Killed.	Remarks.
Northern Column.						
British Officers ..	35	12	..	9	1 (*a*)	Major Gordon Cumming, Cheshire Regiment.
British troops ..	252	277	3	32	1 (*b*)	Private Watson, 1st Cheshire Regiment.
Native " ..	1,380	1,031	30	109	5	
Public followers ..	1,300	359	39	207	..	
Southern Column.						
British Officers ..	61	33	1 (*c*)	26	1 (*d*)	(*c*) Captain Grimshaw, Royal Fusiliers.
British troops ..	310	484	21	276	..	(*d*) Lieutenant Foster,
Native " ..	1,315	1,238	17	257	1	King's Own Scottish
Public followers ..	2,073	1,738	96	1,206	..	Borderers.
Total all ranks both columns	..	..	207	2,122	9	

It had originally been intended that the combined march on Falam should take place in January, but the movement had been necessarily postponed, and the date now fixed for the simultaneous arrival at the Tashôn capital of the two columns was the 11th March.

At this stage it will be as well to leave the Southern force, and bring the account of the northern operations up to the date of marching on Falam. In November, shortly after the commencement of the field operations, a column under the command of Major Edge, Cheshire Regiment, advanced from Fort White to attack the villages of Shwipi, Dimpi, and Dimlo. The Chins set fire to the villages on the British approach, and then engaged Major Edge's men, killing one and wounding two Gurkhas. The following day some live stock was captured and some standing crops destroyed by the column, which then returned to Fort White followed by the enemy, who succeeded in killing a private of the Cheshire Regiment. On the 3rd January preliminary orders were received for the advance on Falam, and the next day the troops and coolies started improving the mule track to that place. The road was made for twelve miles to the southern slopes of the Ledaw range at Yawlu. Here an advanced post was built, rations were stored, and orders awaited for the general advance. No orders were received, however, during February and March, owing to the delay caused by the slow advance of the Southern Column.

Progress in the northern hills.

Experience had taught us that nothing was attained by simply burning the Siyins' houses. Endeavours were consequently made by the Assistant Political Officer to secure their submission by negotiations. These negotiations were so far successful that the Sagyilain Chief (Mang Lon) surrendered on the 17th January. His surrender was important as being the first, and through him all future negotiations with the Siyins were managed. Mang Lon informed the Political Officer that the conduct of the Siyins would depend entirely on the result of the Tashôn expedition, and that if the Tashôns did not fight, the Siyin tribe were not prepared to continue the struggle alone. Owing to the false impression we had at that time, that the Tashôns had unlimited control over the Siyins, this appeared reasonable, and what amounted to an armistice was then arranged until the advance should be made on Falam. During these two months that the Northern Column were waiting for the advance, friendly relations with the Siyins and some of the Sokte Chiefs improved daily. Dok Taung, the Chief of Molbem (called Mobingyi by the Burmans) could not, however, be induced to surrender, although he had twice left his village for that purpose. Finally it was arranged that a column should visit the village in order to enable the Political Officer to meet him. Every precaution was taken to ensure a peaceful visit, and messengers were sent on in front to assure the villagers that we would do them no harm if only they would receive us in a friendly manner. The column advanced from Fort White on the 28th February under the command of Colonel Skene, and consisted of fifty men of the Cheshire Regiment, 150 men of the 42nd Gurkhas, and one mountain gun. Several unheld stockades were passed, and all went well until the column was three miles from the village, when the Dabon Chief met the force and warned the Political Officer not to advance any further. This advice could of course not be listened to; the Chins dived into the *jungle*, and, a few minutes after, a volley was poured into the column from the hills on the right, at a range of about 200 yards. A sharp skirmish resulted, as the troops drove the enemy out of their position. The column then continued its march, the Chins keeping up a desultory fire from the bush, and when the two villages were reached they were found in flames. Thirty-seven houses, which escaped the flames, were burnt that night by the enemy themselves, who avowed that all must suffer alike. Such was the temper of the Chins at that time that they wantonly destroyed all houses which we had passed by and left untouched. Our losses on this occasion were one havildar and one private, both severely wounded.

Negotiations.

On returning from Molbem, orders were received to advance on Falam, and the Northern Column, consisting of 350 rifles and one gun, commanded by Colonel Skene, marched out from Yawlu on the 9th March. The Southern force advanced from Haka *viâ* Minkin, while Colonel Skene marched *viâ* Shinsi and Bwekwa to Pate.

On the 11th March, the two columns arrived almost simultaneously on opposite banks of the Manipur or Nankathé river, without having met with any opposition *en route*.

Arrival at Falam.

Elaborate preparations for the defence of their capital had been made by the Tashôns. Innumerable stockades, breastworks, and obstructions, extending over some nine miles of country, but chiefly intended against an enemy advancing from the north, had been freshly erected at every commanding point.[1] Large numbers of armed men watched both columns as they advanced, but there was no collision. It is difficult to estimate their numbers, but on the south of the Manipúr river, near the Ywama, there were not less than 5,000 men, of whom two-thirds were armed with guns and the rest with spears.

The Southern Column, notwithstanding the emphatic protests of three of the chiefs who had come out to meet it, continued its advance to within 1,000 yards of the village, and there encamped. An assembly was called, and the chiefs were asked if they would agree to our terms. To every one's great surprise, after permitting the columns to approach their capital unopposed, they firmly declined to acknowledge the supremacy of the Government by paying any tribute; and, without absolutely refusing, thought it very unlikely that they would be able to pay any portion of the fine of Rs. 10,000 imposed on them by the Chief Commissioner of Burma.

The situation thus became as strained as it well could be. Having warned the chiefs to think well over the consequences that their persistent refusal of submission would entail, General Symons dismissed them. The next two days were spent in prolonged negotiations, which severely taxed our troops' patience, but which resulted in the formal submission of the tribe and the attainment of all our demands. The tribute due for 1889 was paid as well as the fine, the latter reduced to Rs. 5,000 at the earnest solicitation of the Tashôn Chiefs.

1 These stockades had, however, been built without regard to military requirements, and showed the Tashôns to be more deficient than the Burmans in military training. By moving off the road the whole line of fortifications could have been enfiladed and turned.

A small reconnoitring party having been sent down to Sihaung, both columns withdrew from Tashôn territory without mishap, the Southern force returning to Haka and the Northern to Fort White.

From Haka, General Symons started to explore the country to the south, and succeeded in penetrating as far as Naring. This tour was entirely successful; a large tract of hitherto unknown country was surveyed, and the inhabitants were everywhere friendly. On the return of the column the Hakas no longer evaded the surrender of their slaves, who were soon after restored to their homes in Burma.

When the expedition closed, the only village which openly appeared hostile was Thetta. This village resolutely refused to surrender its slaves, and behaved badly when visited by the Political Officer, but the rains prevented an immediate punitive expedition being sent against it.

On the return of the Northern Column the Siyins were at once called upon to redeem their promises—as the Tashôns had surrendered—and to tender their submission. The Siyins, however, temporized, and the villages of the Bweman clan were forthwith attacked and destroyed by seven parties from Fort White and the Yawlu post. The Yawlu post was then evacuated and burnt, the garrison, under Major Gordon-Cumming, proceeding to Fort White on the 23rd March. On the way Major Gordon-Cumming was shot through the stomach by a Chin lying in ambush, and died almost immediately.

Pimpi was now attacked by two parties, one starting from Kalemyo and the other from Fort White. The Chins burnt the village on our approach, and our return march was one steady fight in which we lost two sepoys killed and a havildar wounded.

Towards the end of April the Siyins at last submitted, and each clan was allowed to rebuild its village as soon as all slaves had been surrendered.

Result of the campaign.

The campaign was now brought to a close and all troops were withdrawn, with the exception of the garrisons of Haka, Fort White, and the three stockades in the latter's neighbourhood, where permanent posts were established.

The result of the operations of the Southern Column was the submission of the Yokwa, Haka, Tlantlang, and Tashôn tribes, and of several independent villages; the recovery of seventy-seven captives; and the enforcement of the payment of fines and of an annual tribute. Roads practicable for baggage animals were constructed from Kan to Haka and from Haka to Fort Tregear. All the tribes who submitted gave assurances that they would abstain from raiding on the adjacent British districts.

In the north, four Siyin clans and some Sokti villages had tendered their submission; sixty-two slaves had been surrendered; and the heads of sepoys which had been taken were given up. Though the Siyins had submitted, however, and though they refrained from ambushing convoys and firing into posts, the Political Officer (Mr. Carey) was not sanguine that their submission would be permanent.

The Chin Hills were now treated as two districts, the Northern Chin Hills, with head-quarters at Fort White, under Mr. Carey, and the Southern Chin Hills (including the Tashôn tribe and the independent villages), with head-quarters at Haka, under Mr. Ross.

EVENTS OF 1890-91.

The Northern Chins.

During the greater part of the year of 1890 Captain F. M. Rundall, 1-4th Gurkhas, was in charge of the Northern Chin district, as Political Officer at Fort White. All the tribes under his control were more or less unruly, with the single exception of the Siyin village of Sagyilaing, and even the chiefs of this village could not prevent their tribesmen from cutting the telegraph wire and otherwise annoying our troops.

Towards the end of the year, however, some of the wire-cutters were captured, and at a durbar held by Brigadier-General Wolseley who was on inspection duty in the Chin Hills, the Siyins made formal submission, and surrendered all their captives in return for the prisoners in our hands.

Kanhow raids.

With regard to the Kanhows, the former small expeditions against this tribe had produced no lasting effect. On the surrender of the Siyins, however, whom the Kanhows had always looked upon as a buffer state between themselves and us, Yatwel, an important Kanhow

Chief, came into Fort White to ask what terms would be given to his tribe if they surrendered. The terms offered, though exceedingly light, were evidently not acceptable to this bellicose tribe, for, shortly after Yatwel's return, they made four successive raids into Burma, the last one, on Pinthawa, being of a very serious character, accompanied by many murders and much destruction to property. On account of these raids Captain Rundall was ordered to take a punitive column against the Kanhows.

The objects of the expedition were to liberate the Burman captives, to punish the raiders, to subdue the whole tribe, and, lastly, to survey the Kanhow country with a view to the opening up of a trade route through it to Manipur.

Kanhow expedition.

The plan of operations was to form a subsidiary base at Tiddim, and from there to work through the Kanhow country with as strong a column as possible, if necessary attacking Tunzun by the way. The village of Mwelpi was fixed on as the objective of the expedition, because it was thought this was the furthest point the column, with its limited transport, could reach, and that it was the most accessible place for a second force, operating from Auktaung, to co-operate with the Fort White troops. This second force, which consisted of seventy men of the 12th Burma Infantry, under Captain Presgrave, moved on Mwelpi simultaneously with the Fort White column, but, owing to lack of guides, could not find its destination, and was forced to return to Auktaung.

2 guns, No. 2 Mountain Battery.
150 men, 2-4th Gurkhas.
150 ,, 39th Garhwalis.
50 ,, 4th Madras Pioneers.

Captain Rundall left Fort White on the 20th January 1891 with a force consisting of the marginally named troops, with 300 Gurkha coolies under Lieutenant Festing for transport. Arriving at Tiddim on the 24th without having met with any opposition, the column was forced to delay their further advance for a few days to await the arrival of supplies. The time was occupied in making a strong post for a garrison of 100 men, the largest number that Captain Rundall could afford to leave behind him. This post was made doubly strong so that, if necessary, a permanent garrison might safely be left there after the end of the operations.

At this time another Kanhow Chief presented himself to ask what terms the British would give his tribe if they surrendered, and was told that the conditions of surrender were the submission of the tribe, the restoration of all captives, the payment of a fine of Rs. 4,000, and an annual tribute of Rs. 300.

By the 10th February all the rations required were stored at Tiddim, and, on the next day, Captain Rundall advanced for Tunzun and Mwelpi, leaving 100 men, under a native officer, in the defensive post.

By dint of very careful management the 300 coolies were just enough to carry the kits and fourteen days' rations without employing transport mules. Men's kits were cut down to 12½ lbs., and only 60 lbs. was allowed for a mess of nine officers, most of the officers carrying their own plates, knives, etc., in their havresacks. The march to Tunzun proved so difficult that, although the distance was but twenty miles, the column only reached their destination on the evening of the third day. On the 16th Captain Rundall left Tunzun for Mwelpi, leaving Lieutenant Persse with two guns and 140 men to overawe the Kanhows at the former place. Before starting his advance he again warned the Kanhows that if they did not conform to the British terms within six days he would attack their town and level it to the ground. Mwelpi was reached without opposition on the 17th, but, finding no trace of the Auktaung Column at this place, Captain Rundall pushed on to Shielmong, which was reached the next day. The inhabitants of this village said that they had heard of the Auktaung force, but did not know its whereabouts. As his column was now eighty miles from Fort White and the rations would carry it no further, Captain Rundall was now forced to retire, and, on the 21st, rejoined Lieutenant Persse at Tunzun. The British terms not having been complied with, it was decided to attack the town the following morning, and, with this intention, the place was quietly surrounded by daybreak. A messenger was then sent in to tell the inhabitants that further opposition was useless and that their town would certainly be destroyed if they did not immediately give up their three chiefs as a guarantee that all the terms would be complied with. This action met with complete success, and, after a little desultory firing in which about twelve Kanhows

Attack on Tunzun.

were killed, the three chiefs came out and surrendered. The following day many slaves were given up and the whole of the fine was paid, and on the 24th February the column set out on their return march to Fort White, which was reached without opposition on the 28th. A garrison of 100 men was left at Tiddim, and this post was afterwards made a permanent one.

The result of these operations, which were most successful, may be summed up as follows :—

(1) The Kanhow country was penetrated and surveyed.

(2) Punishment was inflicted for the raids, and the chief instigators were taken prisoners.

(3) Thirty-nine Burman captives were recovered and the fine and tribute was paid in full.

The tribes under the control of the Political Officer at Haka were the Tashôns, the Hakas, the Tlantlangs, the Yôkwas, and the independent Baungshè tribes lying to the south of the latter.

The Southern Chins.

Throughout the year of 1890 the Myittha valley was remarkably free from raids. The Hakas and the Yôkwas were apparently friendly to us, and on the whole behaved very well. The conduct of the independent Baungshès was not, however, so satisfactory.

Thetta.

About the end of November 1890 the Thetta villagers again began giving trouble by shooting men on our line of communication, and it became necessary that a column should proceed to that place as early as possible. Arrangements were accordingly made for a start from Haka about the 1st December 1890, but a sudden outbreak of fever, which prostrated nearly the whole of the Haka garrison, necessitated the movement being put off for a time, and this gave the Thetta villagers time to stockade and put their village into a thorough state of defence. From the month of November onwards, the Thettas adopted an attitude of open hostility to our troops and committed a series of outrages, culminating, on the 21st December, in the murder of Mr. Wetherell, Assistant Superintendent of Police, and the attempted murder of the Political Officer himself.

The head-quarters of the company, Burma Sappers and Miners, having reinforced Haka on the 30th ultimo. on the 1st

January 1891 Captain Carnegy proceeded to the village of Thetta with a force, strength as per margin, accompanied by Mr. D. Ross, Political Officer, Haka, and by Lieutenant B. A. James, R. E., Burma Sappers, who volunteered to accompany the column as Intelligence Officer. Thetta was reached the following day, and proved to be far more strongly fortified than had been anticipated. After some desultory firing, in which Lieutenant James and two men were killed, the villagers sent to ask whether we would give them terms if they submitted. Captain Carnegy, feeling that his force was not strong enough for him to capture the village and dictate his own terms, agreed to this; the village forthwith surrendered, and there and then paid up the fine agreed upon. The column then returned to Haka, which was safely reached on the 4th January.

The Thetta Column.
Lieutenant C. Ainslie, R.E.
6 Sappers, Queen's Own Sappers and Miners.
2-4th Gurkhas.
Captain P. M. Carnegy.
Lieutenant A. Grant.
Lieutenant H. C. Ducat.
3 native officers.
1 bugler.
129 rifles.

It was felt, however, that the results of this expedition were not satisfactory, and that our failure to take the village and impose our own terms must result in some loss of prestige among the Baungshè villages, several of which, moreover, had not yet been visited. Arrangements were accordingly at once made for a second expedition on a larger scale, with the object of more thoroughly exploring the Baungshè country, of receiving the submission of the villages still unvisited, and of convincing the Thettas, and their neighbours, of our ability to coerce them when necessary.

Combined Baungshè Columns.

It was therefore determined that a combined movement should take place on Shurkwa, a large village situated about twenty-two miles south-west of Thetta, which still remained defiant. Arrangements were made for two columns, one from Haka and another from Gangaw, to meet at Thetta, and then move on Shurkwa and adjacent villages.

The composition of the two columns was as shown in the margin. The column from Gangaw started on the 29th January 1891, and arrived at Thetta on the 5th February, where it was joined the same day by the column under Captain Carnegy. The two columns waited at Thetta, laying in supplies and improving the road to

Haka Column.
Captain Carnegy, Commanding.
147 rifles, 2-4th Gurkhas.
49 „ 4th Madras Pioneers.
Gangaw Column.
176 rifles, 39th Garhwalis, under Col. E. P. Mainwaring.

Rawvan, until the 13th February, on which date a reinforcement of two guns, No. 2 Mountain Battery, arrived from Mandalay. By the 10th February the Thetta villagers had paid up the whole of their fine, and gave assistance to our troops for the advance on Shurkwa.

On the 14th February the combined force, total strength 300 rifles with two guns, under the command of Colonel Mainwaring, marched from Thetta for Shurkwa.

Meeting with little or no opposition *en route*, Shurkwa was reached on the 17th, and the villagers surrendered without firing a shot, promising to give up all their slaves. After two days' halt at Shurkwa to allow the slaves to be collected and given up, Colonel Mainwaring returned to Haka, which was reached without incident on the 22nd February.

The expedition had been entirely successful, and had resulted in the submission of eight villages, including Shurkwa, and the surrender of thirteen slaves.

Second visit to Falam.

During Captain Rundall's absence on the Kanhow expedition a new source of trouble appeared; the Soktes who live on the west bank of the Manipur river, and who are commonly called Nwengals, having crossed the river in several parties and fired into our posts. The Siyins, too, had been cutting the wire and stealing from our posts. As it was believed that the Nwengals were a part of the Tashôn tribe, it was arranged that the matter should be enquired into by Mr. Ross, who had already been instructed to visit Falam from Haka. At the same time Captain Rundall was ordered to co-operate with the Southern Column and meet it at the Tashôn capital.

The column from Haka left that post on 10th March, and consisted of 300 men and two guns under Colonel Mainwaring, who was accompanied by Mr. Ross as Political Officer. On the 13th they arrived, after a peaceful march, at Falam, where they were met by the force under Captain Rundall. At a durbar held the next day the Tashôn Chiefs paid the annual tribute, promised to hand over the offending Nwengals, and further agreed to be responsible for the future good behaviour of that tribe; we in return promising, on these conditions, not to send a punitive expedition against the Nwengal villages.

The two columns then returned to Haka and Fort White, respectively, which were reached without further incident.

The Tao Column.

On the 29th March a force under the command of Lieutenant Mocatta, 39th Garhwalis, consisting of 100 men, 39th Garhwalis, and two guns, with Lieutenant Macnabb as Political Officer, started for Tlantlang and Tao. The object of the expedition was entirely friendly, firstly to meet the Tlantlang Chiefs and enquire into some raids which had been made in Lushai, and secondly to meet messengers with letters from the Superintendent of the Southern Lushai Hills.

The column reached Tao without opposition, but on the road several armed Chins were met with. As this tribe, however, was believed to be friendly, and as each Chin had explained that he was merely going to a conference at Tlantlang, the head village, no suspicions were aroused.

The day that Tao was reached, the Political Officer was informed that the Chins had intended to attack the column, but, not having been able to collect a sufficiently large force in time, they had abandoned the idea. This seems to have put the British on their guard, but their reception at Tao was so friendly that the officers began to discredit the report.

The return march begun on the 2nd April and all went well till about 9 A.M., when, while the column was halting to water the mules, a heavy fire was suddenly opened by the Chins from the hills on both sides of the road. A brisk fight ensued, in which the Garhwalis behaved most pluckily. The Chins, however, could not be driven from the strong position which they had taken up, and Lieutenant Mocatta consequently decided to continue his advance along the road. Hampered as he was by the dead and wounded, for whom he had only two *doolies*, he was soon obliged to halt for the purpose of burning the corpses of the killed sepoys. The advance was then continued, the Chins still hanging doggedly on the heels of the rear-guard; and a running fight was kept up till evening, when the column halted and built a rough *zariba* for the night. There was no water, nor could fires be allowed, but the troops met these privations without murmur.

Unmolested during the night, a start was made at 6-30 next morning, and with the advanced-guard almost continually in action, and the rear-guard keeping off the Chins who incessantly harassed the rear, the column slowly fought their way towards Tlantlang.

Meanwhile Colonel Mainwaring had received information at Haka of the intention of the Chins to attack Lieutenant Mocatta's force, and immediately marched out to his assistance. He occupied Tlantlang without opposition on the afternoon of 2nd April, and sent a message to Lieutenant Mocatta, which the latter, however, never received. The following day, hearing firing, he got into communication with the Tao Column a few miles from Tlantlang, and sent out a small party to their assistance. The Chins now disappeared, and Lieutenant Mocatta's column reached Tlantlang about 8 o'clock that night, after having had nearly forty hour's continual fighting without food.

The following morning the combined force returned to Haka, which was reached without incident on the 5th April. The casualties in the Tao Column amounted to five men killed, and Lieutenant Forbes, one native officer, and thirteen men wounded. The casualties of the Chins, whose force amounted to 500, were unknown, but it was ascertained that the Chief of Tunzun was among the killed.

At the beginning of May, Colonel Mainwaring took out a large column to enforce a heavy fine from the villages implicated. Owing to the rains, however, it was found impossible to deal with all the villages, and further operations were abandoned for the year.

The only military column that was sent out in the winter of 1890-91 against the Independent Chins in the neighbourhood of Yawdwin was the Chinbôk Column under Captain E. S. Hastings, D.S.O. In January 1891, a serious raid was made on Yawdwin post by Chins from Panchaung, and it was evident that severe measures were necessary for the punishment of this tribe. Captain Hastings was consequently ordered to proceed from Myingyan with 112 mounted infantry, and ninety-six rifles of the 4th Burma Battalion, 32nd Madras Infantry, to effect the release of captives and chastise the Chins. He arrived in Yawdwin on the 4th February, and succeeded in severely punishing all the villages implicated in the attack, and in reducing the whole Yaw district to subjection.

The Independent Chins.

OPERATIONS IN 1891-92.

The most important event of the summer of 1891 was a durbar held at Fort White, at which all the Kanhow Chiefs took the oath of allegiance to the British Government, and swore to abstain from raiding in Burma. The captive Kanhow Chiefs and all Kanhow prisoners were then released, and they amply repaid the Government for this clemency by staunchly abstaining from the rebellion raised eighteen months later by the Nwengals and Siyins.

The rest of the summer past without serious incident.

With a view to the further pacification of the Chin Hills, the following operations were decided on for the open season of 1891-92. In the south a column, to be called the Baungshè Column, strength 250 men and two guns, was to operate in the vicinity of Shurkwa; a second of the same strength was to inflict punishment on the Tlantlangs; while a third was to co-operate with a force from Fort White in the country of the Tashôns, Nwengals, and Yahows. The column from Fort White for this purpose was to consist of 300 men and two guns, and a similar force was to operate from that place against the Kanhows. A temporary post was to be made at Shurkwa as a centre for the operations in the south, and a permanent post was to be established at Falam to dominate the Tashôns. The political officers were instructed to make plain to the chiefs that they were to be held responsible for the payment of tribute and for the maintenance of peace, and that so long as they obeyed orders their authority would be upheld.

It had been realized that, until a post was built at Falam and the Tashôns thoroughly brought into subordination to the Government, it was hopeless to expect the minor tribes to respect our authority. The construction of this post was therefore, politically, the most important work of the season. The various tours arranged were intended to comprise a thorough exploration of the whole of the hills, in addition to bringing the various tribes under control.

At this time many villages had held entirely aloof and had not submitted, while the bad characters of the northern tribes within our sphere of influence imagined that they could always avoid us by retiring to the borders of the Lushai tract, to which remote regions they believed we were unable to penetrate.

The first operations in the northern hills were to open up the Sokte tract throughout its length to Manipur, to its western border in the Lushai Hills, and to the Kabaw valley on the east.

Operations in the northern hills.

An advanced base was established at Lanacot, some eighty miles north of Fort White, from which this work was satisfactorily concluded without opposition by troops under the command of Captain G. B. Stevens. One party pushed right through to Manipur, thereby creating a great impression in the Chins accompanying the column, who for the first time realized that the white men in the Chin Hills and Manipur were one and the same race.

In the south, after the close of the active operations of 1890-91, much time was spent cultivating cordial relations with the Haka Chiefs, and the peace of the hills near our posts was only broken by an attack by the Hakas on their tributary village of Kusa.

Progress of events in the south.

Further afield, however, the people were still restless; a present of powder and shot (the Chin method of declaring war) was sent us by the southern independent villages, while the Yahow and northern Tlantlang tribes were still openly hostile.

On the 25th December the Baungshè Column left Minywa under the command of Major Gunning, 60th Rifles. Having reached Shurkwa without opposition, an advanced base was formed at Lotaw, from whence a tour of the surrounding country was made. The column then returned to Haka, with the exception of a small party left at Lotaw to visit some outlying districts which had not been touched by the main body. This work was successfully accomplished, and the party were on their return march to Haka, when the Chins suddenly assumed a threatening attitude, and the Shurkwa Chief refused to supply the column with coolies. After some fruitless negotiations the villagers fired at the troops, and an engagement ensued, as the result of which the village was destroyed, and about fifty Chins were killed and wounded. The British party, whose casualties amounted to one killed and one wounded, then returned to Haka, which was reached without further incident. As a result of these operations thirty-three villages had tendered their submission, and twenty-five Burmese captives had been released.

The Baungshè Column.

The Tlantlang Column under Major A. G. F. Browne, D.S.O., operated in the neighbourhood of Tlantlang between February and April, during which time the whole tribe was brought under control without incident.

The Tlantlang Column.

Early in March preparations were made for the despatch of the two columns into the Tashôn country. Throughout the Chin Hills the Tashôns were regarded as powerful rivals to ourselves, and it was therefore necessary to bring this tribe under our full control. As the Tashôns, however, had never been actively hostile to us, instructions were issued to our column commanders to use every endeavour to attain their object without bloodshed. Owing to the Tashôns being reported to be able to place 10,000 men in the field, it, as has already been stated, was decided to send two columns against them, one from Haka and the other from Fort White.

The Tashôn Expedition.

Previous to the start of the expedition the attitude of the Tashôn Chiefs was most hostile, and it was ascertained that they had endeavoured to induce the Siyins and Soktes in the north to join in a general rising. These endeavours were, however, unsuccessful, and the Tashôns, not daring to face us single-handed, appeared to have then given up all idea of resisting us, and sent messages to Fort White promising that the troops would not be opposed.

The Haka Column left Haka on the 10th March, and occupied Falam without opposition on the 13th, being joined there by the Fort White force the following day. The Falam Chiefs were then informed that their village had been occupied as a punishment for their attempting to organize a general rising, and that a permanent post would be established there. They were forbidden to levy tribute from the Kanhows, Siyins and Sagyilains, but were told that, so long as they remained loyal to the British, their rights would be respected and their authority over the Tashôns assured. Leaving a temporary post at Falam, the Southern Column then proceeded to visit the Yahow country, returning to Haka on the 2nd April.

Occupation of Falam.

The Northern Column under Captain Rose was to have explored the whole of the Nwengal country on the west bank of the

Manipur river, but, on hearing that there had been severe fighting in the Lushai Hills, it was arranged that the Kanhow Column should visit the north of the Nwengal tract, while Captain Rose's force should only visit the south of that country, and should from there push on into Lushai with the intention of preventing the Eastern Lushais from joining their western neighbours in the attack on Mr. McCabe, Political Officer of the Northern Lushai Hills. Captain Rose consequently advanced through Molbem and Botaung as far as the village of the Chief Nikwe, which was reached on the 3rd April. The column, being short of rations, then returned, but on its way back they were ordered to proceed to the assistance of Captain Shakespeare, who, having advanced north to the assistance of Mr. McCabe, was now reported to be in a critical position at Vansanga. Captain Rose, therefore, after proceeding to Botaung for supplies, retraced his steps and marched for Daokhana, in the heart of the Lushai country, and the centre of the rising. The column marched 104 miles in twelve days through unknown and hostile country, and succeeded in joining Captain Shakespeare at Daokhana. That village and several others which had joined in the revolt were then destroyed, and the column, continuing their march to Lungleh, returned to Burma by sea *viâ* Chittagong. There were few casualties on the side of the British, but the march was a notable one.

Lushai Relief Force.

Meanwhile a party of Chins from Hele had attacked the post of Botang, which on the departure of Captain Rose's column had been garrisoned by a party from Fort White under Lieutenant Henegan. In consequence of this the village of Hele was attacked and destroyed by Captain Stevens. Apart from this action no raids were committed during the year, either in the hills or in Burma, and it was thought that considerable progress had been made in the establishment of satisfactory relations with the Chins.

From the 2nd July 1892 the Chin Hills Tracts were formed into one administrative charge with head-quarters at the new Falam post.

THE SIYIN–NWENGAL REBELLION.

During the rains of 1892 a plot was concerted by the Nwengals and the Siyins to overthrow the government in the hills. The cause of the rebellion was the fear of total disarmament, consequent on the British policy of inflicting fines in guns on offending villages and individuals. This system of fining had been adopted in the hope that it would gradually effect the disarmament of the Chin Hills without causing the general rising which it was known that any drastic measures to this end would involve.

The rebellion broke out on the 9th October when *Myoôk* Maung Tun Win was proceeding with a small escort to visit the Chief of Kaptyal at that Chief's request. The party had just reached the neighbourhood of Pomba village when they were treacherously ambuscaded by a large force of Chins, who poured a volley into them at point blank range. Tun Win and eight of his men were killed, and seven were wounded, but the havildar, sending three men to cut their way back to Fort White with the news, collected the remainder of his little party, and, fighting his way to a small knoll, kept the enemy off until the arrival of reinforcements.

Steps were immediately taken by Captain Caulfield (Commanding Northern Chin Hills) and Mr. Carey, Political Officer, to take the offensive, and to prevent the rebellion spreading to the, at present, disaffected tribes. Communications were opened with the Kanhows and Soktes, who all promised their loyalty and support; and though the Soktes, hemmed in as they were on both sides by rebels, afterwards wavered a little in their allegiance, the Kanhows remained loyal to the end.

Reinforcements now arrived at Fort White, including 100 men from Falam under Lieutenant Wardell; and towards the end of October Captain Presgrave arrived with the head-quarters of his regiment and took over the command of the Northern Chin Hills from Captain Caulfield.

The enemy's plan of campaign was that the Nwengals should operate in the neighbourhood of Tiddim while the Siyins confined themselves to the Fort White country. They decided never to make a frontal attack, but to ambush convoys, snipe the forts, block the roads, cut the telegraph wire, and generally make it impossible for the troops to remain in the hills.

As soon as reinforcements had arrived, numerous columns were sent out from Fort White to destroy villages and to try to inflict a heavy defeat on the enemy. As the Chins, however, would never stand, little damage could be done to them, and it was afterwards found necessary to have small outposts placed all over the country, ambushing the enemy, preventing the rebuilding of villages, and destroying all food supplies that could be found. The following is a brief account of the operations of the various columns :—

On the 3rd November a column under Captain Presgrave consisting of seventy men, 1st Burma Rifles, and seventy-five men, Garhwali Rifles, left Fort White and captured Dimlo and Shwimpi, both of which places were burnt and evacuated by the enemy on our approach. The Chins offered little opposition, contenting themselves with firing at the column from long ranges, but on the return march to Fort White they had prepared several ambushes, in one of which the Subadar Major of the 1st Burma Rifles was severely wounded.

On the 10th November a small column under Lieutenant Henegan captured the village of Tannwe, the enemy here making an unsuccessful attempt to capture the baggage mules and cut up the escort. On the 14th Captain Presgrave with 260 men and two guns proceeded against the Pimpi rebels. On the 20th Captain Caulfield with a force of 200 men proceeded to Montôk, which was found evacuated and burnt. A party of police from Kalémyo acted in co-operation with this column, and, though there was little fighting a great quantity of the enemy's food supplies was destroyed.

On the 28th December Brigadier-General Palmer, C.B., arrived at Fort White and took command of the operations. Though generally satisfied with the plan of campaign he immediately asked for reinforcements, and the troops in the Northern Chin Hills were now brought up to 2,600 men.

The Falam Chiefs were at this time neutral, for, though they did not actually side with the rebels, they made no efforts to help us to quell the rising, nor did they give us any information.

By the end of December British posts were established at Phunam, Pimpi and Montôk, and the garrisons at Fort White, Dimlo, and Tiddim were also in a position to operate against the rebels. On 1st January the General proceeded with a force of 450 men to attack the village of Kaptyal, the seat of the rebellion. Great delay was caused by the crossing of the Manipur, an operation which took nine days, but on the 14th all was ready for the advance, and a move was made on Kaptyal, which was, as was always the case at this time, fired and evacuated by the enemy on our approach.

The next fortnight was spent in sending small parties in all directions over the country; and, though the enemy rarely offered any opposition, much damage was done to their crops. They made a determined stand near Hele, but flanking parties soon dislodged them, and they retired without having inflicted any casualties on the British column.

Meanwhile operations had been carried out successfully in the Siyin country, and, the worst of the rebellion being now over, terms were offered to those of the rebels who wished to surrender. By the end of March most of the ringleaders had either been captured or had surrendered, hostages had been given for the future good behaviour of the tribes, and 1,647 guns had been recovered, and the General now returned to the plains, taking most of the troops with him.

The British casualties in the rebellion amounted to seventy of all ranks, including Lieutenant Geoghegan, 6th Burma Battalion, and the Subadar Major, 1st Burma Rifles, severely wounded.

During the rebellion all the southern tribes behaved well except the Baungshè village of Tlantlang, which continued to harbour a proclaimed outlaw and former chief. A column was consequently sent against this village with Captain Beale in command, and the villagers were heavily fined in guns for the offence. No opposition was met with by the column either on its march to Tlantlang or on its return journey.

EVENTS OF 1893-97.

In the open season of 1893-94 a small and stubborn remnant of disaffected Siyins in the neighbourhood of Pimpi was finally suppressed. The northern Chin tribes were also finally disarmed, and have since given no trouble. The southern Chin tribes were, on the whole, quiet, but an inter-tribal quarrel was only settled by prompt action, and the village of Thetta committed a couple of raids towards the close of the year.

Final subjugation of Thetta.

After a full enquiry, an expedition against this, the most turbulent village in the south, was sanctioned at the end of 1894. The force, which consisted of 150 men, 6th Burma Battalion, fifty of the 1st Burmans, and two guns, left Haka on the 1st January under the command of Major Keary, D.S.O. The main force advanced against the village, while fifty men under Lieutenant Henegan made a detour, taking the position in rear. The Thettas made no opposition, and the village was occupied on the 2nd January, the fourth anniversary of the previous attack. Eighty guns were demanded and were promptly delivered, and, following this, all the southern tribes were disarmed, the amount of guns withdrawn being 1,938.

In all, nearly 7,000 guns were taken from the Chins between the years 1893 and 1896, and since the latter date the hills have enjoyed peace, and there has been an almost total absence of serious crime. The growth of trade and intercourse between the Chins and the people of the plains has been rapid, and considerable numbers of Chins have settled in the Kale valley.

The Yawdwin Chins.

Only a narrow fringe of the tribes bordering on the Yawdwin and Pauk sub-divisions of Pakkoku were administered. They remained quiet for some years, but, in 1896, Chinbôks from Kyingyi committed some raids, in consequence of which three parties of Military Police were sent against them in 1897, one coming from the northern hill tracts of Arakan. No opposition was encountered; the offending villages were punished, and compensation was paid to the people who had suffered in the raids. Tours were made throughout the whole district and feuds and disputes were settled in many parts beyond the administrative boundary.

Police operations in 1897.

Chin Hills constituted a scheduled district.

In 1896 the Chin Hills were declared by proclamation to be a part of Burma, and were constituted a scheduled district; the chiefs, however, are allowed to administer their own affairs in accordance with their customs, subject to the supervision of the Superintendent of the Chin Hills.

BIBLIOGRAPHY.

The Chin Hills.—B. S. Carey, 1896.

CHAPTER XXIII.

THE KACHINS.

The country.

THE Kachin hills proper may be considered to be that part of the hills in the Bhamo and Myitkyina districts which has been taken under administration. This country, which for administrative purposes has been divided into forty tracts, lies between 23° 30′ and 26° 30′ north latitude, and 96° and 98° east longitude. It comprises about 19,000 square miles and consists of a series of ranges, for the most part running north and south, all leading towards the Irrawaddy.

Beyond the district above described there are many Kachins in Katha, Möng Mit, and the Northern Shan States, but though they are often the predominating, they are not the exclusive population, and they are comparatively recent settlers.

Myitkyina, to which place the Irrawaddy is navigable for steamers, was the most northerly point to which Burmese jurisdiction extended, and beyond this the whole country remains Kachin. From Sinbo to Myitkyina the country may be briefly described as a well-watered plain, with an occasional low hill rising out of dense *jungle.* The Shans and Burmese Shans who used to cultivate it were driven away by Kachin raids and are only now beginning to return. The land is very fertile and is capable of supporting a large population. From Myitkyina to the confluence of the Mali and 'Nmai Hka the country becomes gradually wilder and the *jungle* more dense. Above the confluence the appearance of the country entirely changes. No more flat ground is met with, and as far as Hkamti Long there stretches a mass of low hills formed into valleys by high parallel ranges of mountains bearing generally north and south.

Still further to the north, about latitude 28° or 29°, lies the Hkamti Long country, which is practically the valley of the Mali

Hka. To the east and north of this rises a snow-clad range of hills, up to the present unexplored, which would appear to be the watershed between the 'Nmai Hka (locally called Tamai) and the Salween.

The country to the immediate north and north-east of Bhamo is, generally speaking, a rugged mass of mountains varying in height from 1,000 to 12,000 feet above sea level. The main ranges run north and south and, except where they have been cleared for cultivation, are covered with dense forest. Deep valleys separate the spurs, at the bottom of which are rocky streams full of excellent water. Towards the hill tops water is scarce, though many of the villages are situated there.

West of the Irrawaddy, and traversed by one of the high roads from Assam to that river, lies the Hukong valley. It is about fifty-four miles long by thirty-five broad, is covered with dense forest, and supports a considerable population. It drains into the Tanai river, which, when it leaves the valley, is known as the Chindwin.

The Tanai Hka, rising in the hills south-west of Thama is a clear swift stream ranging from fifty to 300 yards in breadth, and is fed on both sides by numerous tributaries, chief of which are the Tarong and the Tawan.

Of other rivers, the chief on the left bank of the Irrawaddy is the Taping, which, rising in China, is, at the point where the Nampaung joins it, a raging impassable torrent. Boats of a large size, however, can navigate it as far as Myothit.

The Nampaung is a small river easily fordable all through its course. Its chief importance is that it forms the boundary line with China.

North of the Taping is the Molè, which the Kachins call Manli Hka. It joins the Irrawaddy about five miles above Bhamo and is navigable for large country boats as far as Hngetpyawdaw.

On the right bank the Mogaung river is the chief tributary of the Irrawaddy. It rises in the north-west of the Hukong valley and as far as Kamaing retains its old Shan name of Nam Kawng. It is navigable for steam launches as far as Laban.

Little is known of the streams in the Kachin hills north of the confluence, but none appear to be navigable and they are all very much alike, with deep rocky gorges and precipitous banks covered with deep *jungle.*

Rope-bridges are common, but, except in the rains, most of the rivers seem to be fordable, except the 'Nmai Hka.

In the early morning, in December, the low lying hills and plains are covered with a dense raw fog, and there are very heavy dews. In the higher country, from the end of November to the end of March, there is a cool breeze during the day and a frost at night. In January, the sun in the middle of the day is hot and a haze begins which gradually thickens till it is laid by the rains. The rainfall during the wet season is heavy but has not been registered.

The people.

The Kachins are essentially a hill people, though there are many instances of Kachin villages being built in the plains. In many cases their cultivation is in valleys, but they generally live above it, very often at heights and distances which to any one but a Kachin would seem prohibitive of proper work.

The name Kachin is purely Burmese, but has become firmly attached to the race. The Chinese, however, call the Kachins Yejen (wild men), as a rule, but use the term Shan-teo (heads of the hills), when they think it to their interest to be polite.

Of the national division into two families, the Chingpaws and the Hkaku, it may be briefly said that the former name applies to a southern, while the latter applies to a northern, Kachin. This division has the convenience of corresponding with the present Burma administrative boundary.

The race includes a great number of tribes, sub-tribes and sub-divisions, most of which, owing to the isolating nature of the hills, and to the Kachins' maintenance of blood feuds, are supported by very marked distinctions in dialect. To give an account of all these numerous sub-tribes would be beyond the scope of this chapter, and for such information the reader must be referred to the official Gazetteers. It will suffice to say here that the five principal tribes, all of which are divided into about fifteen sub-tribes, are the Marips, the Lahtawngs, the Lepais, the 'Nkhums and the Marans. Besides these there are several cognate tribes regarded by the Kachins as descended from the same legendary ancestors, but differing in manners, customs, and language from the true

Chingpaw. The chief of these are the Sassons, the Marus, and the Lashis.

A brief account of the above mentioned tribes is appended :—

THE MARIPS.—This tribe is found west of the Mali Hka; round the Jade and Amber Mines; and to the west of Lake Indawgyi. West of the Irrawaddy they are a powerful tribe, but on the east they have only a few scattered villages. These people have from the first been the most consistently friendly to British authority.

THE LAHTAWNGS have spread southwards over all the country north of the upper defile of the Irrawaddy. With the exception of the Sana sub-tribe, they have not come into collision with British authority.

THE LEPAIS are probably the largest and most powerful of the Kachin tribes; they are scattered about all over the Kachin country, but are found principally to the north and north-east of Mogaung, in the tract of country between the two arms of the Irrawaddy, near Myitkyina, and in the Pônkan hills east and south-east of Bhamo.

THE 'NKHUMS.—This tribe inhabits the country on the east of the Irrawaddy north of Maingna. There are a few scattered villages along the frontier; on the borders of the Chinese Shan States of Ho-Hsa and La-Hsa; and east of Bhamo; and an isolated colony on the Nayin stream in the Mogaung area.

THE MARANS are found in scattered villages all along the frontier. They are also found in the Kaukkwe valley, and have spread southwards as far as Möng Mit and Mohnyin.

THE SASSONS.—This tribe, sometimes confused with the Marips, inhabits the country to the north and west of the Amber Mines and extends to Assam. They have never come into collision with the British, and their dress in no way differs from the true Chingpaw.

THE MARUS in dress and appearance resemble the Chingpaw, but they themselves deny that they are Kachins. Their country is on the borders of Burma and China, but they are also found in North Hsenwi and in the Mohnyin sub-division of Katha.

THE LASHIS are mixed up with the Szis and, with them, are spread along the frontier north, east, and south-east of Bhamo.

THE KACHINS have no acknowledged chief; each headman governs his own village.

The Kachin dwellings are long low thatched huts, each often containing a family of three generations, some twenty or more people.

In religion the Kachins worship *nats* or spirits, of whom the number is endless, for anyone may become a *nat* after his death. As a rule the *nats* are considered malignant, and are not, therefore, worshipped as long as everything goes smoothly.

Kachin methods of fighting.

Of war proper the Kachins have no notion; their hostilities are mere desultory raids. Against British troops they have generally fought behind stockades, and though as a race they cannot be called courageous, they have often held their ground with great determination.

Their stockades are, as a rule, made of split bamboos woven into a kind of trellis work, with sharpened points on the outside; while the ground in front is studded with *pangyis* or spikes. These *pangyis* are bamboos sharpened to a triangular point, and placed in the ground in such a way that they are extremely hard to see. They will go through a boot as easily as through cloth, and the natural oil of the bamboo adds irritation to the wound.

Sometimes more complicated defences, including earthworks, have been made by the Kachins; and a line of retreat is always provided for, generally down a steep ravine into thick *jungle.*

Pitfalls are often used. They are two or three feet wide, six feet long and about three feet deep, studded with *pangyis,* and neatly covered over. Another defensive measure is to destroy the hill path, so as to make the passage of animals or coolies impossible.

The spot chosen for the defence of a village or road is usually in thick *jungle,* the favourite place being in a ravine with steep sides; trees are cut down to block the road for the attacking force, and on this spot the Kachins have their guns ready laid. The *jungle* or ravine is densely spiked, and beyond the fallen trees is the stockade or, perhaps, a series of stockades; and, in the latter case, as fast as the enemy are driven out of one stockade they retire into the one behind. The Kachins, however, rarely protect their flanks, so a frontal attack should never be undertaken

The best attack formation is one originated by Captain O'Donnell, D.S.O., while he was in command of the Mogaung Levy. It is very similar to that which was employed against the Ashantis, and is as follows:—An advance party of six men lead the way. Two flank parties of varying strength are told off to follow some little distance in rear, and immediately behind them comes a mountain gun. Directly a stockade is encountered the advance party passes the word back; the flanking parties make straight for the flanks; and the gun opens fire on the centre of the work. This generally has the effect of dispersing the enemy, who, as a rule, retire precipitately in the direction of one or other of the flanking parties. Kachins usually attack at night, and the time chosen is just before the rise of the moon. This enables them to deliver the attack in a half light, and have the moon to light them home with their booty; their system of fighting is in fact nothing but raiding developed.

Weapons.

A few of the more powerful *duwas* have *jingals* and swivel guns but they are very rare. Guns are of every kind, from the flint lock to converted Enfields and even repeating carbines, obtained from Yünnan. Powder is made locally and is coarse and dirty. Four fingers' breadth is not an uncommon charge. Cross bows are also used; they are made of hardened bamboo and are a serviceable weapon. The arrows are but rarely poisoned and metal tips are uncommon. Their other weapons are the ordinary Kachin *dah*, sheathed in wood and slung over the right shoulder; and a broad bladed spear with a shaft about six feet long.

The Kachins were the first of the frontier tribes of Burma with which we came in contact. They are broken up into small communities, each under its own *duwa*, and, though wild and savage they make very good agriculturists. Their disunion was at once a cause of weakness to them and trouble to us, for there was no central authority which could be subdued or conciliated with a view to securing general peace. Each petty tribe raided according to its own inclination or interest, and, owing to the size of the country, the process of establishing satisfactory relations was not effected without considerable trouble.

The Burmese and Shans stood in great awe of the Kachins and for some time previous to the annexation it was a common thing for villagers in the Bhamo district to sleep in boats on the river for fear of sudden raids. Bhamo itself had been attacked by a combination of Chinese and Kachins in 1884, and was almost completely destroyed; the Shan traders were the victims of excessive blackmail which the Kachins levied on all who passed through their territory, and above Bhamo no village, Burman or Shan, could exist without putting itself under the protection of some chieftain in the adjacent hills.

British occupation of Bhamo.

Bhamo was occupied by us on the 28th December 1885, and at first the Kachins seemed more curious than hostile. Our first direct relations with them began with the occupation of Mogaung and our connection with the Jade Mines, which will now be considered.

MILITARY OPERATIONS.

At the date of the arrival of the British Expeditionary Force at Mandalay the Mogaung district was governed by the elder *Sawbwa* of Wuntho, who had been deputed there by the Burmese Government in 1883 (two years after he abdicated in Wuntho in favour of his son) to put down a Kachin rising which had devastated the whole neighbourhood. Successful both in the restoration of order and in his subsequent administration, he left Mogaung at the end of 1885, and the government was then carried on by a council of three persons. The chief of these was Maung Kala, who belonged to a family of Chinese extraction, long resident in Mogaung, and closely related to the Mogaung Tu-ssu, who had ruled that district when it was tributary to China. He possessed an ancient Chinese seal, which had always been found by the Burmese Government a potent means of controlling the Kachins. The other members of the council were Maung Shwe Gya and Maung Sein. The former, of mixed Kachin and Burman blood, was in charge of the defence of the town, and the latter, a Burman, aided Maung Kala in the civil administration. The council appears to have governed wisely and to the satisfaction of the people; they beat off the attacks of Li Win-sho, a Chinese dacoit, who had a large and well-armed gang, and they kept up friendly relations with the Kachins.

OPERATIONS IN 1886.

In February 1886, a British force, accompanied by Major Cooke, Political Officer, proceeded to Mogaung *viâ* Sinbo, and met with no opposition either in going or on the return journey. Major Cooke appointed Maung Kala to be *Myoôk*, and Maung Shwe Gya and Maung Sein to be his assistants, retaining the Burmese title of *Nakhan*.

First expedition to Mogaung, 1886.

Two months later, Maung Kala was assassinated, and it was discovered that Maung Sein had hired men to commit the murder, intending to hand over the town to a self-styled prince who had appeared in the neighbourhood. Maung Shwe Gya and the elders of the force arrested and promptly executed Maung Sein and his accomplices, and the Deputy Commissioner then appointed Maung Htun Gwye, a Bhamo official, to be *Myoôk*, and Maung Po Saw, a son of Maung Kala, to be *Nakhan* of Mogaung. Maung Htun Gwye was badly treated on arrival at Mogaung, and, declining to stay there without the support of troops, he was directed to remain at Sinbo and take charge of that part of the district which adjoins the Irrawaddy. In September, a man named Npa Kyi entered Mogaung territory and produced a patent of appointment as *Sawbwa*, purporting to have been issued by the Wuntho *Sawbwa*. The Mogaung officials answered his invitation to them to submit by attacking and killing him, and, in consequence of this exhibition of spirit, Maung Htun Gwye was recalled and Maung Po Saw was appointed *Myoôk*.

It was intended to send an expedition to Mogaung at the end of 1886, but the attitude of the Wuntho *Sawbwa* was at that time so suspicious that the column was diverted to Mawlu to watch him instead.

Meanwhile the Pônkan Kachins began to be troublesome near Bhamo. On the first occupation of Bhamo, friendly relations had been entered into with the Kachins inhabiting the neighbouring hills, and they were allowed the benefit of despatching their goods by steamers from that place without paying taxes. Whilst the garrison was considerably reduced, owing to the absence of troops on the Mogaung expedition, rumours of an outbreak were brought in by a Chinaman to the intent that they (the Kachins) had killed

The first Pônkan expedition, 1886.

buffaloes and invoked their *nats*, which appears to be one of their preliminary preparations for war. A short time after this, two attacks were made on the village of Sawadi. The *Myothugyi* (headman) of Sawadi was written to, but replied that the affair had been greatly exaggerated. Major Cooke, the Political Officer, and the whole of the Mogaung party then returned to Bhamo; more enquiries were made and it appeared that the Pônkan *Sawbwa* was the man who had attacked Sawadi. A party under Captain Lyle, Royal Welsh Fusiliers, strength fifty rifles, Royal Welsh Fusiliers, and twelve rifles, Bengal Sappers and Miners, was consequently sent to the village of Chaung Dauk at the foot of the hills in which the *Sawbwa* lived. The expedition was received at this village in a friendly manner, and letters from Major Cooke and General Norman were sent to the *Sawbwa* ordering him to come into Bhamo by the 11th April 1886. The *Sawbwa* refused to comply with these orders, and in consequence an expedition under Captain Wace (who had reinforced Captain Lyle's party) was sent against him. The force, which left Chaung Dauk on the 12th April 1886, consisted of two guns, Hazara Mountain Battery, forty-three rifles, Welsh Fusiliers, eight rifles Mounted Infantry, thirty-eight Sappers and Miners, and thirty-six of the 26th Punjab Infantry.

Constant barricades were found across the road, and about 9 A.M., on arrival at a particularly large one in a rocky defile, a heavy fire was opened on the British force from an ambuscade. Captain Wace and a lance-corporal were wounded, but the barricade was successfully carried, and the column, meeting with no further opposition that day, halted at Kara, 1,750 feet above Chaung Dauk, for the night. The advance was continued on the 13th. Captain Wace was not fit to proceed, so the command devolved on Captain Lyle, who took with him the two guns, eight mounted infantry, thirty-eight Welsh Fusiliers and twenty sappers. After a steep ascent, the column was met with a heavy fire from a stockade which the Fusiliers promptly charged, putting the enemy to flight. The British casualties were—Captain Lyle, one man Welsh Fusiliers, two men Royal Artillery, and two sappers, wounded. Owing to the lack of carriage for the wounded, the British force then retired to Kara and thence to Mansi, having only got to within two and a half miles of the *Sawbwa's* town of Karwan.

In consequence of the continued hostility of the *Sawbwa*, it was decided to send a second expedition against him, and it was further decided that Karwan this time must be occupied, and that, unless the *Sawbwa* surrendered without opposition, his palace should be destroyed and all the fortifications of Karwan levelled to the ground.

Second Pônkan expedition.

Colonel FitzGerald was placed in command of the expedition, and Major Cooke accompanied him as Political Officer. The following was the strength and composition of the column, which advanced from Mansi towards Karwan on the 22nd May:—

	Officers.	Guns.	Rifles.
Sappers	3	..	75
Royal Welsh Fusiliers	3	..	100
Hazara Mountain Battery	3	4	..
26th Punjab Infantry	7	..	340
Mounted Infantry	1	..	6

Lieutenant-Colonel FitzGerald's account of the expedition is appended in detail.

4 guns, Hazara Mountain Battery.
80 rifles, Sappers.
180 ,, Royal Welsh Fusiliers.
180 rifles, 26th Punjab Infantry.
8 Mounted Infantry.

I have the honour to report, for the information of the Brigadier-General Commanding, that, in accordance with the instructions conveyed in Brigade Orders, dated 17th May 1886, I proceeded to the outpost of Mansi, with the force shown in the margin, on the 19th May.

2. Early on the morning of the 20th May, it having been reported that the *Sawbwa* of Karwan, and about 1,000 men, some of whom were Chinese, were assembled in the hills close to and above the burnt village of Chaung Dauk, I reconnoitred in force with the whole column in that direction, but, finding the report to be unfounded, I returned in the afternoon to Mansi.

3. Heavy rains and the necessity for a rest for the baggage ponies detained the column at Mansi until the 22nd May, when I marched for Karwan.

4. Owing to the recent rains, the road was very heavy and broken, and required constant repairing by the sappers, to enable the battery mules

and baggage ponies, etc., to keep with the column, and this of necessity rendered its progress very slow.

5. The advance of the column was unopposed by the enemy until arrival at the ford over a small stream that joins the Thenglin river, about four miles below Mansi. Here a heavy but badly-directed fire was opened by the enemy who, however, gradually retired before us to their first stockade, some distance up the road, which was found to be formidably obstructed for quite 100 yards before each position, of which there were four.

6. The first three of the enemy's positions were turned and the enemy forced back up the hill with ease by the advanced party; the Afridis and other Pathans of the 26th Punjab Infantry, whose scouting capabilities are quite equal to those of the Kachins themselves, being in front of all. The fourth, however, was somewhat more formidable, the road in front of it, which originally led down into a ravine and up again on the other side, having been entirely destroyed by the enemy. Before any attempt could be made to turn this position, about fifty yards of road, completely commanded by two stockades, had to be traversed. This was accomplished in two rushes by the Afridi Company, 26th Punjab Infantry, led by Lieutenant Dillon and Lieutenant Couchman, Madras Infantry. The position was then turned, and was occupied by the Afridis, who covered the sappers whilst repairing the road and pulling down the stockades. No further opposition was met with, and the column arrived at our camping-ground at Pan Yaung about 4 o'clock P.M., having taken from 5-30 A.M. to accomplish about eight miles.

7. The next day (23rd May) all available transport animals were sent back to Mansi escorted by fifty rifles, Royal Welsh Fusiliers, twenty-five sappers, and 100 rifles, 26th Punjab Infantry, Lieutenant Anderson, 26th Punjab Infantry, in command, to bring up supplies for the troops.

8. It was my full intention to have advanced the next morning (25th May) on Karwan, leaving two guns, Hazara Mountain Battery, forty rifles, Royal Welsh Fusiliers, and fifty rifles, 26th Punjab Infantry, under the command of Major Hadden, Royal Welsh Fusiliers, for the protection of the post and stores. Orders for the advance had been issued, when information received by Major Cooke, the Political Officer with the force, caused that officer to urgently represent that any further advance would be detrimental to the policy which Mr. Bernard, Chief Commissioner, had laid down as desirable in regard to the Pônkan Kachins and their *Sawbwa*. Major Cooke, however, recommended that, as the force was furnished with ample provisions, it should be detained where it was for several days. This I considered most advisable, as it enabled me to communicate with Brigadier-General Griffith, reporting how matters stood, and admitted of Captain Hobday, Assistant Superintendent of Survey, continuing his survey of the adjacent country, and also of my sending small reconnoitring parties in various directions.

9. On the 28th May, only two days' provisions being left, the return march to Mansi was commenced.

10. Subsequent to the advanced-guard, baggage, and main body having re-crossed the river the enemy opened fire on the rear-guard and continued firing in a desultory manner from long ranges until the arrival of the column at the open plain close to the post at Nankin.

11. The enemy's loss, as far as could be ascertained, was as follows :—

	Killed.
During the advance	4
Whilst camped at Pan Yaung	3
During retirement	3
TOTAL ..	10

It was impossible to estimate the number of wounded, but it is probable there were many.

12. The behaviour of the troops composing the force was admirable throughout, and the hardships arising from exposure to the inclemency of the weather night and day (for no tents were taken) were borne most cheerfully by all.

13. In conclusion I beg to attach * * * a letter in original from Major Cooke, Deputy Commissioner, urging cessation of operations and the return of the column to Mansi.

The following is the text of the letter referred to in paragraph 13 of the above report :—

Regarding this advance on Karwan and the burning of the Pônkan *Sawbwa's* house, which Mr. Bernard wishes to have done, I have been endeavouring to obtain further information as to the responsibility of the *Sawbwa* for the dacoities on Sawadi, which are the origin of this trouble with that clan of Kachins.

I had heard that the *Sawbwa* was not present in his country when the dacoities were committed, but at the time that the force last went up, I did not believe that story. I have, however, since been informed that he was really away from his village at the time, and was absent for some weeks or months ; in fact, that he has only lately returned ; and as a Kachin *Sawbwa* has at any time but little control over his subjects, it is quite possible that the dacoities were committed without his sanction and consent. This information I first heard at Mansi, but it has been further confirmed by questioning the Kara Kachin prisoner who was captured on the first day we advanced.

So long as a hostile force is in their hills or threatening them at Mansi, the *Sawbwa* will never come in and make friends. He sent me a message to that effect just before we started.

The *Sawbwa* has been punished by his village of Chaung Dauk on the plains having been burnt and some 3,000 or 4,000 baskets of paddy having been carried off or destroyed. This represents a fine of Rs. 1,500 or Rs. 2,000; so, whatever may be his responsibility as chief of the clan he has, in my opinion, been sufficiently punished by the fine that has already been inflicted. Indirectly, also, he has lost the tolls on caravans since the beginning of April last, which represents another Rs. 1,000 at least to the clan, and he has had to pay heavily for mercenaries to defend his villages during the last six weeks. The demonstration and advance up to this point has shown the Kachins that if we wish to do so, we can come up into their hills and remain there as long as we choose, and they have lost some three or four men killed, besides several wounded. Any further advance is, I think, inadvisable on political grounds, and will tend rather to cause irritation than to bring about a reconciliation, which Mr. Bernard wishes me to do, as I understand the matter; as a further reason, I may mention that the villages of Kara and two others have to be passed through before reaching Karwan. These villages, I understand, cannot be left unnoticed, as the party advances, and must be destroyed; this means the destruction of sixty or seventy Kachin houses before we even reach Karwan, and will render a great number of women and children homeless at a time when the rains have set in. This, I hear, from all the people about Mansi, will have the effect of making the Kachins of those villages desperate, and they will probably worry the villagers in the plains during the whole of the monsoon.

If Mr. Bernard disagrees with my view of his instructions, a force can, if necessary, be sent up after the rains with orders to burn crops and to occupy the country for a month or so. In the meantime the Kachins will begin to know more about us, and possibly the Pônkan *Sawbwa* may be induced to come in.

All the captives taken from Sawadi were surrendered before the first expedition started. They were ransomed at a nominal price by their own relations.

I am very anxious to avoid any act that may drive the *Sawbwa* into the hands of China and make him their ally, and if he feels he has been unjustly punished, this will probably be the effect.

As a further cogent reason why the force should not advance on Karwan, I must mention that I now learn for the first time that it is situated on the Chinese side of the ridge of hills, and it is quite possible that the ridge is regarded by China as her frontier. Any way it will give the Viceroy of Yünnan an opportunity of urging that we have violated her frontier, and may lead us into serious political difficulties. The actual marauders of Sawadi were the villagers of Chaung Dauk and the Kachin hamlets around

Their leader was a Pônkan Powmaing, known to the Burmese as *Boh* Lôn. Three Kachin hamlets have been already burnt before this expedition started, and Chaung Dauk also has been destroyed. There still remains *Boh* Lôn's village close to Chaung Dauk, which might be burnt, but I do not recommend that more than this should be done.

The cause for the abandonment of the advance was not, however, understood by the Kachins, and they made frequent raids on the plains during the rainy season, and in November made a determined attack on Bhamo. There were several encounters with marauding Kachins in the plains in 1887, but the hills were left practically unexplored.

SECOND MOGAUNG EXPEDITION, 1887-88.

In September 1887 the Chief Commissioner, in consultation with the Major-General Commanding the Upper Burma Field Force, considered that the time had come for the occupation of Mogaung.

The despatch of the expedition was delayed by various causes, and many conflicting stories about the intentions of the *Myoôk* Po Saw were received. In the middle of December, however, he came down to Sinbo with several Elders. He met the Deputy Commissioner there, and professed to be pleased at the approach of our troops. On the 27th December, the expeditionary force, as per margin, with Captain Triscott, R.A., in command, and with Major Adamson as Political Officer, left Bhamo and marched up the left bank of the Irrawaddy. They reached Nethagon on the 5th January, Sinbo on the 7th, and Mogaung on the 14th, at which place they were received in a friendly manner by the inhabitants. In the meantime, however, an unfortunate incident had occurred. One of the captains in the Irrawaddy Flotilla Company's service had received permission to go up the river to see if it would be possible to establish a steamboat service above Bhamo. This gentleman took advantage of the permission given him to go to Mogaung, and took with him Lon Pien, the farmer of the jade mines duties. It appears that Lon Pien made himself obnoxious to

LAND COLUMN.	Mounted Infantry	.. 12 rifles.
	Cheshire Regiment	.. 50 ,,
	No. 1 Bengal Mountain Battery.	2 guns.
	12 Kalat-i-Ghilzai Regiment.	101 rifles.
RIVER COLUMN.	Native officer	.. 1
	Rank and file	.. 66

the Chinese jade traders; as a result the house he was staying in at Mogaung was attacked in the night, and he received wounds from which he afterwards died. The *Myoôk* Po Saw is believed to have been implicated in this crime, and left the town just before the arrival of the British. He was induced to come in on the following day, but absconded again on the night of the 21st, and though he was pursued, made good his escape and thenceforward remained in open rebellion. He was formally deposed, and his cousin Maung Hpo Myo was appointed *Myoôk* in his stead, but Maung Shwe Gya remained the most useful and powerful auxiliary we had in Mogaung.

Major Adamson then visited and explored the jade mines and interviewed many of the surrounding Kachin Chiefs with satisfactory results. Thence he went to the Indawgyi lake, and, after exploring the surrounding country without incident, returned to Mogaung. It is probable that the Mogaung country would have remained quiet but for Po Saw. This man, however, instigated the Lepai Kachins to attack the column on the return march to Mogaung, at the village of Nyaung-chidauk. Information of this move having reached Captain Triscott, he made a double march in the hope of capturing the ex-*Myoôk*. While marching at night, however, he fell in with a picquet of the enemy, and the exchange of shots having destroyed all chance of surprising the village, he halted till daylight. He then advanced, engaged the Kachins and completely routed them, killing several.

About the same time the Kachins, instigated by Po Saw, attacked the mail between Mogaung and Sinbo, and even made an attack on Mogaung itself, but were easily beaten off. In these combinations Po Saw had been chiefly assisted by the Punga *Duwa*, to whose village a successful punitive expedition was made on the 17th February by Lieutenant O'Donnell and Mr. Twomey, Assistant Commissioner.

Major Adamson then left Mogaung for Katha on the 28th. The road from Mogaung to Katha was *viâ* Mohnyin. On the first day the column, after marching seventeen and a half miles, was about to halt for the night, when it was confronted by a strong stockade from which a heavy fire was opened. The stockade was taken with a loss of two men killed. The next day a few shots were fired at the column, but after that no further opposition was encountered, and the force reached Mohnyin on the 4th and Katha on the 6th.

The objects of the expedition were three. Firstly, to occupy Mogaung and to establish British authority there; secondly, to inspect the jade mines; thirdly, to explore the country round Mogaung and, especially, to discover a good land route to Mogaung from the south.

The expedition was successful in all three objects. The flight of Maung Po Saw was unfortunate, but it is probable that he had hoped to establish himself in semi-independence at Mogaung, and that no steps which Major Adamson could have taken would have secured his continued submission.

The establishment of order in the sub-division was, however, not possible until more posts were stationed there. After the departure of Major Adamson, a party of about 400 Shans under Bo Ti, Po Saw's Lieutenant, attacked Mogaung, and the garrison under Lieutenant O'Donnell had to take several positions occupied by the enemy during the night before finally driving them off. The affair was one of the most severely contested fights that the military police had up to that time been engaged in, and the men showed conspicuous gallantry and dash. The enemy's loss amounted to over forty killed, while the police lost eight killed and fifteen wounded. After this engagement the garrison was reinforced with two guns, and an application was made to have the number of troops in the sub-division raised to 800.

OPERATIONS IN 1888-89.

Operations against the Lapais, Ithis, Sana Kachins and Makans, 1888-89.

After Bo Ti's attack the Mogaung sub-division of the Bhamo district was not seriously disturbed. It was, however, found necessary, in the cold season of 1888–89, to undertake further operations to bring the Kachin tribes to submission, and to punish them for many outrages committed in the early part of the year.

The operations embraced four separate expeditions—(1) against the Lepei tribe north of Mogaung, the principal chief being the *Sawbwa* of Thama; (2) against the Ithi or Szi tribe south of Mogaung, the leading chief being the *Sawbwa* of Panga; (3) against the Sana Kachins of the Lahtawng tribe, who had raided near Mogaung in May; (4) against the Makan tribe and other tribes in the neighbourhood of Sinbo, who were responsible for the attack on Nanpapa in May, and for a later attack on trading boats at Hlegyomaw on the Mogaung river in August. The direction of the whole of these operations was undertaken by Sir George White, and all the military police in the Mogaung sub-division were placed under his orders. While the plans for these operations were being matured, and while preparations were being made, notice was given to the Thama and Panga *Sawbwas* requiring them to tender their submission to the sub-divisional officer at Mogaung, and to make reparation for damage inflicted by them on traders and others. The Regent of the Makan tribe, the widow of the late *Sawbwa*, had already been warned that punishment would be inflicted if compensation was not made for the raids at Nanpapa and Hlegyomaw.

The troops for these expeditions were composed of Regulars and the Mogaung Police Battalion, the whole under Lieutenant (shortly afterwards promoted Captain) O'Donnell, of the Mogaung Police, who was given army rank to enable him to take command of the mixed force.

1st Battalion, Hampshire Regiment ..	52 rifles.
No. 2 Bengal Mountain Battery ..	69 men, 2 guns.
17th Bengal Infantry	203 rifles.

The regular troops of the force assembled at Bhamo, and on the 21st and 22nd December 1888 the guns and transport and the infantry respectively started on their march to join the remainder of the column at Mogaung, the infantry joining the guns and transport on the second day of the march. The strength of the column on the 1st January 1889 was as per margin. This column, which was under the command of Captain Brooke, 17th Bengal Infantry, arrived at Mogaung on the 4th January 1889.

Operations against the Lepie tribe.

On the 8th January, the offending tribes having failed to comply with the British terms, Lieutenant O'Donnell marched for Kamaing, a village held by the rebellious Lepei tribe; the fighting column moved by land; the garrison for Kamaing and the stores by boat. On the 11th, Kamaing was taken after a slight resistance, and Lieutenant O'Donnell was preparing for further operations when a severe outbreak of smallpox kept the force stationary until the 15th. During this period, though unable to move his whole force,

Lieutenant O'Donnell sent out two small expeditions to burn the villages of Hwetun and Se-ing.

On the 15th February Captain O'Donnell (promoted Captain 31st January 1889), resuming active operations, marched with a force as per margin against the Lepei tribe.

Hants Regiment	.. 51 rifles.
No. 2 Bengal Mountain Battery	.. 2 guns.
Mogaung Levy	.. 320 rifles.

On the 16th three villages were destroyed; on the 17th Paowela was captured after some fighting, and was burnt, Tangorbum was entered without resistance, and the force then marched for Thama, the capital of the tribe. A letter from the Thama *Sawbwa*, saying that he would do nothing but hide in the jungle, put the force on their guard, and on approaching the village they were fired on by the enemy from a stockade, three men of the Hants Regiment being wounded. This stockade and another were rushed and taken, and Thama was burnt. In the charge on the second stockade, both Captain O'Donnell and Captain Macdonald of the Hants Regiment were spiked through the foot. Wawang, where the column came upon a cleverly contrived ambuscade of the enemy, Muklon, where Lieutenant Hawker, Hants Regiment, received a mortal wound from a spike whilst leading a charge of his men, Naikumgyi, and several other villages, were taken and burnt.

On the 4th March Captain O'Donnell returned to Mogaung, leaving Captain Macdonald, Hants Regiment, to command the column on its return march. On the 5th Captain Macdonald detached a party under Subadar Kalu Thapa of the Mogaung Levy, which destroyed the village of Hkaungpa, the column reaching Mogaung on that day. On the 6th Captain O'Donnell commanded an expedition by boat against Pontu, which was burnt. This ended the operations against the Lepei tribe, whose villages, grain, cooking, and agricultural implements had all been destroyed. The Thama *Sawbwa*, however, still remained recalcitrant.

Punishment of the Ithi tribe.

Captain O'Donnell next directed his attention to the Ithi tribe, who, under the leadership of Bo Ti, had in the previous year given much trouble. The column, strength as per margin, marched on the 11th March, and on the 13th occupied the Shan and Kachin villages of Nyaungbintha. No opposition was offered to this column, for Bo Ti had left the neighbourhood, and the people were leaderless. Small

2 guns.	
44 men,	Hants Regiment.
340 „	Mogaung Levy.

columns burnt all the villages of the tribe. On the 22nd March the detachment, Hants Regiment, left for Bhamo, and on the 28th the remainder of the column returned to Mogaung, leaving a garrison in the Shan village at Nyaungbintha.

Operations against Lahtawng tribe.

2 guns.
260 rifles, Mogaung Levy.

On the 1st April Captain O'Donnell, taking with him a force as per margin, proceeded to punish the Sana *Sawbwa* of the Lahtawng tribe. On the 4th, after a march through the stony bed of a stream and a very difficult gorge, in which the enemy had stockaded themselves, but were outflanked by the Gurkhas of the police, the column reached Paulaung, the Sana *Sawbwa's* chief village, which was burnt. The column then returned, reaching Mogaung on the 7th. The country traversed was very difficult, the amount of flanking that was required made the work very harassing, and the long marches through the plains under an April sun were most trying to the men. Captain O'Donnell therefore gave his force a few days' rest.

Punishment of the Marans.

2 guns.
220 men, Mogaung Levy.

There still remained the tribes to the east of Sinbo, the Maran tribe, and the Hlegyomaw dacoits to be dealt with, and to reach them a march of fifty-six miles from Mogaung to Sinbo had to be made through the plains. Taking a force as shown in margin, Captain O'Donnell left Mogaung on the 10th April, and arrived at Sinbo on the 15th. On the 20th operations commenced, and the villages of Makan, Lasha, Pinzon, and Lwekyo, where a stout resistance was met with, the enemy replying to the artillery fire with *jingals*, were taken and burnt. Watu, the remaining village of the tribe in that part of the country, was spared, as it was on the confines of the Kaukkwe tribe of Kachins, whom it was considered impolitic to disturb. The force returned to Sinbo on the 23rd. Two other villages belonging to the Maran tribe were destroyed on the 26th April, thus completing the punishment of the tribe.

Operations against Hlegyomaw dacoits.

Before attacking the Hlegyomaw dacoits, Captain O'Donnell found it necessary to apply for reinforcements, as the hard work of the last two months had told upon his men, and many of the police were sick. On the 29th April the following troops arrived at Sinbo from Bhamo in reinforcement—32nd Madras Infantry, fifty-two rifles; Mogaung Levy, fifty rifles.

On the 1st May Captain O'Donnell, with the troops as shewn in margin, marched against the Hlegyomaw dacoits. The villages of Karwan and Assin were taken and burnt on the 3rd May; on the 4th, after some stubborn fighting, Kachaing, a large village of forty houses, was also taken and burnt, the enemy again attacking the force on its return march; and on the 5th May the force arrived at Pulaung, having completed its field operations.

No. 2 Bengal Mountain Battery	..	2 guns.
32nd Madras Infantry		52 rifles.
Mogaung Levy	..	200 ,,

British casualties.

In the four expeditions forty-six villages, containing 639 houses were destroyed, together with large stores of grain. The British casualties amounted to one officer killed and two officers and thirty men, including followers, wounded. The column engaged the Kachins twenty-two times and captured forty-three stockades.

Results of the expedition.

The results of the expedition were satisfactory; the occupation of Kamaing and the establishment there of a military post had the effect of opening the road to the jade mines, which had been interrupted; and up to the end of May 1889 no less than ninety-eight villages had tendered their submission to the Sub-Divisional Officer at Mogaung. These included the whole of the villages subordinate to the Chief of Thama, except Thama itself and two other villages; the whole of the Ithi Lepais, including Panga; all the Lahtawngs, except one village; all the tribes round Sinbo with the exception of two small villages; and the Lakun tribe south of the Ithi country. In the case of villages which resisted the column, submission was only accepted after the payment of moderate fines and the surrender of a small number of guns. The Marip tribe and the Sassans submitted from the first and have never given any trouble.

The Pônkan expedition, 1889.

Since the two abortive expeditions to Karwan in 1886, the Pônkan *Sawbwa* had declined to submit, or to visit Bhamo, and from time to time reports had been received of gatherings of disaffected persons in his territory. At the beginning of March 1889 the Pônkan Kachins, probably incited by the Burman remnants of the gathering which had collected there in January and February, again descended to the plains, and later in the month burnt the village of Mansi. Towards the end of March the return of the troops who had been engaged in the Mogaung expedition furnished a convenient opportunity for dealing with this troublesome tribe, and a force under Brigadier-General C. B. Wolseley, C.B., was sent against it.

The objects to be obtained by the force were summarized—

(*a*) to attack and break up the Pônkan tribe of Kachins and occupy the *Sawbwa's* capital;

(*b*) to destroy all hostile villages, and do as much damage as possible to the tribe, until such terms as the Political Officer accompanying the force should dictate were submitted to;

(*c*) to open up a good road from Mansi to the Pônkan capital;

(*d*) to endeavour to open up communication with Lieutenant Daly, Superintendent of the Northern Shan States at Namhkam, and let the presence of troops be felt in and about the Ponkan territory.

Three roads were known of as leading to Karwan from Bhamo, *viz.*, (1) a path direct from Mansi; (2) a path which branched off from No. 1 a few miles beyond Mansi, and ran in a more southerly direction *viâ* Peta and Warapum; (3) a road running north of No. 1. The Kachins, believing that the force would move on Karwan by path No. 1, the route attempted by the two previous expeditions, had strongly stockaded positions on it, which they held in force; the other roads ran for some distance through friendly tribes, and were not supposed to be blocked.

General Wolseley determined to divide the force entrusted to him into two columns, as per margin, and to advance by the north and south roads, Nos. (2) and (3), returning by the most direct road after occupying Karwan. Judging from the available information, it seemed probable that the Northern Column

(1) *Southern Col.* under Captain E. A. Smith, R.A.—
2 guns, No. 2 Bengal Mn. Battery, under Lieut. W. M. Illes, R.A.
100 rifles, 1st Battalion, Hants Regt., under Lieut. M. de Montmorency, Hants Regt.
100 rifles, 52nd Gurkha L. I., under Lieut. W. G. Majendie, Rifle Brigade.
50 rifles, Burma S. and M., under Cap. E. S. Hill, R.E.

(2) *Northern Col.* under Maj. C. H. St. Paul, Rifle Brig.—
2 guns, No. 2 Bengal Mn. Battery, under Lieut. W. H. Robinson, R.A.
150 rifles, 4th Battalion, Rifle Brig., under Mai. St. Paul, 4th Battalion, Rifle Brigade.
150 rifles, 17th Ben. I., under Major J. S. Spencer, 17th Ben. I.

would take one day less than the Southern one to march from Bhamo to Karwan. The Southern Column therefore started on the 15th April; the Northern on the 16th. General Wolseley and staff and Mr. Shaw, Deputy Commissioner, accompanied the Southern Column. On the 16th, when the Southern Column had advanced about two miles beyond Mansi, the advanced-guard found the enemy concealed in a strong position on either side of the road, which here ran up the side of a steep hill covered with dense jungle and bamboos. Captain Smith, R.A., while shelling the enemy's position, was slightly wounded. The troops drove the enemy from their position, and occupied the ridge on the crest of which Nos. (1) and (3) paths were found to branch, the first running along the ridge, the other descending the far side. Some police and a detachment of the 17th Bengal Infantry, who had been brought on from Mansi, and formed part of the garrison of that place, were now sent back, and the column, after a severe march under a hot sun and without water, reached their camping-ground, which was about one and a half miles beyond Peta, a friendly village, without further opposition. On the 17th the march was continued to Warapum.

Action of 16th April near Mansi.

On the 18th the column marched for Karwan. There was a difficulty in obtaining guides; but these being at last forthcoming, the column descended into a deep valley, on the hills above which were Karwan and other Pônkan villages. Arrived in the valley, the guides refused to proceed any further, but pointed out the different paths up the hill; and the column, leaving its baggage under a guard, climbed the hill by a very steep path and entered Karwan unopposed, the Kachins having concentrated to oppose the attack at another entrance to the village. On the alarm being given, the Kachins attempted to resist, but the troops, occupying point after point, drove the enemy off the ridge. During the remainder of the day and night, the enemy, creeping up to close quarters, kept up some desultory firing from the jungle.

March on Karwan.

On the 19th the Northern Column arrived, having found the road much blocked, and having suffered from scarcity of water.

On the 20th the whole force marched by the direct road to Mansi as far as the villages of Ka-u and Pantat, both of which were unoccupied. Pantat was burnt and Ka-u occupied by a force under Captain Smith, while General Wolseley pushed on with the remainder of the column and all the transport to Mansi. The path was found to be steep and in bad repair, and could have been easily blocked by felling trees. On the 22nd General Wolseley's column commenced its return march to Ka-u, establishing intermediate posts under Captain Hill and Lieutenant Oldfield, R.E., at points from whence the work of putting the path in order could be most conveniently carried on. The column reached Ka-u on the 23rd, and on the next day the force moved on to Karwan, where the camping-ground was less cramped, and where the men began to build huts. The enemy meanwhile had not been left in quiet, for small parties had been sent out daily to scour the country, capture cattle, and destroy or bring in grain. The work on the direct path from Mansi was pushed on rapidly, and the road was reported as completed on the 30th April.

Submission of the *Pawmaings.*

Up to the 23rd the Kachins, though they had offered no opposition since the night of the 19th, had shown no signs of submission; but on the afternoon of that date a deputation consisting of the *Sawbwa* of the Kara village of Washa, with his Elders and *Pawmaings* (headmen), came into Ka-u, and undertook to produce within two days all the Pônkan *Sawbwa's Pawmaings* to make their submission.

General Wolseley decides to visit Namhkam.

The terms of submission laid down by Mr. Shaw were slowly, but steadily, carried out, and by the 10th May the fine had been paid, and there remained only seventeen guns and one captive to be handed over. General Wolseley, when he found that there was no chance of any further resistance, and that the Kachins seemed to be making submission in earnest, decided, if he could do so without entering Chinese territory, to push south with a small escort as far as Namhkam. The civil officers with the force discountenanced the expedition and refused to accompany it; but, having despatched a letter by messenger to Lieutenant Daly, the Superintendent of the Northern Shan States, General Wolseley started with an escort, as per margin, on the 2nd May, and reached the village of Namkai in three marches, passing through

2 guns, No. 2 Bengal Mountain Battery.
100 rifles, Rifle Brigade.
100 rifles, 42nd Gurkha Light Infantry.

a friendly country. On the 5th a letter from Lieutenant Daly arrived, brought by two trustworthy guides, who undertook to bring the General to Namhkam by a route which did not touch Chinese territory. As Lieutenant Daly did not consider a large escort necessary, General Wolseley took on with him only forty-five rifles of the Rifle Brigade and twenty of the Gurkhas, sending the remainder of the column back to Karwan. The General and his escort marched on the 6th, and arrived at Namhkam on the 7th. Lieutenant Daly and 150 of the military police had arrived there two days previously, and the arrival on the scene of the troops from the Bhamo side made a deep impression on the people.

General Wolseley, after having been present at the ceremony of the presentation of a patent of office to the *Sawbwa* of Northern Hsenwi, started on his return on the 10th March using a different route to that by which the party had come. The General and his escort camped for one night on the Nam Wan river, which forms for some distance the boundary line between China and the Kachin country, and, marching *viâ* Loilaw and Nien-sin reached Karwan on the 11th May.

The field force returns to Bhamo.

On his return General Wolseley found that the Pôn̦kan *Pawmaings* had entered into a solemn treaty of allegiance, and that the Deputy Commissioner had gone to Bhamo, taking with him a *Pawmaing* as a hostage that the terms of the submission would be carried out in full. On the 13th the General started on his return march to Bhamo, taking the detachment of the Gurkhas for escort as far as Mansi. On the 15th the remainder of the force under Major St. Paul marched for Bhamo. Throughout the expedition the health of the troops, who were without camp equipage, beer, or spirits, was excellent.

Bhamo frontier affairs.

Meanwhile, on the frontiers of the Bhamo district, events of importance were happening. A band, consisting for the most part of Chinese brigands and deserters from the Chinese army, which had gathered on the Molé Hka, north-east of Bhamo, was attacked by military police on the 9th January 1889, and entirely dispersed with the loss of at least fifty killed. The effect of this action was to secure the peace of the district north of Bhamo and to stop further alarms of the gathering of Chinese marauders in that direction during the remainder of the open season. About this time the air was full of rumours concerning projected attacks on the Upper Sinkan township and on Bhamo. These rumours related mainly to the designs of Kan Hlaing (Hkam Leng), whose earlier doings will be noted in the next paragraph. On the 4th February 1889, at Malin, a village on the Sinkan stream about twenty miles from Si-u, a patrol of fifty military police proceeding to Sikaw came upon a large body of rebels strongly stockaded. The stockade was attacked, but without success, and the police were compelled to retire with the loss of two men killed and ten wounded and all their baggage. A strong military force under Captain Smith, R.A., consisting of sixty men, Hampshire Regiment, 150 men, 17th Bengal Infantry, and two guns, was then sent out from Bhamo, and engaged the dacoits at Malin on the 7th February. The dacoits occupied a strong position, from which they were not dislodged without a severe contest, in which Lieutenant Stoddart and four men were killed and seventeen men wounded. The gathering then dispersed as suddenly as it had appeared. After the defeat of the rebels at Malin, the villagers for the most part returned to their homes, and the nucleus of the gathering dispersed, probably returning to Maingpun. Orders were issued imposing fines on the villages which had joined in the rising, and increasing the force of police at the expense of the township. The township was also effectually disarmed. Beyond the imposition of fines, no punishment was inflicted on the rank and file of the insurgents, who were permitted to return peacefully to their villages. Kan Hlaing (Hkam Leng) retired to the hills east of Si-u. On the 23rd March a detachment of troops was sent to Sikaw to remain there during the rest of the dry season in case this man should attempt further hostilities. At the end of May an attempt was made to capture Kan Hlaing (Hkam Leng) in his retreat in the hills, but it was frustrated by the action of the Lwesaing and Tônhôn Kachins, who afterwards descended in some force and occupied Si-u. They were there attacked on the 2nd June 1889 by a party of troops and police, and driven back with loss; in July, however, they again advanced and attacked Sikaw itself. The villagers and the Gurkha police beat them off, but the lateness of the season made it impossible to venture on further punitive operations before the cold weather.

AFFAIRS IN MÖNG MIT AND MÖNG LENG, 1885-90.

We must now retrace our steps a little to notice events which had been happening in the States of Möng Mit (Momeik) and Möng Leng (Mohlaing). These States are nominally Shan, but they have never been administered with the Shan States proper; the Shans only inhabit the valleys, and are greatly inferior in numbers to the Palaungs and Kachins who occupy the hills, which form the greater part of the territory. At the time of the annexation a member of the ruling family of Möng Leng, named Hkam Leng or, in the more commonly used Burmese form, Kan Hlaing, claimed to be the *Sawbwa* of both Möng Leng and Möng Mit. His claim to be chief of Möng Mit was resisted by the ministers of that State on behalf of the rightful heir, who was aminor. In October 1886 Kan Hlaing was induced to come to Katha, where he remained for some time pending the consideration of his claims. Towards the end of the year, however, he absconded and remained a bitter rebel ever after. In April 1887 the Chief Commissioner visited Mogök, received the Möng Mit officials, settled the conditions under which Möng Mit was to be administered, and fixed the boundary between that State and Möng Leng. In contravention of orders Hkam Leng shortly after invaded and occupied part of the territory of Möng Mit, but was expelled by a force sent from Katha. Subsequently the territory of Möng Leng was partitioned between Möng Mit and Bhamo, while Möng Mit was administered under the control of the Deputy Commissioner of the Ruby Mines from Mogok. Hkam Leng took up his residence in the Kachin hills east of Möng Leng and fomented disturbances in the Upper Sinkan township as has already been noted. Towards the end of 1888 he established relationship with Saw Yan Naing, a son of the Metkaya Prince, who had established himself in an almost inaccessible position in the mountains on the borders of Tawng Peng and had gathered about him a large band of dacoits. These two rebels endeavoured to arrange a simultaneous movement on a large scale at various places on the northern frontier. Möng Mit itself, the capital of the State, was now threatened, and fifty men of the Hampshire Regiment were sent to assist in its defence.

On the 14th January 1889 Lieutenant Nugent, Hampshire Regiment, with sixteen of his men, attacked a body of the dacoits a few miles out of the town, but the enemy were far stronger than his information had led him to suppose, and the party was driven back with heavy loss, Lieutenant Nugent himself and one man being killed, and six men wounded. On the 19th Lieutenant Ozzard, with fifty men of the Hampshires and twenty mounted police, attacked the same band of dacoits and killed twenty of them, including their leader.

Reinforcements were then sent up and an attack was made on Manpun, the head-quarters of Saw Yan Naing. Four stockades were taken without loss and the position was occcupied, but owing to a misunderstanding the column returned before the country had been thoroughly settled. The result was that Saw Yaw Naing almost immediately re-established himself at Mantôn, a few miles from Manpun, and remained there for the rest of the year. Hkam Leng remained with the Lwésaing Tônhôn Kachins, with whom he was connected by marriage, and incited them to keep the southern part of the Bhamo district in a state of ferment. Other minor leaders, of whom the most important were Nga Maung of Twinnge and Heng Nga Maung of Möng Long, derived support and encouragement from these centres of disaffection, and in Tawng Peng, which had not been cleared of dacoits, Nga Zeya was still at large.

The Tônhôn Expedition, 1889-90.

It was therefore decided that as soon as the season was favourable for active operations, measures should be taken to effectually settle the country dominated by these leaders who had acquired a fictitious importance by the immunity which they had so long enjoyed. It was necessary (1) to expel Saw Yan Naing and Kan Hlaing from their retreats, and to punish the Kachin tribes who had harboured them, and who had taken part in the raids on Sikaw and Möng Mit; (2) to establish the power of the *Sawbwa* of Möng Mit in the outlying parts of the State.

The Chief Commissioner, Burma, applied for the services of two columns operating from Bhamo and the Ruby Mines District, respectively, for the above objects, and the despatch of these columns being sanctioned they were constituted as follows :—

Bhamo Column—Under Major Blundell.

2 guns, No. 2 Mountain Battery.	250 men, Mogaung Levy (Gurkhas).
75 men, Hampshire Regiment.	150 „ 17th Bengal Infantry.

Mōng Mit Column—Under Major Greenway.

2 officers and 76 men, Hampshire Regiment.

3 „ „ 200 „ 8th Madras Infantry.

The whole force was designated the Tônhôn Expedition, Major Blundell being in chief command of both columns.

Besides these two columns, Mr. Daly, Superintendent of the Northern Shan States, with a detachment of the Shan Levy of military police, was directed to co-operate from the side of Hsenwi, communicating as far as possible with the other columns. At the same time a party of military police under Mr. H. F. Hertz, Assistant Superintendent of Police, was detailed to visit Mainglong, and thence march along the Tawng Peng border, for the purpose of dealing with any bands of dacoits or rebels which might be in that quarter. It was also expected that the *Sawbwas* of Tawng Peng and Hsenwi would do their best to stop the passage of fugitives through their States, and orders calling on them to do so were issued.

The scene of the operations was very difficult country, chiefly in the southern part of the old State of Möng Leng, in the valleys of Sinkan and Nampaw streams, and in the north-eastern part of the State of Möng Mit, known as the Myaukko daung, the "northern nine hills," whose area is about 2,500 square miles.

The Bhamo column, under Major Blundell, with Mr. G. W. Shaw, Deputy Commissioner, as Civil Officer, started on the 15th December 1889. At Sikaw the column was met by representatives of twelve Kachin hills of the Lakun tribe, which, though invited to do so, had declined to assist their fellow-tribesmen of Lwésaing and Tônhôn. The leading man among the Kachins who thus tendered their submission was the *Sawbwa* of Kanlun, who volunteered to accompany the expedition, and informed the Deputy Commissioner that Saw Yan Naing was living at Mantôn under the protection of Wara Naw, a *Sawbwa* of the Tônhôn Kachins and brother of the *Sawbwa* of Tônhôn. Si-u was occupied without opposition by a detachment of the 17th Bengal Infantry in order to open the road between that place and Sikaw. On the 20th December the column left Sikaw and marched on Lwésaing, which was reached on the 23rd December. No opposition was encountered till the column

Commencement of hostilities.

was within a mile of Lwésaing, where the Kachins had erected a stockade across the road and endeavoured to stop the advance of the troops. The stockade was taken with the loss of one private, Hants Regiment, and one native officer killed, and five men wounded. The column then occupied Lwésaing, which was found deserted; but Kachins fired into the village from the slopes of the hill, and wounded two men of the column. Next day, after burning Lwésaing, the force marched to Tônhôn, being again opposed at two stockades half-way between the two villages. These stockades were turned with the loss of two Gurkhas wounded, and Tônhôn was occupied without further resistance. Shots were, however, fired by Kachins into the village, and one Gurkha was killed and another wounded. Before the troops reached Lwésaing on the 22nd December, Captain O'Donnell, with a detachment of Gurkhas, was sent to occupy the ferries across the Shwéli, which were reported as the only places where Kan Hlaing and other fugitives could cross. Shots were fired at Captain O'Donnell's party as soon as it reached the banks of the Shwéli, and a Gurkha native officer was killed. It was found that there were many points besides the three ferries at which the passage of the river was practicable, and there were signs that fugitives had already crossed in rafts. The plan of stopping the passage of the Shwéli was therefore unsuccessful. The column remained at Tônhôn till the 3rd January. On the 28th December eight Elders of Lwésaing, Tônhôn, and other neighbouring villages came in. The Political Officer informed them that a fine amounting to Rs. 2,500 with fifty guns must be paid by seven specified villages which had opposed the march of the troops, harboured rebels, and otherwise rendered themselves liable to punishment. By the 30th December representatives of the villages in the jurisdiction of Lwésaing-Tônhôn had come in, and part of the fine had been paid. The *Sawbwas* of Lwésaing and Tônhôn still held aloof. On the 3rd January the column left for Manpun, a detachment of the 17th Bengal Infantry, with a Burmese officer in subordinate political charge being left to enforce the payment of the fine. The passage of the Shwéli was effected on the 3rd, 4th, and 5th January, and the column was met by one

Arrival at Tônhôn.

of the Chiefs of Humè, a Palaung circle subordinate to the *Sawbwa* of Möng Mit. The presence with the column of an official sent by the *Sawbwa* had the effect of preventing resistance on the part of the people of Humè and the adjacent circles. Marching through the circles of Humè and Mangkwin, north-east Möng Mit, and some Kachin villages subordinate to the Kanlun *Sawbwa*, the column reached Mantôn on the 11th January without encountering further opposition.

Möng Mit Column.

The Möng Mit Column under Major Greenway with Mr. Daniell as Political Officer reached Mantôn on the same day, in ignorance of the movements of the column from Bhamo. Major Greenway had marched unmolested over difficult country through Yabon and Gamaw, but on approaching Mantôn his advance had been opposed and Captain Sewell, Norfolk Regiment, had been wounded. It was afterwards ascertained that Saw Yan Naing had left Mantôn the day before the arrival of the British, and had fled, *viâ* Laochein or Lwésaing, to Chefang in Chinese territory.

The combined columns now halted at Mantôn to await supplies. On the 17th January two detachments were sent against Laochein, where a large body of Kachins and Palaungs were said to have collected. Both columns, converging on the village, were strongly opposed. The village was, however, successfully captured, though Major Forest was severely wounded while leading the advance. After destroying Laochein the troops returned to Mantôn.

From this date numerous parties were sent out to try and capture the two important rebels, and various fines were imposed on the villages who were proved to have harboured them. In spite of every effort, however, the capture of these men, the principal object of the expedition, remained unaccomplished, and it seemed unlikely that further operations on these lines would meet with any better success.

Early in March, at the Chief Commissioner's request, with a view to ascertaining what was the best plan of operations during the remainder of the open season, General Gatacre visited Si-u, Tônhôn and Lwésaing, and with Mr. Shaw proceeded *viâ* Molo and Sipein to Mantôn, which he reached on the 14th March. Finding the country through which he passed tranquil and the people submissive, he arranged to leave a party of 100 men, including forty mounted infantry, with Mr. Shaw, to work the Mabein–Si-u circles, north of the

Shwèli, with head-quarters at Sipein, and 100 rifles with Mr. Daniell at Mantôn to work south of the Shwèli. The remainder of the troops were withdrawn. In consultation with the Political Officers and with the Chief Commissioner's approval General Gatacre issued proclamations warning the people of the consequences of opposing the troops, and promising reduction or remission of the fines imposed if Kan Hlaing and Saw Yan Naing were surrendered. On the 28th March Mr. Shaw took an oath from the headmen of Tônhôn and the neighbourhood to observe the terms of proclamation, and then returned to Bhamo. The troops were then withdrawn from Tônhôn. Before the close of the operations and the withdrawal of the troops at the end of April, the headman of Mantôn was brought in to Mr. Daniell by the Kachins of the neighbouring circles and deported to Mogôk. On the withdrawal of the troops an official (*Amat*) of the Möng Mit State was left in charge of the Myaukkodaung tract, with 100 men of the *Sawbwa's* militia to enable him to keep order. The *Amat* himself fixed his head-quarters at Yabon, and outposts garrisoned by Shan militia were established at Mantôn and Manpun. Before the troops were withdrawn the Kachin *Sawbwas* entered into solemn engagement to keep the peace, to refrain from harbouring Saw Yan Naing, and to obey the orders of the Möng Mit *Sawbwa* to whom they were subject.

Results of the expedition.

Although the operations did not result in the capture of Saw Yan Naing and Kan Hlaing, they cannot be regarded as fruitless. The Kachin supporters of the two rebel leaders received a severe lesson; full knowledge was obtained concerning the hitherto unknown tract in which the troops were engaged; and the authority of the *Sawbwa* of Möng Mit, which had long been merely nominal, was re-established.

Yabon attacked.

There was, however, still a certain amount of unrest in Möng Mit; in October 1890 Yabon was attacked, and the *Amat* and his followers, after a feeble resistance, abandoned their post and fled. The attack was probably due to this man's bad management of the surrounding tribes, but Saw Yan Naing is thought to have had a hand in stirring up the trouble. The *Sawbwa* then sent out a fresh force to Yabon, but the outbreak was left to be dealt with by Mr. Daniell, Assistant Commissioner, who at once visited Yabon with a column and was successful in securing the speedy submission of the chiefs and the people. The restoration of the guns and ponies taken in the attack was required, fines were imposed, and the turbulent Lahkum Kachins were directed to move back and live among their own people. The leader of the attack was cleverly captured by a night surprise, and the whole district was satisfactorily settled and placed in the charge of the several *duwas,* who agreed to pay tribute and bring it to Möng Mit twice a year.

Outbreak in Möng Leng.

Meanwhile on the 9th December another outbreak had occurred. The Möng Leng *Myoôk* was attacked at Etkyi by a band of forty men, believed to be acting under the orders of Saw Yan Naing, and several of his followers were killed and wounded. Mr. Daniell was sent to Kahôn to punish this outrage, and as it was evident that organized opposition would be met with, his party was reinforced by British Infantry from Bernardmyo and Shwebo, and by a company of military police under Captain Alban. On the 28th January the combined force under the command of Major Kelsall, Devonshire Regiment, effected the capture of Kahôn with the loss of one man wounded, the enemy's casualties amounting to five killed and many wounded, including the *Duwa* himself. After this the troops worked through the country with the result that seven villages under Kahôn were destroyed and the remaining villages in the Manmauk circle formally submitted.

The Tônhôn Column under Major Yule now came up from Bhamo, and the village of Loikon was attacked and burnt, upon which the Tônhôn *Sawbwa,* who had been out since the previous year's operations, came in and surrendered.

The best arrangements possible were made with the various Kachin and Palaung Chiefs, who were held responsible for keeping order in their respective districts and were required to acknowledge the authority of Möng Mit by the regular payment of tribute.

OPERATIONS IN 1890-91.

Lieutenant Barton's Lana Kachin Column, 1890-91.

At the close of 1890, the Lana Kachins were blocking the main trade route into Namhkam; and all the routes leading eastwards from Bhamo to Manwaing on the road to Yünnan were the scenes of constant attacks on caravans. Of the valley of the Molé little was then known, and at the beginning of the cold season of 1890-91 arrangements were accordingly made to send out a punitive column to settle the whole of the tribes to the immediate east of Bhamo who had been guilty of attacks on traders. This column, consisting of seventy-five men of the Mogaung Levy under Lieutenant Burton, started on the 24th December 1890, and proceeded to visit the hills north of the Taping, finally returning to Bhamo on the 21st May 1891 from Lana.

The work was thoroughly done. Every village that had any case reported against it was visited and duly punished by fine. Disarmament was insisted upon as far as possible, and fines were taken by preference in guns. Owing, no doubt, to the operations of the column, the attacks on caravans were reduced to two. One of these was perpetrated by the Kalunkong Chief, who was arrested and sentenced. The other attack, though it was made in British territory, was conducted by Kachins from across the border.

Unfortunately, owing to the negligence of a sentry, the camp was rushed by Han Ton and other Kachins on the night of the 1st March. Two sepoys were killed and nine wounded, and Mr. French, Assistant Engineer, also received a severe wound. Lieutenant Burton sent in for reinforcements, and 100 men of the Devons were despatched under the command of Major P. H. Smith, with whose help the villages implicated in the attack were destroyed and Han Ton was killed.

Operation in Sinkan valley.

Towards the close of the year a further series of operations were entered on in the Sinkan valley, in the south-east of the Bhamo district, which had for some time been the abode of a nest of robbers.

Much work was done by this column, under the command of Captain Gastrell, but owing to the expedition having been sent out too late in the season, operations had to be suspended before the country was entirely subdued.

During the cold season of 1890-91 Lieutenant Eliott and Major Hobday of the Survey Department, with an escort, were engaged in exploring the hitherto unknown northern and north-eastern borders. Sadon had originally been the objective of their eastern explorations, but owing to the hostility of that sub-tribe of the Sadans, this part of their project had to be abandoned.

To enable this northern tract to be administered a Sub-Divisional Officer was for the first time established at Myitkyina with a police guard, and the military police at Bhamo and Mogaung were strengthened.

The condition of Mogaung at the beginning of 1890 was far from satisfactory; the Thama Chief and the Sana Kachins were in turn giving refuge to Po Saw and other bad characters, while dacoities and attacks on friendly villages were frequent. The only place where a real and permanent improvement had followed the operations of 1889 was in the tract west of the upper defile, where the inhabitants were thoroughly subdued and quiet. During the summer there was comparative quiet, but directly the rains were over there were evidences of further disturbances in these neighbourhoods. A column consequently started for Thama in February, and succeeded in securing the submission of that chief.

EVENTS OF 1891-92.

In spite of the punishment that had from time to time been inflicted on the Kachins, much internal disorder still prevailed, and it became evident at this time that something more than punitive expeditions was necessary to bring them entirely under our control.

Tribes west of the Irrawaddy.

Columns had proceeded into various districts to punish raiders and burn villages, but large tracts of the country had never been visited at all; nothing had been decided as to what British claims were, and what the position of Kachins was to be, and the tribes of the Kaukkwe valley evidently believed that they might carry on their feuds exactly as they had done in the days of the Burmese Government. It was therefore now resolved that all the tribes west of the Irrawaddy lying inside the circle of our settled villages must be taught that they were amenable to our orders, and with this view the following procedure was decided on. While allowing them to retain village customs and not interfering with their usual payments to their *Duwas*, each tribe was to pay a moderate house-tax. Petty crime was to be settled by tribal custom, but all cases of murder, dacoity and robbery were to be reported to the nearest British Officer. All blood-feuds and inter-tribal raids were to cease, and differences with neighbouring clans were to be submitted to our officers. Certain hill roads were to be opened and maintained. In return each chief was to receive a *sanad*, or certificate, recognizing

Plan of British Administration.

him as Chief and setting out his obligations. All villages lying within the district limits, where they were not exposed to trans-frontier raids, were to be deprived of guns, except in the case of well-disciplined chiefs, to whom they might be re-issued after having been registered and numbered.

To carry out this policy one military and four police columns were employed to the west of the Irrawaddy during the open season of 1891-92.

Tribes east of the Irrawaddy.

Up to this time little had been done with regard to the country east of the Irrawaddy, but frequent outrages committed by the tribes there now showed us the necessity of bringing these districts under our control. In approaching these tribes we had to deal, not with nationalities, but with groups of independent savages with no inter-tribal coherence. Besides this difficulty, the Kachin hills along the Chinese frontier served as a screen for bad characters, who were in the habit of assembling on the Yünnan side of the frontier and making periodical raids into British territory. Mogaung had been repeatedly threatened and the india-rubber trade had been completely disorganized, while rumours of the presence of armed bands rendered a revival of trade between Burma and Yünnan impossible.

It was therefore decided to deal with the Kachins east of the Irrawaddy in the same way as with the tribes in the west. To carry out this policy the whole of the North-Eastern Bhamo Frontier from Namhkam in the Shan States to Sadon was visited during the cold season of 1891-92 by four columns. Only one of these, the Irrawaddy Column, met with any opposition. This column explored the section of the frontier between Nam Tabet and the 'Nmai Hka, in which district it had been previously decided to establish a post at Sadon, a village lying at the junction of the two main routes from China.

The Irrawaddy Column.

Leaving Myitkyina on the 23rd December 1891 the column marched without opposition as far as the Tingri stream. A mile beyond this was a strong stockade which was carried after half an hour's fighting, with the loss of one Gurkha wounded. On the 30th December Sadon was attacked on two sides and was taken after some opposition. The building of a post was immediately started, and after ten days the main column left Sadon to explore the country to the north and north-east. The tribes of these districts were informed that they would have to pay tribute, and our intentions towards them were explained. The tract, however, was not disarmed, it being thought sufficient to inform the tribes that they were British subjects.

The column then returned to Sadon, where they stayed till the 4th February, and during this time the construction of the post was pushed on as fast as possible. On the 5th the main part of the force again left the post with the intention of engaging a body of Kachins reported to be collecting on the 'Nmaihka. Several small engagements were fought and two villages were burnt. On the 14th the column started on its return journey, and on arrival at Sadon, on the 23rd, found that the garrison had been besieged since the 7th of the month. The Kachins to the north, west, and south had risen on that day and surrounded the fort, and had harassed it with repeated attacks by day and night. The small garrison under Lieutenant Harrison had, however, held out most pluckily, and after having been under arms for thirteen nights in succession had been relieved on the 20th by the North-Eastern Column under Captain Davies of the Devonshire Regiment. A remarkable incident of the siege was the skill the Kachins showed in their sapping operations. It is almost certain that they were assisted by the Chinese in this siege; one report mentions that Chinese words of command were heard during some of the attacks. During the remainder of February and the beginning of March the Irrawaddy Column was engaged in subduing the country round Sadon which had furnished men for the attack on the fort.

Siege of Sadon Fort (Fort Harrison).

EVENTS OF 1892-93.

The programme for the open season of 1892-93 included the establishment of frontier police posts at Sima and Namhkam, the settlement of the tribes within the limits of the Bhamo and Katha districts, and the completion of the work of previous seasons. A limit was determined on beyond which direct administration was not contemplated. The tribes were to be divided into two classes—those within our line of outposts and settled villages, and those without it. The first mentioned were to be disarmed and taxed in the same way as other subjects. Those in the second category were to be dealt with on the principle of political as distinguished from administrative control. As long as they kept the peace all unnecessary interference was to be avoided, only a nominal tribute was to be levied, and disarmament was not to be enforced.

Lieutenant Master } Mogaung Levy.
" Newbold }
Surgeon-Major Lloyd.
Lieutenant Dent, Intelligence Officer.
Mr. Hertz, Civil Officer.
Magwe Battalion, 200 men.
Mogaung Levy, 350 men.
Two 7-pr. guns.

On the 3rd December a column under the command of Captain Boyce Morton, strength as per margin, left Talawgyi on the Irrawaddy for Sima, near which place the post above-mentioned was to be constructed. Opposition was met with at 'Nkrang, which was reached on the 12th of the month. Two sepoys and a mule-driver were killed at this place, and Lieutenant Dent, the Intelligence Officer, was badly wounded in the neck. Two days later Sima was reached after thirty stockades had been taken on the way, and intermittent fighting went on until the 5th January 1893, during which time the post was being built.

Myitkyina raided.

On the very day on which Sima was reached Myitkyina was suddenly raided without a word of warning. The court house and Sub-Divisional Officer's house were burnt to the ground, and a Subadar-Major of the Mogaung Levy was killed. The raiders, who were driven off with the loss of three killed, were the Sana Kachins from the north-west of Myitkyina. While measures were being taken to collect sufficient force to punish this tribe, the hostilities at Sima assumed very formidable proportions. Rumours that a general attack on the fort was intended were so prevalent that on the night of the 5th January orders were given for the withdrawal of all the outlying picquets. At 6 A.M., on the 6th, the Kachins made a sudden attack, and it was then discovered that one picquet had been overlooked and was still out, in a very exposed position. Captain Morton, seeing the danger this picquet was in, started out to withdraw them, but no sooner had he reached their position than he fell mortally wounded. He was

Sima Fort attacked.

with difficulty brought inside the fort by Surgeon-Major Lloyd, who afterwards received the Victoria Cross for his gallantry. Five sepoys were killed at the same spot. After the death of Captain Morton the command devolved on Lieutenant Dent, who was still disabled as the result of his wound at 'Nkrang, the other European officers with the force, Mr. Hertz (Civil Police) and Lieutenant Newbolt, having gone out with a reconnoitring party a few days before. Later in the afternoon Lieutenant Master, who had been left at 'Nkrang, fought his way into Sima and took over command of the fort. The enemy were driven off from the vicinity of the fort, but succeeded in hemming the garrison in, with the result that, except for helio communication, Sima was practically cut off. Constant sorties were made, but the destruction of stockades in one place was followed by the erection of fresh works elsewhere, and the rising gained strength daily.

On the 16th January a party under Lieutenant Newbolt attacked Mali to the south of Sima and destroyed it, but on their return march they encountered strong opposition, Mr. Brookes-Meares of the Civil Police being mortally wounded, and seven sepoys killed. After this the force acted on the defensive.

Reinforcements for Sima.

Lieutenant Drever, who had collected 100 military police at Myitkyina to punish the Sana Kachins, was now ordered to join the Sima force and open up communications; while the Eastern Column, which was working south of the Taping, was ordered to effect a diversion by the Molé valley and was strengthened by 100 men under Captain Atkinson, summoned from Namhkam to take command. The Kaukkwe Column, under Captain Alban, was at the same time sent across *viâ* Talawgyi, and these measures had the effect of opening up Sima.

On the 30th January the relieving columns *en route* to Sima, and the Sima garrison, made simultaneous attacks on a formidable stockade at Kamja (or Sumjar). The Kachins were scattered with heavy loss, and the village burnt. Our loss was five killed and six wounded, including Lieutenant Master, who died from the effects of his wound five days later. The next day Palap and Mali were burnt and many stockades destroyed by a party of 175 men under Captain Alban. On the return to Sima, however, the Kachins made several attacks on the Gurkha rear-guard, the behaviour of the

Gurkhas on this occasion being particularly praiseworthy. Our losses during the day consisted of four killed and twenty-two wounded, including Lieutenant Cooke Hearle, Somerset Light Infantry, wounded. The strength of the garrison of Sima was now 622 men and three officers. There were seventy men and two officers garrisoning Kamja, four officers and 220 men *en route* from Bhamo, and 220 men at 'Nkrang and Kazu, making a total of nearly 1,200 men in the Sima district.

On the 3rd February a force of 300 men under Captain Atkinson again visited the neighbourhood of Palap, where a bullet-proof stockade and blockhouse held by Kachins and Chinese was successfully captured after a spirited resistance. The British casualties were two killed and six wounded, while the enemy lost thirteen killed, eight of whom were Chinamen.

After this the fighting was more of a desultory character. Our opponents were the Kumlao Kachins, whose principal characteristic is that they do not own the authority of any chief, even in single villages.

Many of the enemy came from the Hkanona valley, the ownership of which at that time was uncertain, and these could not be touched, but all the villages within our undoubted boundary line were brought to submission, while a few from the other side came in with presents of their own accord. The work of the column was brought to a close in the last week in March, having experienced the heaviest fighting encountered in the Kachin hills. The enemy had received a severe lesson, but it had required 1,200 men to administer it. The casualties for the seven weeks were exceedingly heavy, consisting as they did of three officers killed, three wounded, and 102 men killed and wounded.

The Eastern Column.

Previous to being despatched to the assistance of Sima the Eastern Column had visited the whole tract to the east of Bhamo, and except for some show of hostility at Pansé, where a sepoy was wounded, there was no trouble.

Namhkam post established.

The Namhkam post was established in the beginning of December with Captain Marrett as Civil Officer; to put a stop to the hitherto uninterrupted inroads from across the border of freebooters, who had persistently troubled the Sinkan valley.

Early in January news was received at Namhkam of the gathering of malcontents on the Chinese frontier to the north-east, and fifty men were sent to occupy Se-lan, thirteen miles from Namhkam.

British patrol attacked.

Notwithstanding this precaution a large number of marauders crossed the Wanteng and settled at Man Hang, a Kachin village in the hills above Musé. A patrol of thirty-five men, under a native officer, was shortly afterwards attacked at Musé by the inhabitants of Man Hang, who were, however, beaten off with the loss of thirteen killed.

In punishment for this attack a party of seventy-five military police, under Lieutenant Williams, was sent to burn the village of Man Hang. The village had been succesfully captured when Lieutenant Williams was killed by a chance shot, and the party then retired without either burning the place or destroying the stockades.

Upon this a military column was hurried up from Bhamo, but on arrival at Man Hang they found that place had been evacuated.

The Kaukkwe Column.

The Kaukkwe Column had had its operations interfered with by the Sima outbreak, but during December it had disarmed all the Leka villages, and on its return from Sima it passed through the Kara range, completing the disarming of villages on its way.

EVENTS OF 1893-98.

1893-94.

With one exception the open season of 1893-94 was uneventful. A number of parties went out into the Mogaung, Bhamo, and Shwegu subdivisions to collect tribute, to settle disputes between villages, to withdraw or register fire-arms, and generally to show the Kachins that our control was to be permanently maintained. The officers were everywhere received in a friendly way, except in the hills east of Bhamo. There the village of Pansé on the frontier was visited, to punish it for firing on the eastern columns of the year before. The Pansé people made no open resistance, but most of them went across the border into Lung-ch'wan territory with their cattle and property. Part of their village was therefore burnt as a punishment, and two other obstinate villages shared the same fate. The result was an attack on the column while on the march between

Maipat and Hkinmun and again on the following day, the 16th January 1894 ; a number of stockades had been built at difficult parts of the road, and in the fighting three sepoys and a compounder were killed, and eleven men wounded. Among the Kachins who were killed was Lemaing Tu, the leader of the rising, and in consequence of his death the gathering immediately dispersed, and the punishment of the villages implicated in the attack was effected without further trouble.

1895.

The continued misconduct of the Sana Kachins from beyond the administrative border rendered punitive measures again necessary, and in December 1895 two columns were sent against them, one of 250 men from Myitkyina, the other of 200 men from Mogaung. The resistance met with was very slight, but Major Atkinson, commanding one of the columns, unfortunately died of fever at Sabaw. Apart from this the operations were entirely successful, twenty-four villages being punished, four of which, including Sabaw (whose chief had led the attack on Myitkyina) were burnt.

Punishment of Sana Kachins.

After this date the rest of the hills were so peaceful that officers were at last able to go about with only a small personal escort. The only part where dacoities of any note occurred was in the neighbourhood of the ruby tract of Nanyaseik, where the large sums of money carried about by traders attracted bad characters.

Early in 1898 the Kara *Duwa* caused the only trouble with the Kachins which had occurred for some years. Mr. Brown, Sub-Divisional Officer at Katha, who, with a small escort, was collecting guns from the Kara Kachins, sent his interpreter with five men to the village of Mawatauk, to tell the Kara *Sawbwa* to come into his camp. The reason he wanted to see this man was to complain of the bad state of the roads in his country. The *Sawbwa*, however, was under the influence of a Kachin outlaw whom he had been harbouring for two years ; deducing from Mr. Brown's message that the arrest of this man was contemplated, the *Sawbwa* decided to rebel, and made a treacherous attack on the small party, all of whom were suddenly cut down without having a chance of defending themselves. The next day Mr. Brown proceeded to Mawatauk to see

Murder of escort by Kara Kachins.

what had become of his party. He was ambuscaded on the way, but after a sharp fight succeeded in beating off the Kachins and destroying their village. A column under Captain Harvey was now sent to the district and destroyed all the villages of the clan, the *Sawbwa* and all the principal rebels escaping into the Shwegu sub-division. Here he was hunted down and killed by a small column under the Sub-Divisional Officer of Shwegu, and the Kara country was completely pacified.

The last operations in the Kachin hills were connected with the ejection of an armed force of Chinese-Shans from the Bhamo district.

In March 1898 the *Sawbwas* of Möngwan (Lungchwan) and Möngna (Kangai) sent an armed force to establish posts at Sadon, Seingmye, and Maipat, in the Bhamo district, on the British side of the provisional boundary, and at the same time endeavoured to persuade the Kachins to build stockades and to refrain from paying their accustomed tribute to the British. These villages, in addition to falling to Great Britain under the agreement of 1897, had long been under our administration, and it was considered that if active measures were not taken at once to stop such incursions, the Kachins, especially in the S'zi district, might side with the Chinese, of whose importance they held an exaggerated idea. It was consequently decided to send a party of police under Lieutenant Langtry, with Mr. Hertz as Civil Officer, to eject this force and to destroy their stockades.

Leaving Bhamo on the 23rd March the police, numbering 150, arrived at Sadon on the 28th. The Chinese having refused to retire the stockade was attacked and captured, with a loss to the enemy of four killed and fifteen taken prisoners. The British casualties amounted to three slightly wounded. The next day the column proceeded to Seingmye and Maipat and destroyed the stockades there, both of which had been evacuated before their arrival. Four more prisoners were captured by friendly natives, and the whole sent to Bhamo, the police remaining in the Pansé neighbourhood to prevent a repetition of the incursion.

On the *Sawbwas* implicated destroying all the stockades between the Kulong and Chapak Khas, and promising to refrain from further attempts to coerce the Kachins, the prisoners captured were eventually released. These operations were noteworthy in that our

Kachin recruits, about whose soldierly qualities very diverse opinions existed, were for the first time engaged on service, and were said by Lieutenant Langtry to have behaved particularly well.

CHAPTER XXIV.

THE SHANS.

The country.

THE Shan [1] country occupies all the eastern part of Upper Burma between the 19th and 24th parallels of north latitude. The area is over 40,000 square miles, or about half the whole area of Upper Burma. In shape the country roughly approximates to an equilateral triangle; its base near the 96th meridian, east longitude, marked by the line of hills which begin near Bhamo and run south till they sink into the plains of Lower Burma; its apex on the Mékong, near the 101st meridian. About half-way between its base and its apex the deep narrow Salween sharply divides the country in two. Covering as it does the whole flank of our Burmese territories from north to south, this river is the most important military feature of the region.

The cis-Salween country is a highland region, partly intricate hill country, partly rolling upland, well watered by numerous streams, some of which are of considerable size though none are navigable for any distance. In many parts the valley widens out into level tracts cultivated with paddy. To the southward of the cis-Salween country extends the wide billowy plain known as the Shan plateau, which, with an average height of from 2,000 to 3,000 feet, forms the most important part of the Shan States

The Trans-Salween country may be said to consist of a confused and intricate mass of hills. It is covered with abrupt and lofty mountains with no elevated plateaus, though here and there extensive flat-bottomed valleys occur, the largest being that in which the capital of Keng Tung is situated.

1 Geographically Mōng Mit (Momeit), the Ruby Mines district, and the hilly parts of the Mandalay district form part of the Shan country, while in the administrative division of the country they are apart from the Shan States.
[NOTE.—*Shan* is the Chinese for *mountain*.]

The borders of the Shan country within British territory extend on the north to the southern borders of the Bhamo and Katha districts, and on the west to the Irrawaddy, and to the plains of Mandalay, Kyauksé, Meiktila, Yamethin, and Toungoo. On the north and north-east the country is bounded by various Shan-Chinese States of the province of Yünnan. The country on both sides of the line is mountainous and difficult, and military interest is chiefly centred in a few points where it is crossed by routes of any importance leading to China. These are Namhkam on the route to Yung-chang Fu; Möng-ting on the route to Shun-ning Fu; Panghsang and Kenglaw on routes to Ssu-mao and Pu-erh Fu. On the south-east and south the Shan States are bounded by French Indo-China and Siam. The boundary with French territory is formed by the Mékong for a length of about 125 miles, from a few miles below the point where the boundary with China meets the river, south-west to the Siam border. This is a good natural frontier line. The country on both sides is again mountainous and difficult; this and its remoteness from good bases on either side lessens its military importance, and interest becomes focussed upon the central point of crossing at Keng Lap. The boundary of the Shan States with Siam is an irregular line nearly 300 miles long, from the Mékong to the Salween. Through the greater part of its length it follows the crests of ranges,—many peaks of which rise to over 6,000 feet, and it is a strong natural frontier line. The country on both sides is mountainous. Routes cross the frontier into Siamese territory from Hawngluk, Möng Hsat, Möng Hang, Möng Hta, Möng Mau, and Ywathit.

In the northern Cis-Salween country the main Irrawaddy-Salween watershed rising near the latter river sends out lateral ranges which bar the Northern Shan States across from east to west. There are numerous peaks over 6,000 feet and several over 7,000 feet. Southwards the main watershed culminates in Loi Ling, 8,842 feet, the highest peak west of the Salween, before sinking to the Shan plateau. The parallel ranges by which the central plateau is seamed from north to south have an average height between 4,000 feet and 5,000 feet with peaks rising to over 6,000 feet. In Cis-Salween Karenni the most conspicuous ridge is that between the Nam Pawn and the Salween with an average altitude of almost 5,000 feet. In the Trans-Salween country the main Salween-Mekong watershed is the most conspicuous range. Its crest marks the boundary with China from a little south of the Nam Ting. A westward spur from the main range here forms the Möng Ling Shan group with peaks of 8,665 feet, 8,600 feet, 7,920 feet and 7,573 feet. In the southern Trans-Salween country the main watershed breaks up into many branches and the drainage systems are very involved. Many peaks on or near the Siam border rise to over 6,000 feet, and in the Loi Lan range of Eastern Karenni there is one peak 7,109 feet.

Though the Shan country is watered by many considerable rivers, none of them are navigable, except occasionally by country boats. The rivers of the Shan country belong to three different drainage basins, those of the Irrawaddy, the Salween and the Mékong. Of the first named rivers two large tributaries water the northern Cis-Salween country, the Shweli (Nam Mao) and the Nam Tu or Myitngé. Each flows for a considerable part of its course through mountain gorges, where it is much broken by rapids, and is navigable only for short distances along the still reaches that occur in the open parts of its valley. The Salween with its tributaries takes by far the greater part of the drainage of the Shan country. The Salween itself runs in a deep rocky bed between steep jungle-covered mountains. Though the volume of water is very large, its course is frequently broken by rapids, which have baffled all attempts at navigation. On the right bank the chief affluents are the Nam Pang and the Nam Teng, both rising in the Northern Shan States, flowing parallel to and at no great distance from one another and the Salween, and entering it in Keng Hkam and Mawkmai, respectively. The chief left bank tributaries are the Nam Ting, which rises in China and joins the Salween some miles below the Kunlong ferry, and the Nam Hka which rises in the north-east corner of the Wa country, marks the frontier with China for a few miles of its central course, and falls into the Salween at Maw Hpa.

The Mékong, where it forms the boundary between Keng Tung and French Indo-China, is about the same size as the Salween in the corresponding latitude, and in parts flows through similar deep mountain gorges, in others its valleys open out and there are fairly extensive plains on its banks. It is as unfavourable for navigation as the Salween, and in spite of the efforts of the French to prove the contrary, it is never likely to be a waterway for commerce. Its chief tributaries in the Shan States are the Nam Lwi and the Nam Hkok. The Nam Nga and the Nam Huok, though much smaller, deserve mention as marking the boundaries with China and Siam, respectively.

The largest lake in the Shan country is the Inlé Lake (also known as Ang Teng, Indein or the Yawng Hwe Lake). Fort Stedman, known to the Burmans as Maingthauk and to the Shans as Möng Hsawk, is situated on its eastern shore. It is about eleven miles long, and three and a half miles broad at the widest point. It is shallow and thickly bordered with weeds.

The Northern Shan States road and the Southern Shan States road are the two most important routes leading from Burma into the Shan country. The first of these is the cart-road from Mandalay *viâ* Maymyo and Hsipaw to Lashio. It follows the old trade route from Mandalay to China by the Kunlong ferry, which from Lashio onwards is still only a pack route. The road is well bridged throughout, but the newly-made Mandalay–Lashio railway has greatly discounted its importance and accounts for its not being improved and kept in better repair.

The Southern Shan States road leaves the railway at Thazi (Meiktila road), and leads to Taunggyi, 106 miles. It is a cart-road, bridged throughout, and nearly the whole length has been metalled.

In addition to these, there are several other routes into the Shan States from the Irrawaddy valley. There is a network of cart tracks over the greater part of the Shan country, and besides these, the whole of the region is traversed by tracks over which bullocks or mules can travel with more or less difficulty. The chief obstacle to communication from west to east is the Salween river. It can, however, be crossed by ferries at frequent intervals, wherever, in fact, approaches to its banks exist. Country boats afford the only means of crossing at all the ferries. The width of the river varies from 100 yards to 250 yards. Mules and bullocks can generally swim, but at most of the ferries this is attended with risk owing to the swiftness of the current and the rocky nature of the banks, and it is advisable to raft them across when possible. The approaches to the ferries are generally by steep zigzag paths.

The Mandalay-Kunlong railway is open for traffic as far as Lashio. Like the rest of the Burma system it is a metre-gauge line. The point of junction with the main line of the Burma railways is Myohaung just south of Mandalay. The line follows the general direction of the old main highway through the Northern Shan States to the Kunlong ferry, whence the valley of the Nam Ting gives access to the centre of Yünnan.

The hilly nature of the Shan country favours communication by visual signalling, but in many cases a great deal of jungle clearing has to be done in order to obtain freedom of view. The most serious impediment to signalling is the heat haze which begins to thicken early in March, and from that time onwards prohibits signalling between stations more than from ten to fourteen miles apart, and often stops it altogether.

The general climate of the Shan Hills, with the exception of the Terai, may be said to be good, the minimum temperature ranging from 30° to 55° in the cold weather, and the maximum from 75° to 90° in the hot weather, though some inclosed valleys may run to 100° and over. In the winter the nights are very cold, and hoar frosts are common. Thick mists, which are not dispelled by the sun till 10 o'clock or later, are prevalent and serve to keep the temperature cool till late, and render marching pleasant. When these mists have been dispelled the air is still cool and bracing.

In the hot weather, March to June, the heat is never excessive, except in the narrow valleys, and a cool breeze generally blows during the day, making marching comfortable. The nights are always fairly cool and pleasant, with a light breeze from the south or south-west.

During the rains the temperature is cool as a general rule, *i.e.*, 70° to 80°, but this is sometimes increased when a spell of fine, sunny weather intervenes, when the air becomes muggy and 90° to 95° may be registered. The roads being all practically fair-weather roads or tracks, are soon cut up, and marching becomes fatiguing to men and beasts. At this season of the year fever becomes prevalent and dysentery and diarrhœa of a virulent type are common. Cholera is practically unknown, except in sporadic form. *Surra*, anthrax, etc., are common diseases, especially at the regular caravan halting-grounds.

The Terai which, extending along the whole of the west of the Shan Hills, between the Irrawaddy and the highlands, consists of a tract about fifty miles broad, has a particularly bad climate, especially in the rains. So much is this the case that neither Burman nor Shan can live there. In the rainy season the roads in this tract are nearly impassable and *surra* is so prevalent that Government mules are not allowed to travel.

The rainy season may be said to last from the middle of May to the middle of November. Except in the Terai travelling is easy for small parties at this time, but owing to the soft nature of the soil, and the speedy way in which the roads get cut up, the transport of a large force would be attended by much difficulty.

There are large numbers of cattle everywhere in the country, and pack bullock owners are to be found in all parts.

Administration.

The administration of the Shan States is under the supreme control of the Lieutenant-Governor of Burma, who has his head-quarters at Rangoon. He is assisted by a Legislative Council, consisting of five official and four non-official members. For convenience of administration the States are divided into the Northern Shan States and the Southern Shan States, each administered by a Superintendent, who is assisted by Assistant Superintendents. The Superintendent of the Southern Shan States is also Political Officer of Karenni, which does not form part of British India. Under the Superintendent, Northern Shan States, are five States, while the Superintendent and Political Officer of the southern country has, including Karenni, forty-three States under his supervision.

Internal political relations.

Each Chief carries out the administration of his own State, but internal political relations between these various Chiefs do not exist. Any political question that might arise must be conducted through the Superintendent. This is provided for in the *sanad* which is granted to each Chief, and which contains a clause to the effect that—"In case of a dispute arising connected with any other part of the Shan States, you shall submit the matter to the Superintendent, and abide by his decision." All correspondence between the *Sawbwas*, *Myozas*, and *Ngwegunhmus* is conducted through the Superintendent; that concerning subordinate States is generally conducted through the *Sawbwa* concerned. The above does not prevent Chiefs from corresponding direct with one another on purely personal matters or on small issues which can be decided in an amicable manner. With regard to Eastern and Western Karenni, which do not form part of British India, the above rules are slightly modified. In both these cases the *sanad* requires that no communications are to be made to States in or out of British India. In the case of the Eastern Karenni Chiefs, the channel of correspondence is the Lieutenant-Governor of Burma through the Superintendent, Southern Shan States, and in the case of the Western Karenni, the Superintendent, Southern Shan States.

The people.

The Shan or Tai race in its different branches, is undoubtedly the most numerous of any in the Indo-Chinese peninsula. Members of it are found from Assam to far into the Chinese province of Kwangsi, and from Bangkok to the interior of Yünnan, and it is possible they may be traced further. The number of names by which the Shans are known is extremely large:—Tai, Htai, Pai-i, Moi, Muong, Tho or Do, Hkamti, and a host of others. In addition to this diversity of names there are six distinct forms of written characters:—

(*a*) The Siamese.
(*b*) The Lao or Siamese Shan.
(*c*) The Lü or Hkun, which might be called Trans-Salween Shan.
(*d*) The Cis-Salween Shan.
(*e*) The Tai Mao, which is Chinese Shan.
(*f*) The Hkamti Shan of the settlement west of the Irrawaddy.

As regards their language, there is a great diversity in the dialects spoken, so much so that the language spoken in one district is often absolutely unintelligible to the Shan coming from another neighbourhood.

There are numerous Shan settlements west of the Irrawaddy, some of which retain most of their original characteristics, while others have become more or less Burmanised. The barrier formed by the Salween has had its effects on the characteristics of the people. As far east as the Salween the various States have been more or less under active Burmese suzerainty for a very long time, and the influence exerted, though very far from being anything like so great as west of the Irrawaddy, has been considerable. Beyond the Salween Burmese control was much less continuously and vigourously exerted. Consequently both in dialect and written character the difference between the Shans east and west of the Salween is very marked.

The Shans are seldom found away from the alluvial basins, and do not look upon themselves as hill-people at all. They are great traders, but hitherto, from want of opportunities, on a small scale only. They are a thrifty people, and the houses of the better class exhibit a cleanliness and comfort not found among Burmans of the same rank.

They have much independence of character, but are given to jealousies which have kept them divided politically and socially. In warfare they are often cruel and vindictive. In peace time they are cheerful, hospitable, and ready to render help to one another.

The Shans are well-formed and muscular, and in appearance resemble the Burman, though they are fairer and taller.

Their dress consists of a pair of trousers which are extremely voluminous, and a jacket. They also wear a turban which in the north is generally white, and in the south is of various colours. The Chinese Shans wear a blue turban. The Shans in British territory nearly all wear the limp, broad brimmed, woven grass hat that is made at Tali Fu.

The people nearly all carry a *dah* and the Shan bag which they sling over the shoulder. They are Buddhists, but east of the Salween their Buddhism is very lax, at least as far as the *hpôngyis* are concerned, some of whom trade, wear skull-caps, and smoke habitually. In western Yünnan the *hpôngyis* only differ from the laymen in the fact that they do not actually live with their wives, though they support them, whereas in Burma and elsewhere a married man who becomes a *hpôngyi* is divorced from his wife *ipso facto*.

In addition to the various branches of the Shans, there are on all the loftier ranges of the Shan States numerous settlements of hill tribes. This is more especially so on the northern and north-eastern frontiers. Some of these are very small, others more extensive, and covering a whole range. Almost all these tribes talk Chinese with some fluency, whereas their knowledge of Shan is ordinarily very slight.

The principal tribes of the Shan States are the Rumaias or Palaungs, the Was, the Karens, the Danus, the Taungthus, the Inthas, the La'hus, and the Yaos. A description of these various tribes with their numerous sub-divisions will be found in the Gazetteer of Upper Burma. The Wa, being the only tribe likely to give trouble, is the only one of which an account is necessary in this chapter. Their country is a block of territory on our North-East Frontier extending for about 100 miles along the Salween and about fifty miles inland to the Salween-Mékong watershed. The inhabitants of this tract are known as "Wild Wa": while those of the race living on its outer fringes have become comparatively civilized and are called "Tame Wa."

The "Wild Wa" have never acknowledged British supremacy, but as they rarely leave their own territory they have up to the present not been interfered with. During certain parts of the year they are systematic head-hunters, looking upon the acquisition of fresh heads as essential to the welfare of the village, and expecting to be visited with all manners of plague, pestilence, and famine if they are unsuccessful in their quest.

Owing to this foible it is dangerous to travel in the Wa country, and at present the Burma Government allows no Europeans to enter it. The Wa, however, cannot be called a ferocious race, and do not as a rule make raids or burn villages.

MILITARY OPERATIONS.

Previous to the arrival of the British, the paramount power in the Shan States had for some hundred years been wielded by the kings of Burma. Their troops were stationed in many of the large states, and Burman officials were appointed to watch the movements of the *Sawbwas*.

The *Sawbwas* were virtually absolute in their own states, but excessive taxation sometimes had to be resorted to, in order to meet the demands of the Burmese King.

The administration of the Shan States was at no time carried on justly or consistently, and after the death of King Mindun, they fell into the same state of disorder as the rest of the Burmese dominions.

The first to break out into open disorder was the Keng Tung *Sawbwa*, who took offence at the appointment by King Mindun of a *Sawbwa* to the Keng Hung State without reference to him. On King Thibaw confirming this appointment, the Keng Tung *Sawbwa* massacred the Burman Political Officer and his guard, and installed his own candidate in the *Sawbwaship*. Thibaw being too weak to punish this insubordination, decided to ignore it altogether.

The next to revolt was the Möng Nai (Moné) *Sawbwa* who was angered at the repeated demands for money. He also massacred the Burmese garrison, which was the largest in the Shan States. The *Sawbwa* of Lawk Sawk (Yatsauk) and the Myoza of Mōng Nawng, induced by sympathy, family connections, and similar exactions, joined him, but were driven by the Burmese to take refuge with the Keng Tung *Sawbwa* in 1884. These exiled *Sawbwas* then plotted to regain their lost dignities, and conceived a plan to place at their head a prince of the Burmese Royal House. They chose the Limbin Prince, a son of the Crown Prince, who was a brother of King Mindun, and the most influential and popular member of the Burmese Royal Family. The Prince accepted, and in October 1885 left Moulmein for Keng Tung. On his arrival, the allies collected their forces and, aided by the Keng Tung *Sawbwa*, proceeded to take steps to regain their lost possessions. By this time the Burmese troops of the Shan States had been recalled to Burma to repel our advance against Mandalay, and an open field was left for the contest of supremacy in each state. The allies attacked Möng Nai in February 1886, and the late *Sawbwa* re-established himself, as did also the Lawk Sawk *Sawbwa* and the Möng Nawng *Myoza*.

Situation in October 1885.

After the former flight of the Lawk Sawk *Sawbwa* the administration of his state had been handed over to the *Sawbwa* of Yawng Hwe. The Lawk Sawk *Sawbwa* now proceeded to revenge himself on this man, who was attacked and compelled to flee. The Limbin faction then nominated Sao Chit Su to be *Sawbwa* of Yawng Hwe, but he was immediately ousted by Sao Ong who thereupon had to defend himself from enemies on all sides.

Meanwhile there was trouble all over the Cis-Salween States.

Hsipaw.

The Hsipaw *Sawbwa*, who had been obliged to flee during Thibaw's reign, had only just reinstated himself, and, taking advantage of the general disorder, had laid hands on the neighbouring principalities of Hsum Hsai and Möng Tung. This was keeping him fully occupied and he had no connection with the Limbin party. The State of

Hsenwi.

Hsenwi had been in chaos for a generation, and it still remained so. In the south things were no better. There the Red Karens had only been kept under by the Burmese garrison at Pékôn, and when this was removed the old raiding between Möng Pai and the Karenni States broke out afresh. On the south-eastern frontier Mawk Mai and Möng Pawn had a private quarrel of their own which they were prosecuting with vigour.

Thus every part of the Cis-Salween States was at war; every-

Red Karens.

where villages were being burnt and property destroyed; whole districts were becoming depopulated, and the emigration of the Shans became something very like evacuation by everyone except the actual combatants.

This was the state of affairs throughout 1886. Yawng Hwe was invested on every side but the west, and hostilities were carried on in the usual Shan fashion, which consist in a sudden advance, the construction of stockades, desultory fighting, and an attempt either to starve the enemy out, or to rush their works when the bulk of the garrison are absent in search of food. In these straits, Sao Ong bethought him of the British, whose strength he had seen in Mandalay; and tendering his allegiance to the British Government, he wrote many letters begging for their support against his various enemies. As a result of these letters it was decided to send a

Colonel Stedman's column.

force to rescue this man, and to maintain order in the Shan States by establishing a post in Yaung Hwe. Colonel Stedman, 3rd Gurkhas, was placed in command of the column, which, assembling at Hlaingdet in December, was composed of the marginally named troops. After many delays caused by the impracticability of the roads and the difficulties of obtaining transport, a start was eventually made on 15th January 1887. The pass used was the Pyinde which enters the hills four miles from Hlaingdet, and continues amongst them for forty-five miles till it débouches on the open plateau ten miles west of Pwehla. The column was opposed more or less by the Limbin confederates in this pass, but after a few skirmishes arrived at Pwehla on the 29th.

2 guns, 1-1 Mountain Battery, Eastern Division, R. A.
250 men, 2nd Hampshire Regiment.
50 men, No. 2 Coy., Bombay Sappers and Miners.
1st Battalion, 3rd Gurkha Regiment.
40 M. I. (joined the column at Pwehla).

It was found that the Lawk Sawk *Sawbwa*, with a following of about 100, had stockaded himself at Kugyo, some ten miles across the Yawng Hwe frontier and within seven miles of the capital, but that he was held in check by Yawng Hwe men, similarly stockaded in front of him. As the column was now on his right within a day's march of Kugyo, it was evident that this force was not in any position to harm Yawng Hwe at present, so a few days' halt was made at Pwehla; the neighbouring chiefs were called in and reconnaissances were pushed out in different directions. It was hoped that the Lawk Sawk *Sawbwa* would be persuaded to come into camp or at least retire from his present position, but he maintained a defiant attitude and informed the Superintendent of the Shan States (Mr. Hildebrand) that after he had carried out his intention of driving the 'dacoit' Saw Ong out of Yawng Hwe he would be glad to parley, but that at present he was engaged. As all the neighbouring chiefs had come in and no further object could be gained by remaining at Pwehla, Colonel Stedman advanced on the 7th to Boiyethat, a fortified pagoda held by the Yawng Hwe *Sawbwa*, about three miles from Kugyo: letters were sent to the Lawk Sawk *Sawbwa* informing him that unless he retired he would be attacked and driven out. No answer was received, and from the preparations which were seen to be going on round the Kugyo hill, it was evident that the *Sawbwa* had no intention of withdrawing. During the night Colonel Stedman marched his force across the front and round to the left rear of the Kugyo position: this position was situated on an isolated knoll at the end of a spur of the hills which bound the Yawng Hwe valley on the east. Colonel Stedman's advance was hidden from view by the *jungle* on the undulating spurs of this range and all alarm was avoided by passing behind the advanced works of the Nyawnghwe position. At daybreak, after a march of about seven miles, he had arrived unobserved within 2,000 yards of the left rear of the chief stockade on the Kuygo hill, and attacked at once. Unfortunately a party told off to cut off the Shans' retreat missed its way and joined in the direct attack. The two guns shelled the position from a knoll at a range of 1,000 yards, while the whole of the infantry made a direct attack; the mounted infantry, by making a detour, got into the outworks on the left flank, and the whole position was abandoned before the main attack was within effective range of the Shans' guns (*viz.*, 250 yards). The enemy's loss was twenty-four killed, and several of them were afterwards reported to have died of their wounds in the retreat to their own state; our losses were three men of the Hants Regiment slightly wounded. The whole position was destroyed and the pursuit was carried out for three miles. The Lawk Sawk *Sawbwa*, with his whole following, retreated back to Lawk Sawk without halting, and the organization of the Limbin confederacy on this part of the plateau completely broke up.

Fort Stedman established.

A fortified post was constructed on the east shores of the Inlé lake, and was named Fort Stedman (called in Burmese, Maing Thauk).

The situation at this time was as follows :—

Situation, March 1887.

Yawng Hwe had been rescued and the site for the military fort and Residency chosen. The whole of the Myelat had submitted, and most of the chiefs had come in personally. South of Yawng Hwe, Samka, the ex-Thigyit chief, Mōng Pai, and his grandson Lwélon had submitted. To the north Lawk Sawk and Mōng Ping might be supposed likely to submit, and letters were sent urging them to do so without further bloodshed. North of these again Lai Hka, Mōng Kung, and Kehsi Mansan had shown their loyalty. There was, therefore, a good basis on which to work for the pacification of the whole country, and letters were sent to the *Sawbwas* of eight eastern states telling them to carefully consider the terms of the Commissioner's proclamation enclosed, and to submit. Letters were also sent to the Karenni Chiefs Sawlapaw, Pobya, Ngwe Daung, Bawlake, and others, offering friendship and suggesting a meeting.

The Limbin confederacy had now withdrawn their troops and retired to their own states. Nevertheless there was no sign of the Eastern States giving in, and it was announced that they had taken a fresh oath to stand or fall together.

A letter from the Limbin Prince had, however, been received announcing a willingness to submit if assured of immunity, and if granted a pardon. A fresh letter was therefore sent to the Eastern States and a letter to the Limbin Prince promising him a pardon, an allowance of Rs. 250, and a house at Moulmein or Rangoon, if he would come in. Two days later a letter was sent to the Lawk Sawk *Sawbwa* telling him he had nothing to fear if he came in and made submission, and also that if the Limbin Prince came in he would be well treated and provided for. To this an unsatisfactory reply was received two days later.

While matters were thus waiting settlement to the east, it became evident that something would have to be done to the south where Möng Pai and Pobya were still fighting. Both had written to the British, asking for the speedy despatch of troops and a political officer. The original Shan column had orders to march to Toungoo through Möng Pai, and as, pending the arrival of answers from the Eastern Chiefs, troops were not wanted for service, Colonel Stedman decided to send down an advance partly to Möng Pai, both to form an advance depôt, and also to act as a guard to the Assistant Commissioner who was despatched at the same time to settle the quarrel between Pobya and Möng Pai.

Expedition to Möng Pai.

Accordingly, on the 26th February, the Assistant Superintendent, accompanied by 100 Gurkhas under Captain Pulley, started for Möng Pai, travelling by water. The small states of Ponmu, Saga, Nam Tok and Sagwe, all of which lie on the banks of the stream, were visited *en route*, and satisfactory interviews were held with the chiefs.

The Möng Pai *Sawbwa* came into the old fort of Pékôn, and expressed his delight at the prospect of the over-lordship of the Indian Government, for which he had waited so long. He was anxious to defray the expenses of building a fort, if the Government would hold it, to protect his country from the raids of the independent Karennis. He also sent letters to some of the Eastern Shan Chiefs, which no doubt paved the way to their submission.

In addition to this expedition to Möng Pai further reconnaissances were undertaken in the Myelat. The troops and officers were everywhere well received.

Colonel Stedman's force was shortly afterwards relieved by a force under Major Swetenham, 27th Punjab Infantry, consisting of the marginally named troops. The two guns of 1–1 Eastern Division, Royal Artillery, and the Mounted Infantry were transferred to Major Swetenham's force, which remained as the garrison of Fort Stedman during the following rainy season.

1 company, 2nd Queen's.
1 troop, 1st Bombay Lancers.
4 companies, 27th Punjab Infantry.

The Pyindé pass was held by the 27th Punjab Infantry, also under the command of Major Swetenham. Colonel Stedman's force was now ordered to return to the plains by this route, and to open up the Taunglobyin pass, some thirty miles further south; consequently the detachment at Pékôn was recalled.

In March, reports were received from Hopong that the Limbin Prince's followers had recently renewed their oath of allegiance. Communications, however, were opened up with the most influential of the eastern cis-Salween Chiefs, *viz.*, the Möng Nai *Sawbwa*. It was proposed that he and his confederates, together with the chiefs of the Lai Hka confederacy, should meet the Superintendent at Haipak, about twenty miles north of the Möng Nai capital. Just as the Superintendent and his escort were starting, a letter was received from the Möng Pawn *Myosa*, one of the most important chiefs of the Möng Nai confederacy. This letter demonstrated the inutility of attempting to effect the proposed meeting, as it stated that the Möng Nai *Sawbwa* was detained on a domestic visit to Sawlapaw in Karenni, and that without him the other chiefs of the confederacy could not attend the meeting.

A letter was received from the Limbin Prince, saying that he was appointed by the Shan *Sawbwas* to rule over them before the deportation of King Thibaw, and hoped that the British would remember that he had never opposed their authority. It was found that this was generally speaking correct, and that the Möng Pai *Sawbwa*, amongst others, had an idea that the Limbin Prince was in some way an agent of the Government of India.

Sawlapaw.

During March various letters from Sawlapaw were received by neighbouring Karenni and Shan Chiefs urging them to have no dealings with the "infidel foreigners." In several cases these letters were sent on to the Superintendent at Fort Stedman. During this month the partisans of the Limbin confederacy showed renewed hostility on the east of Yawng Hwe, and the Lawk Sawk *Sawbwa* was found to be instigating dacoity on the line of communications by the Pyindé pass. A good deal of this disaffection was attributed to the prolonged inactivity of the Fort Stedman garrison, combined with the failure of the proposed meeting of chiefs with the Superintendent at Haipak, and it was consequently determined that some action must be taken. It was evident that as long as the *Sawbwa* remained hostile the line of communications which at present existed, and any line of communication of troops operating further east, would never be free from attack; a letter was accordingly sent to him that the Superintendent was now about to proceed to his capital, that if he (Lawk Sawk) surrendered he would be established as *Sawbwa* under the Government, but that if he resisted he would be deposed.

Negotiations with Lawk Sawk.

At this time another letter was received from the Limbin Prince stating that he would surrender if the Government would make suitable provision for him. The Mōng Pawn *Myosa* also wrote to the effect that he would arrange a meeting of the chiefs of the Mōng Nai confederacy and the Limbin Prince with the Superintendent wherever the latter officer liked; in the same letter he complained of an invasion of his territory by the Lai Hka confederacy. The Lai Hka were accordingly at once ordered to cease from these hostilities, and the several chiefs were invited to meet the Superintendent at Hopong on the 17th April.

British advance to Hopong.

Great difficulty was experienced in equipping the expedition with transport. The column eventually started on the 4th April, taking the circuitous road *viâ* Pwehla and Pindaya so as to frighten the dacoits on the lines of communications and drive in the Lawk Sawk posts on the Pindaya frontier, which were the terror of the whole northern Myelat.

The march north from Pindaya was made by easy stages to allow the *Sawbwa* ample opportunities of reconsidering his decision to offer hostility. Everywhere in Lawk Sawk territory the arrival of the column was hailed with delight by the villagers, who professed that for over a year they had been robbed and raided by the Keng Tung men, who had put up the present *Sawbwa* on the throne.

On the 11th April the town of Lawk Sawk was occupied without resistance, but the *Sawbwa* had already fled. A meeting of the chief men of the state was then held, at which it was decided that the present *Sawbwa* should be deposed and that Boh Saing, an ex-Burman official, should be made interim administrator pending the appointment of a new ruler to be named by the Superintendent.

Boh Saing was consequently installed, and the neighbouring states were told to respect the appointment.

From Lawk Sawk the column marched through Mõng Ping to Hopong, where it had been arranged to meet the Limbin Prince and the Mõng Pawn *Sawbwa*. Neither of these men appeared, but the latter sent a message to the effect that he could not leave his state at that time, as he was being attacked by the Lai Hka and other *Sawbwas*.

The British force consequently moved on to Mõng Pawn where a cessation of the hostilities (which were more of the character of comic opera than real war), and the reconciliation of the chiefs, was quickly effected.

Submission of Mõng Pawn and the Limbin Prince.

The Mõng Pawn *Sawbwa* was a man of much force of character, and had been the practical leader of the Limbin confederacy. Upon his submission all the other Southern Shan States surrendered, and the Superintendent at once returned with the column to Fort Stedman. A party, under Captain Wallace, 27th Punjab Infantry, proceeded to Mõng Nai with the Assistant Superintendent, where the full submission of the *Sawbwa* was received and the Limbin Prince voluntarily gave himself up. At the special request of the Mõng Nai *Sawbwa* the British flag was hoisted in his town and the detachment then returned to Fort Stedman, whence the Limbin Prince was sent to Rangoon, and afterwards, at his own request, to Calcutta, where he lived in receipt of an allowance from Government.

State of the country. June 1887.

Thus, by the end of June 1887, the whole of the Southern Shan States had been brought under the influence of the Superintendent and were free from disturbances. The North, however, with the exception of Hsipaw, was still in a state of anarchy. The Hsipaw *Sawbwa* had visited Mandalay early in 1887, and as he was the first Shan *Sawbwa* to place himself without reserve in the hands of the Government, he was received with much consideration. He was present at the celebration of the Jubilee, and, as a special mark of favour ten years' tribute was remitted. It was also decided that the states of Möng Long, Hsum Hsai and Möng Tung should be considered as subordinate to him.

The prime mover of all the fighting in the Northern Shan States was Naw Möng, the son of Song Naw Hpa who had been *Sawbwa* of Hsenwi until deposed by the Burmese Government. This Naw Möng had been imprisoned by the Burmese King, and, set free by us at the occupation, he immediately set out for Hsenwi, where he gathered together his supporters in the Man Sè neighbourhood. From here he marched to the Lashio valley, and after many months of fighting was defeated by Hkun Sang of Tôn Hông, and fled. Hkun Sang then took possession of Möng Yai, and put himself in communication with the Superintendent, Shan States.

2 guns, Eastern Division, Royal Artillery.
25 British Mounted Infantry.
50 rifles, Royal Munster Fusiliers.
100 42nd Gurkha Light Infantry.

Whilst the Northern Shan States were fighting and generally arming themselves as above described, a column (strength as per margin), under command of Major H. T. S. Yates, R.A., accompanied Lieutenant Daly, Assistant Political Officer, Northern Shan States, on tour, reaching Hsipaw on the 24th December. The immediate object was to obtain the submission of the Tawng Peng *Sawbwa* to whom numerous letters had been sent, to none of which he had vouchsafed any reply. The column left Hsipaw for Namhsan, the capital of Tawng Peng, on the 28th December. Conflicting rumours as to this chief's intentions were current before our advance, and on our entering the state, signs of distrust and apprehension were apparent. On the 29th, the road had been blocked in one place by newly felled trees, and on the 31st, the advanced and rear guards were almost simultaneously fired on. The attack, however, was of a most half-hearted description, and Namhsan was reached on the 1st January 1888, and a halt made. All the villages *en route* were practically deserted as was Namhsan itself, the *Sawbwa* having fled the day before our arrival. On the 10th January, the party left Namhsan, and on the 17th reached Mansam, where the villagers were in expectation of an attack by Hkun Sang's men, two parties of which were reported close at hand. To these parties orders were sent to meet the column at Pang Hkyem. The next day the column was met at that place by Hkun Sang's official with about 400 men. His men were in great straits for want of food, and seemed to hail the order to disperse with joy. The column reached Hsenwi on the 24th, and Hkun Sang expressed himself pleased at our arrival. On the 31st January a move was made, the column marching to Kunlong and Möng Ket, whence, on account of rumours of disturbances in Möng Yai, the Political Officer pushed on to Möng Yaw with the Mounted Infantry, the main column arriving the next day. It was then decided that Major Yates, the Infantry of the column, and the Political Officer should at once push on to the disturbed district, the remainder completing the exploration of the country between Lashio and Möng Yaw. Man Sè was fixed on as the place of rendezvous, and Hkun Sang was invited to meet the column there on the 26th February. After a successful march, all armed parties disbanding on receipt of orders, the party reached Man Sè, where the remainder of the column was awaiting them. Hkun Sang turned up punctually, and a few days later the column returned to Mandalay, their object having been effected. The Political Officer arrived on 1st March at Möng Yai where he met a column from the south. Here a meeting was held at which the Hsenwi *Naw-maing* the Möng Yai *Paôkgyôt*, Hkun Sang, the chiefs of Kehsi Mansan, Möng Hsu, and Möng Sin, and representatives from Hsipaw and many of the Southern States were present. The arrangement arrived at was that Kehsi Mansan, Möng Hsu, and Möng Sin would be independent *Myozaships*, and the Theinni principality be divided into North and South Hsenwi, and be placed under Hkun Sang and Nawt Maing, respectively. In this all present acquiesced, and the column broke up and returned to Mandalay.

Lieutenant Daly, Assistant Political Officer, with fifty rifles, 42nd Gurkha Light Infantry, was left at Hsipaw on the way.

A few days later news was received of troubles in South Hsenwi. This necessitated visiting that State, which was accordingly done, Möng Yai was reached on the 14th March, and on the 25th a general meeting was held of all headmen and Elders of circles, and new representatives were chosen. Of the leaders of the rising, four were deported and the rest were left for the *Sawbwa* to deal with, and the party then returned to Maymyo.

Whilst these events were taking place Sawlapaw, the Chief of Eastern Karenni, had been giving trouble. The prolonged absence of the Superintendent, who had made an extended tour through the Southern and Northern States, coupled with the absence of the bulk of the garrison of Fort Stedman, seems to have given rise to the supposition that the British troops had been or were about to be withdrawn. In March 1888 Sawlapaw, who had declined to meet the Superintendent some months before when requested to do so, took the opportunity of settling a long standing feud with Mawkmai. A band of Red Karens attacked Mawkmai, and captured and burnt it, the *Sawbwa* fleeing across the Salween. Sawlawpaw then proceeded to set up as *Sawbwa* a candidate of his own, who agreed to hold the State as a feudatory of the Karenni Chief.

Eastern Karenni.

This success doubtless emboldened Twet Nga Lu, who shortly after attacked and burnt Möng Pawn, driving out the *Sawbwa.* By order of the Superintendent the Möng Nai *Sawbwa* now sent a party to expel Twet Nga Lu, but they were defeated and pursued up to the gates of Möng Nai. Twet Nga Lu then took up a position opposite Möng Nai, which he captured early in May, the *Sawbwa* flying to Möng Pawn.

In the meanwhile, some minor States in the south of the Myelat were fighting amongst themselves, the Yawng Hwe *Sawbwa* inciting them. Peace was restored and the *Sawbwa* fined Rs. 10,000. A column then marched east, and Twet Nga Lu was captured by a mounted surprise party under Lieutenant Fowler, 1st Baluchis, seven days after he had taken Möng Nai. Six of the leaders were executed after trial by the Möng Nai *Sawbwa*, and Twet Nga Lu was shot by his guards. The column with the Assistant Superintendent then marched to Mawkmai, which was evacuated by the

Karens, whose leader escaped to Siam. The Karens retired to their own country, and a post was established at Mawkmai and a small one at Möng Nai. At the end of June 1888, however, Sawlapaw made another attack on Mawkmai. This was easily repulsed, and Lieutenant Fowler, assuming the offensive, drove the Karens out of their stronghold at Kantu Awn and expelled them from the Mawkmai territory. These disturbances led to a British civil officer being permanently stationed at Möng Nai, and about the same time the North and South Shan States were divided and became eparate charges, each under its own Superintendent.

It must be noted that these risings were purely local matters, and it may be here remarked that the Shan States, as a whole, were the only part of Upper Burma which practically accepted British authority without opposition. Within little over a year of the first occupation of the country the ruler of every state had made personal submission to the Superintendent and had agreed to accept his position as tributary to the British Government under fixed conditions. The intention of the Government of India to maintain order and to prevent private wars between the several states, while at the same time allowing to each chief independence in the administration of his territory, had not only been declared but had been exemplified. Trade began to revive almost immediately, ruined villages and towns were re-occupied and rebuilt, and the people began to resume their ordinary pursuits, which, it may be said, have never since been disturbed except in the frontier states, and only there for reasons which were purely local and differed in each case.

EASTERN KARENNI EXPEDITION.

The season of 1888-89 was principally occupied in dealing with Sawlapaw, the Chief of Eastern Karenni. Immediately after the defeat of his forces at Kantu Awn, and probably before he was aware of it, Sawlapaw wrote to the Superintendent of the Shan States recounting his grievances against Mawkmai and peremptorily ordering the withdrawal of British troops from that state. This letter was returned.

Ultimatum to Sawlapaw.

In August 1888 Sawlapaw seemed to have begun to understand that punishment would follow his attacks on Mawkmai. He then asked the British Government to arbitrate between himself and the *Sawbwa* of Mawkmai from whom he claimed Rs. 2,400,000 as compensation. But as these letters were couched in unsuitable phraseology, they too were returned by the hand of his messengers. In September an ultimatum was sent to Fort Stedman for despatch to Sawlapaw, if he proved refractory. This required him to come personally to Fort Stedman, to pay an indemnity of two lacs for the damage done to Mawkmai and to cover the cost of troops sent to the relief of that state, to surrender 500 serviceable muskets, and pay annually Rs. 5,000 in tribute. Every chance was given to Sawlapaw to submit quietly, and it was not until the middle of November that the ultimatum was despatched.

Start of the Expedition.

On the 19th December, as all our efforts to secure his submission were fruitless, it was decided to send out the punitive expedition which had been under preparation. The preparations included the despatch of a strong column under Brigadier-General H. Collett, C.B., from Fort Stedman, and a second under Colonel J. J. Harvey from Lower Burma by way of the Salween district. The Northern Column was to overcome any resistance made by Sawlapaw and take and occupy his capital, Sawlon, while the Southern Column was to co-operate to prevent his escape to the south, and to protect the Salween district from raids which it was expected the Karens would make: The necessity for this was soon apparent, for two days before the arrival of the Southern Column at Papun, Sawlapaw had plundered and partially burnt the village of Kyaukhnyat, north-east of Papun, where there was a police outpost. The Karens then retired, and on the 26th December Colonel Harvey's force marched from Papun and taking a stockade at Pazaung, south of Bawlake, without difficulty, remained in occupation to cover the Burma Frontier.

2 guns, No. 1 Bengal Mountain Battery.
100 rifles, 1st Bn., Rifle Brigade.
40 M. I., 1st Bn., Rifle Brigade.
240 rifles, 27th Bombay (1st Biluch) Light Infantry.
70 M. I., 27th Bombay (1st Biluch) Light Infantry.
23 rifles, Madras Sappers and Miners.

The Northern Column, accompanied by the Superintendent of the Shan States and by Mr. Barnard, Assistant Commissioner, left Saga, thirty-six miles south of Fort Stedman, on the 29th December. The composition of the force is shown in the margin. No opposition was met with till the 1st January, when, as the advanced scouts of the mounted infantry were approaching the village of Ngakyaing, near Loikaw, they were suddenly fired on by the enemy in some

Action near Loikaw.

broken ground on the left flank. The scouts were immediately supported by the whole of the Biluch Mounted Infantry, under Lieutenant Tighe, who, seeing a large body of the enemy in his front, made straight for them at full gallop, detaching at the same time a section to his left, to cut off their retreat to the hills. The charge was so vigorously executed, that although the ground was unfavourable for mounted men, the Karens broke and fled. Lieutenant Tighe pursued them with great determination to within two miles of Loikaw, and succeeded in killing not less than 150. The British loss was four men killed and eight wounded.

Crossing the Balu Chaung on the 3rd, the column reached Lawpita on the 4th, where some slight resistance was met with from a body of about fifty of the enemy. On the 5th January the force marched to the Pon Chaung, descending some 2,000 feet over a difficult path to the river. The passage of this river was effected by the evening of the 6th, and the next day the column entered the "long defile," which extends for some twelve miles to the Ngwé Daung ferry, within two miles of Sawlôn itself. This defile is of the most difficult nature, and if strongly held by an enemy, could only be forced with great loss. On the right runs the Nam Pawn, unfordable, with a width of 100 to 150 yards; on the left rise rugged hills covered with thick forest, and in places quite inaccessible. The road runs along the bank of the river, for the most part within easy musket shot from the right bank, while on the left the hills continually close in on the river, forcing the road into a narrow precipitous gorge. The column met with slight opposition along the whole length of this defile, but owing to the precautions of the General, who had each height occupied and each defile turned, not a single casualty occurred on the side of the British, and on the afternoon of the 8th the force occupied the town of Sawlôn which was found to be deserted. All opposition now ceased.

Settlement of Eastern Karenni.

Some time before the arrival of the British troops Sawlawpaw had fled. Mr. Hildebrand endeavoured to induce him to return, but without success. He succeeded, however, in securing the submission of all the principal local officials and notables, and on the 28th January, as Sawlapaw declined to come in, and his hiding place was unknown, a meeting was held for the purpose of electing a new chief of Eastern Karenni. The person chosen was Sawlawi, the nephew and heir-apparent of Sawlapaw. Subject to the approval of the Government, Mr. Hildebrand inducted Sawlawi into the *Sawbwaship* of Eastern Karenni, and gave him a provisional order of appointment. Sawlawi agreed to hold the State of Eastern Karenni as a subject of Her Majesty, to abstain from dealings with foreign states, to pay an indemnity of £30,000 in three instalments, to deliver before the end of March 1889 five hundred serviceable muskets, and to pay an annual tribute of £500. The payment of the tribute and the delivery of the muskets were guaranteed by the leading officials and timber traders of Eastern Karenni.

Later events in Karenni.

The troops were withdrawn on the 30th January 1889. From that date the administration of Eastern Karenni was carried on by Sawlawi, who displayed conspicuous loyalty in the observance of his engagements with the British Government. The payment of the first instalment of the indemnity and the deliverance of the full tale of guns were made within a day or two of the prescribed date, and Sawlawi regularly kept the Superintendent of the Shan States informed of the progress of events in his territory. Towards the end of February, Sawlapaw, who had remained in hiding while Sawlôn was occupied by British troops, returned and took up his residence at Ywathit, a village not far from Sawlôn, leaving the administration in the hands of Sawlawi.

Failure of the Siamese co-operation.

It had been arranged that the Siamese should co-operate with the British in these operations, but their co-operation was scarcely satisfactory. It was known that the Government of Siam laid claim to a portion of territory on the east bank of the Salween river, and Mr. Gould, Her Majesty's representative at Bangkok (who had previously suggested the co-operation of the Siamese forces against Karenni, but had not then mentioned that Siam would claim any territory as a reward for assistance), writing on the 10th November 1888, intimated that in return for their assistance the Siamese would probably wish to establish their territorial rights over this tract. On the 22nd November, Mr. Archer, Her Majesty's Vice-Consul at Chieng Mai (Zimmé), wrote that the main Siamese force intended for operations against Karenni would not start till December, when Prince Sonapandit would arrive to take command, but that a force of 400 men would be sent at once to uard one of the ferries on the Salween river. The progress of events was notified to the Siamese authorities through Mr. Gould and Mr. Archer; but the first sign of the promised co-operation was the appearance of a band of Mé Hawng Sawn Shans, part of the Siamese force, on the banks of the Salween, at the mouth of the Mé Pai on the 20th January. Resistance had ceased on the 8th, and the Siamese co-operation was practically useless. On the 4th February Mr. Gould and Mr. Archer were informed of the provisional settlement made with Sawlawi, and it was suggested that the Siamese troops should withdraw. This suggestion the Siamese authorities were unwilling to carry out, and remained. The country occupied by the Siamese contained valuable timber forests, and measures were adopted by them which practically amounted to the confiscation of all timber in these forests. The territory occupied by the Siamese had long been held by the Karens, to whom the presence of the Siamese troops was a constant cause of irritation.

The complete and definite surrender of the Red Karens, in that it was so unexpected, was the most satisfactory part of this expedition. For years they had been the terror of their neighbours, and had extended their raids far into the Myelat, whence they carried off women and children to be sold in the Siamese Shan States.

On the return march Mr. Hildebrand demarcated the boundary between the States of Möng Pai and Namméko and effected a settlement of the disputes there. The only other incident of note was that in 1889 the Möng Pawn *Sawbwa* was formally placed in possession of the Trans-Salween States of Möng Tung, Möng Hang, Möng Kyawt, and Möng Hta, which had been claimed by Siam and until this had not acknowledged the *Sawbwa's* authority.

Progress in the north, 1888.

In the north, where there had been continual war for thirty years, it was hardly to be expected that there would be an immediate absence of disturbances. There was a slight rising in South Hsenwi which was at once suppressed, but it was only after some trouble that Lieutenant Daly succeeded in inducing the Namhkam *Myoza* to recognize the authority of the North Hsenwi *Sawbwa*.

There was a good deal of resentment in the States of Hsum Hsai and Möng Long at their subordination to the *Sawbwa* of

Hsipaw, and the persons he put in charge of these states were not very judicious appointments. This, and their proximity to the plains, which made them an obvious place of refuge for dacoits and outlaws, rendered these two states a source of trouble, and their population tended rather to decrease than to settle down quietly.

Tawng Peng, Loi Long, and Möng Mit were full of elements of disturbance owing to the presence near their borders of the Pretender Saw Yan Naing and Hkam Leng, and there was a good deal of ferment and some fighting in these districts, an account of which has been given in the chapter on the Kachins. On the whole, however, there was steady progress, and the confidence of the chiefs in the Government was confirmed and strengthened.

In the following year (1889) South Hsenwi was undisturbed, but in December 1890 the Northern State was the scene of a rising headed by Hkun Yi, the *Sawbwa's* brother-in-law, and son of Sang Hai, who intended him to be the heir. Hkun Yi was killed before the affair became serious, but later in the year there was trouble between the *Sawbwa's* officials and some Kachins in the northern part of the state. This was smoothed over for the moment but the Kachins were not satisfied, and it was the beginning of the discontent which had serious results three years later. The rest of the Northern States were undisturbed, but the condition of Möng Long as a refuge for outlaws was still unsatisfactory and the population of Hsum Hsai steadily decreased. A good deal of progress was made in the construction of roads from Mandalay to Maymyo and Hsipaw, and from Meiktila towards the head-quarters of the Southern Shan States, and both of these began to be much used by caravans.

In the Southern Shan States in 1890 the most important events were: (1) the submission of the great Trans-Salween State of Keng Tung, with which up till then only an abortive correspondence had been maintained, and (2) the settlement, by the Anglo-Siamese Commission, of the disputes about the territory the Siamese had taken up on the eastern side of the Salween after the Karenni expedition, and about the Trans-Salween States handed over to the *Sawbwa* of Möng Pawn, to which they also laid claim.

During the greater part of 1890-91 and 1891-92, the Superintendents were for the most part engaged in frontier affairs. The Kachins caused some disturbance in North Hsenwi. Unsuccessful attempts were made to secure the submission of West Manglön, the only Trans-Salween State that had not accepted British authority, and turbulence on the Keng Tung–Siam frontier culminated in the murder of a Siamese Survey officer in June 1891. At the end of the year, the Western Karenni chiefs, who had been practically independent, were brought under administration. These chiefs were granted *sanads*, a nominal tribute was imposed, and various inter-tribal disputes were settled. In the year 1892-93, the line selected as the Southern Shan States and Siam boundary in 1890 was settled on, the Siamese Commissioners working in perfect accord with Messrs. Hildebrand and Leveson.

1890-93.

In the Northern Shan States there was a considerable disturbance. The task of administering the constantly increasing hordes of Kachin immigrants proved quite beyond the power of the *Sawbwa* of North Hsenwi. The attempts of the district officials to tyrannize over them exasperated them, and on the 12th December, they made a successful attack on Wing Hsenwi. On the 15th, Mr. W.A. Graham, Treasury Officer at Lashio, proceeded to Hsenwi with a Military Police escort, and dislodged the rebels, who then consented to arbitration. Various disturbances broke out afterwards but the Kachins declared that the rebellion was against the authority of Hkun Sang and not against the British Government.

While these affairs were happening, the Superintendent was settling affairs in Manglön. At the time of the annexation Manglön was divided into two states east and west of the Salween. The west was ruled by Sao Maha, a half-brother of the chief of the east or main state. Sao Maha did not admit the suzerainty of the British Government. In 1892, therefore, the Eastern chief was put in charge of both sides of the Salween. During the rains, however, Sao Maha received support from several minor Wa chiefs, and re-established himself at Na Lau, west of the river, and with the assistance of his allies, Ngek Ting and Loi Löu, burnt some villages in East Manglön. On the approach of the Superintendent he fled, and since then West Manglön has been at peace.

Bré Expedition.

Since 1893 peace and prosperity have reigned in the Shan States, and the only troubles that have occurred have been on the frontier. It will be sufficient to barely note the chief events of each year since 1893. In January and February 1894, Mr. Leveson was engaged in an expedition to the Bré and Padaung country between the Karen Hill Tracts of the Toungoo District and the Western Karenni States. This expedition was undertaken in consequence of a raid committed on Lokadashe, a village on the north-eastern border of the Karen Hill Tracts. Up to the date of starting, very little was known of the condition of the country of the Brés and Padaungs beyond the fact that the people were in a disturbed state. They were found to be practically lawless; the various villages were technically under one or the other of the various Shan or Karenni chiefs but were as a rule out of their control. They were therefore placed under the general charge of the Civil Officer at Loikaw with considerable advantage to themselves and their neighbours.

Another expedition, conducted by Mr. Stirling in the same year along the Keng Tung frontier, also brought us into relations with various hill tribes other than the Shans and settled different frontier disputes.

In the Northern states there were still a few dacoities and crimes, among them being the murder of Mr. Lambert, of the American Mission in Wing Hsipaw.

In both 1886 and 1887 there were minor hostilities with certain petty Wa communities.

Since 1897 peace and prosperity has been unbroken in the Shan States, and trade has increased by leaps and bounds. The most important event, and one which has removed a possible source of trouble and even danger, is the partial delimitation of the Burma-China boundary which was successfully completed in the open season of 1900-1901. The only disturbing element now remaining is the Wild Wa community, which has never acknowledged British suzerainty. As these people, however, do not raid into other parts of the Shan States there appears to be no urgent reason to undertake their subjugation. It may possibly be, and, it is to be hoped, it will be, found possible to gradually induce them to accept our authority without having recourse to force of arms.

APPENDICES.

APPENDIX I.

RETURN OF ORDNANCE CAPTURED AT AND NEAR RANGOON.

May, 1824.

		24-pounders.	20-pounders.	18-pounders.	12-pounders.	10-pounders.	9-pounders.	8-pounders.	6-pounders.	5½-pounders.	4½-pounders.	4-pounders.	3½-pounders.	3-pounders.	2½-pounders.	2-pounders.	1½-pounders.	1-pounder.	¾-pounder.	½-pounder.	Swivels.	Jingals.	Total.
Iron long guns, serviceable.	**Mounted**	1	1	1	..	2	3	1	7	5	1	1	..	..	1	3	..	..	..	..	..	..	27
	Dismounted	..	..	..	..	..	..	..	2	3	4	..	1	..	1	..	..	1	..	..	..	..	12
Iron long guns, unserviceable.	**Mounted**	..	..	..	2	..	..	..	1	5	1	..	..	..	1	..	..	..	..	..	..	..	10
	Dismounted	..	..	..	..	1	8	..	2	1	..	..	..	4	..	..	1	..	1	8	..	..	26
Carronades, serviceable.	**Mounted**	..	..	3	1	..	..	..	..	..	..	..	..	..	..	..	..	..	..	..	..	..	4
	Dismounted	3	..	4	6	..	..	..	..	..	..	..	..	..	..	..	..	..	..	..	..	..	13
Carronades, unserviceable.	**Dismounted**	1	..	..	..	..	..	..	..	..	..	..	..	..	..	..	..	..	..	..	..	..	1
Iron swivel, serviceable.	**Mounted**	..	..	..	..	..	..	..	..	..	..	..	..	..	..	..	..	..	..	..	1	..	1
Brass swivels, serviceable.	**Dismounted**	..	..	..	..	..	..	..	..	..	..	..	..	..	..	..	..	..	..	..	2	..	2
Guns, brass, serviceable.	,,	..	..	..	..	..	..	..	..	..	..	..	..	..	..	..	..	3	2	..	..	..	5
Iron *jingals*, unserviceable		..	..	..	..	..	..	..	..	..	..	..	..	..	..	..	..	..	..	..	..	9	9
	Total	5	1	8	9	3	11	1	12	14	6	1	1	4	3	3	1	4	3	8	3	9	110

Of the above guns, 5 brass and 5 iron were captured at Negrais.

Shot	12-pr.		133
,,	9 ,,		30
,,	6 ,,		276
,,	3 ,,		475
,,	3 ,,	Bar	44
,,	Irregular and Foreign		299
	Total		1,257

Gunpowder computed at .. Cwts. 2,400

(Sd.) W. M. BURTON, *Major,*
Comdg. Division Artillery.

APPENDIX II.

PRESENT STATE OF THE ARMY UNDER THE COMMAND OF BRIGADIER-GENERAL SIR ARCHIBALD CAMPBELL, K.C.B., ETC., SERVING AGAINST THE DOMINIONS OF THE KING OF AVA.

Head-Quarters Prome, 18*th August* 1825.

Corps, etc.	Present for duty.													Sick, present.											
	Field Officers.	Captains.	Subalterns.	Surgeons.	Assistant Surgeons.	Sub-Assistant Veterinary Surgeons.	Staff Sergeants.	Subadars.	Jemadars.	Sergeants or Havildars.	Drummers.	Rank and File.	Horses.	Field Officers.	Captains.	Subalterns.	Surgeons.	Assistant Surgeons.	Staff Sergeants.	Subadars.	Jemadars.	Sergeants or Havildars.	Drummers.	Rank and File.	Horses.
At Prome.																									
Arty. Horse Bde. ..	..	2	6	..	1	..	..	..	..	9	3	84	129	..	..	..	..	..	..	..	..	1	..	17	7
Arty. Foot (Euro.) ..	2	2	1	..	2	..	..	..	..	8	2	128	..	..	..	..	..	..	..	..	..	..	..	22	..
Total Euro. Arty. ..	2	4	5	..	3	..	..	..	..	17	5	212	129	..	..	..	..	..	..	..	..	1	..	39	7
Right Hon'ble the Govr.-Genl.'s Body-Guard.	..	..	1	..	1	1	2	3	7	17	6	207	100	..	..	..	..	..	..	..	..	1	..	31	32
H. M.'s 2nd Batta., 1st (or Royal) Regt.	..	3	12	1	2	..	4	..	..	28	20	481	..	..	..	1	..	..	3	..	..	..	2	89	..
H. M.'s 13th Light Infy. ..	..	2	5	..	..	..	..	..	..	11	5	162	..	..	..	..	..	..	..	..	..	..	..	5	..
„ 38th Regt. ..	..	4	12	1	1	..	2	..	..	23	9	363	..	..	..	1	..	..	..	..	..	2	..	21	..
„ 41st „ ..	1	2	10	..	3	..	..	..	..	21	9	242	..	..	..	3	..	..	..	..	..	..	1	23	..
„ 47th „ ..	1	4	10	1	1	..	4	..	..	30	15	505	..	..	..	..	..	..	..	..	..	5	1	78	..
„ 89th „ ..	..	3	11	..	1	..	..	..	..	31	12	333	..	..	..	..	..	..	..	..	..	2	1	50	..
Total Euro. Infy. ..	2	18	60	3	8	..	10	..	..	142	71	2,087	..	..	..	5	..	..	3	..	..	9	5	266	..
18th Regt., M. N. I. ..	..	2	4	..	..	..	1	3	6	32	10	344	..	..	1	2	..	1	..	1	..	2	..	23	..
26th „ „ ..	..	1	7	..	1	..	..	3	8	38	15	430	..	..	..	..	..	..	2	..	1	4	1	95	..
28th „ „ ..	..	2	4	..	1	..	2	5	3	36	14	321	..	..	..	2	..	..	..	..	..	5	..	42	..
30th „ „ ..	1	2	9	..	1	..	2	6	7	36	14	395	..	..	..	1	..	..	..	2	2	5	1	101	..
38th „ „ ..	1	2	11	..	1	..	2	3	7	40	13	498	..	..	..	..	..	..	..	2	..	1	1	112	..
43rd „ „ ..	1	..	6	..	1	..	2	3	3	37	11	402	..	..	..	1	..	..	..	..	2	2	..	34	..
1st Batta., Mad. Pioneers	..	1	6	..	1	..	1	..	4	22	..	409	..	..	..	..	..	..	..	..	..	4	..	133	..
Total Native Infy. ..	3	10	47	..	6	..	10	23	38	241	77	2,799	..	..	1	6	..	1	2	5	5	23	3	540	..

Corps, etc.	Present for duty. Field Officers.	Captains.	Subalterns.	Surgeons.	Assistant Surgeons.	Staff Sergeants.	Subadars.	Jemadars.	Sergeants or Havildars.	Drummers.	Rank and File.	Sick, present. Field Officers.	Captains.	Subalterns.	Surgeons.	Assistant Surgeons.	Staff Sergeants.	Subadars.	Jemadars.	Sergeants or Havildars.	Drummers.	Rank and File.
At Rangoon.																						
Artillery { European	..	1	3	..	1	1	..	..	2	..	62	..	..	..	..	..	..	..	..	..	..	11
Artillery { Native	..	..	..	..	..	..	2	6	6	3	46	..	..	..	..	..	..	..	..	1	2	10
*Detachment, H. M.'s Royal Regt.	..	..	..	..	..	..	..	..	2	3	62	..	..	..	..	..	..	..	..	..	..	8
* " " 41st Regt.	..	..	1	..	..	..	..	..	4	1	46	..	..	..	..	..	..	..	..	..	..	9
* " " 86th Regt.	..	..	1	..	..	..	..	..	3	1	47	..	..	..	..	..	..	..	..	2	..	14
" 1st Madras European Regt.	..	..	1	1	..	..	..	..	1	1	29	..	..	..	..	..	..	..	..	2	..	10
9th Regt., M. N. I.	1	4	11	..	..	1	8	10	52	19	596	..	..	..	..	..	..	..	..	1	1	31
12th " "	1	3	9	..	1	2	9	10	51	19	776	..	..	..	..	..	..	..	..	2	1	97
34th " "	1	..	9	..	1	2	6	10	46	29	672	..	..	..	..	..	..	..	..	..	..	26
*22nd Regt., Left Wing, M. N. I.	..	3	4	..	1	..	4	4	22	8	388	..	..	..	..	..	..	..	..	..	..	109
*Details of corps	..	1	11	..	1	2	8	8	41	19	784	..	..	..	..	..	..	..	..	6	1	143
Total ..	3	12	50	1	5	8	37	48	230	103	3,280	..	..	..	..	..	..	..	..	14	5	468
At Donabyo.																						
1st Madras European Regt. ..	1	1	6	..	1	2	..	..	25	15	227	..	..	..	..	..	..	..	..	..	..	9
22nd Regt., M. N. I.	1	1	7	..	1	2	6	5	33	10	354	..	..	..	..	..	..	..	..	1	..	43
Total ..	2	2	13	..	2	4	6	5	58	25	581	..	..	..	..	..	..	..	..	1	..	52
At Martaban.																						
3rd M. L. I.	1	2	9	..	1	1	8	8	57	30	360	..	..	1	..	..	..	..	..	1	..	21
At Tavoy and Mergui.																						
7th Regt., M. N. I.	1	2	7	..	1	2	9	10	59	20	730	..	..	..	..	..	..	..	..	..	..	19
From Rangoon, omitted in the above.																						
*Detachment, H. M.'s 13th Light Infy.	..	2	5	..	1	..	..	..	9	7	120	..	..	..	..	..	..	..	..	3	1	35
*Detachment, H. M.'s 38th Regt.	..	..	1	..	..	..	..	..	3	1	71	..	..	..	..	..	..	..	..	..	2	37
* " 47th Regt.	..	..	..	..	..	..	..	..	2	2	39	..	..	..	..	..	..	..	..	2	1	38
Total ..	..	2	6	..	1	..	..	..	14	10	230	..	..	..	..	..	..	..	..	5	4	110

N.B.—The corps and detachments marked thus * were either on the way to join head-quarters or ordered to do so by water.

APPENDIX III.

TREATY OF YANDABO.

ARTICLE I.

THERE shall be a perpetual peace and friendship between the Honourable Company on the one part and the King of Ava on the other.

ARTICLE II.

His Majesty the King of Ava renounces all claims, and will abstain from all interference with the principality of Assam and also with the contiguous petty States of Cachar and Jynteea. With regard to Munnipore, it is stipulated, that, should Ghumbeer Singh desire to return to that country, he shall be recognized by the King of Ava as Raja thereof.

ARTICLE III.

To prevent all future disputes respecting the boundary between the two great nations, the British Government will retain the conquered provinces of Arakan, including the four divisions of Arakan, Ramree, Cheduba, and Sandoway, and His Majesty the King of Burma cedes all rights thereto. The Unnoupectowmien, or Arakan, mountains will henceforth form the boundary between the two great nations on that side. Any doubts regarding the said line of demarcation will be settled by the Commissioners appointed by the respective Governments for that purpose, such commissioners from both powers to be suitable and corresponding in rank.

ARTICLE IV.

His Majesty the King of Ava cedes to the British Government the conquered provinces of Yeh, Tavoy, and Mergui and Tenasserim, with the inlands and dependencies thereunto appertaining, taking the Salween river as the line of demarcation on that frontier. Any doubts regarding their boundaries will be settled as specified in the concluding part of Article III.

ARTICLE V.

In proof of the sincere disposition of the Burman Government to maintain the relations of peace and amity between the nations, and as part indemnification to the British Government for the expenses of the war, His Majesty the King of Ava agrees to pay the sum of one crore of rupees.

ARTICLE VI.

No person whatever, whether native or foreigner, is hereafter to be molested by either party, on account of the part which he may have taken, or have been compelled to take, in the present war.

ARTICLE VII.

In order to cultivate and improve the relations of amity and peace hereby established between the two Governments, it is agreed that accredited ministers, retaining an escort or safe-guard of fifty men from each, shall reside at the darbar of the other, who shall be permitted to purchase or to build a suitable place of residence, of permanent materials; and a commercial treaty, upon principles of reciprocal advantage, will be entered into by the high contracting Powers.

ARTICLE VIII.

All public and private debts contracted by either Government or by the subjects of either Government, with the others previous to the war, to be recognized and liquidated, upon the same principles of honour and good faith as if hostilities had not taken place between the two nations; and no advantage shall be taken by either party of the period that may have elapsed since the debts were incurred, or in consequence of the war; and according to the universal law of nations, it is further stipulated that the property of all British subjects who may die in the dominions of His Majesty the King of Ava shall, in the absence of legal heirs, be placed in the hands of the British Resident, or Consul, in the said dominions, who will dispose of the same according to the tenour of the British law. In like manner, the property of Burman subjects dying under the same conditions, in any part of the British dominions, shall be made over to the Minister or other authority delegated by his Burman Majesty to the Supreme Government of India.

ARTICLE IX.

The King of Ava will abolish all exactions on British ships or vessels in Burman ports that are not required for Burman ships or vessels in British ports; nor shall ships or vessels, the property of British subjects, whether European or Indian, entering the Rangoon river, or other Burman ports, be required to land their guns, or unship their rudders, or to do any other act not required by Burmese ships or vessels in British ports.

ARTICLE X.

The good and faithful ally of the British Government, His Majesty the King of Siam, having taken a part in the present war, will, to the fullest extent, as far as regards His Majesty and his subjects, be included in the above treaty.

Article XI.

This treaty to be ratified by the Burmese authorities competent in the like cases, and the ratification to be accompanied by all British, whether European or native, American, and other prisoners, who will be delivered over to the British Commissioners. The British Commissioners on their part, engaging that the said treaty shall be ratified by the Right Honourable the Governor-General in Council, and the ratifications shall be delivered to His Majesty the King of Ava, in four months or sooner if possible ; and all the Burmese prisoners shall, in like manner, be delivered over to their own Government, as soon as they arrive from Bengal.

Additional Article.

The British Commissioners, being most anxiously desirous to manifest the sincerity of their wish for peace, and to make the immediate execution of the fifth article of this treaty as little irksome or inconvenient as possible, His Majesty the King of Ava consents to the following arrangement with respect to the division of the sum total, as specified in the article before referred to, into instalments, *viz.* : upon the payment of twenty-five lakhs of rupees, or one-fourth of the sum total (the other articles of the treaty being executed), the army will retire to Rangoon ; upon the further payment of a similar sum at that place, within one hundred days from this date, with the proviso as above, the army will evacuate the dominions of His Majesty the King of Ava with the least possible delay ; leaving the remaining moiety of the sum total to be paid by equal annual instalments in two years, from this 24th day of February 1826 A.D. through the Consul or Resident in Ava or Pegu, on the part of the Honourable East India Company.

APPENDIX IV.

MINUTE BY HIS EXCELLENCY THE VICEROY AND GOVERNOR-GENERAL OF INDIA, DATED 17TH FEBRUARY 1886.

HAVING now visited Mandalay and discussed the affairs of Upper Burma with Mr. Bernard, the Chief Commissioner, with Lieutenant-General Sir Harry Prendergast, Commanding the Expeditionary Force, with Colonel Sladen, the Political Officer, and with all the chief local authorities, both civil and military, European and native, I proceed to record, for the consideration and orders of Her Majesty's Government, the conclusions at which I have arrived regarding the future administration of that country. These have been already communicated in general terms to the Secretary of State for India in my telegram of the 13th February. I propose in the present minute to explain the position more fully, and to give some account of the measures which I venture to think are best calculated to ensure peace and order in Upper Burma, and to promote the welfare and prosperity of its inhabitants.

It is unnecessary for me to deal with the causes of our quarrel with the late King. They have been sufficiently set forth in previous despatches to the Secretary of State; but the removal of Thibaw having become a necessity, it was manifestly desirable that it should be effected under such circumstances as would convince both him and his adherents that resistance was hopeless. With this view, General Prendergast was supplied with a large and efficient force, and was recommended, by the celerity and decision of his movements, to anticipate and confound the defensive measures of his opponent. He was also instructed not to be beguiled by any evasive replies or pleas for delay, but, as soon as the time allowed for answering our ultimatum had elapsed, to march straight upon Mandalay. In doing this, however, he was to adopt such tactics as were best calculated to avoid direct collision with the Burmese forces, so far as was compatible with the safety of his troops and the attainment of his object. He was also reminded that the country to be dealt with was not inhabited by a hostile people, but by a community identical in race and religion and in all its material interests with those who were already our own subjects. The successful manner in which General Prendergast complied with these suggestions is now a matter of history. As a consequence I have been able to pass up the Irrawaddy and to enter Mandalay amidst the greetings of a friendly and reconciled population.

In further proof of their good feeling I may mention that, since we occupied the capital and the other chief towns of Upper Burma, although our soldiers freely mix with the people and might frequently be taken at a disadvantage, not a single murder or act of violence has been committed against them, while our detached parties, on their arrival at the various villages of the outlying districts, are spontaneously furnished by the inhabitants with supplies of water, and received with every token of goodwill. Nor can there be any doubt that the prospect of the substitution of a strong and orderly Government for the incompetent and cruel tyranny of their former ruler is regarded with general satisfaction by the inhabitants of all those parts of the country to which we have penetrated.

The removal of the late King to a place of security in India having been duly effected, it becomes a matter of urgent necessity to decide under what kind of Government Upper Burma is to be placed. The Proclamation of the 1st of January declared the province to be from thenceforth an integral portion of Her Majesty's dominions. It has also placed the administration under the personal superintendence of the Viceroy. The latter part of this arrangement, however, manifestly possesses a provincial character, and must be replaced by a more satisfactory and permanent régime. I will now proceed to discuss the alternative dispositions which have presented themselves to my mind.

Being most reluctant to add unnecessarily to our Imperial responsibilities, I first considered the possibility of restricting our interference to the barest minimum by confining it to such precautionary measures as would do no more than prevent for the future the open or surreptitious introduction of inconvenient foreign influences into the upper valley of the Irrawaddy. In other words I asked myself whether it might not be possible to transform Burma, to use an expression now become familiar, into a "buffer" state. Under this arrangement, the Native Alompra dynasty would have remained upon the throne; the ruling Prince, like the Amir of Afghanistan, would have been perfectly independent in matters of internal administration, and all that we should have required would have been the right to supervise his external relations. In fact, he would have become what the late King would have remained had he accepted our original proposals, an autocratic, though confederated sovereign. On closer examination, however, and with more detailed information at my disposal, this scheme did not appear feasible. The kingdom of Ava has neither the elasticity nor the ultimate power of resistance which a "buffer state" ought to possess, as our recent expedition has clearly shown. The maintenance by artificial means of its independence on the great line of communication between our Burmese possessions and

China was evidently a contrivance of more than doubtful utility. It would certainly prove an obstacle to free commercial intercourse, and its weakness might tempt the Government of Pekin to assert over it, in a serious manner, those shadowy and, as I believe, unfounded claims to suzerainty which the Chinese Ambassador has recently put forward for diplomatic purposes. Under any circumstances it is a question whether a semi-protected state can be advantageously established on the confines of the Empire. The very principle of protection, even in its most attenuated form, implies responsibilities out of proportion to our means of discharging them, and goes very far towards placing it in the power of the ruler we patronised to drag us into a war against our will by provoking his neighbours into aggressions, which, whether justified or not, it might become necessary for us to resist. Nor must we forget that only a year ago a band of Chinese adventurers took and kept possession of Bhamo for some weeks, while so weak was the Native Government that its troops were unable to recover the place until bribery came to their assistance. A similar enterprise might be undertaken hereafter on a larger scale and under more formidable auspices. In such an event, our intervention would become a necessity, but it would be exercised under the worst possible conditions as long as the military command and resources of the country remained in the hands of a chief alike incapable of husbanding his revenues or disciplining his battalions. Moreover, such a personage would always be jealous of our interference, and would probably prove at the most critical moment unreasonable and obstructive, and perhaps disloyal. The country is not rich enough to support a British auxiliary contingent in addition to the court and army of a king, and as we certainly could not well garrison the frontier at our own expense, it would of necessity be left exposed to such risks as I have indicated.

The next alternative which I examined was that of maintaining Upper Burma as a fully protected state, with a native dynasty and native officials, but under a British Resident, who should exercise a certain control over the internal administration, as well as over its relations with foreign powers.

According to this scheme Upper Burma would assume a status similar to that of many Native States in India proper. I was the more induced to favour such an arrangement, as I had been very favourably impressed by the attitude of the princes and by the condition of the native communities I had recently visited in Rajputana and Central India; but it soon became apparent that there was very little real analogy between the territories in question and Upper Burma. The princes of India are for the most part highly civilised, intelligent, and capable persons, and are generally anxious not only to cultivate the most friendly relations with us, but to assimilate the administration of their states with that of the adjoining provinces under direct British rule. The Burmese rulers, on the contrary, belong to a totally different world ; the order of their ideas has been as incomprehensible to us as that of ours to them, while their conception of their own superiority to all created beings has rendered even ordinary diplomatic intercourse between themselves and other nations impossible. Even those of the Burmese dignitaries who, in their own personal interest and as established court favourites, are anxious for the maintenance of a native dynasty on the throne, frankly admit that there would be no hope of improvement so long as the real power was wielded by a descendant of Alompra. It would be necessary, they assert, to place all effective authority in their own hands under the direction of a British Resident, and to maintain the king as a mere puppet. To any arrangement of this kind there are manifestly grave objections. A puppet king of the Burmese type would prove a very expensive, troublesome, and contumacious fiction. Nor do the notables who thus propose to rule in the Royal name as Mayors of the Palace present the necessary guarantees that the power entrusted to them would be properly exercised. Under King Thibaw some of them undoubtedly took an active part in the massacres which justly roused the indignation of the civilised world, and some of them are well known to have been in league with the dacoits who ravaged the country.

But even were the establishment of a Protected state a measure desirable in itself, we are met by the difficulty that there is no prince of the Royal House to whom the trust could be safely confided. Had the Nyaung Yan Prince lived, such a course might perhaps have deserved, in his interests, a certain amount of serious consideration. The only living member of the Alompra family whose abilities and influence would make him even a respectable candidate is the Myngun Prince now resident at Pondicherry. But the principal claim of this personage to notoriety is the fact that he tried to murder his father, and succeeded in killing his uncle. In any case, it is probable that his feelings towards us are unfriendly. Having been brought over from Burma to India, where he was interned, he escaped and took refuge with the French, whom he now naturally regards as his patrons. Even did we countenance his accession, he could not without the aid of British bayonets, restore order to Upper Burma or maintain himself upon the throne against the numerous other aspirants of his House, and the successful assertion of his authority would be certain to prove the signal for the re-integration of commercial, if not of political, intrigues and jobbery at Mandalay adverse to British interests. The Nyaung Oke Prince, now in Bengal, is unpopular in Burma, and of unsatisfactory character. The difficulty of establishing him in power at Mandalay would be even greater than in the case of the Myngun Prince, and the result of the experiment would probably prove disastrous. None of the other adult princes are men of any note or influence, or command any substantial following in the country.

Having rejected, then, the idea of placing on the throne a prince endowed with the ordinary status of an Indian feudatory, I proceeded to consider whether it might not be desirable to set up the minor son of the late Nyaung Yan as the destined occupant of the vacant throne, with British officers administering the state in his name and on his behalf until he should come of age fifteen years hence; but it was at once apparent that this would impose upon us all the trouble, anxiety, and cost of a British occupation, without securing us any corresponding advantages in the present, while we should be committing ourselves in the distant future to an arrangement which, in the end, would probably disappoint our expectations, and to a prince who might prove totally unfitted to play the part designed for him. It was with considerable regret that I thus felt myself constrained to abandon the idea of maintaining the old dynasty in one form or another on the throne of Burma, for I had always understood that the prestige of the Alompra family had great influence with the Burmese, and I had hoped to utilise it in the cause of order. It is to be observed, however, that the loyalty of the people is exhibited as often by their tendency to support successive ephemeral pretenders, whenever a son of the Royal House is able to escape from the prison in which all the king's children are generally confined, as by any exhibition of active devotion to the *de facto* sovereign.

The foregoing alternatives not affording a desirable solution of the question, the possibility occurred to me of permanently placing the civil administration of the country in the hands of British officers, at the same time that the position occupied by its former kings was assumed by a Llama or some similar ecclesiastical dignitary such as is found in other Buddhist States. By this means it might be possible, I imagined, to give a certain amount of satisfaction to that national sentiment with which the Burmese, in common with all other people, must be credited, to console them for the disappearance of their own Royal House and to secure a satisfactory channel for maintaining those ambiguous relations with China which, though proved by the Burmese to have been devoid of any recognition of inferiority, are asserted by the Marquis Tseng to have implied the acknowledgment of his Emperor's suzerain rights; but such a dignitary, though a less sensitive centre than a king and his court in respect to foreign influences, might very possibly have proved a source of future embarrassment. At all events the idea possessed too experimental a character to have justified its proposal as a practical solution of the problem.

On the whole, therefore, I am convinced that annexation, pure and simple, and the direct administration of the province by British officers, offers the best prospect of securing the peace and prosperity of Upper Burma and our own Imperial and commercial interests. This decision no doubt imposes upon us serious obligations and responsibilities and is for a time certain to involve a great increase of anxiety, and possibly considerable extra expenditure. But no other course is really open to us, and in the end I have no doubt that we shall be repaid for any temporary trouble and annoyance by increased security within our own districts and upon our eastern frontiers, as well as by the development of trade and of the general resources of the new province.

It has not unnaturally been suggested that the deposition of Thibaw and the absorption of his territories may raise uneasy feelings in the minds of our Indian feudatories. This is a matter as to which I have made very careful enquiry, and I am quite convinced that the objection is unsubstantial. The Indian Princes take but little interest in our proceedings in Burma. They are not linked by either political or religious sympathy with the Burmese dynasty, whose sole connection with India in past ages was that of a hostile and aggressive power. They recognise clearly that Thibaw's position was essentially distinct from their own, and that their relations to the British Government stand upon a perfectly different footing. If the rapid subjugation and summary punishment of the Burmese King has had any effect whatever upon their minds, I should anticipate its serving to convince them that hostile or dubious intrigues with foreign powers are not likely to be tolerated by the British Government, and can only bring ruin upon those who engage in them.

Again, it is only by annexation and the establishment of a British administration that we can hope to rescue Upper Burma from the state of lawlessness and anarchy in which many parts of it are plunged. The country has at all times, and even under its best princes, suffered from the depredations of gang robbers or dacoits--recruited not only from among the bad characters of the towns and villages of Burma proper, but from the Shans and other hill tribes of the surrounding mountain tracts. Under Thibaw's maladministration these chronic outbreaks were greatly intensified and extended; and the ill-directed efforts of his Ministers have failed to suppress them, even in the neighbourhood of the capital. Indeed it is universally believed that the relations of more than one of the *Hlutdaw* with dacoits were friendly and mutually profitable. Nor can it be denied that recent events, the disbandment of the late King's troops, and the confusion and uncertainty which the overthrow of the Native Government must for a time engender, have supplied them with additional recruits and a fresh stimulant. There is indeed a curious element of restlessness in the Burmese character which gives a great deal of trouble in Lower Burma, and invariably develops into crime under the influence of popular excitement or of any inviting opportunity. Nothing is more common than for a young man who was yesterday tilling his fields, to all appearance a respectable and well-disposed cultivator, suddenly to disappear from his home and attach himself for a time to a gang of professional dacoits, in order to test the novelty and delight of an adventurous onslaught upon villages in another neighbourhood. When men of settled occupation can thus behave, it is of course quite natural that the unemployed or idle members of the community (and in Burma the industry of the women supports a large idle class) should join such gangs when dacoity is rife. The people generally, while light-hearted and engaging in many ways, have a strain of savagery and cruelty in their disposition which breaks out at times into wanton exercise, and can only be repressed by firm and even severe handling. It is a mistake to suppose that the dacoits who are now disturbing the peace of many districts in Upper Burma, and whose incursions into Lower Burma caused for a time so much anxiety to the local officers, are chiefly bands of patriots or partisan warriors opposing the invasion of their country by a foreign power. Their object for the most part is plunder, and their attacks are principally directed, not against our parties or posts, as the fact of only seven British rank and file having fallen during the whole campaign sufficiently proves, but against the defenceless villages of their own countrymen, who apply for and welcome our patrols and columns as their only defence against their inroads. It is true that larger bodies, recruited from the disbanded soldiery and the more necessitous and adventurous portion of the population, may occasionally gather to a head under the standard of some prince, and in right of their numbers be entitled to claim a more honourable designation than the bands of pillagers technically known as "dacoits," but it must be remembered that even these princes are fighting each for his own hand and his own personal ascendancy, and are not banded in a common cause against us. Whether, however, we call them dacoits, robbers, partisans, insurgents, rebels, or patriots, it is equally certain that in the interests of the community at large they must be summarily put down, though the execution of this task should be conducted in as humane, forbearing, and considerate a manner as possible.

Much has, I am glad to find, been done by Mr. Bernard and General Prendergast to restore order, and the tracts to which they have been able to post British civil officers with an adequate protective force are now for the most part quiet and safe. When the districts which have been thus far left in charge of the *Hlutdaw*, or supreme native council, are similarly taken over, I have no doubt that similar results will follow, at any rate in the more open and accessible parts of the country.

We must not, however, anticipate that we shall be able to repress or prevent disturbance all at once, or a recrudescence of disturbance hereafter. The very causes which made our conquest of Upper Burma an easy task render difficult its complete and permanent pacification. The Burmese are credulous and childish, and appear to be unable to appreciate facts until these have been unmistakably brought home to them. There is, apart from the Royal House, no aristocracy or leading class in the country. All are, owing to the monastic schools, at about the same level of education. There are no rich men,[1] just as, thanks to the sparseness of the population, there are no poor. Even the priesthood has no special power, since any man may assume the *hpongyi's* robe, and all must do so once at least in their lives, while any *hpongyi* can at his pleasure renounce his vows and return to lay life, "becoming," as the phrase is, "a man again." We have therefore to deal with a population made up of disintegrated units, each thinking and acting for himself, rather than with masses or class combinations on whom the influence either of advantage or of fear can be brought effectually to bear. It will be a work consequently of time, as we know from experience in Lower Burma, to convince the disorderly and ill-disposed that we intend them to receive us as their rulers and to respect our standard of civic discipline and political morality. The situation, moreover, is undoubtedly complicated by the fact of any Alompra Prince under the Native Government having been always able to obtain some sort of following whenever he attempted to raise his flag and strike a blow for the throne. Hence the jealousy with which the reigning monarch kept his near relatives shut up within the palace, and hence the terrible massacres of the royal kin which from time to time took place in Mandalay. Hence also the close seclusion of the King himself within his palace, as any excursion outside exposed him to the risk of attack from some one or other of his relatives who might have gathered round him a band of followers. On one of the rare occasions when Thibaw's father, who was undoubtedly a respectable ruler, had proceeded to a summer-house at no great distance from the city, he was attacked by his own son, the Myngun Prince, to whom I have already referred. The heir-apparent was killed, and the King barely escaped with his life by the back-door of the summer-house in which he was sleeping. The monarchy not being strictly hereditary, every prince was a possible king, and never abandoned the hope of being able some day to secure the throne. There are now wandering about the jungle not less than five of these princes, to say nothing of pretenders, each with his small party of followers. But the objects and procedure of these gangs differ little from those of ordinary dacoits. The princes themselves are men of no importance or influence apart from the accident of their birth, and when the ammunition of their followers fails, their adherents will probably disperse of their own accord, if they are not sooner broken up by our troops. Mr. Bernard consequently anticipates that order will be more or less restored in Upper Burma before the setting in of the rains, if British officers are placed at once in charge of all the districts; but he is

1 According to the Buddhist custom of obtaining merit for future existences by building pagodas, monasteries, etc., any Burman who became rich invested his money in these public works, which now abound all over the country.

afraid that some months afterwards, when the crops are sown, and the season of idleness returns, there may be some reiteration of our present troubles. In a year or two, however, we ought to have the whole country reasonably quiet. When we remember how long dacoity lasted after our occupation of Bengal; that thirty years ago the neighbourhood of Calcutta was rendered unsafe by gangs of dacoits; that within a still more recent period it was impossible to wander three or four miles out of Poona without a guard; and that there is at the present moment a dacoit leader at large in the Central Provinces who has for years defied all the efforts to capture him put forth by our own police and by those of several Native States, there is no reason to be dissatisfied with the prospect before us, or impatient at the progress already made.

In dealing with this part of the subject, the Government of India has been naturally anxious to assure itself that in repressing the disturbances which have been troubling the peace of the country, no unnecessary rigour has been employed. I have already noted the strong injunctions laid upon General Prendergast to act, not merely with humanity, but in an exceptionally kind and conciliatory manner towards the people. These injunctions appear to me to have been conscientiously fulfilled. For a brief period, and while our troops were actually in the presence of an enemy, martial law of necessity prevailed, and martial law is always a hateful expedient, and liable to abuse in the hands of inexperienced or excitable officers; but the moment the military situation was assured, Mr. Bernard was invested with full civil jurisdiction over the province and directed to administer it accordingly. A number of civil officers have been placed at his disposal, and the Chief Commissioner assures me that the captured dacoits have been invariably tried and sentenced by the latter, though the carrying out of the capital sentences has necessarily been entrusted to the military authorities. He adds that none but men caught red-handed, and fresh from rapine and murder, have been subjected to the penalty of death. However terrible the necessity for such a procedure, it is the most merciful course in the end. Violent crime can only be controlled by a certain amount of rigour, and the peaceful inhabitants of the country, whom we are now bound to protect by every means in our power, would have a just right to complain if, through undue leniency, the burning and plundering of their villages, accompanied, as it often is, by cruel forms of torture and murder, were encouraged rather than suppressed. Subject, however, to the foregoing considerations, I have requested Mr. Bernard to be extremely cautious in sanctioning any death sentences whatever. In doing this, I have only suggested the course to which the well-known humanity of his nature is already predisposed.

It would have been more satisfactory before proceeding to arrange our future organization had we been in the possession of fuller information as to the resources, revenues, and internal administration of the country under its Native Government. We are at present, moreover, somewhat uncertain in regard to the attitude likely to be assumed by the Shan States, as well as to the probable action of China upon our northern frontier. I hope, before leaving Mandalay, to arrange for the early despatch of an officer, with a small protecting column, to bear conciliatory messages to the Shan Chiefs; and I understand that the Foreign Office has reason to anticipate that China is disposed to meet us in a friendly spirit, and will assist in the re-establishment of the frontier trade.

The attempt to restore order and to govern through the *Hlutdaw* has, in the opinion of all competent observers, hopelessly broken down. It was indeed hardly possible to expect otherwise. Men trained in an atmosphere of palace intrigue, whose sole object in life has been their own security and advancement, and who had notoriously failed to manage the country efficiently under the late king, hardly constituted an agency on which reliance could be placed under the novel and difficult circumstances in which they were called upon to act. I have satisfied myself that, although we may make use of a few of the best of the *Hlutdaw* as a consultative body, to be associated with the head of the British administration in Upper Burma, and may find place for some of the inferior members in district offices throughout the country, the *Hlutdaw* must, as an Executive Council of State, be broken up and abolished.

It is the unanimous opinion of all the officers whom I have been able to consult that it is not desirable to attempt to administer Upper Burma by executive orders issued under the authority of the Viceroy. The legal position of British officers acting under such orders is obviously precarious, and I see no sufficient ground for declining to annex the country formally to British India, provided only that nothing be done, in the present state of affairs, to extend to it any portion of the Indian Statute Law. Simultaneously, therefore, with the declaration of annexation to British India, I would ask the Secretary of State to make an order in Council under 33 Vic., cap. 3, section 1, extending that section to the whole territory of Upper Burma outside the Shan States. This will enable the local administration to frame simple regulations for the approval of the Governor-General in Council, providing for all matters which it is desirable to settle upon a definite legal basis, such as the administration of justice, the judicial powers of officers, the powers of the police, and the collection of the revenue. The Regulations should be so shaped as to leave to the local administration a large discretionary power of settling details by rules which can be amended from time to time as experience may dictate. The spirit of the Indian Code would be followed as far as practicable in framing the Regulations, but nothing so elaborate as the Indian judicial system is called for at present, and any attempt to introduce it would be mischievous.

I propose to administer the country at first in a simple way and as far as may be upon indigenous lines, so as to render the change of Government as little irksome and disturbing to the people as possible. The Shan Chiefships will be treated as feudatory or tributary states without attempting to bring them under any direct administrative control.

Legislation would, under any circumstances, be necessary to give validity in British India to the decrees and sentences of the Upper Burma judicial authorities. There are now in Lower Burma jails numerous dacoits sentenced by the civil officers in the Upper Province. Effect must, of course, be given to these sentences, even if the new territory is not to be annexed to British India. There are no jails in Upper Burma suitable for the confinement of long-term prisoners. If the Statute 33 Vic., cap. 3, section 1, is extended as I propose, the matter can easily be met by regulation under that statute. It will also be necessary to provide that European British subjects committing offences beyond the power of European district officers to try shall be committed to the Court of the Recorder of Rangoon. I would limit the powers of the district officers over European British subjects to those enjoyed by District Magistrates in India before the late amendment of the Criminal Procedure Code. This seems desirable, as no juries can be constituted in Upper Burma.

I propose that the Chief Commissioner of British Burma shall be also Chief Commissioner of Upper Burma. It appears to me both unnecessary and inexpedient to appoint a separate Chief Commissioner for the new territory. Lower Burma must continue to be the base of our operations, both civil and military. Upper Burma will, for instance, be mainly officered from the Lower Burma Commission; and it is important for this, if for no other reason, that the superior authority in both provinces should (subject to the control of the Government of India) remain in the same hands. On the other hand, the work in Lower Burma, though heavy in amount, runs upon lines which are thoroughly recognized and defined. In the present state of communications, and while the task of organizing the administration of the new province engages the energies of the Chief Commissioner and detains him in Upper Burma, it will be necessary to give him assistance in Lower Burma. This can best be done by appointing one of the Divisional Commissioners to be special assistant to the Chief Commissioner to carry on the ordinary work in the Chief Commissioner's name and upon his responsibility—referring to the Chief Commissioner any matters of importance, keeping him generally informed of what is going on below, and being guided by his instructions in the discharge of his duty. The Chief Commissioner would himself also from time to time visit Rangoon and keep himself acquainted with all matters affecting the well-being of his original charge. I consider it to be of great importance to take advantage in the settlement of Upper Burma of Mr. Bernard's remarkable energy and talent for organization, and I should hope that, when this task is successfully accomplished, the united provinces may very easily be administered by a single officer, the services of the special assistant being dispensed with.

I am inclined to accept Mr. Bernard's view that there should be at the outset no authority, such as Divisional Commissioners or Sessions Judges, interposed between the Chief Commissioner and the district officers. I would adopt, as I have already said, the simplest and cheapest system of administration open to us. There will be in each district or circle one British civil officer and one police officer. The civil officer will work through the indigenous agency of the country, *Myo-wuns*, *Thugyis*, and others, confining his efforts in the first instance to the restoration of order, the protection of life and property, and the assessment and collection of the ordinary revenue. I see no objection to the exercise by the police officer of magisterial powers in cases where he has not taken part in the preliminary investigation. This has been legalised in Assam and will be useful in Upper Burma. But most of the unimportant criminal work and nearly all the civil suits must be disposed of by the native officials, subject to the check and control of the district officer. Fortunately the people are not litigious, and I see no necessity for the establishment of distinct civil and criminal courts (except perhaps at Mandalay and in some of the larger towns) or for the encouragement of regular appeals and the introduction of pleaders and all the paraphernalia of our Indian courts. The native revenue officers will, in accordance with the existing custom of the country, be vested with civil and criminal powers. I do not propose to introduce our Indian Stamp Law, but would sanction the imposition of an *ad valorem* institution fee upon plaints in civil suits. This has been practically always levied under the native Government, but was usually appropriated by the Judge. It will now be credited to the State.

As regards revenue arrangements, we have been unable to discover any fiscal records or accounts. The *Hlutdaw* admit that such records existed, but allege that they were destroyed by the soldiery or other ill-disposed persons. The information gathered orally from different quarters is extremely indefinite and often contradictory. I propose to maintain at full rates the capitation or house-tax, which was the main source of revenue under the native Government. It is of vital importance that the necessary census or assessments should be carried out at once in order that the people may know what they have to expect from us in the shape of taxation. We shall engage that the rate of demand will not be liable to fluctuation from year to year, and that no unexpected cesses will be imposed upon them in the course of any year. Should it be necessary to increase the house-tax, six months' notice will be given before the commencement of the year in which the change is to take effect. The royal lands will, at the same time, have to be settled. The initial arrangements regarding those lands will be of a temporary character, but by degrees, as time permits, the district officers will lease them for adequate terms of years. I am not in favour of introducing the system of land settlement now being carried out in Lower Burma. I think we should complete the work there first, and hereafter, should it be deemed advisable, extend the system gradually and cautiously from below upwards, that the people may not be disturbed by the sudden introduction of a régime of which they have no knowledge or experience. As regards currency, I have authorized the temporary acceptance in Upper Burma of the native silver coinage, which is but slightly inferior in value to that of British India. But arrangements for calling this in will be elaborated hereafter in communication with the Financial Department.

Mr. Bernard proposes to constitute 15 Deputy Commissioners' charges and 5 Assistant Commissioners' charges. All to be officered by Europeans, *viz.* :—

District or Deputy Commissioners' charges ..	1. Minhla. 2. Myingyan. 3. Mandalay. 4. Ava. 5. Sagain. 6. Shwebo. 7. Myadaung. 8. Upper Chindwin. 9. Lower Chindwin. 10. Ningyan. (Pyinmana.) 11. Yamethin. 12. Bhamo. 13. Mogamey. 14. Tabayin. 15. Shan States.
Sub-Divisional or Assistant Commissioners' charges..	1. Taungdwingyi. 2. Pagan. 3. Kyauksé. 4. Sabenago. 5. Myinmu.

Large as this number of charges appears to be, it is probably not more than is requisite for the control and efficient management of such wide tracts of country where the means of communication have for the most part to be created. It is, I believe, true economy to start at once with an adequate staff, as in this way we shall the sooner pacify the country and the more effectually realise our revenue demands. It will be possible, by placing selected police officers in charge of the Arakan Hill Tracts and the Salween Hill Tract in Lower Burma, to reduce the number of Deputy Commissioners there by two, and Mr. Bernard further proposes to officer the Sandoway district entirely with Burmese officials. This reduces the number of extra civil officers demanded by Mr. Bernard to 13 Deputy Commissioners, 5 Assistant Commissioners for sub-divisions, 3 Assistant Commissioners to fill furlough vacancies, or 21 in all. It appears probable that the Upper Chindwin district may for a time be managed by the Political Agent in Manipur, and I am considering the propriety of handing over the Kubo valley to the Manipur State as a reward for the services rendered by the Raja's troops on the Chindwin river. This, if carried out, would reduce the number of Deputy Commissioners by one, but such an arrangement would in any case be only temporary, and I agree that we must find 21 additional civil officers for the Burma Commission. It is proposed to distribute them as follows :—

	Present strength.	Proposed addition.	Total.
Deputy Commisionars, I Grade..	4	2	6
" " II "	4	2	6
" " III "	6	4	10
" " IV "	6	5	11
Assistant Commissioners, I "	5	1	6
" " II "	6	2	8
" " III "	5	3	8
" " IV "	18	2	20
	54	21	75

As most of the higher appointments will fall to officers already in the British Burma Commission (who, from their knowledge of the language and people, must be employed in Upper Burma, in preference to untried men), it will be unnecessary to give at once the whole of the 13 steps among the Deputy Commissioners or of the six steps among the Assistant Commissioners of Grades I to III. If 10 of these steps are given now and 9 two years hence, there will be a considerable money saving at starting. Some Assistant Commissioners may temporarily work as district officers with the hope of eventual promotion before them. But service in Burma is, under all circumstances, unpopular, and the province is very expensive as a residence. I do not, therefore, think that we can permanently place the staff on any lower scale. Indeed, if the revenues develop as we hope they may do, it will be necessary hereafter to strengthen and enlarge the staff. If only half the steps are given now, those officers in the Commission who make sacrifices in going to Upper Burma can be suitably rewarded, and the recruits who will come in at the bottom of the list will not receive promotion until they have become qualified for it two years hence. One of the Deputy Commissioners provided in the scale will be Superintendent of the Shan States. The actual number of new districts thus created in British Indian territory will therefore be only 14.

As regard the Police, it will be necessary to appoint a European Superintendent to each of the 14 civil districts and to allow 5 Assistant Superintendents, including those required to supply the places of absentees. There must also be a separate Inspector-General for Upper Burma. It is proposed to arrange the increased Police staff of the United Provinces thus :—

	Present strength.	Proposed addition.		TOTAL.	
Inspector-General	1	1	1	2	2
District Superintendents, I Grade	2	2	1	4	3
,, ,, II ,, ...	2	2	1	4	3
,, ,, III ,, ...	2	2	1	4	3
,, ,, IV ,, ...	4	4	2	8	6
,, ,, V ,, ...	8	4	2	12	10
Assistant Superintendents, I ,, ...	3	3	3	6	6
,, ,, II ,, Class A ..	9	2	9	11	18
,, ,, ,, ,, ,, B ..	9	..	..	9	9
	40	20	20	60	60

In the same way as with civil officers only about one-half the extra steps would be given at once, the remainder being held over for two years. The figures in antique show the number of posts that would have to be added immediately to each grade of the present Police cadre under this arrangement.

For the hill tracts of the Chindwin and for the posts along the Shan frontier I propose to raise two military police battalions, each 500 strong, under a smart young military officer as Commandant. The majority of the men would probably come from the Punjab and Upper India. Their duties would be essentially military, and they would relieve the troops of outpost duty in jungle tracts in the way recently carried out with much success on the Assam frontier. Under the District Superintendent of each civil district would also be placed a small body of military police to repress disturbance and put down dacoity. But I propose to keep the civil constabulary within the lowest limits possible, as such an institution is very expensive. Each *Wun* and *Thugyi* would have a few Burman police peons attached to his court to execute processes and deal, under his orders, with petty crime. A few Burmans would also be at the disposal of the District Superintendent for detective purposes. But experience in Lower Burma has shown that the Burmans make perhaps the worst and most costly policemen in the world, and I do not wish to have more of them than is absolutely necessary. All the military police should be well drilled, be kept under strict discipline, and be armed with Snider rifle carbines. The Burmese police should be armed only with batons, and perhaps *dahs.*

I have allowed both civil and police officers employed in Upper Burma to draw daily travelling allowance up to the 30th June next, as some small compensation for the exposure and hard work they are at present undergoing. When the rains set in, their work will be reduced and ordinary rules may begin to apply. I have also agreed to assist officers in housing themselves by granting them a subvention at the rate of one-half the total cost of any house built by an officer up to a maximum subsidy of Rs. 1,500 in the case of a district officer, and Rs. 1,000 in the case of sub-divisional officer or police officer.

The public works expenditure must for the present be limited mainly to the construction of the buildings absolutely necessary for the accommodation of troops, and to the development of military communications. Civil buildings will be as few and as cheap as possibie, but proper arrangements must be made for the safe custody of treasure. The Chief Commissioner will be left a wide discretion in the disposal of any sum set apart for this purpose. Generally, in the matter of expenditure, I propose to allow the Chief Commissioner the same powers as he now exercises in Lower Burma in respect of provincial charges, the only essential limitation being that he must not exceed the total amount of the Budget grant. It is not proposed to make any provision for educational expenditure or for outlay under the head of Minor Departments; and the expenditure on civil hospitals and dispensaries must be kept as low as possible. The jail accommodation will be limited to the provision of safe sleeping wards for prisoners. The convicts retained in the province must ordinarily be employed on extramural work, dangerous and long-term men being transferred to Lower Burma. I shall arrange to relieve the jails of Lower Burma by transfers to the Andamans and to the central jails of India. The number of our prisoners, I regret to say, is very large, but as soon as the country is settled, I see no reason why a very great proportion of them should not be set at liberty. Indeed, I have thought it good policy to authorize Mr. Bernard to make an announcement to this effect, as all those interested in their welfare will thus have an additional inducement for ranging themselves on the side of order.

I consider it a matter of the utmost importance to commence at a very early date the construction of the railway from Toungoo to Mandalay. This line is necessary, both on political and military grounds, placing, as it would, Mandalay within 24 hours' journey of Rangoon. It will also have a material influence on the early pacification of the districts bordering on the Shan States. It will pass through a tract of country believed to be the richest in Upper Burma, and would not be in immediate competition with the Irrawaddy waterway. I would prefer keeping it as a State railway, but, as perhaps the Secretary of State might object to further borrowing by the Government of India on account of railway construction, it might be necessary to call in the aid of a guaranteed company, transferring to it the existing State lines in Lower Burma. I have authorized the Chief Commissioner to commence the survey of the probable course of the line from Toungoo to Ningyan (Pyinmana). This can be undertaken at once, as that part of the country is now quite orderly. I should be ready to offer reasonable concessions to any company that would construct a steam tram-line from the river to the Palace at Mandalay. The transport of stores over the four miles of intervening road would be greatly facilitated by such a line, and the local traffic would probably make it pay. The line would eventually have to be made over to the Railway Company when the railway is opened to Mandalay.

I have arranged that the regular survey of Upper Burma shall be taken in hand as soon as the pacification of the districts is sufficiently advanced. It is important also to arrive at an early estimate of the value of the mineral wealth of the country, and an officer of the Geological Department will be placed at the disposal of the Chief Commissioner for this purpose. Meantime, I have submitted to the Secretary of State Mr. Bernard's proposal that the Ruby Mines should be made over to the firm of Gillanders, Arbuthnot & Co. on a three-year lease, on condition of their paying to us the annual revenue of two lakhs of rupees which the mines are estimated to have yielded to the former Government.[1] This firm undertakes to employ native agency, to import machinery and to allow a full inspection of their working, books, and accounts. Under these arrangements we shall, at the end of three years, have a good idea of what the mines are really worth and can make more permanent arrangements. It is not proposed to compel the delivery to Government of all stones above a certain size. It is believed that the only effect of this provision under the late Government was to cause the concealment or breaking up of all the large stones. The Jade Mines will, for the present, be left in the hands of the present lessee, a Chinaman, on the same conditions as to revenue and inspection of works and books. In the earth-oil tracts the civil officers will issue prospecting licenses to hold good for one year, and to be superseded thereafter by leases of limited areas for working. Existing wells will continue to be worked as at present, paying as a royalty.

Nearly the whole area of teak forest in Upper Burma is at present in the hands of the Bombay-Burma Trading Corporation. The leases under which they hold are of the most vague and unsatisfactory description. I am

[1] Subsequently higher tenders were made by other firms for working these mines, the highest bid being four lakhs of rupees by Messrs. Streeter & Co. However, it was found that further enquiries must be made before the true value of the mines could be ascertained, and pending this none of these tenders were accepted.

considering what terms we can equitably concede to this company, having due regard to the future of Forest Conservancy in Upper Burma. The Corporation in the meantime continue to pay the rents set out in their engagement with the late King. The claims of other lessees will be similarly dealt with.

Numerous claims against the late Government or against the King and Queen personally are being presented to the Chief Commissioner at Mandalay. Without prejudging the question of the extent to which the British Government is bound to satisfy such claims, I have directed Mr. Bernard to receive all that may be filed before the 1st April next, and to submit as soon as possible to the Government of India a full report upon the whole question as well as upon each individual claim. In the meantime, however, I have authorized Mr. Bernard to take into his immediate consideration the claims of those European foreigners whose departure it is desirable to facilitate, and to deal with them in a liberal spirit. Eventually it will probably be well to place a lump sum at the Chief Commissioner's disposal, and to authorize him to make a fair compromise of all claims which appear to rest upon sufficient evidence, and to be otherwise such as a conquering Government ought equitably to satisfy.

Much consideration has been given to the financial prospects of the newly acquired territory. Upper Burma is poorer and less fertile than Lower Burma; and the Pegu Province, which now yields a large surplus to the Imperial exchequer, did not pay its expenses during the first eight or ten years after annexation. It appears that 100 to 105 lakhs was the largest revenue from Upper Burma that ever reached the late King's exchequer in any one year. Out of this total, 25 lakhs to 35 lakhs were the proceeds of customs, monopolies, and transit dues which we shall not retain. I have asked the Chief Commissioner, assisted by Mr. Jacob of the Financial Department, to estimate as accurately as they can, the receipts and expenditure of Upper Burma for the year 1886–87. Their forecast must be regarded at the best as tentative and imperfect, but it is put forward as the nearest approximation which can be made on the materials at present available.

It is estimated that we may be able to collect 66½ lakhs of revenue during the year if the pacification of the country proceeds satisfactorily. As regards the present financial year, its revenue was forestalled by the late Government; and we do not expect to realize more than two lakhs before the 31st March 1886.

The expenditure side of the Civil Budget comes to a total of about 37½ lakhs, in which the largest items are land revenue 9¼ lakhs; law and justice 5¾ lakhs; and police 15½ lakhs. Half of the land revenue charge is on account of commission payable, by the custom of the country, to *thugyis*, or local revenue officials. The total charge for magisterial and revenue officers and establishments at district and sub-divisional posts is eight lakhs, of which about one-half falls under "Land Revenue" and one-half under "Law and Justice." An outside grant of 10 lakhs is proposed for public works; which for the present will, as already stated, be mainly confined to barracks, military buildings, and military communications. Roads are greatly wanted throughout the country, in which at present not a single mile of bridged or metalled road exists. But until the revenues increase, or more of the Lower Burma surplus can be devoted to the improvement of the sister provinces, we cannot embark upon a system of very extensive road construction. Happily Upper Burma possesses a considerable length of excellent waterways ; and the railway to Mandalay will open up a great stretch of land-locked country.

It is reckoned that the extra military charges due to the occupation of Upper Burma will amount to about 30 lakhs during the year 1886–87. At present there are nearly 17,000 troops in the two provinces of Upper and Lower Burma ; but this garrison will probably be largely reduced when the police are organized and the country is pacified.

The net financial outcome for the coming year resulting from the annexation of the new territory will be somewhat as follows :—

	Lakhs.
Total revenues	66½
Total charges [1]	77½
Deficit ..	11

This financial forecast takes no count of the claims which may have to be paid in respect of the debts due by the late Government, because charges of that kind are hardly debitable to the first year of British administration. In future years we may fairly anticipate a considerable increase to the revenue, while it is certain that there will be a large decrease in the military expenditure. On the other hand, as in all other newly acquired provinces, there will assuredly be a growth in the cost of the civil administration, as well as on account of what it will be necessary to do for the general improvement of the province and the development of its resources.

In the foregoing paragraphs I have alluded, in a very casual manner, to the effect which annexation may have upon our relations with China. I have, however, previously submitted to Her Majesty's Government my strong conviction that it is a matter of great importance to secure the acquiescence of China in any settlement which may be arrived at. When the propriety of issuing the annexation proclamation of the 1st of January was under discussion, the Government of India specially called the attention of the Secretary of State to the possible effect such an announcement might produce at Pekin. They did not, however, consider themselves justified in doing more than this, for the obvious reason that the diplomatic elements of the problem were in

[1] Only the *extra*, not the total Military, charges are here included, as has been explained above.

the hands of the English Foreign Office and were beyond their knowledge and competence. I have already noted the manner in which, at one time, I thought it might be possible to satisfy all the possible requirements of China, without compromising Her Majesty's dignity or interfering with the direct administration of Burmese affairs by British officers. But, if the Secretary for Foreign Affairs, to whom the consideration of the point principally belongs, sees no objection to such a procedure, the Government of India can have, of course, no objection to its representative in Burma continuing the practice of a friendly exchange of decennial presents with the Governor of Yunnan under such conditions as may suit the exigencies of the case. The wording, however, of the agreement embodying such an arrangement would have to be very carefully considered.

On reviewing the whole question which I have thus endeavoured imperfectly to examine, I feel that the circumstances of the case hardly permit me to hope that what I have said will carry anything approaching absolute conviction to the minds of Her Majesty's Government. There is so much uncertainty in all human affairs, and the forces, which may hereafter act upon the situation we are creating in Burma, are so various, uncertain, and remote, that even the most far-sighted and capable person could only give a guess at the best solution of the question. All decisions of the kind must be matters rather of perception than of logical demonstration. But I have the consolation of thinking that at all events, if experience should prove that the proposed régime is not so well calculated as I had hoped, to secure the end in view, the mistake can be more easily rectified than if any other alternative had been adopted. Had we at once proceeded to the constitution of a semi-independent, or even of a protected state, and to the investiture of an Alompra king or any other chief in the room of Thibaw, we should have committed ourselves to a step which could not have been retraced without the intervention of force and the infliction of wrong. No such sinister characteristics would, however, attach to the withdrawal of a Chief Commissioner and his subordinates from the province, should circumstances ever render it desirable hereafter to replace it under the domination of a native ruler.

In conclusion, I append a list of the numbers who have fallen on the field or have died of their wounds during the campaign up to the present date :—

British officers	4
Native officers	0
British soldiers	7
Native soldiers	10
TOTAL ..	21

Of the British Officers, one fell in the field, one was shot when he was reconnoitring, and two were accidentally surprised and cut down.

DUFFERIN.

MANDALAY,
The 17th February 1886.

APPENDIX V.

COPY OF THE LETTER AND ULTIMATUM ADDRESSED TO THE BURMESE ON 22ND OCTOBER 1885.

From E. S. Symes, Esq., C.S., Officiating Secretary to the Chief Commissioner, to His Excellency the Minister for Foreign Affairs at Mandalay, dated Rangoon, the 22nd October 1885.

I AM directed to acknowledge the receipt of your letter, dated the 4th October, on the subject of the decree for 23 lakhs of rupees which was passed by your Government against the Bombay–Burma Trading Corporation. In my letter, dated 28th August 1885, it was stated that the British Government could not acquiesce without further enquiry in the imposition of this enormous fine upon a British company. You were accordingly asked whether the Government of Ava would consent to refer the matters in dispute to an arbitrator to be deputed by His Excellency the Viceroy; and your Government was further requested to postpone for the present the execution of the decree. Your letter definitely rejects the Viceroy's proposal to refer the questions in dispute to an arbitrator, and refuses to permit any postponement in the execution of the decree against the Bombay-Burma Trading Corporation.

2. I am now to inform you that the Viceroy and Governor-General of India in Council is unable to accept this your reply. As the offer to depute an arbitrator has been rejected, the British Government must now insist upon the réception, by your Government at Mandalay, of an Envoy to be sent at once by His Excellency the Viceroy, and upon the settlement of the present dispute with the concurrence of the British Envoy. It will be necessary that the Envoy of the Viceroy should have free access to His Majesty the King, and that he should not be asked to submit to any humiliating ceremonies inconsistent with the diplomatic usage of Western nations.

3. Pending the arrival of the Envoy at Mandalay, I am to request that your Government will abstain from enforcing their claims against the Bombay-Burma Trading Corporation; and I am to intimate that if any action of the kind has been, or should be, taken, the Government of India will act in such way as may seem best to them without further communication to you.

4. I am further to inform you that the present and other recent incidents have shown the necessity for the permanent retention of a diplomatic Agent of the Viceroy at Mandalay. The Agent will be supplied by the Government of India with a British guard of honour, and a British steamer will be

furnished for his use. Your Government will be requested to provide him with a suitable residence near the river, and to accord him the honourable treatment to which he will be entitled as the Agent of His Excellency the Viceroy.

5. There are two other matters which I am to mention to you. The British Government will expect the Government of Ava in future to regulate the external relations of the realm in accordance with the advice of the Viceroy of India; and they will expect your Government to afford complete facilities for opening up British trade with China. These are matters the details of which can be settled hereafter by discussion between your Government and the British Envoy; but His Excellency the Viceroy desires to receive at once an intimation of the general acquiescence of your Government in his wishes on these subjects.

6. The present letter will be forwarded to you by the steamer *Ashley Eden* and will reach Mandalay by or before the 30th October. A second copy has been delivered to-day (the 22nd October) to Sayèdawgyi Maha Mindin Kyaw Thaw, the Commercial Agent in Rangoon of the Ava Government. The Chief Commissioner will expect to receive an answer from you on or before the 10th November. The steamer *Ashley Eden* has been chartered by the Government, and she will remain at Mandalay, provided she be unmolested, until the 5th November, in order to bring away your answer to my present letter. She will leave Mandalay without fail by the 6th November. If she does not bring a satisfactory reply from you, and if no satisfactory reply reaches me by the evening of the 10th November, the British Government will proceed to such action as they may deem fit.

7. Regarding the position of the servants of the Bombay-Burma Trading Corporation, and of other European and British subjects now resident or trading in the dominions of His Majesty the King I am to convey a solemn warning that any detention, injury, or ill-treatment of these persons by officials, soldiers, or other persons under the control of your Government will entail most serious consequences to the perpetrators and also to the officials or others who may countenance such action.

8. In conclusion, I am to request that you will be good enough to state clearly in your reply whether His Majesty the King accepts unconditionally the three first proposals now made, that is to say,—

(1) that an Envoy from the Viceroy and the Governor-General shall be suitably received at Mandalay, and that the present dispute between your Government and the Bombay-Burma Trading Corporation shall be settled with his concurrence;

(2) that all action against the Bombay-Burma Trading Corporation shall be suspended until the Envoy arrives;

(3) that for the future a diplomatic agent from the Viceroy shall reside at Mandalay, who shall receive becoming treatment at the hands of your Government, and shall be supplied by the British Government with a British guard of honour and a steamer.

I am to inform you that the Government of India will not be able to take into consideration any counter-proposals for the despatch of a Mission to Rangoon or Simla, or the like ; or to enter into any discussion regarding the three requirements of His Excellency the Viceroy above summarised. Any reply other than an unconditional acceptance of these three requirements, and a general acquiescence in the wishes of the Government of India on the two subjects referred to in paragraph 5 of this letter, will be regarded as a refusal of the proposals now made by the British Government.

The following is the text of the Burmese reply to the ultimatum.

Telegram from Chief Commissioner, British Burma, Rangoon, to Foreign Secretary, Viceroy's Camp.

My line-clear telegram of this morning told gist of reply to ultimatum. Following is text of translation of important parts :—

On demands 1 and 2, answer runs—

His Majesty was pleased to say that, although the judgment against Corporation was one passed in conformity with the law of the State, yet, if the Bombay-Burma Corporation presented a petition on the subject of the money decreed against them, he would be pleased to look after and assist foreign merchants and traders, so that they should not suffer any hardship. Therefore, with reference to the first and second points regarding the Corporation's forest case the need for discussion or negotiation is at an end.

On the third demand the answer says—

'The Burmese Government, through their wish to maintain friendly relations between the two countries, did not act in such a way as to restrict or put to hardship the British Agent formerly stationed at Mandalay, and yet he left of his own accord and there has been no Agent since. If the British Government wish in future to re-establish an Agent, he will be permitted to reside and come in and go as in former times.'

On the fourth demand, the answer says—

'The internal and external affairs of an independent State are regulated and controlled in accordance with the custom and law of that State. Friendly relations with France, Italy, and other States have been, are being, and will be maintained. Therefore, in the question as to whether one State alone can prefer such request, the Burmese Government can follow the joint decision of the three States,—France, Germany, and Italy, who are friends of both Governments.'

On the fifth demand, the answer says—

'The friendly relations of the two countries are based on assistance to be rendered for the increase of trade and of exports and imports from one country to the other. If, therefore, merchants and traders, whether of English or other races, ask the Burmese Government to endeavour to facilitate trade and the increase of exports and imports with China, they will be assisted in conformity with the customs of the land.'

APPENDIX VI.

THE TEXT OF THE LETTER PRESENTED TO GENERAL PRENDERGAST BY BURMESE MINISTER UNDER A FLAG OF TRUCE ON 26TH NOVEMBER 1885, AND OF GENERAL PRENDERGAST'S REPLY.

From His Excellency the Prime Minister, to Commander-in-Chief of the English War Vessels,—(dated 4th decrease of Tasoungmow, 1247 = 25th November 1885).

1. ALTHOUGH the treaty negotiated at Simla was not concluded, the Burmese Government were under the impression that the former friendly conditions would still prevail, and they could not, therefore, believe that the English Government would make war on Upper Burma.

2. The Burmese Government have always had at heart the welfare and prosperity of the English people. They have all along protected the interests of the Irrawaddy Company's teak trade and the general interests of all British subjects.

3. We are desirous of still further protecting British interests, so far as lies in our power, both at present and in all future time.

4. The last letter (ultimatum) forwarded by the English Government contained very important political matters, and our Sovereign regrets that the time allowed was too short to admit of serious deliberation.

5. The English Government ought to have known that the only reason why the Burmese Government in their reply to the said letter did not fully concede all the demands made was because we were not allowed sufficient time for deliberation. It must have been apparent from the tenour of our reply that the Burmese Government was desirous of remaining on terms of amity and friendship.

6. The Burmese Government did not wholly reject the rights and privileges claimed by the British Government, and we are grieved to find that the English Government, which has always been so friendly, in the present instance have made immediate war on us. We have simply resisted in order to maintain the reputation of the kingdom and the honour of the Burmese people.

7. The English are renowned for their just and straightforward action in all matters (political). We look forward, therefore, with confidence to their doing what is just and proper in the present instance.

8. The country of Burma is one which deserves justice and consideration. We believe that it will receive this consideration at the hands of the English Government.

9. If this is granted, the Kingdom of Burma need not be annexed. It is well to remember, too, that on a former occasion Her Most Gracious Majesty the Queen-Empress was pleased to declare publicly that there was no intention on the part of the English Government to annex Burma, unless such a step was necessitated on good cause shown.

As no such cause exists, the great powers of Europe should not have it in their power to say that the Royal declaration has not been faithfully observed.

10. In addition to the rights and privileges already granted in our reply to your ultimatum, His Majesty the King of Burma has now declared his will to concede all the other demands which were not at first allowed, because we had not sufficient time to bring them under consideration.

11. His Majesty the King is well disposed (in mind and heart). He is straightforward and just, and expects that the English Government will act in accordance with the wishes expressed in this letter.

12. By so doing, the world will have no cause to say that the English have acted unjustly, or with a disregard of international law.

13. The English Government entered our country and attacked us with a number of war vessels. We were obliged to resist. We now desire that hostilities shall cease; and we trust that the English Government will meet us half-way and enter into a treaty by which friendly intercourse may be resumed between the two great countries.

Reply.

General Prendergast begs to inform the Kin-Wun-Mingyi, in reply to his letter of this date, that, acting in accordance with the instructions he has received from the Viceroy and Governor-General of India, it is quite out of his power to accept any offer or proposals which would affect the movement of the troops under his command on Mandalay.

No armistice, therefore, can at present be granted; but if King Thibaw agrees to surrender himself, his army, and his capital to British arms, and if the European residents at Mandalay are all found uninjured in person and property, General Prendergast promises to spare the King's life and to respect his family.

He also agrees not to take further military action against Mandalay beyond occupying it with a British force, and stipulates that the matter in dispute between the two countries shall be negotiated on such terms as may be dictated by the British Government. A reply to this communication must be sent so as to reach General Prendergast before 4 A.M., to-morrow morning.

By order,

S. S. *Doowoon*,
The 26th November 1885.

(Sd.) E. B. SLADEN, *Colonel*,
Chief Civil Officer, Burma Field Force.

APPENDIX VII.

PROCLAMATION MADE BY GENERAL PRENDERGAST ON 15TH NOVEMBER 1885.

To all priests, officials, landholders, traders and other residents in the country of Upper Burma.

In consequence of the refusal of the Burmese Government to grant redress for various injuries inflicted upon British subjects and to accept the proposals made by the Viceroy and Governor-General of India for an amicable settlement of existing difficulties, I have received orders to advance with an armed force upon Mandalay.

The decision of the Government of India to send its troops into the territory of a neighbouring State has been arrived at very unwillingly, and must be regarded as the result of a long continued series of provocations. The reign of His Majesty King Thibaw has been marked throughout by the violation of treaties; by acts of aggression on the British frontier; by outrages upon British subjects and injustice to British traders; and by an external policy systematically opposed to British interest.

Misconstruing the forbearance which the British Government has shown with reference to these serious causes of complaint, His Majesty King Thibaw lately attempted to impose on a British Trading Company an arbitrary fine of ruinous amount, and peremptorily refused the conciliatory offer that the matter should be submitted to an impartial enquiry.

Under these circumstances the Government of India was constrained to address to His Majesty an ultimatum, demanding the acceptance of certain definite proposals for the settlement of this question and for the establishment upon a satisfactory basis of the future relations between the two countries.

These proposals have been met by an evasive reply and by the simultaneous issue of an openly hostile proclamation. The force under my orders has accordingly crossed the frontier for the purpose of exacting compliance with the demands of my Government.

Further, as it has become evident that there can be no hope of improvement in the condition of affairs in Upper Burma so long as the present occupant of the throne remains in power, the Government of India have decided that His Majesty shall cease to reign.

They have had the less hesitation in arriving at this decision from the fact that not only has King Thibaw exercised great oppression and cruelty towards his own subjects but that his administration has been allowed to fall into such a state of disorder as to fill the country with marauders and to expose the neighbouring British possessions to their inroads.

It is the earnest desire of the Viceroy and Governor-General of India that bloodshed should be avoided, and that the peaceful inhabitants of all classes should be encouraged to pursue their usual callings without fear of molestation.

None of you will have anything to apprehend so long as you do not oppose the passage of the troops under my command. Your private rights, your religious and national customs will be scrupulously respected; and the Government of India will recognize the services of all among you, whether officials or others, who show zeal in assisting the British authorities to preserve order.

APPENDIX VIII.

THE SETTLEMENT OF THE CLAIMS OF THE CHINESE GOVERNMENT OVER BURMA.

THE records of both China and Burma, generally speaking, corroborate each other in recounting a long series of wars between the two countries previous to the accession of Alompra, the founder of the last Burmese dynasty. China was in nearly every case the aggressor, and the wars were fought on the ground which now belongs to Upper Burma. The usual motive for these invasions from China was to enforce the payment of tribute. The success of the various campaigns was varied, but when one Chinese army was driven back others were shortly sent, so that, even if at first successful, the Burmese eventually used to buy them off with the desired presents. Alompra ascended the throne about 1782, and, according to the "Supreme Court and Consular Gazette of China" of 22nd December 1886—"A Burmese Embassy went to Pekin in 1790 to congratulate the Emperor on his 80th birthday . . . . Tribute was to be sent every ten years. . . . . Since then there has been no trouble."

The Foreign Department (Simla) is in possession of several Chinese records of the Burmese Missions to China, commencing with the original Decennial Mission of 1790, which contains the text of the Burmese proposals for, and the Chinese acceptance of, Decennial Missions between the two Courts.

From these and other records it is established beyond doubt that since 1790 complimentary presents had been exchanged between the Chinese and Burmese Courts, with more or less regularity, according to the settled or unsettled state of the provinces intervening between Mandalay and Pekin.

It is remarkable that on the occasions of our two first Burmese wars neither the Burmese nor the Chinese made any reference to the mutual relations of the two kingdoms.

On the occasion of the third war the negotiations were conducted in the most friendly spirit by the Chinese, and it was evident from the indifference which they showed on all internal Burmese questions that they neither had exercised nor desired to exercise any sort of control over the internal administration of Burma; but that this tribute, for which they had so often invaded that country, and which had been paid with some regularity for a century according to a Burma-China Treaty, was a much prized appanage of the State.

They expressed no sympathy with King Thibaw, and tacitly acquiesced in the full right of the British Government to overthrow the existing Burmese Government and establish a new one; though they maintained their right to continuance of the Decennial Missions and showed a desire that they should be sent from a King of Burma.

Some Chinese troops were sent to watch their frontier near Bhamo, and letters were exchanged once between the Political Officer there and the Chinese official on the frontier.

Beside the question of the Decennial Mission, the question of the frontier between Chinese and British possessions had to be entered into; and negotiations on this point too were conducted in a friendly spirit.

On the 9th January 1886 Lord Salisbury, who was then Prime Minister, sent the following telegram to the Chargé d'Affaires at Peking:—

Her Majesty's Government are prepared to make arrangements for the continuance of the interchange of Missions and presents between Burma and China in conformity with the conditions of the Burma–China Treaty of December 1769, and will be ready, as soon as practicable, to enter into negotiations for a determination of the frontier which would be to the advantage of the trade between the two countries * * * *

The negotiations continued to be conducted in a friendly spirit, and the following is a *résumé* of the matters discussed:—

(1) Chinese claim the cession of Bhamo and the boundary of the river Shweli; this was not acknowledged by the British Government as admissible; the latter renounce claims to Shan States east of the Salween; the Chinese do not wish to advance beyond their present boundary in that direction.

(2) The French Ambassador twits the Chinese Government on their partiality to the English with regard to the annexation of its dependency Burma.

(3) The British Government declare that they have been unable to find any form of native rule adaptable to the requirements of Burma.

(4) The Chinese complain of their loss of prestige, if Mission to China does not come from a Royal House in Burma, but are willing to accept it from a spiritual chief of the country.

The Treaty of December 1769 referred to is recorded as follows in the records of the Foreign Department, Simla:—

"Fourteen Burmese and thirteen Chinese Officers met at a place a little below Bhamo and settled a treaty; in this there is no allusion to tribute, and no indication of inequality.

'Peace and frindship being established between the two great countries, they shall become one like two pieces of gold united in one; and suitably to the establishment of the gold and silver road (*i.e.*, of commerce), as well as agreeably to former custom, the Princes and officers of each country shall move their respective Governments to transmit and exchange affectionate letters on gold once every ten years.'*"

(5) This proposal is not found feasible by the English.

(6) The British Government make proposals, offering, as a condition of the Chinese immediately accepting terms, the withdrawal of a Mission which, according to the Chefoo Convention, was just starting to Tibet from Darjeeling. This Mission was very distasteful to the Chinese on account of the strong adversion which the Tibetans showed to it. The Chinese were also alarmed for the safety of this Mission if it advanced, as the Tibetans were prepared to resist it, which would seriously involve the Chinese Government.

Eventually on the 24th July 1887 the following Convention was signed :—

***English text of Convention between Great Britain and China relating to Burma and Tibet, signed at Peking, 24th July* 1887.**

Whereas Her Majesty the Queen of Great Britain and Ireland, Empress of India, and His Majesty the Emperor of China, being sincerely desirous to maintain and perpetuate the relations of friendship and good understanding which now exist between their respective Empires, and to promote and extend the commercial intercourse between their subjects and dominions, the following Convention has been agreed upon and concluded :—

On the part of Great Britain by Nicholas Roderick O'Conor, Esquire, Her Majesty's Secretary of Legation at Washington, and lately Her Majesty's Chargé d'Affaires in China, Companion of the Most Distinguished Order of St. Michael and St. George, duly empowered thereunto ;

And on the part of China by His Highness Prince Ch'ing, President of the Tsung-li Yamen, and His Excellency Sun, Minister of the Tsung-li Yamen, Senior Vice-President of the Board of Works.

ARTICLE I.

Inasmuch as it has been the practice of Burma to send Decennial Missions to present articles of local produce, England agrees that the highest authority in Burma shall send the customary Decennial Missions ; the members of the Missions to be of Burmese race.

ARTICLE II.

China agrees that, in all matters whatsoever appertaining to the authority and rule which England is now exercising in Burma, England shall be free to do whatever she deems fit and proper.

ARTICLE III.

The frontier between Burma and China to be marked by a Delimitation Commission and the conditions of frontier trade to be settled by a Frontier Trade Convention, both countries agreeing to protect and encourage trade between China and Burma.

ARTICLE IV.

Inasmuch as enquiry into the circumstances by the Chinese Government has shown the existence of many obstacles to the Mission to Tibet provided for in the separate article of the Chefoo Agreement, England consents to countermand the Mission forthwith.

With regard to the desire of the British Government to consider arrangements for frontier trade between India and Tibet, it will be the duty of the Chinese Government, after careful enquiry into the circumstances, to adopt measures to exhort and encourage the people with a view to the promotion and development of trade. Should it be practicable the Chinese Government shall then proceed carefully to consider Trade Regulations; but if insuperable obstacles should be found to exist, the British Government will not press the matter unduly.

ARTICLE V.

The present Convention shall be ratified, and the ratifications shall be exchanged in London as soon as possible after the date of the signature thereof.

In witness thereof the respective negotiators have signed the same and affixed thereunto the seals of their arms.

Done in triplicate at Peking this twenty-fourth day of July, in the year of Our Lord one thousand eight hundred and eighty-six, corresponding with the Chinese date the twenty-third day of the sixth moon of the twelfth year of Kuang Hsü.

	(*L.S.*) (Sd.)	NICHOLAS RODERICK O'CONOR.
(Monogram)	(*L.S.*)	CH'ING.
(Monogram)	(*L.S.*)	SUN YU-WEN.

This Convention was ratified on the 25th August 1887.